THE WORKS OF SRI CHINMOY

STORIES

VOLUME I

THE WORKS OF SRI CHINMOY

STORIES

VOLUME I

★

THE EARTH-ILLUMINATION-TRUMPETS
OF DIVINITY'S HOME

ILLUMINATION-EXPERIENCES ON INDIAN SOIL

GREAT INDIAN MEALS: DIVINELY DELICIOUS
AND SUPREMELY NOURISHING

INDIA AND HER MIRACLE-FEAST:
COME AND ENJOY YOURSELF

LYON · OXFORD

GANAPATI PRESS

LXXXV

ISBN 978-0-9933080-4-8

See appendix for notice regarding this edition.

FIRST EDITION WENT TO PRESS ON 13 DECEMBER 2015

STORIES

VOLUME I

PART I

THE EARTH-ILLUMINATION-TRUMPETS
OF DIVINITY'S HOME

I shall take you to another world — the world of enlightenment and amusement. I feel that enlightenment and amusement are the obverse and reverse of the same coin. In these volumes, I have related some stories from the Puranas, our ancient Indian texts.

There are eighteen Puranas. Their author was the great sage Vyasa who also dictated the Mahabharata. Millions and billions of people have heard these stories. They deal mostly with the cosmic gods and goddesses. Quite a few stories show how the gods and goddesses used to curse each other in the twinkling of an eye. Other stories, especially stories about Brahma, Vishnu and Shiva, reveal their struggle for supremacy.

These stories are funnier than the funniest. We get tremendous joy from them. Then again, there are scholars who will be able to give elaborate explanations. From these explanations, which are created by the reasoning mind, we will never get any joy. There is joy in reading the stories, joy in hearing them, but no joy in entering into philosophical discourse. Let the philosophers and historians play their role in their own way; we are not interested.

These stories from the Puranas are not for the mind to understand but for the heart to enjoy.

— Sri Chinmoy

THE EARTH-ILLUMINATION-TRUMPETS OF DIVINITY'S HOME

BOOK 1

Lord Shiva and his consort, Parvati, used to live on Mount Kailash. They meditated there and also they used to bless their devotees. They led a very happy and fruitful life.

One day Parvati made a special request to her consort, Shiva, to take her to a grove named Nandankanan.

"Definitely I will take you there," promised Shiva. So they went together to that particular grove. All the trees in that grove were so beautiful. Parvati was extremely moved by their beauty. She asked her Lord, "Please tell me if there is any tree that is more special than the rest. When I look at them, they all seem equally beautiful. But please tell me if there is one particular tree that is most special, or in some way different from the others."

While she was saying these words, Parvati happened to be standing at the foot of one of the trees. Shiva said to her, "The tree that you are now leaning against has something very special to offer."

"What is that special thing?" asked Parvati.

"This particular tree is called Kalpataru," said Shiva. *Kalpa* means 'whatever you desire' and *taru* means 'tree'. "Whatever you wish for, you will immediately get from this tree."

"My Lord, are you telling me the truth, or is this a fib?" asked Parvati.

"If you do not believe me, just ask the tree for something," answered Shiva.

Parvati meditated for a few moments and then said, "O tree, I want to have a most beautiful girl from you." Immediately, a most beautiful young girl emerged from the tree. Parvati was so pleased and happy. She named the girl Ashokasundari.

Ashokasundari said to the goddess Parvati, "You have brought me into this world. Please tell me what I should do."

Parvati looked at her lovingly and said, "You do not have to do anything for the time being. In a few years, however, I would like you to marry a particular prince named Nahusha. He has not yet been born. He is still in Heaven. But he will take incarnation and, in the course of time, I would like you to marry him. I will make arrangements for you."

Ashokasundari was very happy to hear this news. Lord Shiva and Parvati left her there in that beautiful grove, Nandankanan, and they returned to Mount Kailash.

Now, near Nandankanan there lived a demon named Hunda. He used to claim that Nandankanan was the capital of his land. One day after entering the main grove at Nandankanan, Hunda caught sight of this most beautiful girl and immediately fell in love with her.

The demon approached Ashokasundari and said, "You have to marry me, you have to marry me!"

"No, I will not marry you!" said Ashokasundari. "My future husband is Nahusha. I will marry him and nobody else. Go away from this place!"

Unfortunately, demons have a special magic power. They can take any form. After being insulted by Ashokasundari, the demon left the grove. A few days later, he took the form of a most beautiful woman and once more entered the grove where Ashokasundari lived. The beautiful woman behaved as though she was very sad and depressed.

"Why are you so sad?" asked Ashokasundari. "You seem to be quite beautiful. What is bothering you?"

"Yes, I am beautiful," said the strange woman, "but I am so unhappy."

"What is the reason for your unhappiness?" enquired Ashoka-sundari kindly.

In a pitiful voice, the woman said, "I am a widow. My husband was such a good man, but he was killed by the demon Hunda.

Now I am so lonely. Would you like to come to my cottage and stay for a few days? It is a very simple cottage, but I keep it very clean."

"Yes, I shall come with you," said Ashokasundari.

"Please be my guest for two or three days," said the woman. "It will make me so happy."

Ashokasundari followed this woman and they left the grove. When they came to the widow's cottage, the widow immediately changed herself back into a demon and grabbed Ashokasundari. Ashokasundari was so furious that she cursed the demon: "Definitely my husband, Nahusha, will kill you!" Then she managed to break free from the demon's hold and ran away.

Now the demon was cursed. He knew that he was to be killed, and he knew that Nahusha would be the one to slay him. He started searching high and low for Nahusha so that he could kill Nahusha and nullify the curse. Naturally his search proved fruitless, because at that time Nahusha had not yet been born.

In a neighbouring kingdom there lived a very good and pious king. He and his wife prayed to God for many, many years and, finally, his wife was blessed with a child. They decided to name him Nahusha.

When the demon Hunda came to learn that Nahusha had taken birth, he entered the king's palace and kidnapped the child. Nahusha was only one year old. The demon brought him home and asked his cook to kill the boy and cook him. The demon commanded his cook to serve him a most delicious meal made from the meat of the child. The demon thought that if he ate Nahusha, then there would be no possibility that Nahusha would kill him when he grew up.

"Definitely I will kill him," said the cook. "You are my master."

Now, the cook liked the little boy so much that he did not have the heart to kill him. Instead he took the child to Vashishtha's ashram and left him there. On the way back, he killed a deer. This deer he cooked and served to his master in place of Nahusha.

The demon, Hunda, was so happy. "Ah," he said, "now I know for certain that Nahusha is dead! I have eaten him."

Nahusha grew up in the ashram of the saint Vashishtha. Vashishtha gave him spiritual lessons. He also taught Nahusha archery and other skills. From his inner vision, he knew that Nahusha was a prince and that it was Parvati's wish for him to marry Ashokasundari.

A few years passed by and Nahusha did marry Ashokasundari. The two were very happy together. Because Hunda believed that Nahusha was dead, Nahusha was easily able to kill the demon and fulfil his wife's curse.

The story does not end with the death of Hunda. Unfortunately, he had a son by the name of Bihunda. When Hunda was killed, his son felt miserable. He decided to kill Nahusha to avenge his father's death. So he started practising very strict tapasya, or spiritual disciplines. He was praying and praying to the cosmic gods to grant him the power to kill Nahusha once and for all.

When the cosmic gods saw what kind of tapasya Bihunda was doing, they became afraid that his desire would be fulfilled and that he would kill Nahusha. They appealed to Lord Vishnu to help them.

Lord Vishnu took the form of a most beautiful woman and appeared before Bihunda. Bihunda fell in love with her at first sight and asked her to become his wife. The beautiful woman responded, "I shall marry you on one condition. I wish you to bring me a particular flower. The name of this flower is *kamoda*. You must gather ten million of these flowers and worship Lord Shiva with them. After worshipping Lord Shiva, if you can make a garland of these flowers and place it at my feet, then I shall marry you and you will have the capacity to kill Nahusha. I am making this request to you as your future wife."

Bihunda ran to look for the special tree which bore the flower kamoda. He went here and there asking people, "Do you know what the kamoda flower looks like? Do you know where I can find the tree?"

But nobody knew where to find the tree or what the flower looked like. In desperation, Bihunda went to Shukracharya, the Guru of the demons. Brihaspati is the Guru of the cosmic gods and Shukracharya is his counterpart for the demons. Bihunda told Shukracharya what had happened and asked him where he could find the kamoda flower.

Shukracharya explained, "This woman has not made it clear to you at all. The kamoda flower does not grow on a tree. This particular flower comes out of the mouth of a woman. She is so enchanting! When she laughs, these flowers come out of her mouth. The colour of the flowers is yellow and they are full of fragrance. If you worship Lord Shiva with these fragrant yellow flowers, he will definitely grant you the boon of being able to kill Nahusha. But, if the woman is crying instead of laughing, you will see that the flowers which she brings out of her mouth are red in colour and without any fragrance. Be careful! Those flowers you must not touch, or there will be some serious calamity or misfortune in your life. You must gather only the yellow flowers that drop from her mouth when she laughs."

"Where can I find her?" asked Bihunda eagerly.

Shukracharya said, "She lives on the banks of the river Ganga. In the evening you will see her walking along by the side of the river."

The cosmic gods were watching from Heaven. They saw what was happening and once again they became very worried. They asked Narada, the celestial musician, to come to their rescue.

Narada always took the side of the gods. They informed Narada, "If Bihunda obtains these ten million flowers, then he will definitely be able to kill King Nahusha. You must help us!"

Narada agreed to help them. He went to Bihunda and said to the demon, "You are so great! How is it that you have to go personally to this woman to get the flowers; I will ask her to send the flowers to you. You do not have to go and get them yourself. I will ask her to put the flowers in the Ganga and the water will bring them right to your palace. It is beneath your dignity to go and beg for them. This much I can do for you. Since it is I who am asking, she will definitely do it."

Bihunda's pride came forward and he said to Narada, "You are right. Why should I have to go myself? I will wait for the water to bring the flowers to me."

Narada went to the banks of the river Ganga and found the woman who was the source of the kamoda flowers. After she had greeted him with great respect, he said to her, "Now I would like you to cry and bring out of your mouth the flowers that are red in colour and without fragrance. I wish you to place them in the river and let the water carry them away."

She gladly obeyed Narada and began to cry. From her mouth there came thousands and thousands of red flowers, and she placed them all in the water.

The river flowed past Bihunda's palace, where he had been waiting and waiting for the flowers to appear. When he saw them coming, he became so excited that he did not observe their colour and he did not notice that they had no fragrance. Seeing thousands and thousands of flowers floating down the river, he was filled with joy. "Narada was right!" he shouted. "The flowers have come to me, just as he said."

Bihunda was so thrilled and excited that he forgot his Guru's warning. He did not pay any attention to the colour and he did not try to see if the flowers had any fragrance. In his imagination, the flowers were all yellow and fragrant. His joy had transported him to another world.

He gathered all the flowers and started worshipping Lord Shiva. Now, Parvati saw that on earth somebody was worshipping Lord Shiva with flowers that had no fragrance. And the flowers themselves were not charming at all. She said, "This is not the flower that Lord Shiva likes. Who can be so disrespectful to my husband?"

Parvati descended to earth and, with her third eye, she killed the demon Bihunda. She did not need any weapon at that time.

We began our story with Parvati. It was she who asked the Kalpataru tree to give her a young girl. Then this girl's curse brought about the deaths of the demon Hunda and his son Bihunda, who were mercilessly torturing innocent human beings.

EIT 3. *Indra loses his kingdom*

Indra is the king of the cosmic gods. One time, pride entered into him because, while he was supreme in Heaven, he began to neglect Prakriti, who is Mother Earth. Prakriti was so enraged that she cursed Indra. She said to him, "You will lose everything you have — your throne, your kingdom, everything. Even your Guru, Brihaspati, will curse you."

When he was cursed by Prakriti, Indra was so sad and depressed. He was literally sunk in despair. Who should come to him then but his own Guru, Brihaspati, who is the Guru of all the cosmic gods. Because Indra was so depressed, he did not show any respect to his Guru; he did not even stand up. Brihaspati became furious. He said, "How is it possible for you, of all the cosmic gods, not to show any respect to me? Do you not know who is standing here? It is your own Guru! I curse you! You will lose your kingdom, you will lose your throne, you will lose all your prosperity. Everything you have, you will lose. You will become a beggar."

Prakriti's curse and Brihaspati's curse came true. Indra became an utter beggar. Then Brihaspati felt sorry for Indra and he modified his curse a little. He told Indra, "After 60,000 years I will restore your kingdom to you." So Indra prayed and meditated for 60,000 years and his kingdom was restored to him. Unfortunately, he discovered that his kingdom was not as beautiful as it had been previously. His palace needed remodelling and many other places needed construction. Indra was filled with sadness because his kingdom did not have its former perfection. So he employed the Heavenly architect, Vishwakarma, to do the needful.

Vishwakarma worked for many months. The months became years, but still Indra was not satisfied. He was always finding fault with Vishwakarma's work. Every day Vishwakarma had to endure Indra's scoldings and insults. In addition, Vishwakarma had no time for his other important work, so he was miserable.

One day Vishwakarma went to Vishnu and said, "O Vishnu, please save me, save me! Indra has appointed me to rebuild his kingdom. How hard I have been working to please him, but he is not satisfied with my work. He only scolds me and insults me."

"Let me see what I can do," answered Vishnu.

Vishnu took the form of a very striking young boy and came before Indra. "This kingdom is your kingdom?" he asked.

"Definitely it is my kingdom!" said Indra. "Who else could have such a kingdom? This is my creation. Since it is beautiful, you are appreciating it."

The young boy went on, "No other Indra has such a beautiful kingdom or such a splendid palace. Did you receive any help from anyone?"

"Yes," said Indra. "I received some help from Vishwakarma, but it was next to nothing."

"No other Vishwakarma can be of help in remodelling, no other," said the boy mysteriously.

"What do you mean?" cried Indra. "You said 'no other Indra' and 'no other Vishwakarma.' Does that mean there are more Indras and more Vishwakarmas?"

"Yes, yes, there are others," stated the boy. Indra got furious. When he thought that there was more than one Indra, he lost all interest in his kingdom. He did not mind at all if there were other Vishwakarmas. But for Indra to tolerate more Indras was too much.

"I no longer want this kingdom," said Indra in a sad voice. "Now what am I going to do?"

Vishnu once more took his own form as a cosmic god. He said to Indra, "Go and bathe in the river and you will be purified. After you have been purified, you will see that your kingdom, your palace and all your possessions are as beautiful and as perfect as they were before Prakriti cursed you."

So Indra got back his kingdom and he was completely satisfied.

EIT 4. *Twisted in eight places*

This is a story about Krishna and Radha. It was a moonlit night and Lord Krishna was playing on his flute most hauntingly. Radha and the other gopis were all listening. They were admiring the music of Krishna's flute and drinking in his celestial beauty. They were in the seventh Heaven of delight.

After some time, Krishna stopped playing and said, "I have transported you all to a world of purest delight. Now that you are all filled with happiness, I am going to take a walk in the forest." Krishna saw that Radha wanted to accompany him and he said to her, "You may come." The other gopis did not dare to join them. They had the utmost respect for Radha.

So Krishna and Radha walked and walked until they came to a particular place in the forest. Krishna turned to Radha and said, "Radha, I am in the mood to tell some stories. Would you care to listen to my stories?"

"Of course, my Lord!" exclaimed Radha. "Please tell me some stories. I am eager to hear them."

Krishna said, "Anything that comes into my mind, I will tell." Krishna was all ready to tell Radha some stories when, all of a sudden, a strange looking man appeared. His body was bent in eight different places. His legs were crooked, his arms were crooked; everything was unnatural. This man was known as Astabakra — *asta* means "eight", and *Astabakra* means "crooked in eight places".

As soon as Radha saw this unfortunate human being, for some reason she began laughing and laughing.

"How can you laugh at this poor man?" asked Krishna.

"His body is bent in eight different places! I cannot refrain from laughing at such an odd spectacle," answered Radha.

Krishna scolded her: "It is not kind to laugh at others. You should not behave in this way." But Radha kept laughing and laughing.

Astabakra had thought that Radha would be full of compassion for him because she was Krishna's dearest disciple. He simply could not understand why she was laughing at him so heartlessly. He was standing before her with tremendous devotion and love, but her laughter was hurting him deeply.

Krishna said to Radha, "If I tell you about Astabakra, will you stop laughing at him?"

"Of course, my Lord," came Radha's reply.

"Then stop laughing and listen to his unhappy story." As Krishna began to relate the story, Astabakra bowed to Krishna and Radha and silently left their presence.

This is the story that Krishna told. Astabakra was formerly a high-class Brahmin. He was married and he spent quite a few years with his wife. Then, for God knows what reason, he became disgusted with his wife. He took a vow, saying, "From now on I shall never, never mix with any woman! All women are so bad. Here is the absolute proof. My wife has proved that women are unbearable. I will have no connection, no association, with any woman whatsoever in God's entire creation. I shall not even look at a woman."

This was the strict vow that the Brahmin took after his sad experience with his wife. At that time his body was not crooked at all. In appearance he was very strong and handsome.

O God! A nymph in the palace of Lord Indra noticed this Brahmin and fell in love with him. The name of this nymph, or apsara, was Rambha. She was extremely beautiful. She came to the Brahmin and said to him, "I am in love with you. I want to marry you."

The Brahmin became furious. He said, "I have taken a vow that I shall never marry again. My first wife was enough for me. She was the first and the last!"

Rambha began pleading with him. She said, "You have to marry me, since I have declared my love for you."

"Never!" insisted the Brahmin. "I will not mix with any woman in this life."

When Rambha saw that the Brahmin would not change his mind, she became very angry and upset. "You have such a foul tongue! How dare you talk to me like this! I am a dancer in the palace of Lord Indra himself. I curse you for refusing my love. Your body will become crooked in eight different places.

You will be so ugly that no woman will ever want to look at you again."

After cursing the Brahmin, Rambha vanished. The poor Brahmin! His body immediately became twisted and bent. Each of his limbs went in a different direction. He could move only with the greatest difficulty.

In despair, the Brahmin said, "What is the use of keeping this life? Rambha has cursed me and this is what has happened. Why should I remain on earth any longer? I will immolate this body of mine."

Suddenly, Lord Vishnu appeared before him and said, "It is not good to kill yourself. Pray and pray and pray. After some time, I will come to you again and you will be cured. Then you will be happy on earth with your physical body as before. You say that you do not want to look at women. No harm! You will be able to keep your vow. Now start praying and I will soon appear before you."

The Brahmin listened to Lord Vishnu and began praying most sincerely.

"When will Lord Vishnu come and cure the Brahmin?" asked Radha when Krishna had reached this point in his story.

Krishna smiled sweetly. "Vishnu has already come," he said, and began walking home. Krishna was an emanation of Lord Vishnu. They were and they are one and the same. So this was how Krishna cured Astabakra.

EIT 5. *How Shiva got the name* Rudra

Once Brahma and Vishnu were talking and talking and talking endlessly. In everything, they are endless! When they are silent, they do not utter a word for thousands of years; and then again, when they resume talking, they can talk for thousands of years uninterruptedly.

On this occasion, they were enjoying one of their birthless and deathless talks when, all of a sudden, Shiva appeared. For some reason, Shiva sometimes assumes a very rough manner. On that day, everything about him was uncouth. Shiva is not polished like the other cosmic gods. Around his neck there are skulls; he is adorned with snakes; his dear ones are ghosts and his favourite place is the cremation ground. Shiva's manners are also not refined. He is not sociable, let us say.

It was in this unseemly guise that he came to Brahma and Vishnu. Vishnu recognised Shiva, but Brahma could not. In fact, Brahma became furious at the intruder. "How dare you come and stand in front of us!" he exclaimed. "We are two cosmic gods! You have no respect for us!"

"You cannot recognise Lord Shiva?" said Vishnu.

"That is not Shiva!" insisted Brahma.

At that moment, Vishnu opened up Brahma's third eye. "O my God," said Brahma, "it is Shiva!" He said to Shiva, "Please forgive me, forgive me!"

"All right, I forgive you," Shiva agreed. At first, Shiva had been furious when Brahma was insulting him. Shiva wanted to open up his third eye and destroy Brahma then and there. But when Brahma asked for forgiveness, Shiva brought forward his compassion aspect. He forgave Brahma unconditionally.

Still Brahma was not fully satisfied. He said to Shiva, "You have to prove that you have forgiven me."

"What kind of proof do you want?" asked Shiva.

"You have to take incarnation in my family," declared Brahma. "You have to take birth as my son."

"Fine, fine," said Shiva. "I shall take incarnation in your family. I will be your son."

After it was decided that Shiva would be born on earth as Brahma's son, Shiva left the presence of Vishnu and Brahma.

Since Vishnu and Brahma had talked for such a long time, both of them were now completely exhausted. Vishnu said, "Let me enjoy a little rest." Brahma added, "Let me also enjoy rest, a very short rest."

As soon as Vishnu lay down, he fell asleep and started snoring. He was completely in another world. Brahma lay down very near Vishnu. They were practically side by side. Brahma was still partially awake. The moment Vishnu fell asleep, something curious happened. From one of his ears a tiny being emerged, and that being wanted to eat some honey.

A few minutes later, Vishnu woke up. Meanwhile, from his other ear, another being was coming out. This other being was like an insect. The very nature of an insect is to bite, so it wanted to bite Brahma. These two tiny beings were hostile forces, or demons. Their names were Madhu and Koitava. *Madhu* means "honey" and *Koitava* is from the word *kit*, meaning "insect". Our Indian mythology is flooded with these two names.

Madhu and Koitava found that the person nearest to them was Brahma, and so both of them went to kill him. They were evil incarnate. Although one was like an insect and the other was also very tiny, demons can take any form they wish. So Madhu and Koitava suddenly became huge and powerful. They were extremely ugly looking, plus unbearably fat.

After assuming these huge and frightening forms, Madhu and Koitava caught Brahma off guard and started fighting with him. He shouted, "What are you doing?" He fought, but he could not kill them and they also could not kill him. Then Vishnu entered the picture. He became furious.

"From my body you two came out and this is how you are behaving?" he thundered. He then proceeded to destroy the two demons.

Brahma was so happy to see Madhu and Koitava lying dead. He started meditating. All of a sudden, he said, "Shiva promised that he would take incarnation in my family. He said he would be my son. Look at his lies! Shiva never keeps his promises — never, never, never!" Brahma reflected for a moment and continued, "I must pray to Shiva and again remind him of his promise. He promised that he would come to me as my son."

So Brahma prayed to Shiva for five thousand years, but Shiva did not appear at all. One day, Brahma began shedding bitter tears because Shiva had failed to keep his promise. Brahma said, "I cannot go on in vain. Even after seeing my tears, Shiva is not coming. I am crying like an infant, but he is deaf to my prayers. I have now decided to commit suicide. Shiva is a liar. He is not going to come. So the best thing is for me to immolate myself."

After saying these words, Brahma committed suicide. As soon as he had done so, Shiva came out of Brahma's mouth. While coming out, Shiva was crying and crying, and at the same time Brahma was revived. Brahma was so happy to see his son. When he noticed Shiva's tears, Brahma became very concerned.

"Why are you crying, why are you crying, my child?" he asked.

Shiva said that he was crying while taking human incarnation because he was entering into world-ignorance. For this reason Brahma gave him the name *Rudra,* meaning "he who cries pitifully". There is also another aspect to the name, which is "he who destroys". In the course of time, Shiva also manifested this other aspect using the power of his third eye.

So this is the story of how Shiva came to have the name Rudra.

EIT 6. *The many names of Shiva*

There is another version of the previous story. For many stories from the Puranas, there are different versions. Some are even contradictory. You can choose whichever one you like.

Brahma was meditating in order to get a son. All of a sudden, after thousands of years of meditation, he saw a child in his lap. He was filled with happiness, but the child immediately started crying. His body was racked with sobs. Brahma asked the child, "Tell me, my son, why are you crying?" The little boy sighed, "I need a name."

"You need a name?" repeated his father. Brahma immediately gave him the name *Rudra,* which means "one who cries and cries".

A few minutes later, the child started crying again. "Why are you crying?" asked his father.

"I need another name," said the child.

Brahma consented and gave him the name Pinaki. But the child's tears started to flow once more. This time Brahma gave him the name Bibhola. Afterwards, he gained the name *Trishuladhari,* meaning "one who holds the trident". In all, the child received eight names from Brahma.

Finally, he said to his father, "Now you have given me so many names. What shall I do with those names? Which one shall I use?"

It was he who had begged Brahma to give him the names, and now he was asking what he should do with them!

Brahma said to Rudra, "All these names that I am giving you have a very special meaning. Each one embodies a divine quality of yours which I want you to manifest here on earth."

Eventually Rudra did manifest all the divine qualities that Brahma had given him in the form of these various names.

EIT 7. *Krishna's son abducts the Kaurava princess*

This is a story about the irony of fate. When Duryodhana's daughter, Laksmana, came of age, she wanted to choose a husband. According to the custom of those days, when it was time for a princess to marry, her father would hold a special ceremony called a *swayamvara*. All the neighbouring princes would be invited and the princess would place a garland around the neck of the one whom she wished to marry.

So Duryodhana held a swayamvara for his dearest daughter and many princes came from the royal families of other kingdoms. Each prince expected that she would choose him to be her husband.

Krishna's son, Samba, also attended the ceremony. But, instead of waiting to see if the princess was going to put the garland around his neck, Samba abducted her by force in front of everyone. All the other princes as well as the members of the princess's own family were outraged that Samba had dared to do such a thing. For Krishna's own son to behave in such a manner was unthinkable. They all chased Samba in their chariots and, finally, they caught him. Samba was arrested and put into jail in the kingdom of the Kauravas. He was subjected to much humiliation because of his rash act.

Meanwhile, since most of the princes were still present at the gathering, they asked Duryodhana's daughter to choose someone else. The poor princess was already so sad and miserable that for her to choose somebody else in her present frame of mind was an impossible task. Besides, in the depths of her heart, she did like Samba.

Seeing her plight, some people suggested that the swayamvara be postponed until another day. "This is not the time," they said. "Right now the princess is startled. Let her recover from her ordeal before she chooses her husband."

So the princes went home disappointed and Samba remained in jail. The news of his capture soon reached his father, Krishna, who became very sad and upset. "My son has to do me this kind of favour!" he exclaimed. "He knows the Kauravas are our worst enemies. I am not going there to rescue him."

It happened that Krishna's brother, Balarama, was extremely fond of this particular nephew of his. He told Krishna, "I will not allow my nephew, Samba, to be imprisoned in the kingdom of the Kauravas. I will go and bring him back."

Krishna replied, "Do whatever you like. I am so embarrassed by my son's behaviour. You go and do whatever you want to do."

Balarama went to the Kaurava kingdom and said to Duryodhana, "I have come to take my nephew back home."

Duryodhana and his brothers began making fun of Balarama. "Your nephew is so bad!" they said. "Why do you want to be associated with him?"

Balarama answered, "No matter what he has done, I am all love for him. Now kindly release him."

But Duryodhana would not allow Samba to be released. This made Balarama furious. His main weapon was the plough. He started wielding his plough and breaking down the walls of the prison. The soldiers who tried to prevent him were all destroyed.

When the Kauravas saw that Balarama was so powerful, they grew frightened and quickly released Samba. Then Balarama said, "I demand the girl, Duryodhana's daughter. Now that I have defeated all of you, I want Laksmana to marry my nephew."

Once more the Kauravas began laughing at Balarama. "She did not place the garland around your nephew's neck," they contended. "How can you demand that she marry him?"

Balarama said, "No, I know that she loves him."

Duryodhana knew that Balarama had the capacity to destroy all the Kauravas so he was very frightened. He said to himself, "The best thing is to get rid of my daughter. Otherwise, if

I choose to keep her, Balarama may kill everyone. For one daughter, the whole kingdom will be ruined." Out of fear, he let Laksmana go with Balarama and Samba. He did not even consult her before he made his decision. He just told her, "Now go." For her dowry, Duryodhana gave thousands of horses and chariots, together with hundreds of magnificent elephants.

Balarama returned to Dwaraka, Krishna's kingdom, with Samba and Duryodhana's daughter, plus so much wealth from the Kauravas. Once again, Krishna was very happy.

Can you imagine! Of all the princesses to abduct, Krishna's son had to choose the daughter of Krishna's enemy, Duryodhana. Naturally, Duryodhana arrested the boy and put him in jail. But Balarama's love for his nephew was such that he himself went and fought for Samba's freedom. When the Kauravas surrendered they gave Balarama not only Samba, but also Duryodhana's daughter along with immense wealth.

Krishna, Arjuna and Duryodhana all belonged to the warrior caste. They were Kshatriyas. In those days, Kshatriyas were allowed to abduct a bride, but it was generally done by the common consent of both parties. When Arjuna abducted Krishna's sister, Subhadra, it was with Krishna's full approval, because Krishna knew that the two were in love with each other. But when Balarama found out that Arjuna had abducted his sister, he wanted to chase Arjuna in his chariot and kill him. Krishna had to console Balarama by saying that Arjuna was the best of warriors and it was no shame to have him as a member of the family.

This whole practice of abducting a wife started with Vishma. He abducted three sisters for his nephew, Vichitravirya, the grandfather of the Pandavas. The names of these three sisters were Amba, Ambalika and Ambika. Because he took them against their will, Vishma was cursed, and from that day everything started going wrong for him.

EIT 8. *The pride of Brahma*

This is a story about the pride of Brahma, our Creator. One day, Brahma was meditating. In his meditation he had gone higher than the highest, deeper than the deepest. He was in ecstasy. Brahma said to himself, "How I wish I could spend all my time in this sublime meditation!"

Suddenly, there appeared in front of him the most beautiful nymph, or apsara. Her name was Mohini. She said to Brahma, "I want to marry you."

Brahma got furious. "I was in such ecstasy, such bliss, and you have to come here and charm me! Never! Do not come near me. Leave me alone!"

Mohini was deeply insulted. "I am leaving you alone, but not before I curse you. From now on, nobody will worship you, nobody! The other cosmic gods will be worshipped and adored but you will never, never be worshipped by any human being!"

Mohini's curse came true and Brahma was no longer worshipped. He felt miserable, and so he went to Vishnu for advice. While he was waiting in Vishnu's palace, he saw somebody just like himself, except that this figure had ten heads. Then he saw another figure like himself, but with one hundred heads, and a third with one thousand heads. All of them looked exactly like him, but he had only four heads.

When Vishnu entered the room, Brahma asked him who these other figures were. Vishnu replied, "These are all Brahmas, like you. You are not the only Brahma! You have to know that there are many universes and each universe is represented by one Brahma, one Creator. There are hundreds of universes and hundreds of Brahmas. They look exactly like you, but you have only four heads, whereas they have many, many more."

Poor Brahma! He had come to Vishnu for consolation, but Vishnu had smashed his pride. Then Brahma told Vishnu about

Mohini's curse and very humbly asked Vishnu how he could make the curse void.

Vishnu said, "You can dispel Mohini's curse only if you listen to me. You must meditate for 60,000 years and then you must go to the holy river Ganga and bathe. Only then will you be free from the curse."

In Indian mythology, they always say that a curse lasts for 60,000 years and you have to meditate for 60,000 years to get rid of it. So, poor Brahma had to meditate for a very, very long time.

EIT 9. *Krishna prays to have a son*

Lord Krishna was consumed with the desire to have a son. So he went to seek the advice of a particular sage. When the sage saw Lord Krishna, he was overwhelmed with joy. Everybody was shouting, "Krishna has come, Krishna has come!" and they all started worshipping Krishna.

The sage asked Krishna, "Please tell me what I can do for you. Is there anything that you would like me to do?"

Krishna answered, "It is a very simple thing that I want. I want to have a son. Please tell me how I can have a son."

"Only Lord Shiva can help in this matter," said the sage. "You have to pray to Lord Shiva. First, you must gather one thousand flowers. With these flowers you must worship Lord Shiva for many years. When Lord Shiva is pleased with your worship, you will be granted a son."

Krishna left the cottage of the sage and entered into seclusion. He put ashes all over his body and clothed himself in the bark of a tree. For years and years he prayed, only to have a glimpse of Lord Shiva and to ask him for a boon.

With her third eye, Parvati saw that Krishna was praying and praying all alone in the heart of the forest. She said to her husband, "My Lord, what are you doing? Why are you not responding? Lord Krishna has been worshipping you, only you, for so many years."

"What do you want me to do?" asked Shiva.

"Just go and stand before him," pleaded Parvati. "As a matter of fact, let us go together."

Both Parvati and Shiva appeared before Krishna. Shiva said to him, "What are you doing? Why should you, of all people, pray to me? You are Narayana, you are Vishnu, you are the avatar of this era, you pervade everything. Why then are you praying to me?"

Krishna responded, "Lord Shiva, I know that you are the only one who can fulfil my desire."

"Is there any desire which you yourself cannot fulfil?" asked Shiva.

"I was told that only you can fulfil this particular desire. Therefore, I have come to you," answered Krishna.

"What is your desire?" asked Shiva.

"I wish to have a son exactly like you," Krishna said to Shiva. "It has to be exactly like you, otherwise I do not want it."

Shiva and Parvati both smiled and immediately Shiva granted Krishna the boon. Krishna returned home and, after some time, his wife, Jambavati, bore a son. They named him Samba.

What does it mean to have a son exactly like Shiva? On the one hand, Shiva is always lost in trance. But, on the other hand, Shiva's function is to destroy. From destruction comes transformation. This boy, Samba, did many unbearable things during his life. Eventually he brought about the total destruction of Krishna's family. So you can say that Krishna knew that transformation was needed and transformation must be preceded by destruction. That is why he prayed to have a son like Shiva.

EIT 10. *Parvati longs to marry Shiva*

One day, when Parvati was only eight years old, her father, Himavan, took her to see Lord Shiva. From birth, Parvati had always been very spiritual. She always wanted to know about God, so she was thrilled to see Lord Shiva. But Lord Shiva was in a meditative consciousness and he did not pay any attention to the little girl.

After that first encounter, Parvati used to come every day to see Lord Shiva. She would offer him fresh flowers, hoping that one day he would open his eyes and speak to her. In the back of her mind, she had formed the idea that this was the man she wanted to marry.

The days became years and Parvati grew into a beautiful young woman. Still Shiva remained absorbed in his eternal trance. How could anybody disturb Shiva's trance? Once he enters into trance, he enjoys the highest and deepest bliss. So why should he come back?

One day, Parvati confided to her father, "I really want to marry Lord Shiva. He is meditating and meditating. How I wish that I could also meditate like him!"

Himavan was very sad that Shiva was not paying any attention to his beautiful daughter, who was so spiritual in every way. He decided to play a trick on Shiva: he invoked the god of love to disturb Shiva's meditation. The name of this particular god was Madana. Madana had a bow and some arrows that were made of flowers. He used to shoot these arrows at his victims and then they would be filled with feelings of emotional love.

At Himavan's request, Madana aimed his arrows at Lord Shiva and the arrows fell as flowers at Shiva's feet. Suddenly, Shiva opened his third eye and caught sight of the god of love standing with his bow in his hands. Shiva immediately burnt this unfortunate god to ashes because he had disturbed Shiva's meditation.

Meanwhile, Parvati was standing nearby with a most beautiful garland in her hands, but Lord Shiva did not pay any attention to her. It was as if she did not even exist. He simply closed his eyes again and went into trance.

Parvati's parents had witnessed the whole scene and they were furious with Lord Shiva. They felt that he had insulted their dearest daughter. "You cannot marry him, Parvati," they said. "This Shiva has been insulting you for so many years now. You must not waste your time on him any longer."

But Parvati would not budge. "I am going to stay here," she declared. "From now on, I shall eat only leaves, wet leaves." With heavy hearts, Parvati's parents returned home without their daughter.

For several years, Parvati stayed near Shiva, eating only wet leaves. Then she started eating only dry leaves. After a few more years, she gave up eating leaves altogether. When she gave up eating leaves, her name became *Aparna,* which means "one who does not eat even a leaf." Parvati became the goddess Aparna at that time because of her extreme tapasya, or spiritual discipline.

As time passed, Parvati went one step further. She stopped drinking water. She was living on nothing but air. Himavan saw that his daughter was becoming very weak. He knew that it was only a matter of time before she would die. So Himavan went to Lord Shiva and said, "Can you not see what you are doing to my daughter? All her life, she has wanted only one thing, and that is to marry you. But you have never even looked at her. If you are determined not to marry her, at least look at her. Otherwise, she will surely die."

Shiva condescended to look at Parvati, but to himself he said, "Let me test her one last time before I marry her." Poor Parvati had endured so many tests and still Shiva wanted to test her love and devotion. He took the form of an ordinary man and approached her. "You are such a beautiful girl," he said. "Why are you wasting your time here? I have heard that you want to marry Shiva, but what kind of man is he? He spends all his time in the cremation ground in the company of his ghost-friends. The garland around his neck is made of skulls. How can you marry someone as frightening as Shiva? Forget about him! Marry a normal man, like me."

Parvati's eyes burned. "What you are saying is untrue. Go away from here and leave me alone! I know who Shiva is. Do not throw your doubts and suspicions into me. I will never marry you, never! I will marry only my Lord Shiva. If you do not leave me alone this instant, I shall curse you!"

At that moment, Shiva assumed his true form once more. Parvati was so moved and overwhelmed to see him standing before her. Shiva said to her, "Any boon that you want, I shall give you."

"You do not know by this time what boon I want?" asked Parvati. "I want only to marry you."

"Granted," said Shiva.

After Shiva and Parvati were married, Parvati came to know that she had been Shiva's wife in her previous incarnation. Her name then was Sati and she immolated herself because her father, Daksha, insulted Shiva. But that is another story!

EIT 11. *Brahma can swallow everything*

At one time, pride entered into Brahma. He said, "Since I am all fire, I can swallow everything. So now let me swallow everything and prove that I am the greatest of the cosmic gods. Who can dare to stand against me? I can eat fire! I *am* all fire! I am Brahma!"

When Vishnu saw the extent of Brahma's pride, he took the form of a little boy, four or five years old. This little boy came before Brahma holding a dry reed in his hand.

The little boy said, "Lord Brahma, you are the greatest of all the gods. Here is a dry reed. Let me see you burn it or swallow it."

Brahma immediately engulfed the little boy with flames. The flames wanted to devour not only the reed but also the little boy. But although the flames burnt intensely, they could not swallow the little boy and they did not even touch the dry reed in his hand.

"How can this be?" cried Brahma. "I can burn up everything and everybody, but a single dry reed and one little boy are beyond my capacity. I do not understand it."

Then Vishnu took his real form and said to Brahma, "This is all because of your pride I wanted to smash your pride by showing you that you could not do anything to a reed. Now you should not boast anymore. You have to remain silent."

So this was how Brahma was humiliated by Vishnu.

THE EARTH-ILLUMINATION-TRUMPETS
OF DIVINITY'S HOME

BOOK 2

Brahma's son was Bhrigu. Once Bhrigu wanted to know who among the trinity was the greatest: his father, Vishnu or Shiva. He decided that he would be the examiner because he did not want others to make the decision on his behalf.

Bhrigu began his examination with his father. While Brahma was reading the scriptures, Bhrigu came before him in a very haughty way, without bowing. Brahma said, "What! You are coming into my room without showing me any respect? I never thought that you would be so insolent and undivine!" He scolded his son mercilessly.

Silently Bhrigu went away, saying to himself, "This proves that my father cannot be the greatest of the three."

Next Bhrigu went to see Shiva. When Shiva saw Bhrigu coming towards him, he did not know how to greet him. Why? Because Shiva was very unclean, even filthy. In spite of this, Shiva grabbed Bhrigu and embraced him.

"You are so dirty and filthy! Why do you have to make me dirty also?" protested Bhrigu.

Shiva became furious. "You have to call me dirty and filthy? This is what I get for embracing you! I came to you with such affection! I love you. You are Brahma's son. Now you have to say all kinds of things against me?" Shiva was so furious that he wanted to kill Bhrigu.

Bhrigu hastily left Shiva's presence. On the way, he concluded, "Like my father, Shiva is also not good. Both of them have not conquered their anger. Since they have not conquered their anger, what kind of spiritual greatness do they have?"

Vishnu was the last member of the trinity to be examined by Bhrigu. When Bhrigu arrived at Vishnu's abode, Vishnu was fast asleep. Bhrigu thought to himself, "Since both my father and Shiva showed their anger, let me see if I can also make Vishnu angry. I am sure it will be quite easy."

While Vishnu was still asleep, Bhrigu started mildly kicking him. Vishnu did not wake up. Then Bhrigu kicked Vishnu extremely hard right on his chest. Vishnu woke up and immediately grabbed Bhrigu's feet. "Are you hurt, are you hurt, my child? Please tell me. You kicked me so hard! I am deeply concerned that you have hurt yourself. Please tell me what I can do for you."

Bhrigu replied, "My Lord, among the trinity — Brahma, Vishnu and Shiva — you are by far the greatest."

This was Bhrigu's realisation. His father scolded him because he showed no respect to his father; Shiva became enraged because Bhrigu insulted him; but Vishnu, in spite of being kicked ruthlessly, forgave Bhrigu and showed him such compassion and concern.

It is said that the mark of Bhrigu's foot is still visible on Vishnu's chest. Because of this incident, Bhrigu became known as Pada Bhrigu. *Pad* means "foot", so *Pada Bhrigu* means "the sage who used his feet to examine the gods".

EIT 13. *Shiva provides a home for Parvati*

Lord Shiva and Parvati lived at the top of the Himalayas. Sometimes they stayed on Mount Kailash and sometimes they stayed on another mountain named Mandara. One day Parvati said to her consort, "My Lord, everybody has a house. Can we not also have a house? When the weather is hot here on the top of the mountain, I suffer so much. You are in your trance, but I cannot enjoy trance as you do, so I suffer unbearably. Please give me a house to live in."

Shiva was in his own world, and he paid no attention to his wife's request. A few years passed by and Parvati brought up the matter once more. "My Lord, please let us have a house," she begged.

"I am so poor," Shiva replied. "How can I give you a house? Let us go and take up our abode at the foot of a tree. There you will find shade. The tree will protect us."

"Yes," said Parvati, "a tree can give us shade and shelter to some extent. But when it rains heavily, what can a tree do? When there are hurricanes or cyclones or monsoons, what will happen? The rain will come and destroy everything."

"I am very, very poor. What can I do?" answered Shiva.

"Indeed, you are poor!" responded his wife. "But you have made so many people rich. How is it that you have made others rich while you yourself have remained poor? They are lucky. They can get anything they want from you because they are your devotees. But when I want to have something for myself, you refuse me — and I am your wife!" Parvati started weeping pitifully. Then she continued, "I beg you, my Lord, please provide us with a house. Otherwise, I cannot escape from the rain. I can tolerate the heat but not the rain."

Shiva's heart melted. He said to his wife, "Because I am so poor, I cannot give you a proper house. But since I have prayed and meditated for so many years, I can do you this favour. Let us change our abode. Let us move away from this tree on the mountaintop. We shall no longer stay on Kailash or Mandara. We shall enter into the clouds. From now on, the clouds will be our home. We shall remain inside them and we will not be on earth at all. We will not touch the ground. Therefore the rain will not affect us; nothing will affect us."

So Shiva and Parvati entered into the clouds to live. One name of Shiva is *Jimutabahin,* meaning "one who is inside the cloud". Lord Shiva and Parvati still live inside the clouds because Shiva could not afford to have a house.

EIT 14. *Brahma tries to illumine Vishwamitra and Vashishtha*

The sage Vashishtha meditated under water for twelve years. He wanted to become the most powerful person spiritually. When he came out of the water, he saw that his dearest disciple, Harishchandra, was in serious trouble. The sage Vishwamitra had come to Harishchandra's palace and asked him to do certain things. Because Harishchandra could not fulfil his promises, he had to leave his kingdom, sell his wife and child and take up work as an undertaker.

When Vashishtha saw that Harishchandra was undergoing so much suffering, he cursed Vishwamitra: "My dearest king is suffering at your hands," he said. "You are so cruel. I curse you! You will become a bird!"

In reply, Vishwamitra pronounced a curse on Vashishtha: "You will immediately become a bird also!"

O God, both of them became huge birds and they started fighting in the sky! While flapping their wings, they were destroying trees, houses, everything. The whole of creation was being smashed to pieces because they were fighting so ruthlessly.

When Brahma saw the destruction that was being wrought by these two huge birds, he decided to do something. He clipped their wings so that they could no longer fly. Although they could not fly, the two birds continued to fight face to face on the ground. Their fury showed no signs of abating.

Brahma observed them once again and said, "What I have done is not enough. Without wings they are still bent on destroying each other. I can see that my entire creation will be destroyed in the process. I have to do something more."

Brahma meditated for thousands of years to acquire power and finally he was able to transform the two birds back into human beings. When they took the form of men once more, Brahma addressed them: "Are you not ashamed of yourselves?

You cursed each other to become birds and then you fought ruthlessly. You were destroying the whole world because of your personal quarrel. Now at least remain as two ordinary human beings. Even ordinary human beings do not fight the way you have fought. I am not asking you to be saints. Just become decent human beings."

In this way, Brahma tried to illumined the sages. They embraced each other and promised to desist from fighting. Unfortunately, their truce did not last. Afterwards, these two sages once again resumed fighting. Most people say that Vashishtha had the higher wisdom, while others say that he started the whole thing. Each sage has his own supporters. Although they were both great, neither one had conquered anger.

EIT 15. *Krishna's son mocks the sages*

Three very great sages once came to Lord Krishna's palace in Dwaraka. Krishna was resting. When he was informed of their arrival, he said, "Please tell them that I shall be there in a short while. In the meantime, let them be welcomed with proper respect and devotion."

Unfortunately, over the years, Krishna's relatives and others who were close to him had become very undivine. Because they were dear to Krishna, they used to get everything for the asking. As a result, they became corrupted by the pleasure-life. They used to drink and quarrel and do all kinds of unthinkable things.

A few members of Krishna's immediate family did not have any respect for the sages and saints who came to pay homage to Krishna. These relatives felt that as long as they had Krishna, it was enough. To them, all other spiritual people were as worthless as straw.

Krishna's son, Samba, was then twenty-five or twenty-six years old. Even though he was no longer a child, he and some other young men decided to play a practical joke on the three sages. Samba's friends tied an earthen pot on his stomach and dressed him in a nice sari. Then they brought him before the sages.

The young men said to the sages, "This woman is with child. Please, before Krishna comes, can you tell us whether she will give birth to a boy or a girl?"

Since the sages had occult vision, they immediately saw that the young men were mocking them. They became furious. "You are Krishna's relatives! You, Samba, are his own son! You dare to make fun of us! Yes, this 'woman' will give birth, but she will give birth to an iron rod. This rod will bring about the destruction of Krishna's entire clan. You have no respect for spiritual people. We are great sages and you have mocked us."

At that moment, Krishna entered the hall. He was so sad to hear the curse of the sages. At the same time, he knew that his relatives deserved it. The sages also felt sorry that they had uttered such a dreadful curse, but they did not have enough capacity or forgiveness-power to withdraw it. In spite of this unfortunate turn of events, Krishna stayed and had a long talk with the sages, and they received Krishna's blessings. Krishna was beyond, beyond everything. He advised them and illumined them, and then the sages departed.

In due course, the curse came true and Krishna's son gave birth to a heavy iron rod, like a club. Samba and his cousins realised that their destruction was imminent. They went to Krishna and begged him to save them. Krishna said, "You have done something unpardonable, unpardonable. What can I do? All right, grind the whole iron rod into a powder. It will take a very, very long time. When it becomes powder, you must throw the powder into the sea."

With utmost enthusiasm and zeal, the young men started grinding the rod. But after a short time, they stopped and simply threw the rod into the sea. They did not grind the whole rod into powder, as Krishna had told them to do.

Many, many years later, after the battle of Kurukshetra, the iron rod came up to the surface of the sea and the prophecy of the sages came true. Krishna's family members started drinking heavily and fighting among themselves. Krishna's dearer-than-the-dearest friend, Satyaki, who had fought so bravely on the side of the Pandavas during the battle, was killed in a quarrel. One by one, all of the great warriors in Krishna's family were killed in this drunken brawl.

When Krishna saw that his dearest Satyaki had been killed, he said, "There is no need to stay on earth any longer." In the meantime, Krishna's brother, Balarama, had been observing the brawl. He saw the level to which the great heroes had descended and he was disgusted. "Enough, enough!" he said. "Our family has become so corrupt!" He entered into the forest and in his meditation he gave up his life-breath.

When Krishna heard that Balarama had left the body, he said, "My time has also come. Let me go and join him." Krishna went to a beautiful place. There, he sat down under a tree and he started meditating; he wanted to give up his life.

A hunter was passing by. He saw Krishna's form and thought it was a beautiful deer. To him, Krishna's left foot looked like the ear of the deer. The hunter aimed his arrow at the ear and released it. The arrow entered Krishna through the sole of his left foot — and that was the only weak point in Krishna's body. All his limbs and all the other parts of his body were invincible, but his left foot was vulnerable. Whenever he fought, he used to keep that foot well-protected. But he knew that it was weak and Balarama also knew it.

When the hunter came to claim the deer, he saw Krishna lying on the ground with the arrow piercing his foot. The hunter cried pitifully for forgiveness. But Krishna answered him, "No, it is not your fault. My time has come. That is why this has happened. It is all predestined."

"How is it predestined?" asked the hunter.

"This is the curse of Gandhari," Krishna told him.

During the battle of Kurukshetra, Gandhari's hundred sons were all killed by the Pandavas. She was heartbroken. After the battle, she said to Krishna, "You do not know what suffering I am going through! I am cursing you. The same thing will happen to your dear ones. They will quarrel and fight among themselves and they will all be killed."

Krishna said to Gandhari, "Mother, I am not responsible for the deaths of your sons. I begged them not to fight. I begged them to give just five villages to the Pandavas, but they would not listen to me. From the beginning to the end, your sons were so undivine."

Gandhari answered him, "No, no! I know you are God. You could have averted this war if you had wanted to. You could have saved my children and all my dear ones. But because of your partiality for the Pandavas, you did not do it. Therefore, I am cursing you. Exactly the same thing will happen to you. All your dear ones will kill each other."

Gandhari's dreadful curse came true and Krishna's entire clan was destroyed. You may ask how Gandhari could curse someone as great as Krishna. The fact is that Krishna could have nullified the curse, but he chose to accept it. His attitude was, if you want to strike me, then strike.

EIT 16. *Shiva fulfils all boons*

Lord Shiva is usually very calm and poised. He never brags like the other cosmic gods. It is not his way. Again, at one time or another, everybody becomes subject to pride. Since the time of our ancestors, our perennial source, we have all suffered from pride. This story is about Shiva's pride.

One day Shiva said, "People are always begging Brahma, Vishnu and me for this thing and that thing. Why do they have to beg? I have decided that they will only have to ask me once, and then I will immediately fulfil their desire. If I can give them a boon as soon as they utter their prayer, then naturally I will be the greatest, the most kind-hearted of the cosmic gods."

In this way Shiva wanted to prove that he was the greatest and also the best of the gods. To other gods you have to pray for 60,000 years before they will grant a boon, but Shiva promised that he would grant any boon as soon as the prayer was uttered.

One day, a king came to see Shiva. This particular king was very cruel and unkind. He said to Shiva, "Please grant me a boon."

"I shall grant any boon that you want," announced Shiva. At once the king said, "This is the boon that I desire: whomever I touch will turn to ashes."

"Oh, that is easy," said Shiva. "I grant you the boon. The moment you place your hands on somebody's head, that person will be reduced to ashes."

The cruel king was so happy. He said to Shiva, "I am so grateful to you. Now let me put my hands on your head to see whether you are telling me the truth."

Shiva started running away as fast as he could and the king began chasing him. Shiva was in serious trouble. He knew that if the king caught him and placed his hands on his head, he would be turned to ashes in an instant. Shiva ran and ran. Finally, he entered Vishnu's abode.

"Vishnu, Vishnu, what have I done? Save me, save me!" he cried.

With his third eye, Vishnu saw what had happened and he said to Shiva, "Do not worry. Just go and hide in my private room. No one is allowed to enter that room without my permission. I shall deal with that fellow."

A few moments later, the king entered Vishnu's abode. He challenged Vishnu, "Where is Shiva? He gave me a boon and now he refuses to let me test it on him."

Vishnu answered, "I can see you do not know Shiva's nature. He is a liar. When did he get that kind of spiritual power? He is my dearest friend. I know him so well. He definitely told you a lie. That is why he is running away. Here is the proof! If he had told you the truth, he would not be afraid of being exposed. I tell you, Shiva is a liar and a coward of the first order. He has no morality! You are wasting your time chasing him. I can easily prove that he is a liar. Just put your hands on your own head, and you will see that nothing will happen to you, absolutely nothing — I assure you."

The king believed Vishnu. He put his hands on his own head and was immediately burnt to ashes. This is how Vishnu saved his dearest friend Shiva.

EIT 17. *Vishnu takes incarnation as a dwarf*

This story is about Prahllada's grandson, Bali. Bali was an extremely powerful king, but he also wanted to be popular. By becoming powerful, we cannot be appreciated, admired or adored. It is like a superpower country. We may surrender to it, but with hatred instead of love.

Bali was determined to find a way to be popular. He came to the realisation that he would be loved, admired and adored by everybody if he performed a particular kind of sacrifice called a *yajna*. A yajna is performed only by great kings.

When the cosmic gods learned of Bali's intention, they became very jealous. They thought that after Bali had completed his sacrifice, people would worship him and they would no longer care for the cosmic gods. They went to Vishnu for help. "Please, please, do something," they begged. "Bali has become so powerful on earth! Soon the whole world will appreciate, admire and adore him, and our glory will be diminished."

Vishnu consoled them, "Do not worry," he said. "I will deal with Bali."

King Bali proceeded with the sacrificial ceremony under the guidance of his Guru, Shukracharya. Many people came to observe and participate in the function. As part of the sacrificial rites, Bali decided that he would grant special favours to anyone who asked him. He would immediately give whatever that person wanted.

All of a sudden, a dwarf joined the gathering and started chanting from the Vedas, the Upanishads and other holy scriptures. Bali was so happy to see such a tiny person, and he was full of admiration for the dwarf's chanting. He asked the dwarf, "Is there anything that you want from me?"

"Yes, there is something," said the dwarf. At that moment, Shukracharya whispered to Bali, "O my God, I can sense that this is not a dwarf! It is Vishnu, who has come here with some mischievous motive. Please, please, do not fulfil his desire! Whatever he asks you to do, you must refuse. As your Guru, I am telling you not to grant his wish."

"No, no," objected Bali. "I made a promise and I must keep it."

"I am your Guru," said Shukracharya. "You have to listen to me in this matter."

"You may be my Guru, but I made a promise, and I place my promise above everything else," said Bali. Look at Bali's disobedience! Instead of surrendering to his Guru, he bound himself to his promise.

Shukracharya loved his disciple and was determined to save him. Shukracharya had a big heart, and he also had wisdom in boundless measure. He said to Bali, "Before you give something, you have to have a small ceremony. In this detail, at least, you must listen to me. Whatever you want to give him, you can give. I do not know what he will ask you for. But before granting his wish, you must sprinkle a few drops of water on the dwarf's feet. Only then will everything be purified."

The sages used to keep their sacred Ganges water in an earthen vessel called a *kamandalu*. Shukracharya occultly entered into the kamandalu that Bali's wife had brought and sealed up the opening with his body. He felt that if he could stop the flow of the water, the purification ceremony could not be performed and Bali would not be able to fulfil the dwarf's wish.

Bali did not know that his Guru was inside the earthen vessel. When Bali sat at the feet of the dwarf and tried to pour the water, he discovered that the mouthpiece of the vessel was sealed. "O my God!" he said. "What am I going to do?"

Bali looked around for something to pierce the opening. You may think that a knife would have best served his purpose. But instead, he merely used a straw of hay. With the straw he was digging and poking. Unfortunately, the straw pierced one of his Guru's eyes, leaving him blind in that eye. Naturally, Bali did not know that his Guru's eye was there. When Shukracharya emerged from the vessel holding his left eye, Bali felt utterly miserable.

He said to the dwarf, "I am responsible for making my own Guru blind in one eye, just because I wanted to keep my promise. I am filled with sadness, but I still want to grant you your desire. The water is now coming out of the vessel without any obstruction. Let me sprinkle some on your feet and then you can ask me for whatever you want."

After Bali had observed the ceremony, he asked the dwarf to tell him his wish. "You see how tiny I am. Kindly allow me to have the ground that can be covered in three steps," said the dwarf. Bali laughed at the dwarf's wish. "You are so short! How much distance can you cover in just three steps? All right, I grant your request. You can take your three steps in any direction you choose."

Upon hearing Bali's words, the dwarf, who was Lord Vishnu himself, resumed his universal form. With one stride, he covered the whole world; with his second stride, he covered the *Brahmaloka*, or Heavenly world. For his third stride, there are two versions of the story.

One version says that there are three worlds: this world, the higher world and the nether world. In Sanskrit, the words are *bhuloka, bhuvarloka* and *svarloka*. After covering this world and the higher world, Lord Vishnu said to Bali, "Now please tell me, where will I place my foot? There is still one stride left."

Bali answered, "There is no place left for your third stride, so please be kind enough to put your foot on my back." Lord Vishnu then placed his foot on Bali's back and Bali was immediately destroyed.

Another version of the story says that after Vishnu had covered the three worlds, he saw that poor Bali did not have any place to stay. Bali, who had been all-powerful on earth, now had nothing. Vishnu told him, "By birth, you are an asura. Your proper home is in the nether world. I would like you to return to the nether world to live so that Indra and the other gods can enjoy their proper kingdom in Heaven. You have lost all your wealth and power. There is no place for you here on earth now."

Bali was filled with happiness. He said, "My Lord, with your infinite Grace you have blessed me by allowing me to see your celestial form. I was blinded by wealth and power. But now I am so pleased that you are sending me back to my real home underground. I will be happy in that world and the cosmic gods, especially Indra, will be happy once again in the higher world. I do not know how I can thank you for your kindness towards me."

This is the story of Lord Vishnu in his incarnation as a dwarf, who was called Vamana. To me, the most painful part of the story is when Bali pierced the eye of his own Guru while he was trying to get water from the vessel. That is why Shukracharya is known as being blind in one eye. This tragedy happened only because Bali disobeyed his Master. When there is a conflict between the Master and his disciples, very often something happens to the body of the Master.

EIT 18. *The end of the Kshatriya line*

As you know, in India we think of society as a great family. Within that family there are four classes or castes which, ideally, work to make the family function harmoniously. The four classes are Brahmin, Kshatriya, Vaishya and Shudra. Brahmins protect the family from hostile forces by virtue of their prayers and meditations. Kshatriyas are warriors. They protect the family from enemies by virtue of their physical prowess. Vaishyas are businessmen and merchants. They support the family. And Shudras serve others. They do not have money or intellect, but with their strong hands they serve the rest of the family.

The spiritual Masters of India's past have come from either the Brahmin class or the Kshatriya class. Sri Ramachandra, Sri

Krishna, Sri Chaitanya, Sri Ramakrishna and Sri Aurobindo, to name a few, were all either Brahmins or Kshatriyas.

Both Brahmins and Kshatriyas have tremendous pride because of their status in society. Although Vaishyas support the family, they do not show that much pride. They feel that they do not have the prayerful capacities of the Brahmins or the strength and valour of the Kshatriyas. The Shudras, since they are the servant class, do not have any pride.

This story is about the wrath of a Brahmin's son towards the entire Kshatriya caste. There was once a king who prayed to Brahma to make him supremely powerful. Brahma gave him thousands of weapons and the king was truly all-powerful on earth. One day the king went out hunting with his retinue. After hunting for some time, the king became tired. He discovered a small cottage nearby, and he went there to have a glass of water.

The cottage was occupied by a sage named Jamadagni. This sage said to the king, "You have asked me only for some water. But you are the king. If you and your soldiers would like to eat also, I will be able to feed you all."

The king was simply amazed. "You are so poor! How can you provide food for all of us? Do you not see how many soldiers are accompanying me?"

The sage was adamant. "I shall definitely be able to feed you," he said. "Please invite all your soldiers to come."

At the king's command, the soldiers came and sat down, and Jamadagni served them a sumptuous meal. Meanwhile, the king was curious as to how the sage had been able to feed so many people. The king saw that the sage owned nothing save one cow. The name of this particular cow was Kamadhenu. *Dhenu* means "cow" and *kama* means "desire". This cow was able to grant any desire.

The sage had asked the cow to provide a feast for the king's army, and she had brought forth food and drinks in abundance.

The king said to the sage, "A cow such as this should belong only to a king. Please give her to me."

"Even though you are the king, I cannot part with this cow," proclaimed the sage.

The king was stunned by the sage's refusal. He implored the sage to hand over the cow, but the sage would not give her up. Finally, the king, who was a Kshatriya, decided to use force and seize the cow. He and his soldiers all fought with the sage, but the sage was very, very powerful. With his divine weapons, he killed many of the king's soldiers and defeated the king.

Burning with anger, the king returned to his kingdom and assembled a more powerful army. A few months later, he returned to attack the sage and capture the cow. This time, unfortunately, the sage was killed during the ensuing fight and the cow was stolen.

It happened that Jamadagni's son, Parashuram, had been absent from his father's home when this fighting took place. When he returned and found that his father had been killed and the cow taken away, Parashuram was furious. He took a vow that he would kill all the Kshatriyas. "Whomever I see belonging to that caste, I will kill," he said.

According to our Indian mythology, all the Kshatriyas were killed twenty-one times over by Parashuram because the king had killed his father. After wiping out the entire Kshatriya line, Parashuram said, "Now it is time for me to meditate." He started meditating and he gave up his life-breath in a state of trance.

Somehow, though, our Kshatriya line was revived and it came to pass that even the highest spiritual Masters were born into Kshatriya families.

EIT 19. *The power of the Gayatri mantra*

In India, we repeat the Gayatri mantra to gain illumination:

> *Aum bhur bhuvah svah*
> *tat savitur varenyam*
> *bhargo devasya dhimahi*
> *dhiyo yo nah pracodayat*

> We meditate on the transcendental glory of the
> Deity Supreme, who is inside the heart of the earth,
> inside the life of the sky and inside the soul of the
> Heaven. May He stimulate and illumine our minds.

Gayatri is a supreme goddess. She is worshipped by Brahma,
Vishnu, Shiva and all the other cosmic gods. This particular
goddess resides inside each and every human heart in the form
of a swan. If you meditate and dive deep within, you will see a
swan, and that is the goddess Gayatri. The swan is the symbol
of God-realisation.

It is said that if you can repeat the Gayatri mantra seven
times most soulfully, all your sins will be washed away; all your
past wrong karma will be nullified. Again, it is said that if you
can repeat the mantra ten times most soulfully, you will realise
the Highest; you will attain God-realisation. Finally, if you can
repeat it most soulfully seventeen times, you will go beyond
God-realisation.

Our philosophy is also self-transcendence. But in the case of
the Gayatri mantra, the thing that comes after God-realisation,
according to tradition, is quite unexpected. It is said that if
you repeat the mantra seventeen times, you will be liberated
from the sin of killing a cow or a Brahmin. These two sins are
considered the worst possible sins, so their nullification has
been placed even above God-realisation in order of importance.

Again, it comes down to the whole question of Brahmins and Kshatriyas. Because the Kshatriyas are powerful, the Brahmins are afraid of being killed by them. So they have found a secret way to ensure their protection!

EIT 20. *Parvati is jealous of the Ganga*

This is a story about Parvati's jealousy and insecurity. As you know, the river Ganga descended from Lord Shiva's matted hair. When it first came down from the Himalayas, it became entangled in Shiva's hair. Then it passed through his hair and became the Ganga.

During the time when the water was entangled in Shiva's matted hair, Shiva became very fond of the water. He gave it so much of his attention that his consort, Parvati, became terribly jealous.

"My husband spends all his time touching his hair," she said, "He does not care for me at all."

Parvati was consumed with jealousy, and she begged Shiva to somehow get rid of the water that was trapped in his hair. Shiva did not want to comply with her request. He enjoyed having the water in his hair.

Seeing that Parvati was utterly miserable, her son, Ganesha, felt sorry for her. "I cannot bear to see my mother so sad, depressed, morose and miserable," he said. "I have to do something."

Ganesha remembered a particular sage named Goutama. Once, during a famine, there was no food anywhere, either on earth or in Heaven. Only this sage had provisions, and so the cosmic gods came to his place to eat. They all loved him and adored him. Ganesha felt that this sage was the only one who could help him release the Ganga from his father's head and let it flow down onto the land. Ganesha decided to go and see the sage.

Before leaving, he approached one of his mother's assistants. Her name was Jaya. He said to her, "Please do me a favour."

"Definitely," Jaya assured him. "I will do any favour you want."

Ganesha told her his plan: "I am going to the ashram of the sage Goutama, who kept provisions for the gods during the famine. You will kindly take the form of a cow. In the morning, when the sage takes his cows to graze, I would like you to destroy all the grain that is growing in the fields near his cottage. You must destroy all his fields of grain."

Ganesha went to see the sage and he was received with great kindness and hospitality. The sage was deeply honoured that a cosmic god had come to stay at his place.

The next morning, when the sage took his cows out to eat the grass, a strange cow came and started destroying all the fields of grain. The sage begged the cow not to destroy the grain, which was his main provision, but this cow was bent on destroying everything. The sage was unable to stop it.

Finally the sage took a single blade of grass and with it he touched the cow's body. The cow fell down and died then and there. Ganesha and others came running to the spot.

"You are a sage," cried Ganesha. "How could you kill a cow? It is the worst possible sin to kill a cow, especially because you are a Brahmin! You must pay the penalty for your misdeed!"

The sage felt very sorry for his action and he said, "I want to make amends for this wrongful deed. I am willing to pay whatever penalty you suggest. Please tell me what I should do now!"

Ganesha said, "Invoke Lord Brahma. Whatever advice he gives you will be the best." The sage invoked Lord Brahma and Brahma came.

Now, Brahma knew how much Parvati was suffering due to Shiva's preoccupation with the Ganga in his hair. Brahma advised the sage, "If you want forgiveness for what you have done, then you must release the Ganga from Shiva's hair. Let the waters flow down to earth, and then you must take a bath in the river Ganga. If you can do this, you will be purified and all your sins will be washed away."

The sage listened to Brahma. He used his spiritual power to bring the water down to earth. When the Ganga was flowing properly, he bathed in it and became purified. Ganesha's plan worked.

Once the Ganga was no longer entangled in Shiva's hair, Parvati had Shiva all to herself again and she was filled with happiness.

EIT 21. *Vishwamitra begs Vashishtha for forgiveness*

There are so many stories about Vishwamitra and Vashishtha. One of them is deeply moving. Vishwamitra wanted Vashishtha to call him *Rajarshi* or *Brahmarshi,* meaning "one who has attained the absolute highest". But Vashishtha refused to use that title when he was speaking to Vishwamitra. Vishwamitra said, "If you do not tell the whole world that I have realised the absolute Highest, then I shall kill all your spiritual children one by one."

Even then Vashishtha would not address him by that title, so Vishwamitra killed Vashishtha's one hundred disciples, whom he called his sons.

Still Vashishtha would not declare that Vishwamitra had achieved the status of Brahmarshi. His wife, Arundhati, pleaded with him: "What are you doing? If you just say that Vishwamitra has realised the Highest, what harm is there in it? He has killed all your disciples. I am afraid that if you do not fulfil his wish, he will kill you as well."

In spite of his wife's request, Vashishtha remained firm. "No, I cannot do that," he said. "I am ready to be killed, if necessary."

Strangely enough, on that particular night Vishwamitra had come to kill Vashishtha. As he stood in front of the door to Vashishtha's cottage, he overheard Vashishtha's wife say, "Why do you not want to tell him that he has realised the highest Truth?"

Then he heard Vashishtha's words of reply: "Because I love him. If I tell him at this stage of his life that he has realised the Highest, then it will be a lie. He will think that he has realised the Highest and yet he will not be able to get the results of the Highest. He will not be able to drink Nectar. Because I love him, I cannot tell him a lie."

Vashishtha's words touched Vishwamitra's heart, and immediately he fell at Vashishtha's feet and begged for forgiveness. At once Vashishtha forgave him. By touching Vashishtha's feet, Vishwamitra did reach the Highest.

In those days, that kind of spiritual or occult power the sages had. Sri Aurobindo wrote a story about this particular episode. It is called "The Ideal of Forgiveness." He described how Vashishtha forgave Vishwamitra even though Vishwamitra had killed one hundred of his disciples. When I was a young boy, I transferred this story into rhyming verse in Bengali. Many years later, I did it in English verse also.

EIT 22. *Lord Krishna curses his own son*

This is another story about Lord Krishna's notorious son, Samba. Samba misbehaved to such an extent that Krishna became extremely, extremely displeased with him. He told his son, "You have cast a slur upon our family. You have done countless bad things. I cannot tolerate you anymore. The very sight of you is repulsive to me!"

Krishna went on scolding Samba and insulting him in this manner. Krishna's wife, Jambavati, was also present. Finally, Krishna's anger reached its zenith. He said, "I am so disgusted with you that I am cursing you. You will contract leprosy."

Lo and behold, Samba immediately started suffering from leprosy. His body became disfigured overnight and he was in great agony from the disease.

Lord Krishna's wife could not endure seeing her son tortured in this way. With tears streaming from her eyes, she approached her husband. "What have you done?" she said. "I cannot bear to see Samba in such pain. He is, after all, our own son."

Krishna relented and said to his son, "All right, this is what you can do to be cured. First, you have to pray to Surya, the sun god. Then you must bathe in the river Chandrabhaga. When you immerse yourself in the water, you will be cured."

By this time, Samba could not even get up. He asked pitifully, "How can I go there in this condition, Father?"

"You have to go to the river," answered Krishna in a stern voice.

Samba began pleading with Krishna. "I know that you have the capacity to cure me right here. Please lift your curse."

"I am not going to cure you," said Krishna.

Jambavati appealed to her husband. "You are the cause of his disease. Therefore, you must either take him to the river or cure him here."

Finally, Krishna agreed to take his son to the river. Because Samba could no longer walk, Krishna carried him the entire way. When they arrived at the banks of the river, Samba prayed to the sun god and then entered into the river. Krishna bathed his son in the water and, when Samba emerged, he found that he was completely cured. Krishna's curse had been nullified.

In those days, a curse was something to be feared! Nowadays, people curse each other at every second, but their curses do not have any power. Otherwise, so many serious calamities would have taken place. With all the mistakes that we make in our daily lives, we would have died long ago if we had really been cursed. Fortunately, there is no fire inside the words as there was in those ancient times.

EIT 23. *Ganesha encircles the universe*

The two sons of Shiva and Parvati were called Ganesha and Kartikeya. As time passed, both of them became extremely eager to get married. They begged their parents, "Please, please find us suitable wives. You choose. We are dying to get married. Unless we are happily married, we feel that our lives will be empty."

Shiva and Parvati were more than happy to fulfil their sons' request. "We shall find you both beautiful wives," they promised.

Unfortunately, Ganesha and Kartikeya had a terrible argument. Each of them wanted to get married first. Ganesha wanted to marry before Kartikeya because he was the older of the two, and Kartikeya wanted to marry before Ganesha because he thought that the youngest should get the first chance.

Shiva and Parvati now had a serious problem on their hands. They could not decide whom to please and whom to deny. At last Shiva said, "Let us do one thing: whoever can travel to the ends of the earth and come back first will be married first."

Kartikeya immediately set out on his journey. His vehicle was a peacock. Three years passed and still he had not reached the ends of the earth. Meanwhile, the pot-bellied Ganesha stayed at home enjoying himself. He knew that he could not hope to keep up with his athletic brother.

When Shiva saw that Ganesha had not even begun the race, he said to his son, "What are you doing? You have not yet even started! Any day, any moment, Kartikeya will come back. What is wrong with you?"

Ganesha remained silent and Shiva continued, "I know what you are thinking. As long as you can get married, it is enough. You no longer care who is first and who is second. That is why you are not in a rush. You have accepted your defeat."

Ganesha simply smiled at his father and went on with his usual routines. One day, a thought crossed his mind: "I am sure that by now my brother has travelled to the farthest lengths of the earth and is on his way home. Now is the time for me to act."

He went to bathe in the river and then circled his mother, Parvati. After completing one round, he bathed once more and again circled his mother. Seven times he bathed and seven times he circumambulated her.

"What are you doing, my son?" asked Parvati.

"Have you not read our sacred scriptures, Mother?" Ganesha answered. "The shastras tell us that you are the Divine Mother; you are the whole world, the entire universe. I went around you not once but seven times. That means I have gone around the world seven times. So am I not entitled to marry first?"

"What kind of logic is this?" objected Shiva.

Ganesha presented his argument: "If you do not consider my mother to be the Divine Mother, if you do not believe in the Vedas, then why do you tell people to honour the Vedas? You always say that the Vedas are correct and perfect. How can you justify yourself?"

Shiva realised that his son was right. Parvati was the entire universe. To show that they approved of Ganesha's action, Shiva and Parvati found not one but two most beautiful wives for him. Their names were Buddhi and Siddhi. Each wife bore Ganesha a son. Ganesha named his sons Labha and Laksha. He was so proud of his family, and they lived the happiest life together.

The grandparents, Shiva and Parvati, were also extremely happy with their new grandchildren. But sometimes a little sadness entered into them when they thought of poor Kartikeya. He had been gone so many years, and they did not know when he would return.

As Kartikeya drew nearer to home, he saw the sage Narada. He said to Narada, "How is everything? Tell me some news."

"How is everything?" echoed Narada. "Why are you so late?"

"What do you mean?" asked Kartikeya. "Has Ganesha already returned?"

"Yes," said Narada. "He is married, he has two wives and each of them has given him a son. How could you allow him to claim the victory?"

Upon hearing Narada's news, Kartikeya grew furious. He did not accept Ganesha's interpretation of the shastras at all. He reached home and saw with his own eyes that Ganesha was extremely happy with his wives and sons.

Shiva and Parvati tried their best to console Kartikeya. They promised to find him a beautiful bride. But Kartikeya's blood was boiling. He declared, "No! I am taking an oath. Since you all fooled me, I am not going to get married at all in this lifetime."

Henceforth, Kartikeya was known as *Kumara,* which means "one who is unmarried".

Having taken his oath, Kumara left his parents' house to live alone. He did not want to remain with his family any longer because he felt they had all deceived him.

Kumara refused to return home, even to visit his parents. They missed him greatly, so they asked him if they could go and visit him. He agreed that when the night was darkest and there was no moon, Shiva could visit him, and when the moon was at its fullest, Parvati could visit him. He agreed to see them, but only on those two occasions each month, because he was so disgusted with his entire family.

THE EARTH-ILLUMINATION-TRUMPETS OF DIVINITY'S HOME

BOOK 3

This story is about Arjuna, who was the third of the Pandava brothers. He wanted to go on a pilgrimage. Everybody knows that if you embark on a pilgrimage and if you pray and meditate at certain sacred places, then you get special blessings from the cosmic gods and goddesses. In Arjuna's case, he wanted to acquire the power to destroy his enemies.

Arjuna set out alone. There were five very important places of pilgrimage on the shores of the southern sea that he wished to visit. He went to each of these famous places but was extremely disappointed in each place, for he could not find even one person praying and meditating. "Something is wrong," he said. "Either I have come to the wrong places by mistake or something has gone wrong with these holy places."

After visiting the fifth and last site, Arjuna started on his homeward journey. His mind was filled with sadness. He had not gone very far when he saw a sage meditating. Arjuna approached the sage and said, "O sage, I have just visited the five sacred places of pilgrimage. How is it that nobody was praying and meditating along the banks of the rivers there?"

"There is a special reason," answered the sage.

"Please enlighten me as to the cause of this mystery," requested Arjuna.

The sage told Arjuna, "Here is the reason. If you go there, you are supposed to bathe in the river before you begin your worship. But as soon as people enter into the waters, a terrible creature comes and devours them. It lives inside the water. Once you go into the water, you can never come out again. This happens at each sacred place. That is why nobody goes there to pray and meditate anymore. They are afraid. They know that they must first take a bath in the waters, and they do not want to be killed by those water creatures."

"Oh, is that the reason?" said Arjuna. "Then I will go back and see for myself. I am not afraid!"

Arjuna went to the nearest site and entered into the water. Immediately, an enormous crocodile caught him in its jaws and began pulling him down. The crocodile wanted to devour Arjuna, but Arjuna had tremendous strength and he began wrestling with the crocodile. A great struggle took place under the water, and finally Arjuna defeated the crocodile. He came out of the water dragging the crocodile behind him. As soon as the crocodile emerged from the river, it changed into a most beautiful apsara, or divine nymph.

Arjuna was astonished. "How is it possible?" he cried. "You fought with me so fiercely in the form of a crocodile and now you have become so beautiful!"

The nymph bowed to Arjuna. "You have saved me, you have saved me! Now I am begging you to release the four other crocodiles. They are my friends."

"How did this fate befall you?" asked Arjuna.

The nymph replied, "Once a great sage was meditating at one of the sacred sites. He was meditating so intensely that the cosmic gods became worried. They asked us to disturb his meditation, for otherwise he would surpass them in spiritual and occult power. We obeyed those great cosmic gods and came before the sage. But when we tried to disturb his meditation, he got furious and cursed us to take crocodile incarnations. He said that we would be forced to live here in the rivers of these five sacred places, killing and devouring all the pilgrims who entered into the water. We would have to remain here until somebody who was very religious and, at the same time, extremely powerful came to visit the sacred places. The sage told us that we would not be able to devour this man. He would fight with us and defeat us. Then, when he brought us out of the water, we would once again become apsaras. We have waited so long for your coming! Today you have saved me and I am so grateful to you. Please, please save my friends also!"

Arjuna knew that he had to release the four other nymphs from their sad fate. He went to each place, entered into the water and fought with the huge crocodiles that attacked him. One by one, he defeated them all and brought them out of the water. In this way, he was able to release them from the curse of the sage and give them back their beautiful forms.

EIT 25. *The origin of Vishnu's Sudarshana Chakra*

This is the story of how Vishnu's Sudarshana Chakra came into existence. The asuras, or demons, were extremely bad. They always tortured the cosmic gods. At one time, the cosmic gods were suffering so much from the attacks of the demons that they went to see Lord Vishnu. They wanted to seek his help in defeating the demons.

Vishnu said to them, "I do not have enough power to defeat or destroy the demons. I must seek help from Shiva. I will ask him to give me a special weapon that will help me defeat the demons."

When Vishnu went to Shiva, he found Lord Shiva in trance. Vishnu did not want to disturb Shiva's meditation, so he started praying and praying to Shiva with the hope that one day he would come out of his trance.

Every day, for years and years, Vishnu prayed to Shiva, meditated on Shiva and chanted Shiva's name very devotedly. He offered one thousand lotus blossoms to Shiva every day. Each time he offered Shiva a lotus blossom, he would chant Shiva's name.

This went on for such a long time and still Shiva remained rapt in trance. Poor Vishnu was helpless! The gods were being mercilessly tortured by the demons and he was unable to save them.

Finally, after many long years, Shiva came out of his trance. Vishnu's joy knew no bounds. He ran to gather one thousand lotus blossoms so that he could worship Lord Shiva and ask for a special boon.

Shiva had already decided that he would grant Vishnu the boon, but first he wanted to play a trick on Vishnu. He secretly went to the spot where Vishnu had placed the lotus flowers and stole one flower. Now there were only 999 flowers.

After making all his preparations, Vishnu began to worship Shiva most devotedly. One by one, he offered the lotus flowers and chanted Shiva's name. When he came to the end, he realised that one flower was missing. He had only counted 999. That meant he had to go and find one more lotus. Instead of doing that, he immediately plucked out one of his eyes and placed it before Shiva.

When Shiva saw that Vishnu had such devotion for him, he said, "I will grant you anything that you ask for."

"Please give me something that will help me to conquer the asuras," said Vishnu.

Shiva replied, "I give you this round disc. It will help you to conquer all your enemies. No matter how many demons come to attack you and the other gods, you will be able to defeat them all with this disc."

The name of the disc was the Sudarshana Chakra. When Lord Krishna took incarnation, Vishnu gave him this chakra, because Krishna was the embodiment of Vishnu. Krishna could immediately use the chakra at any time; it was his own property. Sri Chaitanya also used the Sudarshana Chakra a few times. He was able to invoke it and it would come to him. When he wanted to kill Jagai and Madhai, for example, he invoked it. These two ruffians saw it coming from Heaven and became extremely frightened. Before it reached them, they surrendered to Sri Chaitanya.

The Sudarshana Chakra is not thrown. With will-power it is sent against the enemy. It rotates very, very fast after leaving the finger and chases the enemy. The chakra itself is round and has something like the points of arrows all around its edge. It has tremendous occult and spiritual power to destroy everything. Nobody can stand against the Sudarshana Chakra.

EIT 26. *The power of Lord Shiva's name*

This story is about one particular husband and wife. Although it is from our ancient Puranas, in many ways the story sounds absolutely like twentieth-century American life!

The husband was from the Vaishya, or merchant, class. He was a very rich trader and he used to travel from village to village. One day, he was returning home all alone when he saw a most beautiful woman by the side of the road. He fell in love with her instantly and began meeting with her frequently. People came to know that he was mixing with this woman and they started speaking ill of him. It was too much for his poor wife.

She pleaded with him, "What are you doing? People are saying such evil things about you. Please do not bring shame upon our family! We have been happily married for so many years. We have such beautiful children. Please do not give it all up for this woman."

Unfortunately, the husband refused to listen to his wife. He continued seeing the woman and even visited her house. For years and years the wife tolerated her husband's misbehaviour. Finally, she threatened him, "If you will not give up your bad life, then I will do the same thing. I will find a boyfriend!"

The husband did not take his wife seriously. He felt it was acceptable for *him* to lead an undivine life, but he could not believe that his wife would do the same. He simply disregarded her threat.

The wife was furious. She was ready to kill her husband. Finally she decided that she would carry out her threat and lead an undivine life. She thought that this would make her husband realise how badly he had treated her and he would give up his girlfriend.

The wife found a boyfriend and began inviting him home. She wanted to teach her husband a lesson. Both husband and wife were now enjoying an undivine life. One day the husband came home only to discover his wife's boyfriend in the house. The husband was infuriated! He struck the boyfriend and wounded him so severely that the boyfriend had to be taken to the doctor. The husband thought that was the end of the matter. After such a thrashing, he was sure the boyfriend would not dare to return.

Unfortunately, the wife started going to the boyfriend's place. During the day the husband would be with his girlfriend, and at night he would come home only to find that his wife was somewhere else. What a story!

This went on for several years, and then the wife's boyfriend lost interest in her. He found somebody to take her place. The wife was very sad and disturbed. "O God," she cried bitterly, "for him I gave up my husband and this is what he has done to me! He has found somebody else!" Then she said to herself, "Ah, it is because I am too old. I am not as beautiful as I was before. That is why he does not want to see me. I cannot regain my lost beauty and I can never get back all the years that I have wasted leading such an undivine life. What am I going to do with my life? I know that I will die soon. Perhaps it is too late for me to become spiritual, but let me see. Let me try to pray and meditate for the brief time that I have left on earth."

The wife left her home and began wandering at random from place to place, praying and meditating. One day she came upon a temple dedicated to Lord Shiva, with a pond in front of it. There, people were reciting verses from the scriptures about Shiva.

She saw a man standing by the pond and she asked him, "What are those people saying?"

"They are praising Lord Shiva," he replied. "These are verses from the scriptures about Lord Shiva's greatness and kindness. Lord Shiva forgives each and every person on earth. There is nobody whom Lord Shiva does not forgive."

"Will he forgive me?" she asked eagerly.

"You heard them chanting, did you not?" said the man.

"Yes, I heard them chanting."

"That means you are already forgiven."

"But I have not prayed to Lord Shiva."

"It does not matter," the man assured her. "Even if one hears Lord Shiva's name, one is forgiven. You have been standing here for a long time and you have heard them chanting Lord Shiva's name over and over, so Lord Shiva has definitely forgiven you."

"How will I know that I have been forgiven?" the wife asked. "I am so bad! I have done so many wrong things in my life."

The man explained, "You will see that you have been forgiven when you die. Your soul will go to Lord Shiva's region, his loka."

"I will not go to hell for the bad things I have done?"

"No, no, no! Now that you have heard Lord Shiva's name, you will go directly to Heaven, I promise you."

In the course of time the wife died and her soul did go to the highest Heaven, as the man had said. She was so happy in that realm.

After some time, she began to make enquiries about her boyfriend, who had also died. The denizens of Heaven said,

"He was such a bad fellow! His soul has gone to hell and he is experiencing tremendous suffering."

"Can you also tell me about my husband?" she asked.

"Your husband and your boyfriend are in the same category," came the reply. "But since your husband started this wrong movement, his soul is suffering even more powerfully than the soul of your boyfriend. Your husband is the worst culprit, so we have sent him to a particular hell which is infinitely worse than all the others."

The wife began begging the Heavenly beings, "Please, please, can you not do something to help my husband? After all, we were both equally wrong. It is only by the Grace of Lord Shiva that I am here. I just heard his name at a temple and I was forgiven. It does not seem fair that I should be enjoying Heaven, while my husband should be suffering so much. After all, we were happily married for such a long time. How can I bring my husband's soul to Heaven? I am ready to pray and meditate. Please tell me what I should do."

"Nobody will dare to go into that lowest hell," said the Heavenly beings. "There is nothing we can do."

"If I pray and meditate, will it make any difference?" asked the wife.

"Yes," they said. "You can certainly pray and meditate. Who knows, one day Lord Shiva may forgive your husband as he forgave you."

So the wife started praying and meditating most fervently. After some time, a messenger from Lord Shiva came and said, "Lord Shiva is very pleased with your sincerity. He knows what you want and he will grant you the boon. If you want to descend into the lowest hell to bring back your husband, he will send someone with you. One of the celestial musicians will accompany you. As you were exonerated by hearing Lord Shiva's devotees chanting his sacred name so devotedly and soulfully, so will your husband be freed from his sins by hearing this musician sing the praises of Lord Shiva. Then you and your husband will be able to stay together in Heaven."

The wife was overjoyed. She took the celestial musician with her to that worst possible hell. When they reached that unbearable place, the musician sang many songs in praise of Lord Shiva. Hearing them, the husband was absolved of his wrongdoings and he went with his wife to live in Heaven. Because of Lord Shiva's compassion and forgiveness, these two were accepted into Heaven.

In India, people still believe that no matter what kind of life you lead, as long as you hear people devotedly praying to Lord Shiva or singing songs in praise of him, all your sins will be washed away.

EIT 27. *Lord Krishna meets Radha*

When Krishna was a little boy of four or five, his father, Nanda, took him to the field where the cattle were grazing. Krishna wanted to spring a surprise on his father, so he created a severe thunderstorm. It began to rain heavily and the trees were tossing wildly.

Although Krishna was responsible for the storm, he pretended that he knew nothing. He started crying and screaming, and he clung to his father for protection.

Nanda was trying desperately to protect his child and also the cattle. He found that he could not manage to do the two things simultaneously, and so he was in a terrible predicament. He had to save his dearest child and again, he had to save the cattle. Nanda could see no way to bring both the cattle and the child home safely.

All of a sudden, a most beautiful woman appeared. Nanda was very relieved to see this unknown woman who had come at such a crucial moment. "Would you kindly take care of my child?" he asked. "I must take the cattle home now. Then I will come back. I am sure that you will be able to protect my son."

"Do not worry. I will definitely take good care of your child," the woman assured Nanda.

Nanda departed for home with the frightened cattle. When Krishna and the woman were alone together, Krishna did something extraordinary. He created a most enchanting scene and took the form of a youth. This youth was dark-skinned; he wore an orange cloth and on his forehead there was a peacock feather. In his hands, he held a flute which he was playing so hauntingly. Krishna looked at the woman and asked her, "Do you remember this incident, when we were in Heaven?"

The unknown woman was Radha, who was Krishna's dearest beloved.

Radha replied, "I do remember this incident. It is very vivid to me." Krishna was showing Radha a scene from their life together in Heaven before they took incarnation on earth. He wanted to remind Radha of their eternal oneness.

The time was fast approaching for Krishna's father to come and take his son home. Krishna stopped the performance in Heaven and became a little child again. He started crying pitifully for his father to come and claim him. After some time, Nanda had still not appeared and Radha became very worried. She was wondering what to do when she heard a voice telling her to take the child to Nanda's house.

Radha was so sad and miserable that she had to return Krishna to his parents after being reunited with him on earth. She was afraid that she would not be able to see him anymore. But the voice told her, "Take the child back to Nanda and Yashoda. If you listen to me, I assure you that you will be able to go and see your Lord Krishna every evening. You will meet him and he will play his flute for you. A part of your heart will always remain with him."

At that moment, there appeared Brahma, the Creator. For 60,000 years he had been praying to the Highest only to have a glimpse of Radha. In his meditation, he had seen Krishna and Radha together on earth and he was deeply moved. So he came personally to see Radha, who was the embodiment of the Universal Force.

Radha obeyed the inner message that she had received from the voice and took the child back to Nanda's house. After that, she used to come and visit Krishna every evening.

That is one version of how Lord Krishna and Radha met for the first time. There is another version of the story. In this second version, it is believed that Radha's father was a very rich king. When Radha was still a little girl, he decided it was time for her to get married. He made all the necessary arrangements for her to marry a neighbouring prince.

But Radha did not want to get married; she wanted only to be with Krishna. So she took her soul out of her body and kept only a portion of herself, a shadow of her real existence, inside her body. The prince for whom she was intended married the shadow.

Radha transported her soul to Nanda's family because she knew that Lord Krishna was being brought up there. She took birth in Nanda's family, and she and Krishna became brother and sister, closer than the closest.

EIT 28. *Kartikeya and the five princesses*

One day, when Kartikeya was three years old, his mother, Parvati, took him with her to the river. Kartikeya was playing happily in the reeds that grow by the side of the river. Parvati thought she would leave him there for a few minutes while she went home to do something.

Alas, when she came back, Kartikeya was nowhere to be found. Parvati was so upset and worried. She searched and searched for him, but to no avail. Finally, she was forced to return home without him and give Shiva the sad news. Shiva was heartbroken that their dearest child was missing.

What actually happened was this: while Parvati was absent, five princesses passed by. They saw the little child playing in the reeds and they could not conquer their temptation. He was so divinely beautiful! They took Kartikeya back to their palace and cared for him as their own.

Now, these particular princesses were very spiritual. Because of their prayer and meditation, the cosmic gods would sometimes visit them in person. One day, soon after they had taken Kartikeya, four or five cosmic gods came to their palace.

"Where did you get such a beautiful child?" asked the gods. "We know that all of you are unmarried."

"We abducted the child," confessed the princesses.

"How could you do such a thing?" cried the gods. "To whom does the child belong?"

"We do not know whose child he is," the princesses answered truthfully. "We simply saw him playing in the reeds and we could not resist taking him. He looked so charming! Now we are bringing him up."

"How much suffering the poor parents must be going through!" lamented the gods. They added, "All right, since you do not know who his rightful parents are, he can stay here. But let us make him very powerful."

The cosmic gods started teaching Kartikeya archery and all the other arts of fighting. As the years passed by, Kartikeya became extremely skilful and powerful. The cosmic gods were so pleased with him. They declared, "We are more than satisfied with your progress. We have taught you so many things and you have learned them very well. You are undoubtedly the strongest warrior. In skill, you have surpassed even us. We now declare you to be the commander-in-chief of the cosmic gods."

Soon the news reached Shiva and Parvati that a newcomer had been made the supreme leader of the cosmic gods. "They are saying that his strength is unparalleled," remarked Shiva to his wife. "I understand that all the cosmic gods have helped him."

"Then let us go and see him," suggested Parvati.

When Parvati saw Kartikeya, she felt at once that this was her long-lost son. Shiva, as usual was hesitant. He doubted that this brave warrior could be the beautiful little son whom he had lost so many years before. But Parvati was convinced. She begged Shiva to make enquiries about Kartikeya's background.

Shiva and Parvati learned that Kartikeya had been raised by five unmarried princesses who had found him playing all alone in the reeds by the side of a river. When the princesses described the location of the reeds, Shiva cried out, "That is the exact place where we lost our child!"

This is how Kartikeya became commander-in-chief of the cosmic gods and was finally restored to his grief-stricken parents.

EIT 29. *Radha's one-hundred-year curse*

One day Radha came to learn that Krishna was talking at great length with one of the gopis named Brinda. Radha became furious. She fully intended to scold and insult both Krishna and Brinda.

Brinda heard that Radha was burning with anger, and she was filled with fear. She did not know what the consequences would be and so she committed suicide.

Krishna happened to be with one of his dearest friends, Sridhama, when Radha arrived to give Krishna his scolding. Sridhama was always for Krishna, and he could not bear to hear Krishna insulted. Sridhama faced Radha and said, "If you scold my Lord even once, I shall curse you."

"It is I who am cursing you!" said Radha, her voice shaking with anger. "You have to take incarnation in a very low family, and you will suffer enormously."

Sridhama immediately responded, "Radha, I am cursing you. For one hundred years you will not be able to meet with my Lord. There will be a great separation for one hundred years!"

Radha and Sridhama exchanged their terrible curses and both the curses came true. In Radha's case, it is said that she was with Sri Krishna for the first eleven years of Krishna's life. Then Krishna left Brindaban and stayed in Mathura and other places for one hundred years. He was a king and a warrior. It was during this time that the battle of Kurakshetra took place and Krishna became the charioteer of Arjuna. Afterwards, Krishna retired and Radha came to be with him for the last fourteen years of his life. According to the Purana that contains this version, Sri Krishna lived for a total of 125 years.

If this story is true, and Krishna's lifespan was 125 years, then the story of the hunter whose arrow pierced Krishna's foot cannot be valid. It is said that this hunter was responsible for Krishna's earthly departure.

Once the battle of Kurukshetra was over, Krishna's son, Samba, was instigated by some relatives to misbehave. As a result, he was cursed by three great sages and Krishna's whole family was destroyed. The curse pronounced on Samba was preceded by the curse of Gandhari. She felt that Krishna could have prevented the war altogether.

In this particular version of the story, Radha does not re-enter Sri Krishna's life at all after their childhood together in Brindaban. Of course, there are some great Indian scholars who say that Radha did not even exist! They say it is all in the imagination-world. So many volumes have been written about the non-existence of Radha!

I am reminded of our greatest Vedantin scholar, Shankara-charya. He went from one end of India to the other, only to preach his philosophy that the world is unreal. People asked him, "If the world is unreal, as you say, why are you wasting your time going from place to place? From your room you can declare that the world is unreal. But we feel that this world is real."

Shankaracharya's answer was, "If I do not go from place to place and offer the message that the world is unreal, people will not hear my philosophy. You live in one place and your friends live in another place. I must also visit your friends to share my realisation with them."

Again, his critics asked, "If this world is unreal, why are you wasting your time and energy? Just pray to God to take you away!"

Shankaracharya said, "No, I cannot do that. God is asking me to tell people that the world is unreal."

There are so many funny, funny stories like this in our Indian history. I find them so entertaining and illumining. In the case of Sri Krishna, who is actually going to know what happened so long ago? Historians say that he lived five thousand years ago; but, according to me, he lived nine or ten thousand years ago. That is my inner feeling.

What we do know is that the supreme Lord Krishna is ever-transcending. Right from his very birth, he performed miracle after miracle. Even today, thousands of years later, his consciousness is guiding us, illumining us and protecting us in unimaginable ways.

EIT 30. *Shiva leaves Parvati behind*

One day Shiva wanted to go and visit Mount Mandara. He was in a terrible rush, but Parvati was not ready. Finally Shiva decided to leave without her. Some apsaras and gandharvas, or celestial musicians, followed him.

When they reached the destination, Shiva began to feel sorry that he had not waited for Parvati to accompany him. So he sent Nandi back to bring Parvati.

Meanwhile, Parvati was sulking. How could Shiva go without her? When Nandi arrived, she said to him, "You have come to get me, but I am still not ready and I do not know when I will be ready. You can go and tell Shiva that I am not ready." Parvati was very sad and depressed.

Nandi went to inform Shiva that Parvati was still not ready. This time Shiva told him, "Nandi, go back and wait for her. No matter how long it takes, wait for her. You have to bring her here."

Nandi returned to Parvati again and waited and waited for her to finish getting ready. In the meantime, some apsaras and gandharvas wanted to fool Lord Shiva. The apsaras were the main instigators. One of them took the form of Parvati and one of the gandharvas took the form of Nandi. They looked exactly like the real Parvati and the real Nandi.

This particular apsara and gandharva appeared before Lord Shiva. The false Nandi said, "I have brought Parvati," and the false Parvati added, "Yes, my Lord, I have come." Shiva was very, very happy. He thought they were the real Parvati and Nandi.

O God, in a few minutes' time, the real Parvati and the real Nandi arrived, and there was great confusion. The second Parvati insisted that she was the real one and the first Parvati insisted that *she* was the real one. A fight broke out between the two sides, but the real Parvati and the real Nandi easily defeated the false ones.

Then Lord Shiva, with his infinite compassion, forgave the false Parvati and the false Nandi.

EIT 31. *Who is the greatest: Brahma, Vishnu or Shiva?*

Our Indian trinity is composed of Brahma, Vishnu and Shiva. Brahma is the Creator, Vishnu is the Preserver and Shiva is the Transformer. According to some, Shiva is the Destroyer, but we say Transformer.

Once it happened that pride entered into Brahma. He said to his devotees, "From now on, you have to consider me as the highest Absolute. I am not of the same standard as Vishnu and Shiva. What do they do, after all? Vishnu just preserves and Shiva only deals with demons. But I am the Creator."

Brahma's devotees bowed to him, saying, "You are the highest."

As they were praising Brahma, Vishnu appeared. "What are you saying?" he asked the devotees.

They replied, "Brahma has informed us that he is the highest and we are repeating his words."

"It can never be!" exclaimed Vishnu. "He just creates, but I take the trouble of preserving. My task is far more difficult because it goes on for years and years. My patience, compassion and forgiveness far surpass Brahma's act of creation. It takes very little time to create, but to preserve the creation goes on indefinitely. I am the one you should be praising as the highest!"

Brahma's devotees did not agree with Vishnu's reasoning at all. They stated Vishnu's case to Brahma, and then Brahma and Vishnu began quarrelling and fighting. Their dispute went on and on.

The four Vedas could not brook this kind of conflict. They took the form of four divine beings and stood in front of Brahma and Vishnu, who were engaged in bitter argument. The Vedas said, "We feel that Shiva is by far the best of the trinity. You two are quarrelling and fighting, but he is far above all this. Only ordinary human beings quarrel and fight in this manner."

At that moment, Lord Shiva was passing by. "What is going on?" he asked.

Vishnu summed up the whole story: "Brahma thinks that he is the greatest and I think that I am the greatest."

Now it was Shiva's turn. "Neither of you is the greatest and highest," he said. "*I* am the greatest and highest."

Vishnu surrendered. "I cannot go on arguing. I will gladly proclaim that you are the greatest," he declared.

Shiva was highly pleased with Vishnu, but Brahma strongly opposed Shiva. He said, "I am undoubtedly the greatest. You deal only with ghosts and demons. You do not take care of your physical existence. You wear skulls around your neck. You do not believe in creation!"

"Enough!" shouted Shiva. "I am no longer going to tolerate your insults. I challenge you to a fight!"

As Shiva prepared to fight, a being came out of his body and said, "I will fight for you." Brahma and this being struck each

82

other very hard, but the being was finally able to cut off one of Brahma's heads and Brahma fell down dead. Originally Brahma had five heads, but this being removed one of the five.

Seeing Brahma lying lifeless on the ground, Shiva felt sad. "After all," he said, "Brahma was once upon a time my friend. What have I done? This being and I are responsible."

So Shiva revived Brahma, but Brahma now had only four heads. Brahma immediately cursed the being: "The head that you have cut off will always remain on your hand."

This is how Brahma's fifth head became stuck to the hand of that being, whose name was Nandi.

Another version of the story says that the head became stuck to Shiva's palm. When Shiva lies down, it can be seen there.

Yet a third version says that Nandi went from one place to another trying to dislodge Brahma's head from his palm. Finally he went to Krishna, who advised him, "Go to Benares. It is the most sacred place of all. There the very sanctity of the place will enter into your palm, and you will see that this head will come off your hand."

Nandi listened to Krishna's advice and went to Benares. As soon as he arrived in that sacred city, lo and behold, the head of Brahma left him.

Shiva was very pleased with Nandi for winning the fight with Brahma. He said to Nandi, "I am so satisfied with you. You were able to kill Brahma. You are extremely powerful. I am compelling you to stay with me. From now on, you will be the leader of all the demons and ghosts that are my subjects."

That was how Nandi became Shiva's chief attendant.

EIT 32. *Shiva insults his wife*

There was an asura who wanted to become immortal, so he prayed and meditated for many, many years. Finally Brahma appeared before him to grant him a boon, and the asura asked for the boon of Immortality.

Brahma said, "I cannot grant you that boon, but at least this much I can do for you: you will not be able to be killed by any male."

The asura was very happy because he would now become the strongest and most powerful of all the great fighters. He immediately invaded Heaven and threw Indra out. Then he began destroying Heaven and expelling all the cosmic gods one by one.

The cosmic gods hurried to Brahma and pleaded, "What have you done, what have you done, my Lord? Now you have to save us!"

Brahma said, "I am the culprit. I granted the boon, but now I do not have the power to protect you. I have to go to Shiva. Only he can save you from this predicament. Let me go and ask Shiva what can be done."

So Brahma went to Shiva and explained the whole situation to him. He said, "I gave this asura the boon of becoming invincible. Now he has thrown Indra and all the other cosmic gods out of Heaven. There is only one way he can be defeated, and that is by a female. Can you not provide a very powerful female to kill this asura?"

Shiva thought for a few moments. "It is a very difficult task," he said at last, "but I will try my best. I will see what I can do for you."

While Shiva was wondering how to solve this problem, Parvati happened to walk by. Now, Parvati was extremely beautiful and her complexion was very fair. All of a sudden, for some unknown reason, Shiva addressed her as *Kali*. As soon as Parvati heard her husband calling her Kali, she got furious.

"Why are you calling me by that name?" she screamed. "You married me because I was so beautiful. Now why are you casting a slur on me? Have I become dark? Am I no longer beautiful? I am so disgusted with you! Who asked you to marry me? I am not going to stay with you. If you think that I am dark-skinned, I will leave this instant!"

Shiva made no attempt to retract his words, and so Parvati left him and entered into the forest. She began praying and meditating and practising very strict spiritual austerities. One day a tiger came near her as she sat meditating. It wanted to kill and devour her. Upon seeing the tiger, Parvati thought, "How kind this tiger is! I am meditating here all alone and it has come to protect me." She entered into the soul of the tiger and, out of sheer gratitude and love, removed all the tiger's ferocious qualities. The tiger remained by her side and became her most favourite devotee.

Parvati continued meditating on Brahma. At long last he came to see her. He said, "I am so pleased with you. Now what can I do for you?"

"I wish to have a better complexion," said Parvati. "Shiva has called me Kali. What an insult! That means my skin is no longer beautiful. I cannot bear to be called dark. I want to be more beautiful."

"All right," said Brahma, "I will grant you this boon. From the cells of your body a dark being will come out. It will be quite black. When your body is rid of this being, you will become beautiful, more beautiful, most beautiful. From now on you will be known as Gauri, she who has the most beautiful complexion."

Immediately, a very dark and very powerful being came out of the cells of Parvati's body. It took the form of a female and Brahma endowed it with all kinds of spiritual and occult powers.

This being fought against the asura and defeated it. Then Indra and all the other cosmic gods went back to Heaven and lived again in perfect joy. Meanwhile, Parvati returned to Shiva and they were very happy together once again.

EIT 33. *The unparalleled beauty of the goddess Parvati*

Once the goddess Parvati wanted to become beautiful, more beautiful, most beautiful. She was already quite beautiful, but her present beauty did not satisfy her. She wanted to become beauty *non pareil*.

Parvati knew that this kind of beauty could be acquired only by virtue of intense prayer and meditation. She decided to leave her husband, Shiva, and go into seclusion so that she could practise spiritual disciplines without interruption.

Before leaving, she asked Nandi not to allow any woman who looked like her to enter Lord Shiva's place. She said, "Many times my Lord has been deceived by women who take my form and try to approach him. You have to be absolutely sure that it is I who have returned, and nobody else. Otherwise, I am sure that in my absence some women will try to fool you."

After issuing her strict instructions, Parvati withdrew into the forest for an indefinite length of time. All her jewellery and lovely garments she left behind so that she could give her full attention to prayer and meditation.

A few months later, an asura or demon, who happened to pass by Shiva's place, noticed the gigantic gates outside it. The demon asked one of the guards, "Whose place is this?"

"It is Lord Shiva's place," the guard replied.

"I would like to be admitted," said the demon haughtily.

"It is absolutely forbidden," said the guard. "I have received special instructions from Parvati and nobody may be admitted."

Outwardly the demon pretended to be detached. "All right," he said, "if you do not allow people to enter, what can I do?"

Inwardly he was seething with rage. He went home and came back to the gate a few days later. This time he took the form of a tiny creature. It was something like a snake. Because this creature was so tiny, it was able to pass through the gate unnoticed by the guards. It was almost invisible to the eye. Once it was inside Shiva's home, the creature assumed the form of Parvati. She was beautiful beyond description.

When Shiva saw his wife standing before him, he was filled with joy. He came forward to embrace her but, as he put his arms around the false Parvati, the demon suddenly resumed its old form. The demon attacked Shiva and a terrible fight took place.

Eventually Shiva gained the upper hand and the demon lay dying on the ground. With his last breath, the demon said to Shiva, "You have killed me, but I am warning you. One day my brother will come and kill you. He will take Parvati's form and kill you. He is much stronger than I am."

It was well known that this demon did not have a brother. His threat was all lies. He wanted Shiva to destroy the real Parvati when she returned from the forest.

The problem of the false Parvatis went on for many, many years. Just as Parvati had foreseen other beings took her form and tried to fool the guards. Sometimes the guards refused to admit them and, at other times, when they were able to enter successfully, Shiva recognised them. Shiva did not want to be fooled a second time.

After a long time, one Parvati came and requested admittance. She behaved so much like the real Parvati that the guards opened the gate. She entered and started walking towards Shiva. Shiva immediately suspected her. "O God," he sighed, "another one has come to fool me."

Shiva prepared to defend himself once again. This time, from his body, countless beings emerged to destroy the false Parvati. But to Shiva's great surprise, countless beings also emerged from the body of this particular Parvati. A huge battle raged between the two sides.

As Shiva gazed at the many beings who were fighting for Parvati, he realised that only the real Parvati could have this kind of spiritual power.

"You are my real Parvati!" he cried, throwing down his weapons. Shiva advanced towards her. As he came nearer, he noticed that his wife was now much, much more beautiful than she had been previously. Because she had prayed and meditated for so many years, she had become beauty unparalleled.

Can you imagine, a divine cosmic goddess, a supreme goddess, dying for beauty! It is no wonder that all women crave beauty at every second of their lives. It all started with our supreme goddess, Parvati.

PART II

ILLUMINATION-EXPERIENCES
ON INDIAN SOIL

BOOK 1

The Mogul Emperor Babar was very kind, very generous and very powerful. Once while Babar was away from his kingdom, his step-grandmother instigated one of his cousins to stand against him. This particular cousin made friends with the chief of the army and a few important figures in the capital. When Babar tried to return to his kingdom, his whole army fought against him. They wouldn't allow Babar to come back. But Babar had quite a few followers outside his kingdom, and they helped him to fight against his own people. Babar was so great and powerful that eventually he won the battle.

After he had won, Babar went and knelt down before his step-grandmother. He said to her with folded hands, "I don't hold anything against you. If a mother likes one son more than another son, what can the less favoured son do? He should not feel miserable. The mother should love all her children equally, but if she does not, the ones that are not in favour must not feel sorry. They should still have the same love for their mother as the ones who stand high in her favour. So I don't hold anything against you. You have done the right thing, according to your light. Now let me have peace of mind." Then he placed his head on her lap and fell asleep.

A few hours later Babar woke up, only to see the main culprit, his cousin, standing in front of him. He had been arrested and brought to Babar by the Emperor's loyal followers. Babar stood up and embraced his cousin. Then he said, "You are at perfect liberty either to stay with me the rest of your life or to leave my kingdom. If you leave my kingdom and want to live elsewhere, I will meet with your expenses. If you want to continue staying here, you are free to do so. I feel no ill will towards you at all."

His cousin said to him, "Babar, I want to stay with you. If I leave you, people will try to kill me. Not your favourites, but

93

those who helped me fight against you will try to kill me in order to make you feel that they have become very devoted to you. So I want to stay with you. I know that you will never kill me. Not only that, I know that your forgiveness and compassion will be my eternal friends, and that you will eventually give me a high post."

Babar gave him a broad smile of forgiveness and assurance.

IE 2. *Babar takes a life*

There was nothing that the great Emperor Babar would hesitate to do for his subjects. He used to regard his subjects as his own children. From time to time Babar used to go out of the palace grounds and walk along the streets to mix with his subjects and see the conditions in which they were living. Often if he saw someone who was poverty-stricken, he would help him out. People did not recognise him because he dressed very simply at those times. Also, he wore a kind of turban over his crown, so it was impossible for people to know what it was by seeing only the outside of it.

Now it happened that there was a young man who cherished tremendous jealousy towards Babar because everybody appreciated, admired and adored him. Everybody always extolled Babar to the skies for his bravery, kindness, nobility and other divine qualities. For this reason the young man had long been harbouring a desire to kill Babar. He had heard that from time to time the Emperor walked in the city all alone. So he always carried a sword, hoping that someday he would meet the Emperor when he was by himself and have the opportunity to kill him.

Usually when Babar went out, his guards would secretly follow him to protect him. Although Babar didn't want anyone to go with him, his guards were afraid for his safety. Babar was the ruler of the whole kingdom, but in this respect his own bodyguards wouldn't listen to him.

On one particular afternoon, the Emperor managed to go out alone, without his guards. As Babar was walking along incognito, he saw a mad elephant coming down the street. People were shouting and running away from the elephant, and everybody was panicking. But there was one little, helpless child who could not run fast enough to get out of the way. Everybody was frightened to death, but nobody dared to try to save the child. Just as the elephant was about to trample the little child, the Emperor ran over at top speed and snatched the child out of the way. Babar saved the child, but as he was running away with him, his turban fell to the ground.

When the mad elephant had passed by, some men ran to pick up the turban of the brave hero. When they saw the inside, they realised that it was actually the crown of their Emperor. The young man who wanted to kill Babar was one of those who had seen the Emperor save the life of the child. Although he himself had known that the child's life was in danger, he had not been brave enough to try to save him, and he had run away, just like everybody else. When he realised what had happened, he fell at Babar's feet and said, "Forgive me."

Babar said, "What have you done?"

The man said, "I have been cherishing the desire to kill you for many years, because I was terribly jealous of the admiration you receive. Now I see that you truly deserve it. As Emperor, you are more precious to the kingdom than any of us, but you were ready to give up your own life to save an ordinary human being. What I have learned from you is that it is infinitely better to give life than to take life. This is what you have taught me. Now, instead of taking your life, I am giving you mine. Please take my life." Then he offered Babar the sword with which he had planned to kill him.

Babar took the sword and said, "I taught you how to give life. Now I am going to take your life. Come with me. From now on you will be one of my bodyguards. I can see that your sincerity is truly remarkable, and I am sure you will be a faithful guard."

So Babar took the man's life, only to make it into a useful and fruitful one. Instead of killing him, instead of punishing him, Babar made the man one of his personal bodyguards.

IE 3. *Babar honours Ibrahim Lodi*

The great Mogul Emperor Babar was once fighting a very bloody battle known as the First Battle of Panipat. Babar's enemy was King Ibrahim Lodi. The armies fought for quite a few days, and finally Babar's army began to overpower the other one.

One of the commanders of Ibrahim Lodi's army said to him, "O King, you stay at the rear of the army. Don't stay in the thick of the battle. As a matter of fact, let us keep fighting to the bitter end while you go and escape. We want you to be safe."

The king said, "How can I do that? If my army, my friends and my relatives are ready to give their lives for me, will I run away in order to save my own life? If they are willing to give their lives, can I not also be willing to give my life?"

The king fought very bravely but finally he was killed. The commander who killed him was full of happiness that the enemy king was dead, and he hurried to tell Babar the news. Babar immediately asked the commander to take him to the dead body.

When he got there, he raised Ibrahim Lodi's head from the ground and said, "I admire you. You fought very, very bravely. Now I will take full responsibility to see that you are honoured as a king should be when he dies. I will give you the grand reception worthy of a king, and I will have a king's tomb erected. I will do everything for you. You are a real hero!"

IE 4. *Babar's concern for the merchant*

Once a merchant was passing through the mountains with his caravan to bring goods to another town. On the way, there was a terrible storm and lightning struck the caravan. The merchant and many other people were killed, and there was nobody to take responsibility for the goods being carried in the caravan.

When Babar heard of the tragedy, he asked his soldiers to collect all the goods and keep them in a safe place. Then he sent for the merchant's relatives to come to him immediately, and he gave everything to them. The members of the merchant's family were overwhelmed by Babar's concern and kindness. They wanted to give the Emperor an expensive present, but he would not accept it. They begged him at least to take some reimbursement for his trouble, but again Babar refused.

He said, "No, I can't do that. You have lost your dearest one. Now I can't take advantage of his death. It is your wealth and property; it is you who deserve it."

So Babar gave everything to the merchant's relatives without accepting any reward for his kindness and concern. The merchant's family was deeply moved.

IE 5. *Babar sacrifices his life*

Once the Emperor Babar's son Humayun had a very high fever. It continued for a few days and the most eminent doctors were called in, but no one was able to cure him. Some people in the palace were saying that perhaps God would be pleased if they sacrificed expensive animals in order to save the Emperor's son. Others said, "No, the sacrifice has to be more precious than animals. The best thing is to sell the Kohinoor diamond to some very rich people and then use the money for religious purposes. The money should be given to the poor."

Finally Babar said, "I can sell the most precious diamond to save my son's life, but I have no idea if it will really save him. Everybody is suggesting that I sacrifice the most precious thing on earth in order to cure my son. I feel that there is nothing dearer to me than my own life. Humayun is my eldest and dearest son. I should sacrifice my life for my son."

After saying this, the Emperor folded his hands and circled his son's bed three times, praying to Allah to take his life and save his son. He said, "Allah, everybody is telling me to offer the most precious thing to You so that You will kindly save my son's life. I feel that my life is the most precious thing that I have to offer. Please take it."

Then Babar cried out, "Allah has granted my prayer! Allah has listened to my prayer!"

From the moment he said that, Humayun started to get better. In a short time the Emperor Babar died.

IE 6. *Humayun forgives his prime minister*

One day the Emperor Humayun was addressing his court. His prime minister was sitting right in front of him, but he was not paying any attention to the Emperor's talk. He was totally exhausted, and he was sleeping soundly.

Finally Humayun became disappointed and disgusted. He said to the prime minister, "What are you doing? You are sleeping right in front of me! What bad manners you have!"

The prime minister said, "Your Majesty, I was not sleeping."

Humayun said, "Then what were you doing?"

The prime minister said, "Your Majesty, wise people say that when an Emperor speaks, you have to listen with folded hands. When a great orator speaks, you have to look at his eyes. And when your loving, compassionate friend speaks, you have to feel his heart. While I was sitting in front of you, I was seeing you as all three persons: an Emperor, a great orator and a compassionate friend. So I was closing my eyes and wondering what I should do — listen to you as the Emperor, as a great orator or as my most compassionate friend."

Humayun said to him, "You are such a clever fellow, such a wonderful rogue, and such a perfect flatterer! All right, you have won the case. Not only do I forgive you, but I will give you a nice reward for your extraordinary ability to save yourself."

IE 7. *The Emperor punishes his son*

There was once a Muslim emperor whose son was undivine to the extreme. One day a very shocking report came to the emperor. A man came to the palace and said that his wife had become unfaithful to him because of the emperor's son. The man's story was proven to be true, and the emperor was disheartened and disgusted.

The man said, "I am embarrassed to have to tell you this shocking news. Now, please do something."

The emperor said, "Yes, I will definitely take some action, without fail. If somebody else had done this kind of thing, what kind of punishment would I have given him? I would have ordered that person to be hanged. But that punishment is only a matter of a few seconds. For the emperor's son, there should be some punishment that is more painful and that continues for a longer time. Then everybody will be able to see it and learn from it. The just punishment is for him to be stoned to death in public. My soldiers will continue throwing stones at him until he finally dies."

The emperor buried his head in his hands. "How can I have a son like this?" he cried. "My subjects are all my children. If my only son behaves like this, if he has become so bad, then how can I expect my other children to be good? He has brought disgrace to the royal family and to the whole kingdom. Justice demands that he be stoned to death!"

IE 8. *The fourth sound of the gong*

There was once a Muslim emperor who was always willing to listen to complaints from his subjects. Sometimes they would file complaints through the proper channels, and then the emperor would do the needful. At other times the emperor had a special way of receiving complaints. Outside the main gate of the palace he kept a big gong. Anyone who had a complaint could come and sound the gong. If the person sounded it only once, that meant that he had lost a quarrel with someone, which he felt he should have won. If the gong sounded twice, it meant that somebody always worked very hard but felt he was not getting proper wages. If it sounded three times, it meant that somebody's house had been robbed, and he was looking for the thief. If the gong sounded four times, it meant that somebody had murdered someone.

The emperor's soldiers used to watch and see how many times the person lodging the complaint struck the gong. Then they would immediately bring the person to the emperor and tell him what the complaint was about. One day a man struck the gong four times, which meant that there had been a homicide.

The soldiers asked him, "Who has killed whom?"

The man said, "Somebody killed my father."

The soldiers asked, "When was he killed?"

"Forty years ago," the man answered.

The palace guards couldn't believe their ears. "So only now you want punishment?" they asked.

"Yes," said the man. "I just came to know that my father had been killed. My mother told me this morning."

The guards asked, "Why did your mother not tell you before?"

The man answered, "Because if she had told me, then I would have killed one of the king's ministers. This particular minister killed my father forty years ago, and he is still in office!"

"Are you saying that the minister should be executed?" they asked.

"Exactly," the man said.

The palace guards brought the man before the emperor, and told the emperor the whole story. The emperor turned to his subject and said, "You have to know who asked the minister to kill your father. The minister was only carrying out my order. Are you saying that I should be punished as well?"

The man said, "I can't go so far as to say that. But I have not seen my father for forty years. Indeed, that is a tragic loss. During these forty years the minister has gotten so much in salary. As compensation for my father's death, may I receive only one month's salary of the minister?"

The emperor said, "I am ready to give you the equivalent of forty years of the minister's salary — whatever money he has earned from the day he killed your father. Go and find out the exact date of your father's death from your mother, and then come back and tell me."

The man's mother had forgotten the day, the year — everything. But the minister had kept a record. It had only been thirty-five years. The emperor summoned the man back to the palace to give him the money, and told him, "Here in my hand is the minister's salary, and here on the minister's body is the minister's head. Which do you want? I can give you either the minister's head or the salary that he has received over the years."

The man quickly said, "The minister's salary, not his head!"

IE 9. *Nasir Uddin and the pandit*

Once a King named Nasir Uddin became very, very pious. He refused to take money from his kingdom's treasury for his own personal needs. To make extra money, he would make copies of the Koran in his own handwriting and then sell the books. He also made a few other things to sell, and in this way he would meet with his personal expenses.

One day a great pandit came to his palace to visit him. Nasir Uddin happened to be copying the Koran, and the pandit watched him for some time. At one point the King stopped writing and started talking to his guest. The pandit said to him, "Your Majesty, unfortunately you have made a mistake in a word you were copying."

Nasir Uddin made a circle around the word that the pandit wanted to correct. Then he erased it and wrote in the word that the pandit told him. The pandit was very happy that the King had listened to him. After some time the pandit left the palace. As soon as he left, the King again erased the word and wrote in the word that he had written originally.

His guards asked him, "Why are you doing that? If it was the right word in the first place, why did you change it?"

The King answered, "Although I may be King, he is a pandit, and he knows much more than I do in this field. Unfortunately, he happened to make a mistake in this case. He was wrong and I was right. But if I had told him that he was wrong, his pride would have been deeply hurt. I know that he knows much more than I do about the scriptures. Therefore, I wrote down the incorrect word so that he would not be embarrassed. But now I don't want to leave the wrong word here. Otherwise, whoever buys this book will have the wrong version.

"It is not good to hurt people even if you are correct. It is nothing for me to make myself humble, when it is a matter of knowledge. But if he had advised me about ruling my kingdom, do you think that I would have listened to him? Managing my kingdom is a different story. But it is always good to show respect to someone if he is very great in his own field."

IE 10. *The son's forgiveness*

A Muslim king once said to a group of his admirers, "I am not in the mood today to chat with you people. Instead I wish you to tell me some inspiring stories. Whoever can tell me the most inspiring and illumining story will be rewarded."

There were two or three who volunteered to tell most inspiring stories. The last man to speak said, "O King, ten years ago I killed one of your very dear ministers."

Everybody was very shocked, and the guards wanted to arrest the man. But the king said, "No, allow him to finish his story."

The man continued, "You sent your soldiers to kill me. For many weeks and months they searched for me. Since they were making such a thorough search, I was afraid I would be caught. So I left your kingdom and went to a neighbouring kingdom. That king happened to be your friend, so there too people were searching for me to arrest me and bring me to you. I went from village to village hiding from the authorities.

"I was haunted by the thought that I would be arrested. One day I was running and running until I fell down and fainted. While I lay unconscious, I was found by a most kind-hearted middle-aged man who carried me to his home. When I recovered, the man asked me what had happened.

"I told him that I had killed a very important person and that I was afraid of being arrested. The man said, 'Oh, I see, I see! You can rest assured that I will always help you. Already I have shown you hospitality, and now your sincerity has touched my sympathetic heart. But I have a secret mission, and I must leave early every morning and return only late in the evening. I will see that the members of my family give you food and meet with all your need's.

"This arrangement went on for six months. One day my host came home very, very sad, depressed and exhausted. I said to him, 'Today you are so sad. What is the matter? True, every day you seem somewhat sad, but today you are extremely depressed'.

"My host answered, 'Some time ago someone killed my father. Now people are saying that he has run away and come to this vicinity. The king has offered to give ten thousand gold coins to anybody who can find him, and now many people are looking for him. That is why I am sad. I took a vow that I would personally kill that fellow. For years I have been looking for him. Every day I go out in search of him, but still I have not been able to find him. It will be a disgrace if someone else catches him and gets the reward. I don't want the money, but I do want to fulfil my vow and kill this man.

"'So you see, you have killed one individual, and somebody else has killed my father. People are looking for you, and I am looking for someone else. This world is like that — a battlefield. I will not tell anybody that you have killed someone. I will always protect you. But how I wish I could find the person who killed my father! I know that he is right in this vicinity'.

"I said to my host, 'I am sure that you will find him someday. I will pray for you'.

"The following morning, when my host came to say hello to me, I said, 'Please do not go out in search of the murderer. It is not necessary'.

"He said to me, 'Without going out, how will I find him?'

"I paused and then I pointed to myself. 'Here is the person whom you are looking for', I said.

"The man couldn't believe his ears. 'You?' he said.

"I said, 'Yes! I am the person who killed your father. Since that time I have changed my appearance totally. That is why you don't recognise me as the person you are looking for. I have lost weight, and I have grown a beard. For many years what agony I have gone through to escape punishment! But now let my suffering come to an end. Just kill me! If you want the reward money first, I will go to the king with you. The king will keep his promise and give you the money. Then you can keep your promise and kill me'.

"The man said, 'Oh no, I can't do that. I was generous to you and you were generous to me. Two generous people cannot suddenly be unkind to each other. But God knows if tomorrow I will be in the same frame of mind as I am in now. Please leave my house immediately. After a few months, if I gain back my anger, again I will go in search of you in order to kill you. In the meantime, if somebody else finds you and takes you to the king, I will not be responsible. I have no idea whether or not my anger will return and I will try to kill you. Now I find it in my heart to forgive you, so I am telling you to leave. But tomorrow I may not be able to forgive you. So go now!'

"So, O King, I left his house, and now, ten years after I killed your minister, I am finally telling you the story."

The king was shedding tears. He said, "What am I going to do now? If the son of the man you killed had the heart to forgive you, how can I have the heart to kill you?"

IE II. *The cow and the pig*

There was once a man who was very, very rich and very, very miserly at the same time, so the villagers used to dislike him intensely. One day he said to them, "Either you are jealous of me or you don't appreciate my lack of generosity — God alone knows. But you dislike me; that much I know. I tell you, when

I die, I won't take anything with me. I will leave it all for others. I will make a will, and I will give everything to charity. Then everybody will be happy."

Even then people mocked and laughed at him. The rich man said to them, "What is the matter with you? Can't you wait for a few years to see my money go to charity?"

Still the villagers didn't believe him. He said, "You don't believe me, but am I immortal? Of course I will die, and then my money will go to different charities." The man could not understand why people were not appreciating him.

One day the rich man went out for a walk. All of a sudden it started raining heavily, so he took shelter under a tree. O God, under the same tree he saw a pig and a cow. The pig and the cow entered into conversation, and the man overheard what they were saying.

The pig said to the cow, "How is it that everybody appreciates you and nobody appreciates me? When I die, I provide people with bacon, ham and sausage. People can also use my bristles. I give three or four things, whereas you give only one thing: milk. Why do people appreciate you all the time and not me?"

The cow said to the pig, "Look, I give them milk when I am alive. They see that I am giving it and that I am very generous. But you don't give them anything while you are alive. Only when you are killed do you give ham, bacon and so forth. People don't believe in the future; they believe only in the present. If you give while you are alive, then only will people appreciate you. That is why I get appreciation."

The rich man got the point. From then on, he started giving everything that he had to the poor. After that everybody adored him and worshipped him.

IE 12. *The two goddesses*

There were two neighbouring families that were very, very friendly and very, very kind to each other. Both the husbands and wives were extremely close. Both families were very rich as well. How did they become rich? In one family the wife prayed to the goddess of wealth, "O goddess of wealth, come and make me rich; come and make my husband rich!" Finally the goddess appeared before her, and the lady begged her, "Always stay with me." The goddess did what she asked, and that is how that particular couple became very, very rich.

The other wife prayed to the goddess of misery, "O goddess of misery, never come to me! I want to be always happy." The goddess of misery appeared before her and said, "I am here to inform you that I will never again come to you." So this couple also became rich, because the goddess of misery never came to them.

It happened that when a third couple moved to the same village, the wife saw that these two other couples were very, very happy. Secretly she asked each of the two wives how they had become so rich. When they told her, she decided also to start praying to both the goddess of wealth and the goddess of misery, hoping that at least one of the goddesses would do the needful. She prayed, "O goddess of wealth, please come to me! O goddess of misery, please never come to me!"

After the wife had been praying for a few days, all of a sudden both the goddesses appeared together. The lady was so happy and delighted. She said to them, "I am so grateful that both of you have come." In her excitement the lady mistook the goddess of wealth for the goddess of misery and said to her, "Please never come here again. I don't want you or need you."

Then the lady said to the goddess of misery, thinking that she was the goddess of wealth, "Please stay here. I will be so grateful to you."

The goddess of misery said, "You want me? Fine, I will stay with you."

The goddess of wealth said, "You don't want me? Then I will go away forever."

So the lady was miserable for the rest of her life. The moral of the story is that you have to know what you are praying for when God finally comes and stands in front of you. Otherwise, if you are excited, you may ask for the wrong thing.

Again, truly advanced spiritual seekers will always ask God for the right things. Vivekananda was so poor that he could not make both ends meet. When he asked Ramakrishna for wealth, Ramakrishna said to him, "I can't ask Mother Kali for wealth, but you go and ask her."

As soon as Vivekananda entered into the temple to pray, he could not bring himself to ask Mother Kali for money. He prayed, "Give me aspiration. Give me the voice of conscience."

When Vivekananda returned, Ramakrishna said, "What were you doing? Why did you not ask for material wealth?"

Vivekananda then went to the temple a second time, but again he could not pray for wealth. Finally he told Ramakrishna, "I can't ask for these kinds of material things." This is the difference between Vivekananda and the unfortunate lady.

Ramakrishna said, "I knew, I knew that you would never be able to ask Mother Kali for material wealth. But Mother Kali is so pleased with your aspiration that she will take care of your family from now on."

After that, Vivekananda never suffered from financial difficulties. Previously he had suffered because his relatives all stood against him and would not help him. Then, because of Mother Kali, he was able to support his family. Vivekananda was a divine soul, so he asked for the right thing and he got the right thing: spiritual wealth. Mother Kali was so pleased that she fulfilled not only his spiritual needs, but also his family's basic material needs.

IE 13. *The king forgives his enemy*

Two kings fought a battle. The victor said to the vanquished, "Now that I have conquered you, I can do anything I want to with your life. Tell me what you would have done if you had conquered me."

The other king said, "I would have killed you immediately."

The first king said, "You would have killed me immediately? So now that I have conquered you, what do you expect from me?"

The other king said, "If you were a businessman, I would expect you to sell me to some rich man and get some money. If you were a butcher, I would expect you to kill me. But you are neither a businessman nor a butcher. I feel that you are a very kind-hearted man. If this is true, then naturally you will forgive me."

The first king said, "Whether I am a kind-hearted man or not, at least for today I want to be kind-hearted. So I am forgiving you and giving you back your throne. Only remember that I am stronger than you. I am physically stronger than you, and my army is stronger than yours. So don't disturb me anymore."

ILLUMINATION-EXPERIENCES
ON INDIAN SOIL

BOOK 2

Once, in the kingdom of the greatest Mogul Emperor, Akbar, the traders were all quarrelling and fighting among themselves. The Arab, Indian and Portuguese traders were all trying to exploit one another.

One day a Portuguese merchant got mad at a Muslim trader, so he tied a copy of the Koran around the neck of a dog and set the dog free. The dog started roaming along the streets, going here and there at random with the book hanging around his neck.

Akbar's mother, Hamida Bhanu Begam, saw the dog and became furious. She said, "It is such a sacred book! How can someone put it around the neck of a dog!" Hamida Bhanu asked her son, the Emperor, to send someone to catch the dog and punish it. She also wanted Akbar to find out who the owner was so that he could also be punished mercilessly.

Poor Akbar! On the one hand he was very devoted to his mother. On the other hand, what kind of punishment could there be for this kind of crime? Suddenly a brilliant idea entered into his mind. He asked one of his servants to bring him a monkey. When the servant brought it to him, Akbar tied a Bible around the neck of the monkey and asked the servant to let the monkey loose in the street. The monkey started wandering along the street, going from one place to another with the Bible hanging around his neck.

When Akbar's mother heard about this, she was not satisfied. She said to her son, "What are you doing? You are making this a fight between a monkey and a dog. Is this what I wanted? I wanted the dog and its owner to be punished."

Akbar said, "Mother, how can I do that kind of thing? Someone has created this kind of mischief to make fun of our religion, but I don't know who the culprit is. The sacred book is innocent, the dog is innocent, and nobody will confess to being the owner of the dog. So, if somebody speaks ill of the Muslims and puts the Koran around the dog's neck, then the best thing that we can do is to put a Bible around a monkey's neck. We can only play the same kind of trick on that person. If he makes fun of us, we can make fun of him. But more than that we can't do. We can't punish people for these kinds of jokes."

IE 15. *The immeasurable wealth*

Once the Emperor Akbar wanted to know how much wealth he had in the treasuries of all the cities in his kingdom. First he wanted to see how much jewellery and gold he had in the treasury of his famous capital, Agra.

He asked his treasurer to give him a report as soon as possible. The treasurer hired one thousand men who used four hundred pairs of scales day in and day out.

After five months Akbar called in his son and asked, "What is the report?"

His son replied, "Father, the treasurer and his men are nowhere near the end of this monumental task. There is still so much wealth left to measure!"

Akbar asked, "How much longer will it take? How much more time do they need?"

His son said, "They have no idea how many more months it will take."

Akbar remained silent for a moment. Finally he said, "Please tell them to stop." He realised that even the wealth of just one city, Agra, was immeasurable.

IE 16. *Boiram Khan retires*

The Emperor Akbar's father died when Akbar was quite young, so for some time a very wise man named Boiram Khan ruled the kingdom in Akbar's name. When Akbar finally took charge of his kingdom, Boiram Khan remained as one of the commanders of Akbar's army. Unfortunately, he became very haughty and undivine and began doing many wrong things.

Akbar was very grateful to Boiram Khan because he had helped him so much during his youth. But complaint after complaint kept coming against this commander because he was killing people for no reason. Finally Akbar said, "The best thing is for Boiram Khan to retire and spend the rest of his life in Mecca."

Even on the way to Mecca Boiram Khan was fighting and killing people. People attacked him because he had been very unkind, so Boiram Khan and his followers fought against the attackers. At one point one of Akbar's great admirers, a brave lieutenant, came and attacked Boiram Khan. The commander and his group counter-attacked and killed the lieutenant. All of a sudden, Boiram Khan's eyes became filled with tears. His soldiers said to him, "You were such a great general. Once upon a time you were Akbar's only adviser. You protected his kingdom. We have never seen you in tears before. Why are you crying today?"

The commander said, "My young friends, what have I done with my strength? I curse my life more than anybody else on earth. Because of my strength and power, today I have caused the death of hundreds of beautiful and powerful human beings. If I didn't have such strength, such capacity, then I would not have been able to kill such powerful people. They had so many good qualities. They were very brave; that's why they fought.

Only because I happened to be stronger was I able to kill them. This strength of mine — is it a blessing or a curse?"

IE 17. *The minister's temple*

Once Jahangir, the Emperor Akbar's son, said to his father, "Father, how is it that you have allowed one of your Hindu ministers to erect a temple and spend so much money? The top of the temple is even studded with diamonds. Why did you allow him to spend so much money for the Hindu religion?"

Akbar said to him, "My son, I love my own religion. Is there anything that I will not do for my religion? Will money ever stand in my way? If I wanted to build a beautiful mosque, would I care about the amount of money it costs? This Hindu minister also loves his religion. If he wants to spend money for his religion, what right do I have to prevent him?

"I love something because it is my very own. Does he not have the right to love the thing that is his very own? His religion is his very own, just as my religion is my very own. I cannot ask him not to spend money on his religion, for I know that I would do the same thing for my religion."

IE 18. *Jahangir punishes his son*

The Mogul Emperor Jahangir once got a severe complaint against his son. What had happened was this. His eldest son had very happily and proudly ridden his elephant from the palace to a particular place in the kingdom. On the way the prince had seen the wife of a low-class man and had thrown a piece of beetlenut at her in a very amusing way. When the husband came to know that his wife had been insulted by the prince, he went to Jahangir's court and made a complaint.

Jahangir got furious and made inquiries to find out if what the man had said was true. After some investigation, he learned that the story was correct. Jahangir immediately ordered that the low-class man should ride on the Prince's elephant from the palace to the same place to which the prince had gone. The Prince's wife would stand at the same place along the street where the man's wife had been standing. Then, when the low-class man passed by, he would throw a piece of beetlenut at the princess.

"This will be the only compensation," the Emperor said.

Everybody said, "How can the Emperor do this? She is the princess and he is just a low-class person." Everybody was protesting that it would be so humiliating for the princess.

But Jahangir said, "No, my son has to learn that he cannot do this kind of thing. My order is my order. You have to execute it immediately. Otherwise, both my son and his wife will be even more severely punished."

Finally the low-class man ran out of the palace, crying, "I don't want them to be punished. I forgive your son."

Then Jahangir said, "Since he has forgiven my son, I have nothing to say." The Emperor turned to his son and told him, "He has forgiven you, my son. That is the only reason why I am forgiving you."

IE 19. *King Firuzshah's generosity*

Once the throne of Bengal was occupied by a king named Firuzshah, who came from Abyssinia. He ruled Bengal with great kindness and generosity. He was especially kind to the poor and was always giving them alms, irrespective of their caste. Even if people were only pretending to be poor, the king would still give them money. When his ministers objected, he would say, "If they say they are poor, what can I do?" His ministers didn't like his generosity and were always trying to save money. But the king would not listen to them.

Once King Firuzshah told his ministers that he wanted to give a very large amount of money to the poor. The ministers were very shocked. They said to one another, "Perhaps he does not know how much he really loses when he gives away his wealth!" So they brought all the gold coins and jewels that were supposed to be distributed that day to one of the rooms in the palace. Then they invited the king to come and see the wealth. They said to him, "O King, you always want to give away expensive things to the poor. We are happy that this time you will be giving away such a large amount of money."

In the back of their minds they thought that when the king saw all the wealth in one room, he would be surprised and shocked at how much he was giving away. They thought he would say, "So much wealth I am giving away? No, I cannot give so much. Give only a quarter of this or half of this." In this way they felt they would be able to stop the king from distributing so much money to the poor.

O God, instead the king said, "You fools, at least four times this wealth I want to give to the poor. Four times this amount will please me."

Then the king ordered them to give away four times more than they had collected in the room.

IE 20. *King Hyder Ali saves a kidnapped girl*

Once a week King Hyder Ali used to receive complaints directly from his subjects. On that day his subjects didn't have to go through the usual channels. On one such day a man came up to the king and said, "Your Majesty, my only daughter has been kidnapped by a high-ranking officer and taken away to his village. Whenever I go to complain to the magistrate, he turns a deaf ear to me. So many times I have told him what this officer has done, but he will take no action. What am I going to do?"

The king sent for the magistrate and asked, "Is this story true?" The magistrate remained silent and then finally admitted that it was indeed true. The king became furious and ordered the magistrate to be whipped two hundred fifty times by the strongest man in the palace. Then he ordered several strong guards to bring back the man's daughter. He told them, "You know what kind of punishment I want you to give. Do the needful!"

So those guards went to that particular village and brought back the girl — along with the head of the culprit. The king was so pleased with them. He said, "This is the punishment I wanted. Now, anything you want from me, you can have. You deserve a reward."

In this way the man got his beautiful daughter back.

IE 21. *The prince's prison term*

There was once a king who had only one son. Unfortunately, the prince was notoriously undivine, to say the least. The king was miserable that his only son was so bad.

One night a report came to one of the ministers that the king's son had been involved in a robbery. The prince and his friends had all been caught. When the minister heard that the prince was involved, he didn't want to take any measures against the culprits without consulting the king. So in the middle of the night he went to the king's chamber and knocked on the door.

The king asked, "What has happened?"

When the minister told him the story, the king got furious. "You are an idiot!" he shouted. "Why do I keep you as my minister? If you were equal to your position, then at this hour you would not have come to bother me. You should be equal to your post."

The minister understood the king and ordered the prince and his friends to be arrested and thrown into prison for six months. The following morning the minister went to the king and told him what he had done.

The king said, "You have sentenced them to six months in prison? For the other culprits six months is all right, but for my son the punishment must be six years. This is my order. His friends will stay in prison for six months, and he will stay in prison for six years."

Every week the prince and his friends were allowed to visit the king. The king was so nice to his son's friends. Each time he would give them beautiful presents and have talks with them. He would tell them, "Never rob again. It is not a good thing." He would show them such kindness and affection. But he would never say a word to his son. He would only say to his son's friends, "How could my son do this kind of thing?"

After six months all the culprits were released except the prince. The prince continued coming to the palace once a week, but the king would never speak to him or show him any kind of affection. The prince would sit in his father's room for some time, and then he would be taken back to the prison.

Finally, after six years, the prince was released. At that time the king had a long talk with him. The king said, "I am the king. I am richer than the richest. If you had asked me, I would have given you anything you wanted. How much wealth could anyone have in comparison to my wealth? My wealth is all yours. Someday I will leave my kingdom in your hands, and then you will get everything. When you become king, you will have to be good to your subjects. People appreciate me because of my kindness, sympathy and oneness. When you, the prince, commit a robbery, what kind of oneness are you showing with your future subjects?"

Because of his father's strictness, the prince turned over a new leaf and eventually became a wise and compassionate ruler.

IE 22. *The pious minister*

Once an old minister did a number of extraordinary things and the king was very pleased with him. The king went to the minister's house and lavished many expensive gifts on him. He gave him jewels and money, as well as horses and elephants.

The minister was very sincere and pious, and he wanted to live a very simple life. So all the wealth that the king had given him he gave away to the poor in the king's name. He kept only a few horses and elephants.

The king's other ministers were very jealous because the king always spoke so highly of this minister's bravery and kindness. So they plotted against him and forged his signature on a letter which showed that he was a traitor. Then they brought the letter to the king.

The king couldn't believe his eyes, but since all the ministers were saying that the old minister was a traitor, what could he do? There was only one punishment for a traitor, so he ordered that the minister be killed. When the old minister was brought before the king, he said, "O King, I used to serve your father most devotedly, and I have also been serving you most devotedly. Now you believe that I have become a traitor. I know that my life is very insignificant, so what is the use of defending myself? Once upon a time, when I used to fight for your father, my beard used to become red. At that time it was red with the blood of his enemies. Now, when you kill me, my own blood will make my beard red."

After the pious minister was executed, the other ministers said, "O King, we should now get back all the wealth that you have given this bad minister."

The king agreed, "Naturally we should get it back." So he sent his soldiers to the old minister's servant. "Show us where he has kept his wealth!" they ordered.

The servant replied, "There is nothing left. He distributed everything to the poor, except for a few horses and elephants."

None of the soldiers believed the servant, so they brought the servant to the king. The king said, "Now, tell the truth."

The servant said, "O King, I will tell the truth. You gave so many things to the old minister, but he gave away everything to the poor in your name. He pretended that you had asked him to distribute the wealth. It was really his, but he gave away everything except for a few horses and elephants."

The king asked, "Why did he keep the horses and elephants?"

The servant replied, "He said that if you were ever attacked by your enemies, you would need them. Then it would be necessary for you to buy back the elephants and horses from those people to whom he had given them. Because you had given them to him out of your affection and love, he kept them only for you to use in an emergency. The rest of the wealth he gave to the poor in your name."

The servant paused. Then he said, "O King, he also told me that what the other ministers said against him is all false."

The king got furious and said to the other ministers, "If this servant is telling the truth, and you confess, then I will forgive you. But if you don't confess, and I find out later that what he is saying is true, then I will kill all of you immediately."

The other ministers confessed that they had forged the letter and that the old minister had given everything away to the poor. About the elephants and horses, they said it was up to the king whether or not to believe it.

The king cried, "What have you done? I knew he was such a good, pious, sincere minister, but you convinced me to kill him. How cruel I have been! I promised that I would forgive you, so I will not punish you. But now I know that good people cannot stay with me. Only bad people like you will force themselves on me and stay with me. To the end of my life I will feel miserable that I have lost such a good, pious minister. I have lost him, and now I am left with only unthinkable rogues like you!"

IE 23. *The punishment is compassion*

In India there was once a Muslim mendicant who had a certain amount of occult power. His name was Bajit Bastami. In Chittagong there is a special place where many Muslims worship him. Even the Hindus have tremendous love for him.

In a pond near his tomb there are fifteen or twenty very large turtles that were actually human beings once upon a time. Bajit Bastami got angry at these people because they were unkind to him, so he turned them into turtles. He gave them all names: Rajali, Majali, Pulali and so on. He said that when the time came, he would turn them into human beings once again — not ordinary human beings, but great human beings. Because they were going through such severe punishment, he said that some time in the future his compassion would help them become great human beings.

There are many stories about Bajit Bastami's compassion. Once at midnight he was walking along the street praying and meditating when he saw a man playing on a flute. The flutist was heavily drunk, but he was playing extremely well. Since he was playing such melodious, haunting tunes, people had gathered around him. But whenever they appreciated him, he would insult them, using very foul language. Some people cursed him and left, while others, in spite of being scolded and insulted, stayed there. They didn't take his insults seriously, since he was obviously drunk. Besides, the man was playing very well, and they were enjoying the fun.

As soon as the musician saw Bajit, he started insulting him, and this time he used the filthiest, absolutely the most foul tongue. Bajit was annoyed and said, "You stop using these kinds of words!"

The drunk flutist got furious. He approached Bajit and struck him mercilessly on the forehead with his flute. The drunkard's flute broke and Bajit went home with his forehead bleeding profusely.

By that time Bajit had many, many disciples and followers, and when they saw their Master's plight, they wanted to kill this flutist. But Bajit said, "No, no! You must not do that. Tomorrow morning I will do something about it." The disciples were very happy that their Master was going to punish the man.

The following morning Bajit gave one of his servants some most delicious Indian sweets plus a few rupees to take to this flutist, along with a message. The message was that Bajit was extremely sorry that his head was responsible for breaking the man's flute, and he was sending money so that the musician could buy a new one. Also, since he had experienced a little bit of the man's foul tongue the previous day, he was sending some sweets to sweeten his tongue.

When the flutist received the gifts and heard the message, he was deeply moved. Immediately the musician and all his friends and admirers ran to Bajit 's cottage and fell at his feet, asking to be illumined by his forgiveness.

In later years they all became Bajit's extremely good disciples. In this way, through his compassion Bajit transformed some undivine drunkards into divine aspirants.

IE 24. *The kind-hearted homeopath*

There was once a very good homeopath who wanted to live in a very simple manner. He had a big heart, so he used to help the poor without charging them any fee. Everybody was very deeply appreciative of his kind-heartedness, except his own father. His father used to scold him and insult him, even in front of his wife.

Once it happened that a very poor man developed a high fever and all kinds of ailments. The homeopath went to the man's house to help him and found that he was shivering violently. The homeopath took off his own shawl and gave it to the poor man, in addition to massaging his whole body and giving him medicine. He spent two or three hours there. His fee for house calls was only three rupees, but as happened quite often, he did not even ask the man to pay him.

When the homeopath went home, he was shivering because he no longer had his shawl. His father insulted him mercilessly for his impractical attitude. His wife shed bitter tears, for she too had a big heart, and she felt very sad when her father-in-law insulted her husband.

One day it happened that the richest man in the city developed a serious disease. Even the doctors in the hospital could not cure him. Finally the rich man's friends pointed out by way of joke that there was only one doctor in the city whom he had not consulted: the foolish quack homeopath. Although they were joking, the rich man said, "Since I am heading towards the other world, it cannot do any harm for me to try him."

So he sent for the homeopath, who came and gave him a remedy. In two or three days it became obvious that the patient was improving, and in a month's time he was completely cured. The rich man wanted to give the homeopath three hundred rupees. But the homeopath said, "You have already paid my fee of three rupees. Why should I take this?"

The rich man insisted, "Three hundred rupees is nothing for me."

The doctor's father began insulting him, as usual, and tried to force him to take the money.

Finally the homeopath started shedding tears in front of everyone. Looking up with folded hands, he prayed aloud: "O God, You have really forsaken me. If I become rich, then I will not think of You. This is just a tricky plan to test me. If I take the money, I will no longer think of You. Only if I remain poor will I be able to think of You at every moment. No, I will not accept this money under any circumstances." In spite of his father's unceasing insults, he remained firm in his refusal to accept the three hundred rupees.

This seeker happened to be one of the foremost disciples of Sri Ramakrishna. He was devotion incarnate. When his Master used to give prasad on a plantain leaf, he used to eat even the leaf, because he felt that the leaf was also a blessingful gift from the Master. No other disciple of Ramakrishna had his kind of devotion. You may call it fanatical devotion, but I call it true devotion.

There are many inspiring stories about this disciple of Sri Ramakrishna. Once some friends of his came to visit him. He was so poor that he didn't have fuel, so he cut off one of the beams that was holding up the ceiling and used it as fuel to cook for them.

When Sri Ramakrishna passed away, for two or three months this disciple was bedridden. He cried and cried, saying, "Now there is nothing to see or feel on earth — nothing, nothing."

Sri Ramakrishna told many, many people that this disciple was a householder who could truly be respected by all. He deserved admiration and adoration from even the purest and most spiritual seekers. This homeopath was a radiant example of purity, simplicity, sympathy and oneness-heart.

IE 25. *I love you more than I love my own life*

Once there was a young boy named Ramesh. His parents were not only rich, but also extremely kind. Ramesh was a very good student. His classes started at nine o'clock in the morning. From nine o'clock until twelve o'clock he studied. Then from twelve to one he had an hour's recess, and again from one to three he studied.

The students used to bring food from home to eat during the lunch hour. One day Ramesh realised that his friend Gopal had not eaten anything for lunch for a few days. As a matter of fact, Gopal wasn't bringing any food to school with him.

Ramesh went to his friend and asked why he was not eating anything. Gopal said, "My mother could not give me anything. She said we had nothing at home."

Ramesh said, "Don't worry. I will share with you."

"No, I can't take your food," said Gopal.

"Of course you can," insisted Ramesh. "My parents give me much more food than I need." Finally Gopal agreed, and for a few weeks the two boys shared Ramesh's lunch.

Then all of a sudden Gopal stopped coming to school. Ramesh was very sad. One day he asked the teacher why his friend was not coming anymore. The teacher said to him, "Ah, he comes from a poor family. His parents can't afford to pay the school fees; therefore, he can no longer come to school."

Ramesh felt sad and miserable. When school was over, he took down Gopal's address from his teacher and went to Gopal's house. Ramesh begged his friend to come back to school, saying that he would ask his parents to pay the fee. Gopal's parents were deeply moved by his kindness, and Gopal again started going to school.

Gopal's father was an old man. In a few years' time he died. When he died, the family became totally poverty-stricken, and Ramesh supported them with his own money. When Gopal's sister was severely attacked by a serious disease, the family could not afford the hospital bills. Again Ramesh helped them out. In every way he was the friend and guardian of Gopal's family.

Both Ramesh and Gopal completed high school and went to college. One day Gopal said to Ramesh, "To say that my heart is all gratitude to you is an understatement. I wish to say that I love you more than I love my own life."

Ramesh said, "My friend, if you love me, that is more than enough for me. You do not have to love me more than your own life."

Gopal said, "But I do, and I want to prove it." Then he opened his penknife and cut his own arm. Naturally he began bleeding. Gopal placed a few drops of blood at Ramesh's feet.

Ramesh said, "What are you doing, what are you doing?" He touched the cut on Gopal's arm, placed a few drops of blood on his own heart and said, "This is the right place for your life-blood. I give you my earthly treasure in the form of money and material wealth. You give me your heart's love, which is heavenly wealth beyond all measure."

IE 26. *Who is stronger?*

There was once a great devotee of Lord Vishnu, a spiritual singer and poet named Surdas. Surdas was blind from infancy. He had six brothers who all died while fighting in a battle against the Muslims. Although Surdas was totally blind, he went in search of his brothers' bodies. While searching, he fell into a well that had no water in it.

For six days Surdas was trapped inside the well. During this time he repeated the name of Krishna, the Avatar of Lord Vishnu, over and over again. At the end of six days Lord Vishnu himself appeared and with his occult power lifted Surdas out of the well. Lord Vishnu also granted Surdas vision so that he would be able to see everything in a normal way.

For a few days Surdas was extremely happy. Then he began to feel miserable because he saw that the world is full of ugliness and that people are always quarrelling and fighting with each other. Finally he said to Lord Vishnu, "O Lord Vishnu, I don't want to see these things anymore. Please take away my vision again. When I didn't see human ignorance so vividly, I was very happy and peaceful. Please make me blind so that I can be happy again." Lord Vishnu granted his prayer, and once again Surdas became blind.

Surdas used to compose most soulful songs. Since he had many good friends and relatives, there was always someone who was kind enough to write down the words and music for him. One day when he was greatly inspired, he began calling out for one of his stenographers, but no one was available.

Suddenly Surdas felt the presence of someone and said, "Please tell me who you are. Announce your name." But the person wouldn't answer. Since Surdas very strongly felt somebody's presence, he tried to grab the person, but immediately the person vanished from his grasp.

Surdas said, "I know, my Lord, it is You who have come to me. You have the power to snatch Yourself away from my grasp on the physical plane. So in this way You are physically stronger than I am. But let me see if You are spiritually stronger than my heart. Let me see if even for a fleeting second You can disappear from Your devotee's heart. This is my challenge. I am sure that spiritually You cannot withdraw from me, because of the heart of love and devotion that You have given me. You will not be able to leave my heart even for a fleeting second."

Surdas was right. Lord Vishnu could never escape from the loving heart of his devotee.

ILLUMINATION-EXPERIENCES
ON INDIAN SOIL

BOOK 3

Once Emperor Sajahan went out on an expedition with some of his friends, relatives and admirers. He was walking quite fast in front of the entourage and, at one point, became separated from the group. The Emperor was not familiar with the area, and unfortunately he got lost. His friends and relatives could not trace him.

After some time the Emperor became very thirsty, but there was no water nearby. All of a sudden, Sajahan saw an old man carrying a container of water on his back, and he asked him if he could have some to drink. The man said, "All right, since you are so thirsty," and he gave Sajahan a large quantity of water. The Emperor started drinking it very fast.

The man became worried, for he felt that it was not advisable for anyone to drink so fast. Since he was also carrying a bag of grass on his back, he took a handful of grass and threw it into the container that Sajahan was drinking from.

Sajahan got furious. He said, "What are you doing? Why did you throw grass into my water? You were so kind to give me water. You saved my life. Now why are you throwing grass into my water?"

The man explained, "My good friend, I have a number of asses, and I never allow them to drink water fast. If I put grass in their water, they drink more slowly. If you drink too fast, you may develop colic pain. I was only trying to be considerate of your health."

In the meantime, Sajahan's friends and admirers had discovered the Emperor. From a distance they saw the man throw grass into Sajahan's water, and immediately they became furious. They wanted to beat and strike the man mercilessly.

But Sajahan stopped them. He said, "No, no, no! This man has saved my life. It was only out of concern that he put grass in my water."

Then the Emperor turned to the man and said, "You don't have to make your living by working with asses anymore. I am making you the head of a village because you have saved my life."

IE 28. *Sajahan teaches his officer a lesson*

Once Sajahan went out on an expedition with some soldiers in his army. All of a sudden, a man came up to him crying, "Your Majesty, your Majesty, I have a complaint to make against one of your officers."

The Emperor asked, "Is he here? Who is it?"

The man pointed to one of the officers and said, "Yes, he is here, sitting on that horse. I work for him, but for the last four months he has not paid me. I assure you, your Majesty, I work very, very hard."

Sajahan asked the officer if this were true. The officer remained silent and then with his head bowed, he admitted that it was.

Sajahan ordered the officer to get off his horse. Then he turned to the servant and said, "Now, you get on the horse. You ride with the others in my army who are coming with me on this expedition. Wherever I go, you follow me on this horse."

The Emperor turned to the officer and said, "You have to run and follow the expedition wherever we go. This is my command."

The officer started running, following Sajahan wherever he rode. Soon he started panting, and after a short time he cried out, "I am dying, I am dying, I am dying!"

The Emperor stopped his horse and said to him, "You deserve to die. I give you money because you serve me. This innocent man serves you day in and day out. How is it that you don't pay him? You must pay him his back salary right now."

The officer said, "I am more than ready, but I don't have money with me now."

The Emperor said, "Then take money from me."

The officer took the money and gave it to his servant. Then Sajahan said, "As you know, I never give loans. Whenever I give something, it is always as a gift. But promise me that from now on you will always pay this man. If you break your promise, I will give him your post and make you his lifelong servant."

IE 29. *Sajahan receives two complaints*

Once a man came to see Sajahan at the Emperor's court. He said to the Emperor, "Your Majesty, I have a serious complaint to make against a particular girl."

Sajahan asked him who the girl was, and then he summoned her. He said to the man, "Now make your complaint."

The man said, "Your Majesty, we were in love for many years. Five months ago we got engaged. Since then, I have spent all my money on her. Because of her, I have become practically poverty-stricken. And now, all of a sudden, she has decided that she no longer wants to marry me. When I had a lot of money, she was all love for me. Now that I have no money, she hates me."

The girl said, "Your Majesty, this is a total lie!"

Sajahan asked the man, "Can you prove what you are saying?"

The man said, "Oh yes, easily I can prove it. You know, we were so close, so intimate with each other that I can tell you where she has marks on her body." Then the man told the Emperor about them.

Sajahan asked two elderly women to take the girl into another room to see if the man was correct.

The elderly women returned with the girl and said, "O Emperor, what he says is absolutely true. There were marks in exactly the places that he said."

Sajahan turned to the girl and said, "You liar! You have to marry this man."

The girl cried and cried. Then she said, "I beg of you, can I wait just three months before I marry him? There are quite a few things I have to do to get ready for the wedding. I will definitely marry him in three months' time, since it is your order."

The Emperor turned to the man and asked, "Will you agree to wait for three months?"

The man said, "Yes, I will wait. But remember that she is promising to marry me in front of you, your Majesty."

Sajahan said, "Yes. She must keep her promise and obey my order. If she does not, then she will be hanged."

In two weeks' time the girl hired three strong, stout women and went with them to the home of her future husband. As soon as he opened the door, they immediately started strangling him and the man was totally helpless. Then the girl put a bracelet into his hand and started screaming.

All the neighbours rushed over to see what was happening. The girl told them, "This man came to my house and stole my very precious gold bracelet. Fortunately, my friends were there, and we chased him to his house. Now he should be punished."

The complaint went to Sajahan that this man had stolen the gold bracelet. The Emperor summoned both the girl and the man to his palace. He said to the man, "You are such a rogue! You must be punished." Then he asked the girl, "How do you want him to be punished? Whatever punishment you want, just tell me. Do you want him to be hanged?"

The man was frightened to death. He said, "O Emperor, I wish to tell you that somebody else also deserves some punishment."

Sajahan said, "Who? What are you talking about?"

The man said, "The maid of this particular girl also deserves punishment. I bribed that old lady with a lot of money so she would tell me something about the marks on the girl's body. That lady was her servant for many years and used to braid her hair. I learned about the marks from her."

Sajahan summoned the maid and ordered that the man and the maid each be whipped one hundred times. Then he said, "This innocent girl doesn't have to marry this rogue. In fact, I am going to give her lots of money to compensate for the suffering she has gone through because of this rascal."

After a few months the girl again came to Sajahan's palace. This time she was full of remorse. She told the Emperor about her trick with the gold bracelet. She said, "I never had anything to do with him, and I didn't want to marry him. Since he told so many lies about me, I wanted to see him punished."

At first the Emperor was shocked to hear her story. Then he said, "Do not worry. You did the right thing. He deserved that kind of punishment for lying and saying that you had been in love. He was the one who started everything. What you did, I admire. I need intelligent women like you in my kingdom!"

IE 30. *The Muslim mendicant*

The Emperor Sajahan had heard many good things about a particular Muslim mendicant in his kingdom. People said that the mendicant always prayed to Allah and that he was very pious and spiritual. Everybody felt that he said and did the right thing at all times, and they greatly appreciated and admired him. The Emperor was also full of appreciation for him and had a strong desire to meet him. Of course, since he was the Emperor, Sajahan could have asked to see the mendicant at any time. But Sajahan never wanted to summon him or in any way force him to come to his court.

One day when Sajahan was on the third floor of his palace with some of his close friends and relatives, this particular mendicant happened to walk by the palace gate. Everybody said to the Emperor, "Look, here is the mendicant whom you have wanted to meet for such a long time."

Sajahan said to his relatives, "Since he is near the palace, please tell him that I would be extremely grateful if he would come to see me for a few minutes. Tell him that he does not even have to walk up the stairs. We will hang a basket off the balcony by a rope and lift him up to the third floor."

The mendicant was very surprised to hear that the Emperor himself wanted to see him. He was very humble and said, "If his Majesty wants to see me, how can I refuse?"

So he sat in the basket and Sajahan and a few others pulled him up. The Emperor said, "I am so happy and grateful that you have accepted my invitation. Today I wish to discuss spiritual matters with you. All the time I am with people who don't practise spirituality, and I am also in that same category. If I wanted to, I could make time for my spiritual life. Unfortunately, I don't have sincere aspiration. But I do appreciate you and admire you very much."

The mendicant said, "Your Majesty, I don't deserve your appreciation and admiration. You and your subjects see only my face; you don't know my mind. My mind is uglier than the ugliest. I have so many bad thoughts. Outwardly I may appear very calm and peaceful, but inwardly my mind is very undivine. So I don't deserve your appreciation."

The Emperor said, "I deeply appreciate your sincerity, but I know that you are truly a very pure and pious man. Please tell me how you have become so close to Allah. Is it because you pray and meditate all the time?"

The mendicant said, "No, no, no! You think that I am close to Allah, and many others also believe the same. But I tell you, I am not closer to Allah than any of his other children. It is like the relationship between an Emperor and his subjects. I am one of your most useless subjects. I have no capacity. Would I ever have dared to request an audience with a great Emperor like you? A beggar, an insignificant subject like me, would never ask you to grant him an audience. It is your kindness, your affection, your love and your concern for a useless fellow like me that enabled me to come and speak to you. I don't deserve to see you at all.

"You wanted to see me and honour me. If I had had pride and haughtiness, I would not have come to you. I would have thought, 'Oh, although you are the Emperor, you don't pray and meditate. So why should I go to you? I don't need you'. But I was humble, and I was also moved by your invitation.

"Similarly, I am moved by the Call of Allah. Allah does not need an insignificant creature like me. Allah does not really need anyone. Out of His infinite Love and Compassion, He calls me and I respond. In this way He calls each and every man in secret. But very few are lucky enough to be able to respond to His unconditional Call. Because I have been lucky enough to respond to His Call, I am becoming close to Him. It is not my capacities or my qualities that have made me close to Allah, but His unconditional Concern and Love for a useless creature like me. In the same way He can, does and will call each and every human being. Unfortunately, very few respond to His Call."

IE 31. *The arrogant officer*

Every evening the Emperor Sajahan had an open audience with anyone who wanted to see him. Hundreds of his subjects would come, and the Emperor would chat with them for about half an hour.

Nobody was allowed to sit right in front of the Emperor. One evening an officer deliberately sat down in the forbidden area. The Emperor and the members of his court were all furious. Sajahan said, "How dare you show such disrespect by sitting right in front of me! I want you to leave this palace right away! I am dispensing with your services, and you will never again be given another job with the government. From now on you can only do ordinary, menial jobs!"

The day after the officer was fired, he again came to the public audience and sat down right in front of the Emperor. The previous day he had at least shown the Emperor a little bit of respect, but this time he had absolutely no respect. His face showed extreme haughtiness.

Sajahan said to him, "What is the matter with you? Yesterday I dispensed with your services. I threw you out of the palace and said that you can't work here anymore. Why are you now being even more disrespectful?"

The man said, "O your Majesty, yesterday I was dependent on you for my salary. Since I was dependent on you, I was always obedient. Now I am not serving you anymore, so I am independent. I can do anything I want to with my life. Previously I was at your mercy, but now I am on my own. I don't have to obey you anymore because I am no longer serving you."

All the people present were shocked at what the officer was saying and they wanted to thrash him. But Sajahan embraced the man and said, "I want everybody to have this kind of independent spirit." Then Sajahan gave him back his job and also gave him lots of money.

The following day everybody was wondering where the officer would sit, now that he had his job back. Finally they noticed him sitting at the very back of the group. Someone asked him, "What are you doing there?"

The officer answered, "An arrogant person can fight with another arrogant person, but he cannot fight with a man of boundless compassion and forgiveness. That is why I cannot fight with the Emperor anymore."

IE 32. *The Taj Mahal*

Everyone knows about the Taj Mahal, the most beautiful mosque in the world. It was the Emperor Sajahan who built it in honour of his wife, Mamataj. Today it is considered one of the great wonders of the world, and everybody appreciates its beauty.

One day a king and queen went to see the Taj Mahal. The king said to the queen, "Tell me, what do you think of this mosque?"

The queen said, "If you ask me what I think about it, I will speak about the architecture, the workmanship and so forth. But if you ask me what I feel about it, then I will tell you my real feelings. Will you honour my feelings?"

The king said, "Definitely I want to know your feelings, and definitely I will honour them."

The queen said, "All right. I would be willing to put an end to my life tomorrow if you would build a Taj Mahal like this one for me. Are you prepared to do so? I am ready to take my life this moment, but are you prepared to build another Taj Mahal for me?"

The king was speechless. The queen continued, "I can fulfil my promise tomorrow, but I can see that you are not ready to build another Taj Mahal for me. You would not even dare to promise to build me another Taj Mahal!"

The poor king looked at his wife in silence.

IE 33. *Let Allah's Will be done*

There were once two princes. When their father died, the older one became king. This older brother was good, sincere and pious, but the younger one was undivine to the extreme. He wanted to dethrone his older brother, so he organised a big army and started fighting against him.

The commander of the king's army said to the king, "We will definitely win. Our army is more powerful, and I am sure it is Allah's wish that we win."

The older brother said, "I do not know what Allah's wish is, but I am praying to Allah that His Will be done. Whomever He chooses to win, I will be very happy. If He thinks that my brother will take better care of the kingdom than I do, then Allah should allow my brother to win and become the king. I want Allah's children — my subjects — to be well protected and well guided.

"Right now my brother may be very undivine. But who knows, if he becomes king, perhaps he will become very nice, kind and pious. I don't know the future. If Allah feels that my brother will far surpass me in good qualities and that under his rule the kingdom will prosper much more, then I feel that my brother should win and not me. I want only Allah's Will to be done so that his children can be really happy."

IE 34. *The mother saves the youngest prince*

Once a particular king died, and his eldest son became king. His ministers immediately advised him, "Kill your five brothers. Otherwise, one day they will try to dethrone you."

So the king killed all his brothers, except for his baby brother who was only two years old. Still the ministers warned him, "It is better to kill the child now. Who knows what will happen in the future?"

The king's mother was sad and miserable that her eldest son had killed his four brothers. But what could she do? The king was the king. When she heard that he was planning to kill her two-year-old son as well, she went to him and said, "You have killed all my other sons. Tomorrow you will take the youngest one's life. What can I do? You are the king, and this is your order. But please give me a day to calm my mind and bring forward my inner strength before my youngest son is killed."

Then, in secret, with the help of friends, the mother found a merchant from another country who agreed to take her youngest son away and bring him up in his own country. She gave him lots of money and asked him to take good care of her son.

One of the mother's servants happened to hear about the plan. She went to the mother and said, "I have heard that you are sending your son to another country. Tomorrow if the king does not see his baby brother, you will be in trouble. Let me substitute my own son for the baby prince. He is your son's age, and he even looks like your son. Please let my son be killed in his place. Who knows, perhaps your son will one day be the king of this land or of some other land."

The queen was so moved and so grateful. She wanted to give the servant a very large amount of money, but the servant would not accept anything. She said, "The prince's safety is my reward."

So the servant's son was killed, and the young prince went to another country. After some time the merchant sent a letter to the mother telling her that her son was all right. He said that he had employed two or three nurses to take care of him.

O God, nothing remains a secret. Ten years later one of the nurses became jealous of another nurse who was getting a higher salary than she was. She became furious with the merchant and wanted to take revenge. This particular nurse knew the story of the child, so she informed the governor of the state that the prince was hiding there. When the governor came to know about the prince, he sent a message to the boy which said, "Give me a very large amount of money or I will send you back to your brother." At that time the prince was twelve years old.

The boy wrote a letter to his mother, and the merchant brought it to her. The mother sent the governor a very large amount of money. But, to be safe, the merchant took the prince to a different country. When the prince grew up, he became the ruler of that country.

IE 35. *Aurangazeb sacrifices grapes*

Once one of the generals of Emperor Aurangazeb fell sick. For months he suffered, and then his case started getting worse and worse. Finally, the Emperor called in a Greek doctor to help the patient. The doctor gave the general some medicine and told him that he should not eat grapes. He said grapes were not good for him and were creating problems. The general kept arguing with the doctor. He could not understand how not eating grapes would help his condition. Since he was very, very fond of grapes and they were one of his favourite foods, he did not want to give them up. But the doctor told him, "I am sorry. You must not eat any more grapes."

The Emperor believed in the doctor. Again, he was very fond of the general and did not want to see his dear friend suffer unnecessarily. So he made a bargain with the general. He said, "You like grapes and I also like grapes. But if you promise not to eat grapes, I also will not eat them. Then, when you are cured, at that time you, Allah and I will all eat grapes together. And if anything ever happens to you, if you do not survive your illness, then I will never eat grapes again."

The general was deeply moved, and he promised not to eat grapes until he was cured.

IE 36. *The Muslim king and the poet*

A Muslim king was very fond of poetry. He used to honour poets all the time, giving them gold and diamonds. Sometimes if a poem was extremely beautiful, he would ask the poet to stand on one side of a scale, and on the other side the king would put gold coins to equal the poet's weight. Then he would give the poet all the coins.

Once a poet wrote a very beautiful poem, and the king was very pleased with him. Unfortunately, the poet was very greedy. When the king was discussing how much the poet would get, the man became so restless that he could not wait to hear the outcome. So he said to the king, "Perhaps you will give me one *lak* of gold coins. May I see how many coins that is and how much it weighs?" The poet only wanted to see the coins. He did not actually know how much he would be getting.

The king was amused and said, "All right, bring one lak of gold coins to show him."

When the money was placed in front of the poet, the king said to him, "Now, what is happening inside you? Tell me!"

The poet said, "I am admiring you and appreciating you for having shown me all these coins. I have never seen so much money in my life, and perhaps I will never again see a lak of gold coins at one time. I have never seen such a huge amount!"

The king said, "I want you to be grateful to somebody else, and not to me."

"Who is that person?" the poet asked.

The king put all the coins in the poet's hands and said, "Look up. Now be grateful to Allah. I am giving you these coins in His Name. So please be grateful to Allah and not to me."

IE 37. *A sincere man's promise*

This is an authentic story about two friends. One day a young man said to his good friend, "I can see that some day you will become great and rich."

His friend scoffed, "Ridiculous! I will become a great man and a rich man!"

The first friend said, "Yes, I can see it. It is written on your forehead."

The second one said, "All right, if I become great and rich, I will give you ten thousand rupees."

"Do you really mean it?" the first friend asked. "If so, then write it down."

The second one wrote down, "I will give you ten thousand rupees if ever I become rich and great," and he signed his name.

The young man kept the note that his friend had written, but he never took his friend seriously. The agreement was made only by way of joke. Now, it happened that in ten or twelve years the one friend really did become rich and great, while the other unfortunately remained quite poor. By that time both friends had drifted apart and were leading their own lives. Even so, the one friend continued to preserve the note, although he felt that since it was a joke, he would never receive the money.

Quite unexpectedly, the poor man fell seriously ill. Just before he died, he called his son, who was only seven years old, and said to him, "My son, please bring me the box that is near the window. Inside it there is something very precious which I have kept for you."

The son was so sad that his father was dying that he didn't want to bring the box. He felt that nothing could be more precious than his father's life. But the father insisted, so the son went and got the box. Then the father said, "When I die...." and immediately the little boy and his mother started crying. But the father continued, "After I die, you go to this man and show him what he has written." The wife and son looked at the paper and were surprised to learn that the rich man had promised to give ten thousand rupees. But at that time they could not think of anything but their beloved one who was about to leave them.

Soon the man died. Friendship is such that the rich man, who was once his best friend, did not even come to see him before he left this world. But after three or four weeks' time the son took the note to the rich man. By that time the rich man had many servants. At first the man's servants didn't want to allow this little boy to bother him. But finally, when they saw he was only an innocent child, they allowed him to come in.

The boy gave the rich man the note. The rich man read it and asked, "Did I write this?"

The boy said, "I do not know. Before he died, my father gave it to me to give you." The son was practically crying.

The rich man summoned one of his secretaries and explained, "I promised this boy's father many years ago that I would give him ten thousand rupees if I became rich and great. I can say that I have been rich for seven years; now you please calculate how much interest I have to give him in addition to the ten thousand rupees."

The secretary told him, "Seven thousand rupees, which makes it seventeen thousand altogether."

The rich man immediately issued a check for seventeen thousand rupees and gave it to the little boy, saying, "Take this directly to your mother. Don't go anywhere else first."

This is how one sincere man kept his promise.

IE 38. *The prince receives punishment*

There was once a king who had only one son. One day a complaint came to the king that the prince had become extremely violent while he was playing with another teenager. He had broken the rules of the game and struck his friend very severely. The other teenager's head had begun bleeding profusely.

When the king got the message, he was horrified. He went to the magistrate and said, "Since he is my son, I don't want to deal with his case. You please look into the matter."

The magistrate summoned the king's son and also the friend who had been hurt. The magistrate saw that both of them were minors. He felt miserable that he had to punish the prince, so he went to the king and said, "Your Majesty, both these boys are minors, and your son is such a good boy. While playing, perhaps he lost control of himself. But he does not deserve punishment."

The king said, "He does not deserve punishment? Then who deserves it?"

The king summoned the prince and his friend and said to the friend, "In front of me you have to strike my son the way he struck you. Only if his head bleeds will I be satisfied. Otherwise, the punishment will not be just."

The boy started trembling. He was afraid to hit the prince.

The king said, "If you do not obey my order, you will be punished! One day my son will rule the kingdom. He has to learn how to control himself."

Still the boy was afraid. The king insisted, "You have to obey me!" he said.

Finally the boy started striking the prince very hard. The king was satisfied only when his son's head started bleeding. The prince was crying, but what could he do? This was his father's order. In this way the king taught his son self-control.

IE 39. *The kind-hearted king*

There was once a very kind-hearted king. He was always considerate, compassionate and generous to his subjects. One day he got a complaint from a teacher who said that his students were so unmanageable that he did not know what to do with them. He even had to strike his students because they would not behave well.

The king summoned the teacher and told him, "It is not good to beat your students." Then he called to his palace all the students who had been beaten and presented them with extremely beautiful and expensive gifts. He also gave them three weeks' leave from school.

Another time the king was supposed to give a talk at a particular hall. When the king arrived, he saw that the door was closed, and the guard was lying down in front of the door fast asleep. The king's friends and admirers got furious. But what did the king do? Instead of scolding the guard, he got mad at his friends and admirers! He said, "Poor fellow, he is tired, exhausted. We can't be unkind to him. I was supposed to give a talk here, but let us go to some other place instead."

Then the king told one of his very faithful officers to watch over the sleeping guard so that nobody would disturb him. In this way he made sure that the man could enjoy uninterrupted sleep.

IE 40. *The king's cousin*

One day a young man came to a certain king and said, "Please, please appoint me to a high post. I am the cousin of the neighbouring king, who is a good friend of yours. This particular king always speaks highly of you. Therefore, I would like to serve you."

The king appointed him to an important post in his army. The man did a very good job, and the king was quite pleased.

In a few years' time it happened that the neighbouring king invited this particular king to come to his palace. Of course, the king accepted the invitation and asked the young man to accompany him. The young man, who by then had a very high post, became very frightened. He knew that he would be caught because he was not really the other king's cousin.

On the day the king was to leave, the high-ranking officer fell at his feet and started crying. The king said, "You are a military man. What are you doing?"

The man said, "Forgive me. I am not the cousin of that other king. I cannot go there."

The king said, "No, you have to go! Everybody respects you and thinks that you belong to a royal family because I gave you such an important post. Now I have to prove to everybody that you really do belong to a royal family. Since you are not the other king's cousin, you have to become a member of my family. You have to get married to a member of the royal family and become my son-in-law." In this way the king saved the officer's reputation.

ILLUMINATION-EXPERIENCES
ON INDIAN SOIL

BOOK 4

The Emperor Timur was an ancestor of Akbar the Great. When Timur was in India, one day he saw a religious mendicant praying and meditating most soulfully at the foot of a tree. Timur was not a spiritual person, but he appreciated spiritual people. He was so deeply moved by the religious mendicant that he told him he could have anything he wanted from him.

The mendicant said, "I do not need anything from you."

Timur asked, "But why not?"

The mendicant replied, "Because God has supplied me with all my material needs. I have got such a beautiful tree and I can draw water from the river. During the day I have the sun, at night I have the moon, and all the time I have such a vast sky over my head! What else do I need?"

Timur said, "You do not have any money!" The mendicant said, "I do not need money."

"Then please come and visit my palace," said Timur.

"There is no need for me to visit your palace," said the mendicant. "It is true that each place has its own outer beauty, but I care only for the inner beauty."

Finally, Timur said, "I am the Emperor. You have to take something from me."

The mendicant said, "Then give me something that will increase my aspiration and my love for God."

Timur said, "I do not have any aspiration. How can I give you something that will increase your aspiration?"

"Aspiration is the only thing I need," said the mendicant. "Anything else that I take I will not be able to appreciate or use."

Timur said, "No, you have to ask me for something else. Since I do not have anything to increase your aspiration, give me another chance to offer you something!"

The mendicant finally said, "All right. When I meditate here, sometimes flies bother me. Can you stop them from bothering me?" The Emperor tried for a few minutes to stop the flies from bothering the mendicant, but they came back again and again. At last the Emperor said, "It is an impossible task! How can I do it?"

The mendicant told him, "Oh, you are a real Emperor, indeed! You cannot even save me from these flies. Yet just now you were bragging about your wealth and capacity."

The Emperor was deeply humiliated. He stopped disturbing the poor spiritual mendicant and went away.

IE 42. *Washing the teacher's feet*

Many years ago, a Moghul prince was studying under a teacher. In those days, the teachers were worshipped by their students. In these days, the story is different, perhaps because teachers are now afraid of their students.

Previously, it was customary for a student to wash his teacher's feet after he had taken a lesson. One day, while the prince was washing his teacher's feet, the Emperor came by. The prince became frightened and the teacher also started trembling. How could the prince wash the feet of an ordinary man?

When the Emperor saw the prince hesitating, he began to scold the prince. "I clearly see that you are not washing your teacher's feet with utmost devotion and humility. Stop neglecting your duty and wash your teacher's feet properly!" So the prince washed his teacher's feet with utmost devotion and the Emperor was very happy. The Emperor wanted his son to learn the lesson of humility. Meanwhile, the teacher was trembling the whole time!

IE 43. *Jahan Ara's last wish*

The Moghul Emperor Shah Jahan's only daughter was Jahan Ara. Jahan Ara was extremely beautiful, extremely soulful and extremely self-giving. When Shah Jahan was incarcerated in the Red Fort by his son, Aurangzeb, Jahan Ara remained in the same prison to serve and console her father. She stayed with her father for eight years. In every way she tried to keep him happy and well.

Long before he was imprisoned, Shah Jahan had built the Taj Mahal, one of the great wonders of the world, in memory of his dead wife, Mumtaz Mahal, whom he had loved very much. Who knows what he would have done if Jahan Ara also had died before him? True, by that time he was no longer the Emperor, but he would have perhaps begged his most notorious son to do something very special for his all-giving daughter, Jahan Ara. When Shah Jahan died, the daughter greatly mourned the loss of her father. With her mother also gone, she had full freedom to come out of her self-imposed prison-life and enjoy life as a member of the royal family. But Jahan Ara said, "How can I be happy when my brother is so cruel and undivine?" She felt her life had no meaning without her beloved father. So she continued living in prison for her few remaining years on earth.

Jahan Ara's last wish was not to have a canopy over her grave. Instead, she wanted only grass to grow on top of her grave. She wanted a most humble funeral ceremony, just like that of an ordinary person. She said, "I have not lived the life of a princess for many years. The life of simplicity, humility and purity I have tried to live. So let my passing also be all simplicity, humility and purity."

IE 44. *Aurangzeb visits the mosque*

Prince Aurangzeb incarcerated his father, the Moghul Emperor Shah Jahan, and also imprisoned and even killed some of his brothers so that he could become Emperor. Afterwards, he felt miserable at what he had done, and he often went to the mosque to pray.

One day he was praying in the mosque, along with many other people, when one of the mosque attendants saw a hole in the carpet. The man cried out, "What will the Emperor think if he sees such a hole?"

The Emperor overheard the attendant and became furious. The man apologised profusely and said, "Please forgive me, O Emperor. Next time when you come, there will be no hole in the carpet. It will be a brand new carpet."

Aurangzeb said, "You fool, that is not why I am angry! Why should you beg my forgiveness for a hole in the carpet? In my palace, if I had seen such a hole in the carpet, I would have been really furious. There I would not tolerate such a thing. But I have come here not as the Emperor; I have come as an ordinary person, as one of you. I have come as a beggar to pray to Allah. This is Allah's special place, and Allah does not care for luxury and pomp. Here, simplicity and poverty are the real perfection. So do not worry about the hole; let it remain. Only if I pray in a simple place will I have true aspiration and true love for Allah!"

IE 45. *Aurangzeb's glass of water*

Late one night, the Moghul Emperor Aurangzeb asked one of his personal attendants to bring him a glass of water. He wanted to have something to drink and also he wanted to wash his face, ears and nose before beginning a special midnight worship. The attendant was half asleep and went out of the room in a terrible hurry to fetch the water. While returning with the water, by accident he fell on the Emperor and almost kicked him. When he realised what he had done, the attendant immediately knelt down in front of Aurangzeb and begged for forgiveness.

The Emperor said, "Forgive you? Why do I need to forgive you? This is only a silly accident. I am planning to ask Allah to give me more inner wealth, so in which way are you inferior to me? In which way are we different? We are both beggars."

IE 46. *The king's humility*

One day a sage came to a king for an interview. The sage had to wait for a long time because the king was very busy. Finally, the king said he could come in.

When the sage entered the hall, the first thing he did was to take off his hat and bow to the king. Immediately the king took off his crown and bowed to the sage. The ministers and others who were around the king asked, "What are you doing? He took off his hat because he is an ordinary man. But you are the king. Why should you have to take off your crown?"

The king said to his ministers, "You fools, do you think I wish to remain inferior to an ordinary man? He is humble and modest. His humility is a peerless virtue. He showed his respect to me. If I did not take off my crown, then I would be showing less humility than an ordinary man, and I would be defeated by him. If I am the king, I should be better than everybody in everything. That is why I took off my crown and bowed to him!"

IE 47. *Maharshi Dayananda's illumination*

Maharshi Dayananda came of a very rich family. At the age of twenty-one he was inspired to leave his house to search for a Guru. As he was leaving, he stood in front of his house and bowed down to his parents and relatives. He said, "I am leaving to become a sannyasin. I am not going to come back again."

Dayananda carried with him two books of Hindu scriptures which he had studied. He carried those scriptures hundreds and hundreds of miles as he went from village to village searching for a Guru.

Ten years passed, but still he found no Guru. He saw many so-called Gurus, but none of them satisfied him. One day, a seeker told him where he would find his Guru. He believed the seeker and travelled a hundred miles, all on foot, to the place where the Guru lived. He found the Guru and was very satisfied. His Guru said to him, "What are you carrying with you?"

Dayananda told him, "Two books of scriptures."

The Guru said, "Scriptures? Then you cannot be my disciple. Go and throw them into the river."

Those two books were Dayananda's most cherished possessions, but what could he do? In obedience to his Guru, he threw them into the river. He returned to the Guru and asked, "Am I now ready to be your disciple?"

The Guru said, "Yes, you are ready!"

Dayananda soon discovered that his Guru was totally blind. But that did not lessen his faith in his Master. Next he discovered that his Guru had never been able to read. Even then he had such faith in his Guru. He used to cook for his Guru and wash his clothes, serving him like a slave. Eventually he became his Guru's dearest disciple. But even when you are the Guru's dearest disciple, you can sometimes make mistakes. Once this Guru was extremely displeased with Dayananda and he struck Dayananda mercilessly with his hands. Then the Guru's hands became swollen and very painful. The Guru was miserable, but Dayananda was much more miserable — not because his Guru had hurt him, but because his Guru had hurt himself. He begged his Guru to beat him with a stick when he became angry with him in the future.

In a few days' time, the Guru again became angry with Dayananda. This time he struck Dayananda repeatedly with a stick. In the course of the beating the stick broke into sharp pieces and again the Guru got hurt.

One of the other disciples said, "Master, what are you doing? This disciple has left a very rich family to come to you. The poor fellow has nobody else except you. And he is so spiritual. He is far better than we are. Why do you strike him?"

The teacher remained silent, but Dayananda got furious. He insulted his brother disciple severely "What right do you have to speak to our Guru in that manner? Our Guru knows everything far better than we do. I may know the scriptures and I may come of a very rich family, but I have given up these things. I do not need earthly possessions. I need only the inner world. That is why I am at his feet." And once again Dayananda begged his Guru to beat him whenever he did something wrong. In fact, he went and brought his Guru quite a few new sticks for that purpose. The Guru simply gave him a soulful and compassionate smile.

In a few years' time Dayananda's Guru said to him, "You are now fully prepared. The time has come for you to leave me and initiate your own disciples."

Dayananda was totally heartbroken. He said, "This is the worst punishment!"

The Guru said, "This is not my punishment; this is my wisdom. You have realised me. Now, while I am still alive, you have to go out and spread my light. Others are not fit. Only you are fit."

So Dayananda left his Guru and gathered quite a few disciples of his own. From time to time, he used to tell his close disciples amusing and soulful stories about his Guru. Quite frequently he would take off his shirt and show his students the big marks on one of his shoulders, where his Guru used to thrash him.

He said, "My Guru was so kind and compassionate to me. He used to strike me mercilessly. These marks were not his punishment but his illumination. You have come to me as disciples because I am illumined. But I wish to tell you that my illumination is inside these marks.

"Either I am a better Guru or a worse Guru than my own Master. In my case, I bark, but I do not strike. But, who knows, my striking might have given you illumination by this time!"

IE 48. *The return of Gorakshanath*

Gorakshanath was a great occultist who lived on earth many hundreds of years ago. Since then, he has taken quite a few other incarnations. This is a story about one of his later incarnations, when he came to earth in a different body and with a different name.

One day, while a certain spiritual Master was having a very powerful meditation, he began shaking his legs. At that time, many of his past incarnations appeared before his inner vision. These incarnations were talking to him with such devotion, saying: "When you took our form, you were a huge wave of the ocean. You could create a sensation — a real commotion.

But now that you have become the ocean itself, your vastness is such that it cannot be fathomed; it cannot even be appreciated. It will take centuries to appreciate the vast consciousness that your illumination-ocean embodies for humanity."

After having this experience, the Master told his disciples some stories about his Gorakshanath incarnation: "Across the vast Indian sub-continent I travelled, visiting quite a few places. Everywhere I used my occult power. If somebody said anything I did not like, O God, either I would destroy that person or I would give him severe punishment. In this incarnation, either God has taken away those occult powers or God does not allow me to use them. Some people believe that I still have occult power, and some people think that I do not have any. Who is right and who is wrong, God knows! But, in those days, to kill someone and then revive him was not a difficult task. Nowadays, I cannot even kill an ant! The ant just hides. Even a cockroach will run away before I can catch it!

"I have had many, many significant incarnations, although the number is fewer than you people have had. Most of you have had many, many more incarnations than I have had, but during my past incarnations I ran a little faster than you did. My Gorakshanath incarnation was significant because it taught me the difference between occult power and spiritual power.

"I always say that God first uses His Compassion. When His Compassion fails, He uses His destruction aspect because that is the only way to take people to the goal. For a few years, when he was younger, Gorakshanath was quite compassionate, but his compassion was exploited. Then, later in life, he only showed occult power. In some places, he created a sensation; in some places, fear. Again, in some places, people loved and respected him. But he did not receive as much love as he did admiration. The admiration he got came most of the time because people feared him, not because they loved him.

"People who did not get a direct experience of Gorakshanath's occult power, but only heard about it from various sources, appreciated him. Others who directly experienced his occult power firsthand were terribly afraid of Gorakshanath. They were reluctant to come near him.

"Sometimes occultists use their power correctly, and sometimes they use it incorrectly. Sometimes, when they use occult power in a negative way, they have the power to change it into something positive. That is their good quality. They break something, but they have the capacity to repair it. But some occultists do not have that capacity. When they break something, it is finished! Then the rest of their lives they are miserable. But some occultists break and remake again. Gorakshanath was one of those who could destroy and rebuild.

"When occultists have tremendous occult power, sometimes they sneer at humanity's weaknesses instead of showing sympathy. It is difficult for most occultists to identify themselves with humanity unless they have achieved God-realisation. Their very existence is fire, fire, fire! But they do not realise that they are setting fire to their own house. If they took the whole world as their own home, they would see that when they use occult power they are definitely destroying their own home.

"Towards the end of his life, for at least forty years Gorakshanath remained meditating inside various caves at the foot of the Himalayas. At that time he stopped using occult power completely; he only wanted God-realisation. Before God-realisation, occult power cannot be guided. It is absolutely like a mad elephant. But once you get God-realisation, occult power can be tamed easily, like a pet dog or cat.

"When spiritual Masters realise God, they see the difference between occult power and spiritual power. Spiritual power is the ocean itself, whereas occult power is either one wave or a few waves. Since in the ocean there are countless waves, when we become the ocean, we get countless waves.

"After realisation, when we get spiritual power, occult powers also increase in number and in strength. But the greatest occult power or greatest spiritual power is oneness-power with God's Will. Continuous, sleepless and breathless oneness with God's Will is the most difficult power to have. It is like becoming God's slave. In this sense, 'slave' means 'child'. At every moment little children want to be dictated to. Although they know how to make decisions, they get tremendous joy if they always get the command from the highest.

"That is the role that I play quite often. I get the message from the Highest what to do with certain individuals or groups of individuals. That very thing I always tell my disciples. You may not know or you may know better than I do what to do with your life on the physical plane. But if you get the sanction from me or even if you make me aware of your future plans, then I do hope you get more joy than when you make your own decision, which may or may not be correct. Once the decision comes from within or from Above, then that decision is your salvation, and it will give you utmost joy.

"Sri Ramakrishna said that if the ego does not go, then that rascal should be kept as a slave. This ego is safer if it has the Supreme as its Master. That is the happier and sweeter way. The other way is to have the Universal Consciousness and feel, 'I am Brahma'. After realising God, the Universal Consciousness becomes yours, but there is no joy in this. You cannot play the sweet obedience-game. After becoming one with God, if you can become both Master and disciple, then there is great joy. But if you play only the role of the Master, only the Universal or Transcendental Self, then you do not get the same joy.

"Realisation I did have before my Gorakshanath incarnation. But that kind of realisation was like sitting near the foot of the tree. Then, in subsequent incarnations, I came to the foot of the tree. Then I started climbing and climbing. Now I have really climbed high, higher, highest.

"There was a kind of height that I achieved in those past incarnations. In each case, to reach that height had been my goal. In this incarnation, there is no such thing as the ultimate height. In previous incarnations, if I could reach nirvana, that was enough. Then, if I could have *sahaja samadhi*, that was enough. In this incarnation, I am seeing clearly that the Absolute Supreme is always transcending His own height. It is not my imagination or sweet dream. No, no, I am seeing it! The very nature of Divinity is to increase its own Divinity. This incarnation is offering me the message of the ever-transcending Reality, and I am offering that message to you, my dearest children."

IE 49. *The beggar gives his all*

Before India gained independence, a few young men from the villages wanted to free India from the foreign yoke; they wanted the British to quit India. They needed material wealth to throw the British out of India, so they started collecting money in the Indian villages.

One day, they got inspired to collect material things as well. They went from door to door carrying a huge bag, which gradually was filled with money and gifts. As they went, a one-legged beggar kept following them. The young men did not mind.

At the end of the day, they entered into a house to see what they had collected. The beggar also wanted to enter, but since he was not a member of the group, they did not allow him in. The beggar pleaded with them: "I walked such a long distance right behind you. You want freedom; I also want freedom. Our Motherland is not only your property. It is also my property."

At first, the young men got mad and told the beggar to go away. Then one of the men felt sorry for him, so they decided to show him the things they had collected. While the beggar was looking at the gifts in their bag, most of them were showing him real contempt. Then suddenly the beggar opened up the bag that he had been carrying. It contained a few coins and some rice. He spontaneously threw all the contents into their bag.

Immediately all the members of the revolutionary group started shedding tears of gratitude, because he had given all that he had to their cause. On that day, they had gone to visit so many rich families, who had given them next to nothing; but this beggar had given them everything that he had! They were deeply moved by the beggar's contribution.

IE 50. *Vidyasagar's sacrifice for his teacher*

This story is about a great Bengali figure named Vidyasagar. His name means 'the ocean of knowledge'. He is well known in India, especially in Bengal. During his lifetime, there was nobody who did not admire him for his wisdom and adore him for his compassion. He did so many things to raise the standard and the consciousness of Bengal!

He used to teach Sanskrit at a Sanskrit college run by the British Government. It happened that a higher post was available, and the principal wanted Vidyasagar to get the post. But Vidyasagar said, "No, I cannot accept it."

The principal asked, "Why?"

Vidyasagar replied, "Because there is someone who knows Sanskrit far better than I do. He is the one who should get this post." The principal said, "You fool, you need money! You have a big family to support. Your brother and sister depend on you. I have such affection and concern for you. You must take this post."

Vidyasagar insisted, "No, there is somebody who is more qualified than I am, and that person is my own teacher."

The principal said, "No, I am sorry. I do not agree with you."

Vidyasagar said, "I am not going to accept the post."

Finally the principal said, "The day after tomorrow is the last day I can accept applications, and your teacher has not yet even applied. It has to be done in an official way."

Vidyasagar said, "I will go to my teacher's house and bring him an application."

To reach his teacher's house, Vidyasagar had to pass through several villages, either by bullock cart or on foot — a distance of fifty miles. Vidyasagar was an ocean of knowledge and compassion, but he was not an athlete. For him to walk fifty miles was really something! He left Saturday afternoon and arrived at his destination the next day. When his teacher heard what Vidyasagar had done, he could not believe his eyes and ears. He started shedding tears and immediately embraced Vidyasagar.

The teacher told him, "If somebody says, 'God', immediately it comes to mind that God is in Heaven. But I will say that God is not in Heaven. God is right in front of me." Vidyasagar's family name was Isha, which means God.

Vidyasagar filled in the form, and his teacher just signed it. Then again Vidyasagar walked back fifty miles. Altogether he covered one hundred miles. When he returned, he was tired and exhausted, but he was also so delighted that his teacher would get the job. The principal did give Vidyasagar's teacher the job. But afterwards, the principal sat down on his chair and could not speak for an hour. How could there be people like Vidyasagar on earth? He could not do anything. He just sat on his chair speechless.

So Vidyasagar continued to receive fifty rupees a month, while his teacher received ninety rupees — practically double.

IE 51. *The horse that wanted more beauty*

A cosmic god had a horse. The horse was beautiful and also it had many good qualities. But it wanted to be more perfect in every way. It especially wanted to become beauty unparalleled.

One day the horse said to the cosmic god, "O Lord, you have given me beauty. You have given me other good qualities. I am so grateful to you. But how I wish you could make me more beautiful. I would be extremely, extremely grateful if you could make me more beautiful."

The cosmic god said, "I am more than ready to make you more beautiful. Tell me in what way you want to be changed."

The horse said, "It seems to me that I am not well proportioned. My neck is too short. If you can make my neck a little longer, my upper body will be infinitely more beautiful. And if you can make my legs much longer and thinner, then I will look infinitely more beautiful in my lower body."

The cosmic god said, "Amen!" Then immediately he made a camel appear in place of the horse. The horse was so disheartened that it started to cry, "O Lord, I wanted to become more beautiful. In what way is this kind of outer form more beautiful?"

The cosmic god said, "This is exactly what you asked for. You have become a camel."

The horse cried, "Oh no, I do not want to become a camel! I wish to remain a horse. As a horse, everybody appreciated my good qualities. Nobody will appreciate me as a camel."

The cosmic god said, "Never try to achieve or receive more than I have given you. If you want to lead a desire-life, then at every moment you will want more and more. But you have no idea what the outcome will be. If you cry for a longer neck and legs, this is what will happen. Each thing in my creation has its own good qualities. The camel is not as beautiful as you are, but it carries heavy loads and has a tremendous sense of responsibility. You stay with your beauty, which is absolutely needed. Beauty is definitely one of my divine qualities. And let the camel remain with its sense of responsibility, which is another divine quality of mine. Do not ask me for anything more. If I decide to give you something on my own, then it will not create any problems. It will only add to what you have. But when you are the one who asks me to add to what you already have, then you are bound to run into serious difficulties."

IE 52. *The great heavenly sage Narada*

The great heavenly sage Narada came from a very poor family. His mother used to serve the hermits in the forest. Some of the hermits were ordinary seekers, while others were highly evolved. Still others had realised the highest heights. Just before Narada's mother left the body, after being bitten by a snake, she asked her son to continue serving the hermits just as she had been doing. So after his mother's passing, Narada also started serving the sages. The sages liked him immensely and they taught him how to pray and meditate.

For years and years Narada prayed and meditated, and then one time he saw God inside his heart. He saw God for only a moment; then immediately God disappeared. Narada cried and cried for God to appear again, but to no avail. Finally, he heard a message from Above: "I came to intensify your aspiration. When your aspiration is intensified infinitely more than what it is now, I will appear again."

Narada eventually went back to the soul's world after completing his earthly sojourn. A few years later, Brahma asked him to take human incarnation again and return to earth to manifest God.

Narada said to Brahma, "No, the world is full of suffering and temptation. I do not want to go back to earth. On earth, when I think of manifesting God, at that time I forget to think of God. I want only to think of God and pray to God, and not to manifest God."

Brahma insisted, "No, you have to think of God and also manifest God; you have to do both together."

Narada said, "One cannot do that. Those two things do not go together!"

But Brahma said, "Aspiration and manifestation can and must go together."

Eventually Brahma forced Narada to come down into the world. This time, when Narada entered into the world, real temptation caught him. He had fifty wives. At the end of that particular incarnation, when he went back to the soul's world, he said, "I am never going back to earth!"

Brahma said "All right!" This time, while Narada was in the soul's world, Brahma taught him how to play on his vina. Then Narada said, "I will come down into the world again only to play on the vina and spread God's Glory, but for nothing else!"

Brahma said, "Fine!"

When he returned to earth, Narada went from one place to another singing of the Glory of God. That was his manifestation. While singing, he would accompany himself on his vina, which was named 'Mahati'. When Narada was travelling all over the world, his special means of conveyance was a machine, which is normally used to husk rice. He would ride on it from one place to another.

This was the incarnation in which he realised God. He always used to bring inspiring messages from Heaven to earth. He was the one who brought the message to Savitri's parents about Satyavan's death, which was described in the Mahabharata. He also helped Dhruva. He asked him to pray to God and he taught him how to realise God. Dhruva realised God through Narada's instructions.

Narada continues to live in the inner world. Even now, in the inner world, he sings songs about his love of God. He is very active; he is always on the move — devotedly, soulfully and powerfully spreading the Compassion and Love of God.

PART III

GREAT INDIAN MEALS:
DIVINELY DELICIOUS AND
SUPREMELY NOURISHING

BOOK 1

GIM 1. *Justice in King Giyasuddin's kingdom*[§]

There was once a great Muslim king named Giyasuddin, who also loved archery. As a king he was great; as an archer he was good. One day while he was hunting, he accidentally sent an arrow through the chest of a little child who was crawling in the bushes. It was the only child of a widow, who had brought him with her while she was praying and meditating in the forest. The archer-king was aiming at a deer, but instead of striking the deer, his arrow entered into the little child. The boy was crying most pathetically and the mother was hysterical.

The mother went to the magistrate of her district to make complaints against the archer, in spite of knowing that he was the king. She felt that there should be some justice. At first the muslim magistrate was hesitant: "How can I punish the King?" Then he said, "No, I shall do my duty."

So he summoned the king to court, addressing the summons to the archer Giyasuddin, not to the king Giyasuddin. On the appointed day the king appeared in court. On other days he would have saluted the king, but it was customary that the judge did not salute anyone summoned to appear in court. So the judge did not salute the king. He remained seated on his bench, and the king stood where convicts are asked to stand.

The magistrate said, "Do you know that you are going to be convicted?"

The king said, "Yes."

The magistrate said, "This is my punishment. You have to beg pardon of the mother of this poor child and, also, you have to pay everything that the child needs for his recovery."

The king immediately agreed. "I will do it." Right away he went to the mother, who was in the court, and begged her pardon. Then he gave her the money necessary for her child's recovery.

The king was then released. As soon as the king was released, the magistrate came down from his bench and bowed to the king, saying, "You are the King, and I am just an ordinary magistrate. It was you who appointed me and inwardly I shall be grateful to you for Eternity. But here justice was playing its role."

The king said, "I am so glad that you are just. I want everybody in my kingdom to be as just as you. Had you not summoned me or taken any notice of the woman's complaint, or had you just called me to court and said, 'He is the King; so what can I do?' I would have waited for a few days and then I would have come and punished you for the lack of justice in your district. This sword I would have utilised to punish you if you had not done your duty."

The magistrate pulled out a cane from under his long gown and said, "If you had not come or if you had not obeyed my order to pay for the child's recovery and also beg pardon from the mother, I would have punished you with this stick."

The king smiled broadly at the magistrate and embraced him, saying, "You deserve my embrace; you deserve my fondest embrace."

GIM 2. *Saradananda's sacrifice*[§]

One day, a long time after Sri Ramakrishna had left the body, his consort, Sarada Devi, was going to her parents' home. She was traveling by bullock cart. One of Ramakrishna's dearest disciples, Saradananda, was accompanying the Holy Mother. The road was full of holes, rocks and all kinds of obstructions. Quite a few times the wheels fell into the holes, and the jerk of the bullock cart increased tenfold each time this happened. The disciple felt miserable because Sarada Devi was not feeling well and she was trying to rest. But the road was so narrow that the driver could not avoid the holes.

Towards evening, Saradananda saw a very big hole in the distance. The Holy Mother was sleeping, and the disciple thought that if the cart had to pass over this hole, the Holy Mother would definitely be awakened and might even be hurt. Saradananda asked the driver to go very slowly, saying he would meet them on the road after a while. Then he ran to the spot where the hole was and lay down, filling it with his own body. Because it was dark and they were using an Indian lantern, the old driver could not see that the disciple lay down in the hole so that his back was level with the road.

When the bullock cart came near the hole, the driver saw the body in the road and screamed. The Holy Mother was aroused and asked what happened.

The driver got furious. "Look at what this man was doing! He was lying down on the road. How could I go on?"

The disciple said, "You fool, I did all this so that our Divine Mother could sleep, and now you have screamed and awakened her. If the wheels had fallen into the hole, there would have been a serious jerk and she could have got hurt."

The Holy Mother blessed Saradananda, "I am so proud that I have a disciple like you. How many disciples are there on earth who would do this kind of thing for their spiritual Masters and Divine Mothers?"

GIM 3. *Two beggars*[5]

There was once a Muslim mendicant, Makdun. Makdun used to roam from one place to another, all the time praying and meditating. Even while walking along the street he would be praying and meditating. He was very poor and depended entirely on the generosity of good and kindhearted people for his material needs.

One day he was walking along the street when he saw thousands of people gathered before a beautiful mosque. "Why are so many people there?" he wondered. Then someone told him, "The Emperor is coming today to offer a special prayer here." When the Emperor came, the mendicant went into the mosque and devotedly watched him pray to Allah most soulfully for more wealth, more name and more fame.

Then the Emperor said to the crowd, "Now come and take anything that you want from me." He started giving away money, clothing and everything, showing his heart's magnanimity and generosity. All the people stood in a line and one by one came up and took from the Emperor whatever he or she needed. Each one went away satisfied with what he had got. Makdun watched and watched, and when everybody had taken what he wanted, he started going away. The Emperor called out, "What are you doing? Why are you going away and not taking anything from me? What is wrong with you?"

With folded hands Makdun said, "Forgive me, O Emperor, but how can I take anything from a beggar? Just an hour ago you were begging God to give you more name, fame and earthly possessions. I don't need anything from a beggar. You are begging to the same Person for name and fame that I am begging to for peace, love, joy and inner satisfaction. The things that you are crying for I do not need, and perhaps the things that I am crying for you do not need. So you pray to Almighty Allah for what you want and let me pray to Him for the things that I need. You and I are just two beggars. Let us beg for our respective things to the One who has them."

GIM 4. *The message of perseverance*[§]

When Bopdeb was a young boy studying Sanskrit, he was the worst possible student. In everything he used to fail. His parents used to scold him mercilessly and his teachers beat him black and blue, but nothing did any good. Finally his teachers gave up and threw him out of school. Bopdeb was such a fool that his parents did not want to keep him either. So poor Bopdeb, feeling miserable, left his home and went to the nearest village.

Bopdeb used to pray and meditate under a tree near a big pond. One day, he saw some village women carrying empty pitchers to the pond and filling them. For quite a few days Bopdeb observed that after the pitchers were filled, the village women would place them on the stone steps by the pond and then go bathe and swim there. After getting refreshed, they returned to the village with their pitchers of water.

One day, when nobody was there, Bopdeb came near the spot where the women always stood and noticed something significant. He saw that the stone where the women would put their pitchers was being worn down. It was no longer level with the rest of the step. Bopdeb said to himself, "If, because the women placed their pitchers here repeatedly, even the stone is wearing down, then what is wrong with my brain?" From this he got the message of perseverance. He said, "Perseverance will always reach the goal."

He started praying and meditating, and after meditating seriously for a few days, he started reading his old Sanskrit grammar books. Previously he had been the worst possible student in Sanskrit, but this time he was able to remember what he read. He continued his studies and, by perseverance, eventually became the greatest Sanskrit scholar, especially in grammar.

GIM 5. *In God's eye nobody is untouchable*[§]

There was once a cobbler whose name was Dipan. Dipan was extremely poor. He was a great devotee of the Lord Vishnu and he had the deepest adoration for all the cosmic gods and goddesses also.

Dipan had a tiny shop where he sold shoes. During the day if there were no customers, he didn't feel sorry. He used to just go on praying, meditating and chanting. In the evening he would take his most beautiful and most expensive shoes and leave them at the doors of religious people. "The religious people deserve these shoes, although they don't come to buy," he said. "Perhaps they don't have enough money." Dipan went on for a long time like this and, with the greatest difficulty, used to make his livelihood.

One day, a sadhu came to Dipan's store. Dipan was so moved to see the sadhu that he fell down at his feet. But he did not dare to touch his feet because the sadhu was of a high class. Just because he was a cobbler, Dipan was not allowed to mix with the so-called aristocratic members of the society. Only lowclass people could he mix with.

The sadhu said, "What are you doing? Why are you not touching my feet?"

Dipan said, "You know that I am an untouchable. How can I touch your feet?"

The sadhu said, "In God's Eye nobody is untouchable. You are God's child. You pray to God all the time. You are dearest to Him. Please touch my feet. I will not be bloated with pride. As a matter of fact, you can even touch my head, if you want to, but do touch me."

Dipan said, "I will dare only to touch your feet, if you allow me." He touched the feet of the sadhu and the sadhu blessed him.

The sadhu said, "I am giving you all the spiritual merits and virtues that I have acquired over the years. One day you will become a great, great saint. Then all those who have neglected you and shown contempt for your profession will see light around you. They will come and touch your feet and worship you. It is only a matter of time."

The cobbler fell at the feet of the sadhu once again and offered his tearful gratitude. Then the sadhu left.

The following day, with tremendous joy the cobbler was working in his store, when all of a sudden he saw a halo of light behind his head. The halo of light was also circling around all the shoes. When the customers came, even with their ordinary human eyes they saw light: not lantern light or Indian village light, but real light, spiritual light. Then they came to realise that Dipan was not an ordinary man. They had known all along that he prayed and meditated day and night, but previously they had regarded him as a crazy fellow. Now they were so moved, and they all started appreciating, admiring and adoring him.

"We do not want you to have to continue working in your shop," they said. "Nothing will give us greater joy than to offer you the opportunity to spend the rest of your life in prayer and meditation." So they gave him a big house where he could pray and meditate, and said, "Please take care of your spiritual life. We shall come and pray with you whenever we can."

GIM 6. *It is my poverty-life that has kept me spiritual*[§]

There was once a great Sanskrit scholar who specialised in logic. He lived a very simple life, and he did not care for money. His wife was also very simple. Both of them were very simple, pure and kind-hearted.

Because he was such a great scholar, everybody had great admiration for him. His friends advised him to come to Calcutta so that he could live a decent life. But he said, "No. It is my poverty-life that has kept me spiritual. If I become rich, then my religious life, my spiritual life, will come to an end."

The king heard much about this scholar, and one day he invited him to come to his palace. But the scholar declined the offer. He said, "O King, you are protecting us. You are doing your duty well. Therefore, I am very grateful to you and very proud of you. But I personally do not need anything from you. But I wish to thank you deeply for your kind offer."

The king was deeply moved, and he decided to come to this man's cottage himself. When he came he said, "Please, please take something from me. You are such a nice man. You are so religious and kind-hearted, and such a great scholar, too. Everybody appreciates you. Please take some material help from me. I am the King and I am asking you to take something from me."

The man said, "No, no. I do not need anything. I can't take your help. But my wife is here. She may need something, so please ask her."

With folded hands the king asked the wife if she needed anything. He said, "I will be so happy and grateful if you will take anything you need." But she said, "No, I do not need anything. I have rice and dal; I have tamarind from the tree; I have water and I have matches. I have everything in plentiful quantity. What else do I need? I am very grateful to you for offering to give me something, but I don't need anything. If I need something, then I will tell you."

The king couldn't believe his ears. He wanted to leave a large sum of money with the woman. The scholar said, "For so long you have been my friend. Inwardly I have always considered you my friend because you are a just King. If you leave money with my wife, we will not take it. If you force us to take it, then we will take it. But you will become our enemy instead of our friend, because this money will bring our spiritual life to an end."

Upon hearing this the king left the man and his wife, feeling great joy and admiration and tremendous peace of mind.

A few months later a great Sanskrit scholar came to Calcutta and challenged all the scholars there. All the other scholars lost to him. Only this particular scholar was left. So the king sent a messenger to his village and asked him to come to the palace to challenge this other scholar. The man said, "I don't want to compete, but to please the King I will do it. The King came to my place and was so kind to me. Only to please him I will compete. The result I will leave at the Feet of God."

So the pious man accepted the challenge of the very great scholar who had defeated all the other scholars in Calcutta. The debate went on for four hours. At the end of the debate it was quite clear that the pious man, the village scholar, had defeated the challenger.

All the Calcutta scholars were so proud of the winner and they wanted to honour him. They wanted to give him money and fine clothes and make him rich overnight.

But the pious man said, "No, I won't take anything from you. I don't want honour and I don't want material gifts. I don't want anything from you. Calcutta is a very bad place. Here everything is temptation, temptation. I need only God. The King was very kind to me when he came to my house, and it was because of him that I entered this competition. If his subjects had been defeated by somebody from another place, then it would have been a disgrace to him. So I accepted the challenge only to please him. I have only done my duty as a subject of the King. I am very happy that I could be of some service to him, but now I want to go back to my village. Here there is nothing but temptation."

So the pious man and his wife together went back to their village, where they continued to live a life of utmost simplicity and purity.

GIM 7. *Yudhishthira's worst enemy*[§]

After the battle of Kurukshetra was over, one day Yudhishthira said to Krishna, "Krishna, we Pandavas have won. Needless to say, it is all your Grace. Otherwise, we could never have won. But you know, Krishna, in spite of our victory, something is bothering me. Do you know what it is? I have no peace of mind. Now that we have defeated the Kauravas, we are supposed to be very happy. But how can I be happy when I have no peace of mind? Why is this so? Why is it that I cannot be happy and peaceful?"

Krishna said, "Yudhishthira, O King, how can you be happy when your worst enemy is still alive?"

"My worst enemy is still alive!" Yudhishthira exclaimed. "Who is he? How is it that I do not know anything about him? Please tell me, Krishna, where my worst enemy is."

Krishna said, "Your worst enemy is not elsewhere. It is inside you. You have been feeding and nurturing that worst enemy for a long, long time. Unless and until you have conquered that enemy, no matter what you achieve, no matter what you do for yourself or for mankind, you can never have happiness."

"O Krishna, for God's sake, tell me who my worst enemy is! Stop your philosophy and now illumine me!"

Krishna, with a loving heart and a smiling face, embraced Yudhishthira and said, "O Yudhishthira, you are by far the best not only among the Pandavas, but among all mortals, all human beings. Yet one enemy of yours, which is nothing short of weakness, is most destructive. And that weakness-enemy of yours is your unfortunate pride. Conquer the iota of pride that you have. Then happiness will flow into your mind, and peace will smilingly settle down inside the very depths of your heart."

Yudhishthira said, "Your wisdom-blessing is my mind's happiness and my heart's peace, Krishna, my Krishna."

GIM 8. *The cyclone*[5]

A middle-class couple from Calcutta were traveling to Europe in a large ship. After a few days, all of a sudden a cyclone of the worst type came, and it began raining heavily. Many tiny boats were capsized. The passengers in the large vessel raised a hue and cry because there was no way they could save their lives from imminent catastrophe.

The wife said to her husband, "Everybody is crying because we know that our lives can be counted in minutes. How is it that you are so calm and quiet? Do you have no worries or anxieties? Do you not think that in a few minutes we shall all die? Why are you so silent?"

On hearing this the man took a pistol from his pocket and aimed it at his wife. The wife said, "You crazy man, what are you doing? Is this the time for you to make jokes? What will people think of you?"

The husband gave a broad smile and said, "Look, you know that it is I, your husband, your dearest one, who was aiming a pistol at you. You know perfectly well that I will not kill you because of my tremendous love for you. Now God, who is the Author of all Good, is infinitely more compassionate than I am or than I ever could be, and we are His children. Do you think that He will allow us to be destroyed, or that He will destroy us? If an ordinary human being like me cannot kill you because of the little love that I have for you, how can God destroy us? He has infinite Love for His children, although we do not know and never will know how His Love works in and through us.

His Love and Compassion work in and through us in a way that we will never understand. May God's Will be fulfilled in God's own Way. Today let us just be observers, and tomorrow let us participate in the fulfilment of His Cosmic Will."

Immediately the cyclone stopped and everything became calm and quiet. The wife, with utmost pride in her husband's wisdom and gratitude that the storm had stopped, fell at her husband's feet.

GIM 9. *Once you realise God, all the cosmic gods become yours*[§]

There was once a great seeker whose name was Gyandas. A few times he had experienced a vision of his family's presiding deity, and this made him very happy.

One day Gyandas and a group of seekers were praying together at the banks of the river Narmada. After some time a spiritual Master came and stood in front of them. He pointed to each one and remarked on their spiritual development. To some he said, "You are ripe, mature and advanced." To others he said, "You are unripe and immature; you are a beginner in the spiritual life."

Gyandas was one of the unfortunate ones. When it was his turn, the Master told him that he was an immature seeker. He could not believe his ears! He had always thought that he was truly advanced, because he had had a vision of his presiding deity a few times. He also felt that there were a few among those whom the Master had called advanced who were not really advanced.

Poor Gyandas felt sad and miserable. He went home and prayed and cried the whole night. In the small hours of the morning he had a sweet dream. In the dream his presiding deity appeared. Gyandas asked her, "How is it that I am not advanced? You have been so kind to me. You have appeared before me a few times. I thought that it was just because I am advanced in the spiritual life that you came to bless me."

The deity said, "The spiritual Master was right. You are not advanced, but that doesn't mean that you will never be advanced in the spiritual life. You too can be a great spiritual Master like that Master, but you have to be initiated first.

"A Muslim mendicant has come to your village. Everybody thinks that he is a simple, ordinary mendicant, but I know that he is a great spiritual Master. Go and be initiated by him."

The deity's words gave Gyandas the shock of his life. He said, "Initiation? Do I need initiation? And from that Muslim? He is so filthy! He doesn't take a bath even once a month. I can't go near him. He smells! I can't have him as my Master."

The deity said, "Then you will remain always unrealised. If you want to become advanced and spiritually mature, if you want to have boundless peace and joy, then go to him for initiation."

For a long time that morning the seeker argued with himself. Finally he decided to go to the Muslim teacher. He went and stood before him with bitter anger, inner disgust, pride and, at the same time, terrible fear. Then, O God! He saw something which puzzled and confused him no end. The Muslim Master was lying down by the banks of the river Narmada, with his feet on a wooden statue of Lord Shiva!

Gyandas said to himself, "Look at this villain! How dare he place his feet on our cosmic Lord Shiva! Lord Shiva is one of our Trinity! Deliberately he is insulting me because he knows that I am a Hindu." To the Muslim Master Gyandas said, "I will never become your disciple!" He was mad and furious.

The Muslim Master said to Gyandas, "My boy, I have not come into your life to confuse you. I know what you are thinking. Now do me a favour. Remove this wooden statue of your Lord Shiva. Place it wherever you want to."

Gyandas grabbed the statue and placed it quite a distance away. But lo and behold, the statue started walking like a human being and went back under the feet of the Muslim Master. Gyandas was astonished and shocked at the same time.

The Muslim said, "Now look, you hold the statue here and let me go away." Gyandas held the statue while the Muslim Master covered about two hundred metres, and then stood still. The seeker felt compelled from within to bring the statue to the Master, but he argued with himself. He said, "No, I won't go! I won't go!" He felt a terrible pressure from within and also an inner command from the statue itself to go to the Muslim Master. But he said, "No, I am not going. I won't go to him. I won't accept him as my Master."

Gyandas put the statue on the ground, and the statue very happily ran towards the Master. So once again the Master was lying down with the statue at his feet.

What could Gyandas do? He was so puzzled. He said, "If I don't take initiation from this Muslim Master, then my presiding deity has said that I will never realise God. But this man is deliberately insulting my Hindu God. Let me go and ask him why he is doing this to me."

Gyandas went to the Muslim teacher. Before he could open his mouth, the Master said, "I will remove all your confusion and illumine you. Once you realise God, the cosmic gods become yours. For a God-realised person, the cosmic gods are like parts of one's own body. It is not beneath my dignity for my hands to touch my feet. Again, I can also touch my head if I want to. Any part of my body I can touch with any other part. There is no question of superiority or inferiority, for all parts of my body belong to me.

"Each limb of my body I claim as my own. In the same way I claim Shiva as part and parcel of my existence. For Shiva to be at my feet is like one part of my body touching another part. Shiva and I are one.

"Realise God. Then you will see that there is neither superiority nor inferiority. We are all one, one, one. Stay with me. I shall initiate you. Once you are initiated, you will go back to that spiritual Master and hear from him that you are far more advanced than all the other seekers who were with you yesterday."

GIM 10. *Vyasa's request*[§]

The great sage Vyasa once went to the Lord Shiva and prayed to him, "Lord Shiva, you are unparalleled among the Trinity. Your Compassion is infinite, your Power is infinite, in every way you are infinite. I have come to you with my heart's prayer: I would like you to initiate my son, Shuka. It is high time for him to be initiated and I know for sure that if you initiate him, then my son and I will be supremely blessed. So do fulfil my heart's desire."

Lord Shiva said, "I can and I shall fulfil your desire. But let me tell you one thing. If I initiate your son, do you not think that he will leave the house and roam along the street, praying, chanting and meditating? You will lose him."

The father said, "I know there is every possibility that I will lose my son. But I must do my duty. When it is time for the son to be invested with the sacred thread, the father must do his duty, even at the risk of losing his son.

"But, my Lord, you are all-where. After being initiated by you, if my son roams around the world chanting and meditating on the supreme glory of the Absolute Supreme, how can I lose him or miss him? If he is meditating on the omnipresent and omniscient Lord, then I will never miss him. That much wisdom you have already given me, my Lord."

Lord Shiva gave the father a broad smile and blessed him: "I am coming to your house to initiate your son. I assure you, he will be the world's greatest God-knower at such a tender age. He has already mastered all the scriptures. Now, from my blessings and initiation, he will gain mastery over his earthly life and become inseparably one with the life of the immortals."

GIM 11. *The king's initiation*[§]

There was a good pious king who ruled his kingdom justly, divinely and supremely. Everybody was pleased with him and proud of him. But there came a time when he was pinched with an inner hunger for initiation. He felt a burning cry for inner peace and inner light, so he gave up his kingdom and went to a spiritual Master for initiation.

The spiritual Master said to him, "I will initiate you when you are ready. Right now you are not ready for initiation."

The king accepted the Master's words. He bowed to the Master and said, "I will do anything that you want me to do. Only please accept me as your disciple."

The Master said, "Yes, I will accept you as my disciple. From now on, every day you will go to the top of the hill and cut down trees along with my other disciples, for we need fuel to cook our food. You will also take the cows out to graze in the field as the other disciples do, and you will do domestic service."

The king agreed. Every day he used to go with the other disciples, who were his spiritual brothers, and perform the domestic tasks to please the Master. Although the king had never done this kind of work, he did his very best and his work was, to some extent, quite satisfactory.

One day he was chopping down a tree, but he was not working fast enough. One of his brother disciples gave him a smart slap and said, "You are working so slowly. Master will be furious if we work so slowly. Don't work so slowly!"

Now, this fellow happened to be of a very, very low caste; he was an untouchable. But the Master accepted disciples from all castes, and in his eyes everybody had the same rank. The king didn't say anything to the untouchable, but in silence he was telling himself, "Does he not know who I was? If he had done this kind of thing when I was king, immediately my men would have killed him. Now I have accepted the spiritual life; therefore, he is saved. God bless his ignorance. He should know who I was and who I am."

Some time had passed and the king again came before the Master. He knelt down and said, "Many people who have come after me have been initiated, but still I am uninitiated. When will my time come?"

The Master said, "One day your time will come, but it has not yet come. It will take time. Still you enjoy the pride of having been a King. As long as you enjoy and treasure your pride-wealth, initiation will remain a far cry. Conquer your pride and I shall initiate you. Unless and until you have conquered your pride, do not expect me to initiate you."

The king touched the Master's feet: "From now on I will most soulfully try to conquer my worst foe, pride, and thus be a fit instrument for your initiation."

The Master said, "Try, my child, you will succeed without fail."

After some time it came to pass that the king did conquer his pride, and he was initiated by the Master.

GIM 12. *The pride of the cosmic gods*

Once Lord Shiva decided to destroy the worst possible demon, Tripura. Some of the cosmic gods wanted to help him in this great adventure. So one of them became his chariot, some became his horses, one became his charioteer, some became his arrows and one became his bow. Each god became something in order to help Lord Shiva.

Unfortunately, pride all of a sudden entered into these cosmic gods. The god who became the chariot said, "If I had not become the chariot, now Shiva would not be able to win." The god who became the charioteer said, "If I had not become the charioteer, Shiva would not be able to win." The god who became the bow said, "If I had not become the bow, Shiva would not be able to win." Each cosmic god felt that he was indispensable.

Seeing this, Lord Shiva smiled and said, "You fools, do I need you? If you serve me devotedly, then indeed I need you. But I don't need you with your pride. You stay with your pride. I can do the needful all by myself. Look what my third eye can do."

Immediately Shiva opened up his third eye and destroyed Tripura. Then he turned to the cosmic gods, "Your service I badly need only when you offer it soulfully and devotedly. But when pride enters into you and you feel that you are indispensable, then I wish to tell you that you are millions and billions of miles away from the discovery of Truth. O so-called helpers of mine, give what you have; give what you are. Give what you have soulfully, give what you are unreservedly. Then you will see what you become: a torrent of Delight, ceaseless and immortal."

GIM 13. *Gratitude is my true wealth*[§]

There once lived a very rich man, who was very proud of his wealth. He used to wear most expensive clothes, and it was impossible for him to walk even two blocks. Instead of walking, he used to take the palanquin carried by four people. He felt that it was beneath his dignity to mix with ordinary people. Most villagers didn't like him because of his haughtiness, but this did not bother him in the least. He thought that as long as he had money-power in his possession, he didn't have to worry about anything; he didn't have to care for anybody else's opinion.

One night, his only son was bitten by a snake. The father became hysterical and insane, and he ran out of the house barefoot and wearing only a dhoti, not even a shirt. He covered two long miles, running like a madman, until he came to the cottage of a shoemaker who could cure people from snakebite.

When the shoemaker opened the door and saw who had awakened him in the middle of the night, he became furious. Although the rich man was crying and lamenting because of his son, the shoemaker only said, "At this hour I am not going to your house. Had it been somebody else, I would have gone. But you have never shown any sympathy or kindness to the villagers. Now, at the time of your need, you have come. But I shall not help you!"

The rich man accepted all this humiliation. He cared only for the safety of his son, and he cried and cried. Finally the shoemaker condescended to come to his home, and he cured the boy. The rich man wanted to give the shoemaker a large sum of money. But the shoemaker said, "I won't accept any money from you. I know it is impossible for you to change your nature. Tomorrow again you will become haughty and scold and insult everybody. This is how you do your duty in your own human way. I also have my own duty to do, and I have to do it with a sympathetic heart, for God has given me the heart to be of service to the needy. In your case, God has given you money-power, which is being used by your arrogant and destructive vital."

The rich man said, "How do you know that I will not change my nature and my whole life after this?"

"I know you, I know you," the shoemaker replied.

Both the parties said, "Let us see, let us see."

Some admirers and flatterers of the rich man, who had come when they heard about his son, got furious. They wanted to strike the shoemaker. "How do you dare to speak so rudely of our chief? You have cured his son. So what? We are more than willing to give you as much money as you want. You won't take money; you are showing your generosity in this way. At the same time you are being brutal. Is this not the height of your pride? You won't accept money and, at the same time, you are criticising such a great man. Was it not enough for you to humiliate him at your shop? Here also why must you speak so badly of him and humiliate him further?"

The rich man said, "No, don't hurt him. I will feel miserable. He has cured my son, he has given my son life. I will eternally remain grateful to him. My son is dearest to me. He is all my hope, all my joy and all my promise. I am ready to accept all kinds of humiliation from this man. What he has given me is infinitely more meaningful and precious than what he is now doing to me. Let him scold me, let him insult me, let him do anything he wants. I have got my son back. All I need is my son; there is nothing else on earth that I need more. So let him go peacefully. I tell you once and for all, my heart of gratitude is following him."

GIM 14. *Silence is the answer*[§]

There was once a very advanced, great seeker. Many people used to come to him for advice, but he would not advise anybody. He always used to say, "If you want to come and meditate with me in silence, I am more than willing to meditate with you. But I will not tell you anything."

People were satisfied with this. They were all gratitude to him for giving them the opportunity to meditate with him. Always they felt a kind of intense delight when they meditated with him, and tremendous inner joy used to envelop them. Sometimes during meditation he would smile at them most soulfully, but he would never talk to them.

One day a young man came to him and touched his feet, pleading with him for advice. "I am in trouble. I have all kinds of emotional problems. You have to save me."

The advanced seeker finally opened his mouth and said, "Look, my boy, why do I not talk? If I tell the truth, the world hates me. If I don't tell the truth, God does not love me. Now where do I stand? Truth is painful for humanity. I can't tell the truth or humanity will have ill will. And if I tell lies, I displease God. I want to please both man and God. So I remain silent.

"If I am deeply absorbed in silence, God is pleased with me. At the same time, humanity sees that I am not involved in anybody's affairs, either individually or collectively. To everyone I am the same. I pray for humanity inwardly, but if I were to become involved outwardly, I would have to open my mouth. And the truth humanity finds impossible to accept. Therefore, I remain silent to please both humanity and divinity. Silence is the answer to please the higher worlds and the lower worlds at the same time."

GIM 15. *I like the compassionate God*[§]

One day a great seeker was praying and meditating at the foot of a tree. All of a sudden, without any rhyme or reason, a hooligan came and struck him mercilessly, leaving him unconscious. In a few minutes' time, a friend of his happened to pass by. When he saw the seeker lying unconscious, he was simply shocked. Immediately he found a doctor, who brought the seeker back to his senses. They asked him who had struck him so badly, and he said, "He who struck me has cured me and is now nursing me."

His friend said, "Even at this hour you are cutting jokes! You were beaten mercilessly, you were unconscious. Why can't you tell the truth?"

But the seeker only said, "I know the person who struck me is the same one who cured me and is now nursing me."

In a few minutes' time, two policemen came dragging the hooligan in chains. They were positive that he was the one who had beaten the seeker. "This is the man. We are sure. You just confirm it," they said.

The seeker said, "What are you doing? Why are you torturing this poor man? The body is the temple of God. If you strike and smash the temple, how can God remain inside? Please, O policemen, let him go. I don't want God's temple to be tortured and destroyed by you. I will feel miserable if you do anything more to this temple.

"It was God who punished me through him and again it was God who cured me. It is also God who is crying through you for justice. But of all the Gods, I like best the compassionate God. Therefore, please let him go. I am happy in my forgiveness, so you be happy by becoming one with God's Will in me."

GIM 16. *The boil-illumination* [§]

There was once a great seeker who was on the verge of realisation. Every day this seeker used to pray and meditate with his friends. His friends were also his admirers and adorers, and they used to beg him to open up an ashram. As soon as he opened up an ashram, they said they would all become his disciples.

"Why can't you become my disciples now?" he would ask.

They would reply, "No, only if you open up an ashram will we become your disciples. If you have an ashram of your own and if we become members, then you will be responsible for the illumination of our lives. Now you are not taking us seriously. So please get an ashram, and we will become your disciples."

The seeker thought about this for some time, and he decided that it would be a nice idea: "Let me have an ashram and all the disciples will stay there."

O God, in the meantime the seeker developed a very painful boil on his right foot. The boil became very big and it gave him terrible pain. The doctor was called, and he got ready to operate. When he was about to begin, the seeker literally cried like a child. "Why is he acting like a child?" the doctor asked. "No, even a child behaves better than this. What will his friends and admirers think of him?"

The seeker's friends, who were gathered around, threatened the doctor: "If once more you insult our friend, we shall strike you. Pain is pain. Only the sufferer knows what the pain is actually like. If it is real pain, why should he not cry? So you remain silent and just do your job!"

With a mischievous smile on his face, the doctor began to operate. While the doctor was operating, the great seeker said to himself, "I could not take care of even one boil on my own body. I suffered so much because it was a foreign element. My friends are also separate human beings, separate from my life. When

197

they enter into my life, it will be the same kind of situation. I don't have the capacity to save myself from one boil, so how will I be able to save their inner lives?"

"O God, I am so grateful to You. By giving me a boil, You have taught me a lesson. It is only You who can take responsibility for other people. One boil is enough to illumine me. I don't need illumination from human beings. Now I know that I will never open an ashram. I want only to pray and meditate and realise You. I will remain in supreme ecstasy, for I want only God-realisation. This boil is my illumination; my illumination is this boil."

GIM 17. *The temple of love* [§]

An old Muslim once went to a fair with his granddaughter. The granddaughter was so happy to be with her grandfather. At the fair she saw many things she liked, but there was one toy which she liked the most. It was a doll representing Krishna. She asked her grandfather to buy it for her, but he said, "I will buy anything else for you, but not this, because this doll is the God of the Hindus. You know how bad the Hindus are."

The owner of that particular shop happened to be a Hindu. He got furious: "Who asked you to buy a Hindu God? Go away from my shop!"

The old man said, "Who needs your toy? I am going." Both the shopkeeper and the old man exchanged a few nasty, foul words. But when the old man started to leave, his granddaughter began crying pitifully. She said, "I won't go home unless I get the doll." The grandfather was helpless, and he had to buy it for her. To the Hindu the old man said, "I am helpless. My love for my granddaughter far surpasses my love of my own religion and my hatred for your religion."

The little child returned home so delighted with her toy. Every day she used to play with the doll, even when she was walking to school. At home also she used to play with the doll most devotedly, and she never played with anybody else.

Some years passed and she became old enough to get married. When her parents told her that they would look for a husband, she said, "How is it that you say you will look for a husband, when all along I have been married to this doll? This doll is my husband."

The parents got the shock of their life, but what could they do? They said, "All right, you have shocked our religious beliefs. Now tell us what we can do for you."

The girl said, "Now build a temple in honour of your son-in-law. He is nobody other than Krishna himself."

As soon as she said "Krishna himself," the parents saw right in front of them the living presence of Krishna. They were so moved. Krishna said, "She is right. Build a temple so that people can come and worship me."

"Let us build it," the parents said. "But this is a Muslim community. No Muslim will come to a Hindu temple, and they will hate us if we build one."

The girl said, "No, if you don't listen to my Lord, my husband, then I am leaving you for good. I will never come back."

They were so attached to their daughter that they said, "Definitely we will do it. You are so beautiful, so spiritual. We can't lose you. We shall build a temple for your husband, the Hindu God Krishna." When they built the temple, to their wide surprise hundreds of Muslims began coming there to worship. The parents asked them, "Why do you come to a Hindu temple?" The devotees answered, "It is not a Hindu temple as such; it is a temple of pure divine love. When we come here, we are flooded with love. We feel its presence everywhere, and we get tremendous joy. But when we go to our mosques, we do not get the same joy. Instead, we get only an austere, rigid, lifeless and meaningless feeling. That is why we come to your temple. The Hindu God Krishna is all love, which we all need. What humanity needs is love and more love, nothing else; only love, love, love."

GIM 18. *Oneness with the Will of God*[5]

The founder of Sikhism, Nanak, was meditating one day with a group of disciples near a Hindu temple. When Nanak wanted to enter the temple along with his disciples, the guards would not allow him; they mistook him for a Muslim. He had a long beard, long hair and a long moustache, and his whole face seemed to be a Muslim face. His disciples told the attendants that he was not a Muslim but the great Master, Guru Nanak. But the guards were so ignorant that they had never heard of him and they refused to allow him to enter.

The disciples were very sad and mad, but they were helpless. They were afraid that if they did anything, the police would come and arrest them. So they left the temple and went to a nearby beach. Evening had set in, and Nanak asked them to meditate with him. They all meditated for some time, but the meditation was not deep, for they were still harbouring anger and humiliation. Nanak felt very sad. It was not because he had been prevented from entering into the temple, for he knew that ignorant people will always do that kind of thing. No, he was sad because he had become one with the sadness of his disciples. He said to them, "Look at the sky. See how beautiful and vast it is. Look at the moon, look at the stars. How beautiful they are! Let us be inwardly and outwardly as vast and beautiful as the sky, the moon and the stars." On other days the disciples would have all cheerfully become one with their Master, but on this day they were still mad, and they were not showing any kind of cheerfulness.

Nanak said, "In this world there will always be people who will insult us, but we should be above their insults. The attendants were not nice to us, but I tell you that the god of that temple is pleased with us. He will do something for us."

To their wide surprise, while Nanak was talking two large dishes full of fruits and Indian sweets appeared before them. They could not account for this, but Nanak said, "It was the presiding deity of that temple who brought this food. I saw him with my inner vision, but you did not see him."

But the disciples were not satisfied. They said, "No, it cannot be." They thought that one of the disciples had gone out and brought these things for them.

"Is this the kind of faith you have in me?" Nanak asked. On other days the disciples would have believed their Master. But today they were doubtful, because they felt that their Master should have shown his spiritual and occult power and entered into the temple. But Nanak did not do anything when the guards insulted him.

"What do you want?" Nanak asked. "Do you want me to show you another miracle? I have shown you so many miracles, but have any of them changed your life? No! Again, if you want one more miracle I can show you, but I tell you it will not change your nature. It will only increase your curiosity. But perhaps in this way you will be silenced. Go and taste the water of the sea."

Some of the disciples hesitated, others went. The water was full of salt. Nanak asked those who had drunk the water to come and sit before him, and those who hadn't drunk to sit elsewhere. Then he asked those near him to drink the sea water again. This time, when the disciples drank, the water was as sweet as honey.

"Really you have performed a miracle!" they cried. "Just two minutes ago it was all salty. We were about to vomit. But now it is all honey, so sweet."

So the people who drank were satisfied with this miracle, and both they and those who, out of fear, didn't drink the water, remained silent.

Nanak said, "I have pleased your curiosity, but I wanted something else from you: compassion-forgiveness, forgiveness-compassion and, the most important thing of all, oneness with the Will of God."

GIM 19. *Oneness with God's entire creation*[§]

A great seeker named Bamadav was known throughout the land for his unparalleled kindness and compassion, not only towards humanity but towards all earthly creatures. Although he was extremely poor, his was the heart of magnanimity and generosity.

One day, Bamadav was preparing his simple evening meal. He had put butter on two pieces of bread, but had not yet buttered a third piece. He was about to eat the two buttered pieces when all of a sudden a dog started barking outside the door to his small cottage. When Bamadav opened the door, the dog ran in, grabbed the unbuttered piece of bread and ran away.

Bamadav ran after the dog, pleading with it to stop: "O dog, I am asking you to return my piece of bread only so that I can butter it and give it back to you. You are a guest, and guests should be treated with utmost affection and love."

As soon as Bamadav said this, the dog changed into a human being full of luminosity, and said to him, "I am the Supreme Deity. I came to you to see your oneness with my entire creation."

Bamadav was overwhelmed with joy and fell at the Supreme Deity's Feet. The Supreme Deity blessed the great seeker, saying, "You saw Me in a dog. Others would have beaten the dog, instead of begging to get the piece of bread back in order to butter it. Your oneness with the animal world, your oneness with all the worlds, your oneness with My entire creation — all have pleased Me beyond your imagination. Therefore, I am granting you the supreme realisation: Eternity's Peace, Infinity's Light and Immortality's Life."

GIM 20. *Ramdas and the buffalo*[§]

One day the great seeker Ramdas met the God-realised soul Tulsidas and prayed to him, "O great soul, do help me realise God. I have been praying and meditating for years and years, but still God-realisation is a far cry. Do help me realise God."

Tulsidas said, "I shall not only help you to realise God, but I shall make you see God tomorrow."

Ramdas said, "Tomorrow? O great soul, perhaps you are cutting jokes with me. Am I fit for God-realisation?"

"Yes, you are more than fit," answered Tulsidas. "Tomorrow, God will come to you. Keep your house clean, prepare nice, delicious food for God and pray and meditate the whole day most soulfully. God will definitely come to you."

The next day Ramdas brought many beautiful flowers to decorate his room and made a delicious meal for God. He remained soulful the whole day and prayed and meditated.

But O God, the whole day passed, and there was no sign of God. Ramdas was lamenting like anything. "Why has God not come? How could such a great soul like Tulsidas deceive me? But there is no sign of God."

All of a sudden Ramdas saw a buffalo standing near his door. He was so mad. "How could that buffalo come here? Where did it come from?" he said.

The buffalo entered into his house and began eating the food and destroying the flowers. The animal ate many of the fruits which Ramdas had kept so devotedly for God. Ramdas was so furious that he took a stick and started beating the buffalo. But the buffalo just kept eating to its heart's content and then ran away.

"Is this my fate?" cried Ramdas. "I wanted God and instead a buffalo has to come and ruin everything. O Tulsidas, is this your God? Tomorrow when I see you, I will give you a piece of my mind!"

The next day he went to Tulsidas, but the God-realised soul was in a very high mood. For some time Ramdas did not dare to speak. Then Tulsidas said, "So, God came to you?"

Ramdas said, "God came? A buffalo came!"

"A buffalo?" asked Tulsidas.

"Yes," answered Ramdas. "It came and ruined everything."

"You fool!" Tulsidas said. "It was not a buffalo. It was God in the form of a buffalo. He wanted to examine you to see if you had established your oneness with his entire creation. If you had been in a very high consciousness, you would have seen and felt that it was not a buffalo but God Himself. God took the form of a buffalo and examined you. You have mistreated God so mercilessly that now it will take a very long time for you to realise God. So you may as well forget about God-realisation."

Ramdas cried and cried before Tulsidas, "How could I have known God would take the form of a buffalo and thus play a trick on me?"

Tulsidas said, "Pray more soulfully, more devotedly, more unconditionally and more unreservedly. Then you will know everything: where God is and who God truly is."

Ramdas said, "From now on, I shall try to be worthy of one day receiving God in God's own Way."

GIM 1. *(p. 175)* 5 January 1979
GIM 2. *(p. 176)* 5 January 1979
GIM 3. *(p. 177)* 5 January 1979
GIM 4. *(p. 179)* 5 January 1979
GIM 5. *(p. 180)* 6 January 1979
GIM 6. *(p. 181)* 7 January 1979
GIM 7. *(p. 184)* 7 January 1979
GIM 8. *(p. 185)* 7 January 1979
GIM 9. *(p. 186)* A story from the Maharashtra. 7 January 1979
GIM 10. *(p. 189)* 7 January 1979
GIM 11. *(p. 190)* 7 January 1979
GIM 12. *(p. 192)* 7 January 1979
GIM 13. *(p. 193)* 7 January 1979
GIM 14. *(p. 195)* 7 January 1979
GIM 15. *(p. 196)* 7 January 1979
GIM 16. *(p. 197)* 7 January 1979
GIM 17. *(p. 198)* 7 January 1979
GIM 18. *(p. 200)* 8 January 1979
GIM 19. *(p. 202)* 8 January 1979
GIM 20. *(p. 203)* 8 January 1979

GREAT INDIAN MEALS: DIVINELY DELICIOUS AND SUPREMELY NOURISHING

BOOK 2

One day an old man walked a long distance to see how the rice was growing in his paddies. When he came home, he was dead tired. His son, who was very, very spiritual, began to devotedly massage his father's feet while the old man was resting. The father was relaxing with his eyes closed, appreciating his son's devotedness and the good massage. After about half an hour, the father fell fast asleep.

All of a sudden the son saw Lord Krishna standing right before him, watching his devotedness with appreciation and admiration. For a few seconds the son folded his hands and then he continued massaging his father's feet.

He said to Krishna, "O Lord, I am so happy that you have come to see me. I pray to you every day most soulfully, but now you have come at a time when I am massaging my father's feet. Look, there is a chair over there. Would you kindly get the chair and sit down? At this moment I cannot bring it to you."

Krishna said, "No, I have been sitting for a long time. I can't sit anymore. And you are massaging your father's feet, so you are unable to come over here to me." The son said, "Krishna, I see your presence inside my father. Since I have already started massaging him, will you not forgive me?"

"What is there to forgive?" asked Krishna. "Nothing pleases me more than to see someone do his duty. You have received illumination. In your father you see my presence, so you don't have to come to me."

While this conversation was going on the father woke up. "What are you doing?" he asked his son. "With whom were you speaking?"

"I was speaking with Lord Krishna," replied the son.

"Lord Krishna! Where is he?" said the father.

The son said, "He appeared here. And I did not go to him because I was massaging you."

The father said, "You fool! I have been crying to see Lord Krishna and you have actually talked to him without even offering him something to sit on."

The son explained, "I did ask him, but he said he was not tired, and he appreciated my devotedness to you."

"What kind of son do I have?" lamented the father. "I am only a mortal, an ordinary human being. The Lord Himself came, but you could not go and see him. O Lord Krishna, forgive my son and forgive me for having such an idiot in the family."

The son said, "Say what you want. But you know that in you I always feel the presence of my Lord Krishna. So when I didn't go to him, he did not mind. On the contrary, he was very proud of me because I was doing my duty. Krishna said that nothing pleased him more than to see someone doing his duty."

The father said, "If what you are saying is all true, then I am really blessed that I have such a nice, wise, soulful and devoted son who can bring Krishna to us. But blind I shall always be. It seems I shall never see him. Even if my eyes had not been closed, perhaps I would not have seen him with my naked, human eyes. You were able to see Krishna because he opened your third eye, the eye that sees. I am so proud that at least my son has seen him. But how I wish I could know for sure that this is all true."

At that moment Krishna appeared and said, "It is all true, all true. It is because of your son's faithfulness and one-pointed devotedness to you that today you are seeing me. In you your son saw me, and that is the supreme realisation. Now you, the father, try to see me also in your son. Then you will also be blessed with the supreme realisation that I am in all, with all and for all. I am the creation, I am the Creator; I am the life of the creation and the Light of the Creator. Again, I am the one who is all light, all life, all compassion, all oneness, all satisfaction and all perfection. See this and feel this in all, and then grow into this realisation."

Both father and son fell down at Krishna's feet and said, "Krishna; O infinity's Lord, you have come to us with a finite form so we can touch you, feel you and become like you. Infinite is your greatness, eternal is your goodness."

GIM 22. *Three categories of disciples*[§]

One day a spiritual Master was meditating with some of his disciples and a few seekers. After about twenty minutes, he looked around and said, "Is there anyone who would like to ask me a spiritual question?" One disciple raised his hand and asked, "Master, could you please say something about your disciples' spiritual development?"

"My child," replied the Master, "I can only tell you that I love all my spiritual children dearly, no matter what their level of spiritual attainment may be."

"Please tell us more," begged the disciples. "Can you tell us more about the different levels of development?"

The Master paused. "Let me tell you a story," he said. "Once there were three dolls. These dolls were conscious dolls. One was made of sugar, one was made of cloth and one was made of burnt stone. Now it happened that each of these dolls entered into the sea. When the one that was made of sugar entered into the sea, it totally dissolved. The second doll entered into the sea, and came out fully soaked. Then the third doll entered bravely into the sea. When it came out it just shook its body, and not a trace of water was left on it.

There also, my children, I have three types of disciples. One type, when he enters into the ignorance-sea, is totally lost, totally melted. When the second type enters into the ignorance sea, he is able to come out. But ignorance is all around his consciousness.

He still carries ignorance with him. The third type enters into ignorance bravely and fights against ignorance. He not only comes out victorious, but he also takes up the challenge of transforming ignorance into wisdom-light.

"I do hope one day all of my disciples will fit into the third category: brave soldiers of the Supreme entering into the sea of ignorance like warriors, fighting against ignorance and coming out victorious, and finally changing ignorance-sea into wisdom-light."

The disciples bowed down to their Master and said, "You have inspired and illumined us. We shall all strive from now on to become brave soldiers of your mission, soldiers of the Supreme, fighting against the forces of ignorance and ultimately transforming them."

GIM 23. *In progress is the presence of Vishnu*[§]

Once Narada, the great devotee of Vishnu, was angry with his Lord. He said to himself, "Who cares for Vishnu? If he is really inside my heart, then why do I have to worship him? Is it not enough that he is inside my heart? And if he is not inside my heart, if he is not anywhere to be found on earth, or if he is non-existent, then why do I have to worship him? So in no way do I need Vishnu. Whether he is in my heart or in this creation, or whether he is nowhere to be found or does not exist at all, I don't need him."

Like this Narada went on for a few days, but all the while he was feeling miserable. Something was killing him inwardly. On the one hand, he was feeling very haughty and proud that he had discovered that he could live without Vishnu. On the other hand, his aspiration-heart was crying and dying for Vishnu's presence and Vishnu's Light.

Finally he went to Lord Shiva for advice. Lord Shiva said, "You fool, how can you live without Vishnu?"

Narada said, "I know I cannot. That's why I have come to you. Vishnu was my all once upon a time. Now he does not care for me; therefore, I have stopped caring for him. But I need him badly. Alas, I don't feel his presence inside my heart. I don't see him anywhere in my consciousness or in my aspiration-cry."

Shiva said, "I feel sorry for you. Now you have to develop devotion. There is nothing as important and meaningful in the spiritual life as devotion. If you develop and increase your devotion, then you are bound to feel Vishnu's presence inside your heart, just as you did before."

"How can I develop devotion?" Narada asked.

Shiva answered, "Mix with the people who have failed in life. Mix with the people who are full of sorrow. Mix with the people who feel that they cannot exist even for a second without Vishnu. Mix with the people who feel that, without God, they are helpless but, with God, they are everything and have everything."

Narada said, "Alas, there was a time when people used to come to me to increase their own devotion because I was all devotion to my Lord Vishnu. Now is this my fate? I have to go to other people and mix with them to develop devotion. What irony!"

Lord Shiva said, "One has to aspire consciously and constantly to make progress. In your case, you were satisfied with what you had. You did not care for further progress. I tell you, in the spiritual world if you do not make continuous progress, then ignorance is bound to pull you down. There is no fixed resting place. Every moment you are going either forward or going backward.

"If you are conscious and constant in your prayer and meditation, then you will always make progress and, while making progress, you are bound to feel Vishnu's presence. So make progress every day, every hour, every minute. Then you are bound to feel Vishnu's presence in yourself and your presence in Vishnu. You will not only feel him but also see him as your Compassion-Lord, Illumination-Lord and Fulfilment-Lord."

Narada said, "My Lord, I shall."

Shiva said, "And you can!"

GIM 24. *The three types of eaters*

One day a spiritual Master was playing his flute while his disciples were eating. He was getting joy from watching them eat. After some time, he asked them if they would like to hear a story from him. They said, "Of course, of course."

The Master said, "I will tell you a very short story. There are three kinds of eaters. One type of eater will eat voraciously no matter how the food tastes. He feels that since God has given him the body, he must eat. The more he eats, the more he thinks that he is pleasing God, since the body is God's creation. So he eats anything he gets.

The second type will eat whatever he is given, no matter what quantity. If the food is good, he is happy. If the food is bad, he accepts this, knowing that every day one cannot eat most delicious food. He tolerates the fact that, from worldly human beings who cook every day, one cannot always receive a delicious meal. After all, not even one day is the food unbearable; always there is some standard. Therefore, whatever he gets is all right.

The third type of person says to God, 'O God, today by Your Grace I am eating. Tomorrow I may not get any food, but that also I shall take as Your Grace. Whatever happens to me I feel is an experience that You are giving me. So if You give me food, it is wonderful, and if You do not give me food, it is also wonderful, for I will feel that You want to give me a specific experience.

I shall be equally satisfied in Your divine dispensation. If You give, I feel that for my progress You are doing so. If You do not give, it is again for my progress. Your Will is my will. I don't want to have any will of my own.'

To the first group the Lord says, 'My Eternity will take care of you.'

To the second group He says, 'My Divinity is pleased with you.'

To the third group He says, 'My oneness-life is all pride in you. Your oneness in My Greatness and your oneness with My Goodness will always satisfy Me. Your aspiration is great, your dedication is good. Your realisation of My highest Height and deepest Depth is not a far cry, but imminent.'"

GIM 25. *Perseverance, patience and self-giving are of paramount importance*[§]

Once two partridges, a husband and wife, were going out on a trip. Before they left, the wife laid some eggs near the ocean. Then the husband said to the sea, "We are going on a sea voyage. You have to take care of these eggs for us. On our return, if we don't find the eggs, then we shall empty you."

The sea agreed to take care of the eggs, and it kept the eggs safe. A few days later the two partridges came back, but they could not find the eggs. They began screaming at the sea. The sea wanted to give the eggs to them, but it could not find them anymore. The birds cursed the sea and started emptying it. The husband and wife each began taking out a drop of water at a time, throwing it onto the land.

"We are going to empty you," they said to the sea.

Some little birds saw all this and they asked, "What are you doing?"

The partridges replied, "We are punishing the sea. The sea is very bad because it didn't keep its promise to look after our eggs."

The little birds thought it was a noble task and they joined the partridges. After a while, some big birds took up their cause. They were very sympathetic and self giving, and they also started taking out water drop by drop. This went on for days and weeks.

One day, the Conveyor of Lord Vishnu, Garuda, came and asked, "What are you doing?"

The birds said, "Can't you see? We are emptying the sea."

Garuda said, "You fools, how long will this take you? You will never be able to do it. The sea is very vast, infinite."

But the birds answered, "No, we have determination and perseverance."

Garuda was very surprised and said, "Let me show them some compassion. Let me ask Lord Vishnu to help them. If Vishnu helps them, then certainly they will be able to find their eggs. If the eggs are still in good condition, Vishnu will be able to return them. But if they are destroyed, he can do nothing for them."

He went to Vishnu. "Vishnu, I have never seen fools like these. If you really care for fools, then will you do them a favour?" Garuda then told him the whole story.

Vishnu said, "No, they are not fools. They are showing the spirit of patience and perseverance. This is how human beings must try to empty the ignorance-sea, drop by drop. It is what the seekers must and should do. Ignorance-sea is very vast. If sincere seekers want to empty it to replace it with knowledge-light, then they have to do it the same way, drop by drop. So I am very pleased with those partridges. I am commanding the sea to return the eggs."

Garuda said, "The sea wanted to give them the eggs but it misplaced them and feels that they are all destroyed."

Vishnu said, "I am using my own occult power to show the sea where it has kept the eggs."

He used his occult power and the sea immediately found the eggs and returned them to the partridges. Then Vishnu said to the birds, "Perseverance, patience and self-giving all are of paramount importance to fulfil one's divine task."

GIM 26. *The Buddha's message*[§]

There was a great King named Vindusar who ruled his kingdom wisely. When he died, his eldest son, Ashoka, became King. Ashoka's brothers were all handsome and strong, but Ashoka was not at all beautiful. His brothers always used to cut jokes with him because he was not good-looking.

When Ashoka became King with the help of the minister, he wanted to take revenge. So when he got the throne, he killed his brothers one by one. Then he killed all his relatives who spoke ill of him. Whoever spoke ill of him, he killed. He also wanted to be the lord of a vast kingdom, so he went and conquered a place called Kalinga, destroying many Buddhist temples and killing many Buddhists.

One day he was in his palace-fortress when he heard some most pitiful cries. The relatives of the thousands of people whom he had killed were cursing him and lamenting and grieving for their dear ones. Ashoka felt sorry. Suddenly he heard a voice chanting, *Buddham saranam gacchami,* "I take refuge in Lord Buddha." Again and again he heard this voice chanting the same words. It was so soothing to him. He thought of the Buddha's Compassion and he felt that a change was taking place in his life, but he could not account for it.

When he went outside into the streets, he saw one of the greatest followers of the Buddha, Upagupta, chanting nearby. Ashoka approached him and said, "Please forgive me, but I have

217

heard some chanting, and now I wish to be initiated. I want to be a follower of the Lord Buddha."

Upagupta told him, "It was I who was chanting before." The King was deeply moved. Upagupta initiated him and he became Upagupta's disciple.

After that, Ashoka took refuge in the Lord Buddha — in the Buddha's Compassion and in the Buddha's Light. He no longer paid any attention to his Kingdom nor to his throne. Eventually he became a religious mendicant. He put on an ochre cloth and roamed from place to place all over the world, chanting the Buddha's glory and establishing Buddhist temples. He opened up free hospitals for the poor and unreservedly gave away things to the poor and the needy. He became compassion incarnate. Even his own daughter went to Ceylon to spread the Buddha's Light. Everywhere Ashoka went — even inside mountain caves and on pillars — the Buddha's message was inscribed: *Ahingsha parama dharma*, "Non-violence is the greatest virtue."

GIM 27. *Babar's sacrifice*[§]

The first Mogul Emperor Babar was a good poet, a great hunter and a man of wisdom. Very often he had to fight against his enemies in order to maintain his own kingdom, but he had a good army and he always won.

Babar had a son named Humayun, which means "fortunate." Sad to say, a series of unfortunate events took place in Babar's and Humayun's lives.

When Humayun was sixteen years old, his father wanted to conquer a particular place ruled by Ibrahim Lodi. The son said, "Father, you know our army is nothing in comparison to Ibrahim Lodi's army. How can you dare to fight with them?"

But Babar replied, "No, my son, we shall conquer them. Let them have the number; we have the quality and the capacity."

The son said, "Father, I will always abide by your will. Let us go."

Both the father and son were great heroes and with their small army they went to conquer Ibrahim Lodi's army. Surprisingly, they defeated the enemy. The people were very pleased with their new conquerors, for the old ruler had not been at all nice. One of the local governors owned India's most precious diamond, which was called *Kohinoor* (the British government later took this diamond away from the Indians.) The governor gave Kohinoor to Babar's son, Humayun, because of his bravery. Humayun showed it to his father and said, "Father, this is for you."

But Babar replied, "No, my son, you deserve it. You have got it and you should keep it. I am very proud of you. You have fought so bravely. That's why you have been given this diamond. Now you keep it. I will be so happy if you do."

Father and son were extremely kind to each other and they returned to their own kingdom. Alas, in a few hours' time Humayun fell sick. Day by day his condition grew worse. Many doctors came to try to cure him, but none succeeded. They all said that his days were numbered. Many people prayed to Allah for Humayun's recovery, but to no avail.

Then a saint came to Babar and said, "If you make a great sacrifice, if you sacrifice something most precious, only then your son will be cured."

Babar asked, "What kind of thing should I sacrifice?"

The saint said, "Give away Kohinoor. It is most precious."

But Babar said, "Kohinoor is my son's possession. What kind of sacrifice would that be? I have to sacrifice something of my own. I have so much wealth and prosperity, and such a vast kingdom. But the most precious diamond Kohinoor is not mine; therefore, I cannot sacrifice it. "And even if I did own Kohinoor, it would not be a real sacrifice to give it away. Even if I give away my wealth, power and kingdom, I don't think this is the most precious sacrifice I could make. My life alone is most precious. I am ready to give my life."

Then he walked around his son three times, praying to Allah, "For me, my most precious thing is my own life. The saint said to sacrifice something most precious, so take my life instead of my son's. This is my only prayer, and I sincerely mean it."

To his wide surprise, after he completed three rounds his son stood up completely well. But immediately Babar fell deathly ill.

Humayun cried and said to Allah, "My father is going to die, but I shall eternally treasure my father's fondness for me and my father's implicit faith in Your Compassion."

Allah listened to the father's prayer, and in three months' time Babar died. This is the love that a human father can have for his son.

GIM 28. *Satyavama's perfect husband*§

When Satyavama reached the age for marriage, her parents wanted to find a husband for her. Satyavama said to them, "I will only marry that person who always listens to me. If I say sit down, he will sit down. If I say stand up, he will stand up. If I say eat, he will eat. If I say run, he will run. It has to be that kind of man; only then I will marry him."

The parents said, "Who needs that kind of wife?"

Satyavama insisted, "No, if you do not find that kind of husband for me, then I am not going to marry."

Her parents pleaded with her. "We want you to get married. You are grown up. Now that you are of age, what will people think of us? It is not good to keep an unmarried girl at home."

Satyavama said, "I agree with you, and I am ready to get married, but my husband has to be at my beck and call."

The parents were helpless. They looked everywhere for a husband for her. They found many handsome and learned men who were willing to marry their daughter. But then they would say, "There is only one unfortunate thing. You have to be at her beck and call and always listen to her."

"Shame, shame," the men would reply. "We shall have to listen to our wife's command? It is the husband who is supposed to lord it over the wife."

So everybody got angry with the parents. Some laughed at them, some insulted them. "Why are you coming with this kind of proposal?" they asked. The parents were helpless. They were not getting anybody to agree to their proposal.

Then Krishna happened to hear about the situation. He said, "I am the right person for her." So he went to their home and said, "Satyavama, you are looking for a husband. I am ready."

At that time Krishna already had a few wives, but he said, "If she wants that kind of husband, I am ready. If she wants me to do something, I am ready to be her perfect slave."

Satyavama was so happy to have Krishna as her husband. She had said that she would marry anybody who agreed to this proposal. Now, of all people, Krishna wanted to be her husband. He was so venerated by everyone. Although Krishna had other wives and children, he married Satyavama.

As soon as they were married, Satyavama started telling Krishna, "Do this, do this, do this!" Whenever she asked him to do anything, he did it. But Krishna's smile conquered her. Each time he smiled, she would forget to give him a new job. "O Krishna, what am I going to do?" she said. "As soon as I see your face, as soon as I see your smile, I feel that it is I who have to listen to you. You are all love and joy. By asking you to do things, do I get any joy? Only by looking at your face, do I get satisfaction."

Krishna said, "I knew it, I knew it." So Krishna and Satyavama were very happy together.

GIM 29. *Renunciation is not the answer*[§]

There was once an Indian spiritual Master whose disciples were extremely fond of him. They were especially fond of his infinite wisdom.

One day the Master gave a talk on the acceptance of life. Everybody was deeply moved. Only one person did not fully appreciate it. She came up to the Master and said, "Master, you know that I have been worshipping you soulfully ever since I accepted your spiritual path — of course, according to my own capacity. But today I simply can't accept your advice.

"You know I have been cursed by God with two sons. They make demands on me in season and out of season, and they don't allow me to pray and meditate. I feel miserable. If I had not been married like my spiritual sisters, I would have made very fast progress. I am sure that renunciation is the easiest way to make the fastest progress. One should reject life right from the beginning."

The Master said, "My child, don't be a fool. With boundless compassion I am telling you something. There are many women on earth who were once upon a time married, but whose husbands and dear ones left them one by one. Now they have nothing on earth to bind them, but they are not meant for the spiritual life. What they do is this. They tame a cat or a dog or some pet animal. Some of them are very poor; with greatest difficulty they maintain their livelihood. Yet they buy milk for their cats. They manage to feed their dogs with utmost love and concern.

"And then, if the cat leaves their house and goes to eat elsewhere, they search and search for the cat. Then if they find the cat at a neighbour's house, they accuse the neighbour of tempting the cat to come and eat there. They scold the neighbour mercilessly, and the neighbour insults them like anything: 'Who needs your cat?' Often there are fights between the owner and the accused neighbour. Nobody else needs the cat, but the owner feels that her cat was tempted and that this is the reason it goes elsewhere to eat. In this way their disputes never end, and village quarrels have no mother, no father, no beginning, no ending.

"Now isn't a child of your own flesh and blood infinitely more important than a cat? You will give up your sons, but if you don't conquer attachment, then you will feel compelled to replace them with cats, dogs and pets. It is better to have human beings, who are much more evolved than animals. To deal with an evolved being is infinitely more meaningful and fruitful.

"The best way is to see God inside your own children. If you could see God and your Master inside your children, then you would regard them in a different way. You would not feel miserable, but you would show them more affection, more love and more concern. In this way you would have more peace of mind.

"So try to see me inside them. Then all your problems will be over. Renunciation is not the way. For if today you renounce something, then tomorrow you are bound to get attached to something else. Just accept what you have, and illumine your sons with your inner light, if necessity demands. That is the correct way, the spiritual way."

GIM 30. *Play your role as a daughter of God*[§]

A spiritual Master was with some of his disciples when an elderly woman came up to him one day and said, "Master, I am not now totally devoted to you. But I assure you, in the course of time I will become totally devoted and dedicated. I will aspire infinitely more than I do now."

The Master said, "How will you do this?"

The woman said, "Right now my sons are studying, but once they complete their studies I will be free. One will practise medicine, the second will practise law and the third will be in gymnastics. It is only a matter of time, and then you will see how devoted I will be."

The Master said, "God bless you. First of all, your children have to complete their studies, and then they will enter into their respective professions. At that time you will say, 'Oh, now that they are mature and established, let me help find proper marriages for them. They have to get married and be bound to one individual; otherwise, they may not lead decent, faithful lives. The best thing is for them to get married!'

"After you marry them, you will say, 'Marriage is not enough. They should have children!' When you have grandchildren, you will have tremendous joy. But then you will say that it is your duty to bring them up in the same way you have brought up your own sons. The grandchildren will go to school and grow up, and some of them will listen to you while others won't. So every day you will be in the world of worries and anxieties. This is how your life will end."

The woman said, "No, Master, you wait and see. Even if what you say is true, one day, when my grandchildren grow up, I will be ready."

"Yes," said the Master, "at the age of ninety you will be ready for the spiritual life."

The woman insisted, "No, I will accept spirituality in this life."

"When you have one foot in the grave," commented the Master.

"Duty is duty," said the woman. "These are my sons. God brought them into my family."

The Master said, "Yes, you are doing your duty. Again, you have to know that it is God who brought you to me. Your children now want you to stop worrying about them. You have played your role as a mother. Now you should play your role as a seeker."

"It is very difficult for me to accept what you are saying," said the woman.

The Master explained, "Look at the sea. If you go to the sea and wait for the waves to subside, will this ever happen? There will always be waves. If you want to swim, you have to dive into the sea. In the spiritual life also, you have to brave all kinds of opposition. Because of your sons, you are unable to meditate all the time. But if you really want to see God, then this opposition you have to face and conquer. You have to dive into this opposition and be very brave. And for God's sake don't create any more obstructions for yourself by thinking of your sons' jobs, careers, marriages and children. By doing this you are only inviting more waves of obstruction to enter into your life. If you are wise, you will stop here.

"As a mother you have played your role. As a daughter of God, as a spiritual daughter of mine, you now have a new role to play. Think of God alone. God will take care of your sons. He is the only one who can take care of His creation, not you nor me nor anyone else."

The disciple said, "Your words are most illumining, but my capacity is very limited."

The Master said, "Your capacity is limited but my Compassion is unlimited. So you stay with your limited capacity and let me stay with my Eternity's Compassion-Capacity."

GIM 31. *Three mothers*[§]

Once an elderly lady was illumining her grandchildren by telling them stories. The grandchildren wanted to hear stories from their grandmother, so she decided to tell them a beautiful story. She said, "We human beings use the term 'mother' to refer to the one from whom we came into existence. We also call a cow 'mother' because it is associated with the cosmic gods. Again, we speak about 'Mother Earth.' So there are three mothers. These three mothers help us at each step of life.

"When we are born, we take our mother's milk for some time. Then we take cow's milk, and then we eat vegetables that we get from Mother Earth. Mother Earth produces food and we eat her food. We appreciate, admire and adore these three mothers, but we have to see them in a different light and deal with each of them in a different way. They can't be put together.

"The physical mother cannot eat the same food that nourishes Mother Earth. The earthly ground needs cow dung and manure for its food. Again, the cow cannot live on human milk or be kept in a house. And a human mother cannot live on grass or be put in a cow shed.

"Each of the three mothers has her own way of pleasing us. No one can please us at every moment in our own way. Even your own father cannot please you at every moment in your own way. He has many interests in life. He has to go to work, he has to mix with his friends and there are so many things that he has to do. So do not expect the same thing from each individual, and do not expect everyone to please you in your own way. Also, do not think that you will be able to change the respective roles of human beings. If people are doing different things, you cannot just change them. Each one has to do his and her duty in a different way. And it is you who have to receive from each individual according to the way that he wants to give, not according to the way that you want that person to give.

"Your mother is your friend, the cow is your friend and earth is your friend. But you cannot ask these three friends to always help you all at the same time or to change their respective roles. So, my grandchildren, when your mother gives you something, be happy at the time she gives and feel that this is the only way you can be satisfied. And when the cow gives you milk or when Mother Earth gives you something in the form of food and fruits, you have to be satisfied in the same way. Accept everything from each individual in the way the individual wants to give it, and never expect all earthly beings collectively to please you in your own way. Be happy with what you get, and make others happy in your cheerful acceptance."

GIM 32. *Everyone has his own role*[§]

A great spiritual Master once asked his close disciples to come and meditate with him. When they came and sat in front of him, he said, "Today I have a special request to make, and I hope each of you will fulfil my request. God has made a serious mistake, and I want all of you to help me in rectifying the mistake."

Some of the disciples bowed down, puzzled, while others burst into laughter. Then the Master said, "I am serious. Please take me seriously, all those who are laughing. And others, I am telling you not to be so puzzled. You will see that this is something truly illumining.

"You know that in God's creation there are tigers, lions, bears and other animals that eat only meat. Again, in God's creation there are also cows, buffaloes, goats and animals that eat only grass and leaves. Now, why should it be that one party will eat only meat while another party will eat only grass? Let us have both parties eat both meat and grass. Or let us reverse it, so the tiger, lion and bear will eat grass and the cow, buffalo and goat will eat meat. In this way we shall fulfil them." Again, some of the disciples laughed; others grew more puzzled.

The Master continued, "There is nothing to laugh at, and there is nothing to be puzzled over. Now, for God's sake help me."

"What kind of help would you like?" asked the disciples. "We don't understand."

"You don't understand?" said the Master. "Is it such a difficult thing that I am speaking about? In a family one brother may be sick and another may be healthy and strong. So the mother will not give the same food to both. To the one who is really sick the mother will give one type of food and to the one who is strong and stout the mother will give another type.

"Again, usually we eat ordinary food at home, but when a relative or friend comes, we make a special meal. Now, rich people eat richer, more fattening food. Poor people, on the other hand, eat simple food. When rich people come, I try to give them rich food because they are in the habit of eating it. But since you people have accepted the spiritual life, an austere life, you do not need that kind of food. Still, some of you feel miserable that I don't give you the same food that I give rich people. But God is not that kind of communist. He feels that what you need is best for you and what I need is best for me. Your needs are different from my needs. That does not mean that either your need or my need is superior or inferior. Only we are meant for two different things.

"So God wants to please each individual in his own way. If for everybody God has to do the same thing, then individuals will start doing everything wrong. Everybody has to perform his own role and fulfil God's Will in God's own Way. Some of you find fault with me because to some I give rich food, to others I give simple food. To some I give a smile, to others I don't give a smile. Always you find fault, wondering why I am not doing the same thing for each person. But all human beings cannot be treated in the same way, if one really cares for humanity's progress. Even in a family each member has to be treated differently so that he can make the best progress. It is absolutely necessary that a little child be treated one way and a grownup another. The child cannot be treated like an older person and an older person cannot be treated like a child.

"Each soul evolves, starting from the stone life. From the stone consciousness it goes to the animal world and then to the human world. Many of us once upon a time were tigers, lions and bears or cows, buffaloes and goats, and the food was different for each of us. Each one has to eat according to his own nature. Some people eat ignorance-food, some people eat knowledge-food. People who need aspiration are of one type, and those who need desire are of another type. So aspiration-lovers and desire-lovers cannot go together. They have to be kept separately, like the animals who need different food. That is how all parts of God's creation fit together and that is why God's creation is perfect. God wants to be pleased in many ways by many people, and each individual in His infinite creation is pleasing God in the special way that God wants to be pleased."

At this point two of the Master's disciples came forward and bowed down to the Master, saying, "You have read our mind. This morning we were criticising you because you gave rich people richer food than poor people. We felt that you were partial to some and cruel and indifferent to others. Now we see that you are neither partial nor indifferent; you favour neither the rich nor the poor. You are only dealing with each individual according to his necessity. Now we have understood. Please forgive us."

The Master said, "I have already forgiven you. That's why I took the time to illumine you. Had I not forgiven you, I would not have taken the time to illumine you. And I am saying this in front of the others so that they do not make the same deplorable mistake.

"Live in the sea of my love. Then only there will be no confusion, no misunderstanding and no problem. Nothing can separate you from my love, from my oneness and from my satisfaction in you, if you please me in my own way."

GIM 33. *Brother, come and save me!*[§]

The Emperor Humayun was in his palace one day when he heard a commotion. He asked his guards, "What is happening?"

The guard said, "A messenger has come from Chittor. Queen Karmavati of Chittor has sent a message for you."

"How strange!" exclaimed the Emperor. "Let him in. I am curious to know what a Hindu Queen has to say to a Muslim Emperor."

When the Emperor opened the letter, he found a special bracelet. It is traditional for sisters to offer this kind of bracelet to their brothers once a year on the Indian festival day of Rakhi. When offering the bracelet, the sister asks her brother to protect her honour and save her if anything should happen during the coming year.

The message read: "To Emperor Humayun, this bracelet is given by your sister to her adopted brother. Your sister needs your help to save Chittor from Bahadur Shah of Gujarat."

Humayun said, "Karmavati! Karmavati is a Rajput Queen, a Hindu Queen, and I am a Muslim. She calls me her brother? If I am her brother, this means that all Hindus and Muslims are of one family, that Hindus and Muslims will not remain enemies forever but will one day live together as a single family. This is the happiest day of my life."

Humayun immediately rushed to Chittor with his army. Before he reached Chittor, he heard the horrible news that Karmavati had taken her life. When her husband had been killed in battle, she had written to Humayun and had been waiting for his arrival ever since. But when she was about to be captured by the Muslim King Bahadur Shah, she threw herself into fire rather than surrender to him.

Humayun was shocked and horrified. He felt miserable that he had not come in time to save her. He cried out, "I shall take revenge. Karmavati called me her brother. A Hindu Queen called a Mogul Emperor 'brother'. This brother shall not rest until he avenges his sister's death. This is my promise."

As soon as Bahadur Shah heard about Humayun's arrival in Chittor, he fled and went into hiding. But Humayun made a pledge, both to himself and before the Hindu Queen's subjects: "O Bahadur Shah, no matter where you go in Allah's entire creation, I shall find you and keep my promise to Karmavati. Now, my Hindu sister, you are in the other world, but I shall carry out my promise. I shall be worthy of your trust in me."

GIM 34. *Akbar is saved*[§]

Humayun promised his father on his father's deathbed that he would always be kind to his brothers. When Humayun became Mogul Emperor, his brothers turned very greedy. They betrayed him many, many times and wanted to dethrone him, but Humayun forgave them time and again. When his only son, Akbar, was a baby, one of Humayun's brothers, Carmen, set a cannon in a tricky way in order to kill the child. But when Akbar's nurse came to know of it, she shielded and protected the child, saving his life by giving up her own.

Akbar would one day become the greatest of all Mogul emperors. In his court there were many Hindus with high posts, and he even married a Hindu princess. It was he who made the Hindus and Muslims one. He ruled his Kingdom with compassion and truth. In every way he was the greatest of all Mogul emperors.

Everybody wanted Humayun to kill Carmen for the attempt on baby Akbar's life, but Humayun said, "I have forgiven my two brothers Carmen and Hindal many times. This time also I have to forgive him." But his subjects said, "No, this time you have to listen to our request. We are so faithful to you. We offer you our constant admiration and adoration. It is your duty to listen to us."

Finally the Emperor said, "All right, what do you want?"

His subjects said, "Blind him, so that he cannot be of any harm to us any more."

Humayun said, "I am ready to send him into exile, but it would be so difficult for me to blind him."

But they said, "No, if you send him into exile, in some tricky way he will escape and form an army to attack you. So the best thing is to blind him."

Humayun finally listened to his subjects' request.

GIM 35. *The water carrier's bravery*[§]

Once the Mogul Emperor Humayun was fighting a terrible battle against his enemy. The enemy's army was extremely powerful and outnumbered Humayun's army. What was worse, Humayun's treacherous brothers, Carmen and Hindal, had turned traitors to the Emperor. In their greed to capture his kingdom and dethrone him, they had joined forces with the enemy. As

Humayun's army was falling back, the Emperor's horse slipped and fell into a nearby river. The horse drowned and Humayun, badly hurt, was being tossed around helplessly in the rough current.

A water carrier named Nizam, who was a humble man of low caste, saw the Emperor's plight and cried out, "I fear for the Emperor's life! His subjects admire him and adore him as such a just and great Emperor. If the Emperor drowns, we will lose our only hope for a better and more illumining life. I can see that he is wounded and will not be able to save himself."

The water carrier dove bravely into the river and held out his leather bag so the Emperor could float across the river to safety. Both men held the bag, and the water carrier protected the wounded Emperor until they reached the other shore. The Emperor was so moved. He said, "You have come and saved me. Now I am helpless, but I promise you that when I go back to Agrah and am once more seated on my throne, I shall give you my throne for one day. Believe me, this is my solemn promise. You are not a mere water carrier. You are the saviour of the Mogul Emperor Humayun."

The water carrier Nizam was overwhelmed. He fell at the Emperor's feet: "Please, I did not expect any reward. My reward is your safety."

But Humayun insisted, "You, a water carrier of low caste, have shown such loyalty and love for your Emperor, whereas my own brothers have become traitors. I will always be kind to them and forgive them, for this is the promise that I made to my father Babar when he was on his deathbed. But of all of my subjects, you are the one who deserves my throne for one day. You deserve not only my throne, but my eternal gratitude. All my subjects should show you admiration and adoration for your heroic bravery."

The Emperor kept his promise, and Nizam did sit on his throne for one day.

GIM 36. *Akbar's birth*[§]

The Mogul Emperor Humayun was fighting a terrible battle against his enemy in a neighbouring Kingdom. The battle was raging and Humayun was leading the attack. Suddenly Humayun saw his faithful palace messenger trying to make his way towards him, but the soldiers were not allowing him to come to the front of the army. Humayun ordered that the messenger be allowed through.

Humayun took shelter for a moment in a secluded spot to receive the messenger. The messenger bowed to the Emperor and said: "O Great Emperor Humayun, the Empress Hamida Bhan has delivered a son."

Humayun was so delighted and excited. Across the battlefield he cried out, "Allah be praised! We shall call him Akbar."

Then he said to the messenger, "Alas, this is my fate! My son was born, yet I am still fighting my enemies and no victory is in sight. I have nothing with me to give you, O messenger, for bringing me the happiest news. All I have is a small quantity of musk in this tiny box. This is the only thing I can afford to present you with. But I tell you, one day my son's fame will cover the length and breadth of the world as the fragrance of the musk fills the air here. Like perfume, my son's fame will one day spread throughout the world."

When Humayun was finally able to return to his palace to see his son, he was so moved and excited. He said to his son, "My father gave me the name Humayun, which means 'fortunate.' He was right. I am truly fortunate, for I see in you, my son, all the world's fortune. I clearly see that you will be the greatest of all the Mogul Emperors. I see it and I feel it."

He said to his wife, "I am once more leaving you with our child, for I have to go and fight against the enemy again. I am a warrior. I fight with the outer enemy, while religious mendicants, spiritual people, fight with the inner enemies: anger, pride and so forth. I do not have time to fight against the inner enemies. Outer enemies are more than enough for me to cope with. But our son, Akbar, will also fight against the inner enemies. He will be inwardly and outwardly great and good."

GIM 37. *Humayun's death*[§]

One day the great Mogul Emperor Humayun came back victorious from a battle. His subjects were extremely happy and excited that the Emperor had won. The whole Kingdom had turned out to cheer him, lining the streets to the palace. All his subjects wanted to touch his feet and sing his praises.

When the Emperor got to his palace, he said to his army, "We have won, but it is all by Allah's Grace. Otherwise, we would not have won. Let me go and offer my gratitude to Allah in the mosque."

In the mosque Humayun offered his soulful prayer and heart's gratitude to Allah: "Allah, You have always been kind to me. Even my own brothers, not to speak of kith and kin, have deceived and betrayed me many times. But I promised my father on his deathbed that I would be kind to them. Therefore, I have forgiven them every time. I myself have also done so many things wrong in this life and, Allah, You have forgiven me as I have forgiven my own brothers and relatives. You have always taught me that forgiveness is the answer, not revenge. To satisfy oneself, forgiveness is the only answer. Allah, accept my gratitude-life and my gratitude-heart for this great victory."

After offering his prayers of gratitude, Humayun knelt down with folded hands and began praying again most soulfully. Suddenly he collapsed on the floor, and everybody rushed over to him. He said, "This is my last prayer to Allah. Allah, I am soon going to be with You. My father died while praying to You. I was dying and he prayed that you would take his life instead of mine. You listened to his prayer. He died in my place and I was cured.

"Now I am dying while praying to You. My father died while praying to You for my life. I am dying praying for my kingdom, for my people and for my son. I know that there is only one way to gain victory, and that way is through prayer. Without prayer, there is no success and no glory. No prayer, no satisfaction! Allah, Allah, may Your Glory be praised in all human hearts throughout Your creation!

"I leave my son here on earth in Your care. You save him and protect him. You give him world-glory. My last prayer is not the prayer of the great Emperor Humayun, but the prayer of a soulful Muslim mendicant-seeker who needs no one but Allah for eternal peace and eternal satisfaction. Satisfaction is what I have always needed and shall always need forever and forever.

"Allah, You have given me that satisfaction now, not in the victory of the battlefield, but in allowing me to utter Your compassionate name. Your name is all Peace. Satisfaction abides and shall always abide in peace. Peace is satisfaction, satisfaction alone."

GIM 38. *The fight is for the brave*[8]

One day, a new disciple approached his spiritual Master and said, "O Master, O Master, before I accepted the spiritual life, it seems I was quite happy."

"Then, my child, why did you accept the spiritual life?" the Master asked.

"Oh, I accepted the spiritual life thinking that I would be happier, infinitely happier," the disciple said.

"Then what is the matter with you?"

"The thing is, now I have problems every day. Today somebody is sick in the family, tomorrow some other calamity will take place in the family and the day after tomorrow something else will happen. I am so restless. Previously I didn't have any insecurity problems or jealousy problems and so forth. Now everything has come into my life."

"My son, previously you were not conscious of your problems. Now you have become conscious of them. So it is good. You have made progress."

"But how can I get rid of these problems, Master?"

"You can get rid of these problems through your prayer and meditation."

"But Master, around me I see a ferocious tiger. The tiger represents such destructive qualities. Previously I did not see any tiger around me. Also I see inside myself a snakelike quality. I see all animal qualities inside myself. Previously, I didn't have these."

The Master said, "Previously you did have all these qualities inside you, only they had not come to the fore. Now that they are coming to the fore, you should be happy."

"Master, how can I be happy when God seems to be testing me like anything?"

"No, my son, God does not test you. You may think that He is testing you, but God only encourages you to become stronger. And even if He did examine you, you have to feel that it would be worth sitting for His examination, for if you did not pass the examination, you would not be happy. So if there are examinations, be happy that you are given the opportunity to take them and pass them. And if there are no examinations, feel that what you are going through is only an experience."

"O Master, Master, what am I going to do with myself? It seems that problems will never end in the spiritual life."

The Master said, "Problems will only end in the spiritual life. If problems come to you, so much the better. They have appeared in front of you only so that they can be removed. If they always remain hidden inside you, then you will never be able to cast them aside. But if they are standing right in front of you, then you can see them, face them and fight them. So you should be happy and grateful to God that they are right in front of you and not inside. When they are outside, they are infinitely easier to fight. So be happy, be happy. Fight! The race is for the swift, and the fight is for the brave. So dive deep within to run the fastest, and look all around to be the bravest."

GIM 39. *Master, stay in your reality-boat!*[§]

One day a spiritual Master was answering a few questions asked by his disciples. Suddenly he paused and said to one of his stenographers, "Look, I can easily see that these questions and answers and the talks I give will be like Sri Ramakrishna's *Kathamrita*, Sri Ramakrishna's gospel."

All of the disciples remained silent, but two or three inwardly laughed, because they felt that Ramakrishna was far superior to their own Master.

The Master immediately pointed to those unfortunate ones, and said, "You fools! If you think that Sri Ramakrishna is far superior to me, then why have you accepted my path? Go and follow Sri Ramakrishna's path. If you think that just because he is not in the physical, you have to be satisfied with an infinitely inferior Master like me, then I want to tell you that you are making a deplorable mistake. Ramakrishna is definitely still alive; he is immortal. So go and follow him and worship him."

The disciples who had implicit faith in their Master and who felt that he was by far the best stood up and said to those few unfortunate disciples, "Go away from here. We don't want you. If you feel that our Master is inferior, then go and become Sri Ramakrishna's disciples."

Then the Master said, "I know why you think that Sri Rama-krishna is superior. Sri Ramakrishna used to enter into trance quite often, whereas I don't go into trance. But do you think that I don't have the capacity to enter into trance? I do have the capacity. A few days ago I showed you people my trance-capacity. The only thing is, when I enter into trance, I see more vividly your lower vital and emotional problems, and all kinds of problems. Who wants to see this? When I am in a simple, ordinary consciousness, I do not pay attention to your emotional problems and other problems. But when I enter into trance I see them very vividly, and at that time I find it more painful to have disciples like you. Therefore, deliberately, I don't like to go into trance. But I tell you, it is not a difficult task to enter into trance."

Some of the disciples said, "O Master, we knew it, we knew it. Who wants to see you in trance? If you are in trance, then we are totally lost. We enter into our own trance, which is all sleep. When you are in trance, you say that you are more conscious of what is happening in our lives. But we feel that this is the time for us to relax and enter into our own world, since you are not consciously seeing what is happening. That used to be our feeling, but now we see that this is not the case."

Now the bad, unfortunate disciples said, "O Master, forgive us, forgive us. We will never compare you with anybody. You will always remain our best and highest."

The Master said, "That should be your attitude. Even if your Master is not as high as another Master, if you accept him, then you have always to feel that he is the highest. If you accept a spiritual Master, it is because you feel that he is absolutely the highest and the best. If you do not feel this, if you have only limited faith and not implicit, one hundred per cent faith, then it is useless to accept a particular Master; for at every moment your mind will be thinking of somebody else. You will think, 'Perhaps if I had the other Master, I would be making better progress. If I had been fortunate enough, I would have got that Master.'

"No, no! If you accept a Master, you have to accept him wholeheartedly and give him all your devotion. Otherwise, you can't expect anything great or good, not to speak of your total transformation and complete illumination from that Master."

All the disciples bowed down and said, "Master, we do not want your trance, we want only your wakeful consciousness. Of course, there is no difference between your trance-life and wakeful consciousness. But when you are with us, when you talk to us in our own human way, when you cut jokes with us and tell us all kinds of juicy stories, when you answer our spiritual questions, at that time you make us feel that you are one of us and that you are for us. When you are mixing with us and cutting jokes, you make us feel that we are really in your boat. We want to be in your boat, and not the other way around. We don't want you to be in our boat where there is constant fear, anxiety, worry, doubt, insecurity and impurity. No, we want you to be in your boat.

"We wish to be in your reality-boat all the time and not in your trance-boat. When you are in your trance-boat, we are totally lost, for we do not know what you are doing. We may feel that you are acting like a stranger to us and consciously or unconsciously neglect you. Or we may feel that this is an opportunity to deceive you, or that you don't care for us. All these things are not helpful at all. So you remain with us in a human way. If you deal with us in a human way and mix with us and show us your utmost compassion and affection, we will feel blessed. This is the only way we feel that we will be able to reach our own highest heights."

The Master said, "You are right, you are right. Because I act like a human being with you, in most cases you are able to talk with me and mix with me. But if I remain always in a divine consciousness, a trance-consciousness, then nobody will be able to understand me or approach me; nobody will be able to have higher goals. Strange feelings and fear will always assail you.

"But I am with you and for you. I am with you and beside you. I am right among you, so you can run with me and climb with me and take me as your comrade and friend. That is the easiest and the most effective way for you to reach your highest, which is my real height."

GIM 40. *Make only one promise*[§]

There was once a rich man who took an oath that he would never invite Sanskrit scholars, learned people or seekers to his home. His best friend, who was also a very rich man, had once invited some scholars and seekers to come to a function and neither group came. So his friend was very sad. This particular rich man went to his spiritual Teacher and said, "I don't care for knowledge; I don't care for the pride of the seekers. I promise I shall never invite scholars and seekers into my home."

The Master said, "Have you done the right thing? It is not good to make this kind of promise."

"Why?" the rich man asked.

"If you fulfil your promise," the Master said, "pride will enter into you. And if you don't fulfil your promise, you will feel sad and disturbed. Who knows, one day you may want to invite some scholars and sincere seekers to your house. Then your pride will go and you will feel sad and depressed. And depression is destruction. Again, if you don't invite them, you will feel very proud that you kept your promise, but pride is also destruction. You are the loser no matter what you do. So it is better not to make promises.

People say it is good to make promises; then only your inner capacities come forward. But I wish to tell you that only one promise is good: your promise that you will conquer ignorance and realise God in this life-time. That promise alone is worth making; other promises are all dangerous and destructive."

The rich man said, "But look what happened to my best friend when he invited some seekers and scholars to his house. How badly he was insulted! If those people were sincere seekers, why did they not come to please my friend? And if they were real scholars, they should have had humility."

The Master asked, "How do you know why they did not come? They may have thought that the rich man was inviting them only to add to his own glory. Perhaps they felt, 'He does not care for knowledge or aspiration; he is just inviting us to show off to society. So why should we falsely glorify him? Again, they may have thought that he was inviting them to honour them. But then perhaps they felt, 'We don't need honour. We want only to remain in our own prayer and meditation.' Especially the seekers may have felt like this.

"If scholars don't come because of their pride and vanity, it is they who will be blamed. Again, if seekers don't come because they feel that glory is nothing short of temptation and they do not want to be glorified, then they are doing the right thing. But whether they are doing the right thing or the wrong thing, whichever way they want to please themselves, let them do so. Your business is only to invite them, if that is what gives your heart joy. Again, if it is only your vital that wants to be glorified, then you are making a mistake by inviting them. And if you want to invite them because your vital feels that they are inferior and you are in a position to bless them and glorify them, then again you are making a mistake.

"This world is full of misunderstanding. So the best thing is not to make any promises. Only try to see the situation. Don't have any specific hard and fast rules. When necessity demands, do something spontaneously, but don't make it a law that you will do it. Wait for the inner command."

"Master, Master, yes, I see that you are right. I will always wait for the inner command," said the rich man. "Now, what is my inner command?"

The Master said, "In your case, the inner command is that you have to conquer your pride. If in the inmost recesses of your heart, at times you have the desire to invite people, then do so. Then, if they want to come, well and good, and if they don't want to come, don't say anything. But do not promise to yourself that you will not invite any scholars or seekers because certain ones have insulted your friend. Human knowledge you know, but there is also the supreme knowledge. The supreme knowledge is oneness, oneness with God's Will. If you have oneness with God's Will, then whether they come to you or you go to them is of no importance. What is of importance is only to remain in God's Will. Then, no matter where they are and no matter where you are, all of you will please and fulfil one another.

"So my advice is not to make promises. Fulfilling your promises brings in pride, and the failure to fulfil your promises unnecessarily brings in sadness and frustration. Keep only one promise, and that is your promise to achieve God-realisation. And then modify that promise also."

"How can I modify that promise?" asked the rich man. "I need that promise badly. I want only to realise God. No other promise will I make, Master."

The Master said, "That promise also has to be made in a certain way. Your wish is to realise God, but it is up to God whether He will make you realise Him in this incarnation or in some other incarnation. So when you make this promise, add, 'This is my wish. If Your Wish is otherwise, then please fulfil Yourself in and through me in Your own Way.' That is the best promise: 'I will fulfil my Beloved Supreme in His own Way, and for that only I shall pray to Him.' That promise is the only promise which at every moment all seekers must treasure."

GIM 21. *(p. 209)* 8 January 1979
GIM 22. *(p. 211)* 9 January 1979
GIM 23. *(p. 212)* 9 January 1979
GIM 24. *(p. 214)* 9 January 1979
GIM 25. *(p. 215)* 9 January 1979
GIM 26. *(p. 217)* 9 January 1979
GIM 27. *(p. 218)* 9 January 1979
GIM 28. *(p. 220)* 9 January 1979
GIM 29. *(p. 222)* 9 January 1979
GIM 30. *(p. 224)* 9 January 1979
GIM 31. *(p. 226)* 9 January 1979
GIM 32. *(p. 227)* 12 January 1979
GIM 33. *(p. 230)* 13 January 1979
GIM 34. *(p. 231)* 13 January 1979
GIM 35. *(p. 232)* 13 January 1979
GIM 36. *(p. 234)* 13 January 1979
GIM 37. *(p. 235)* 13 January 1979
GIM 38. *(p. 236)* 13 January 1979
GIM 39. *(p. 238)* 13 January 1979
GIM 40. *(p. 241)* 13 January 1979

GREAT INDIAN MEALS:
DIVINELY DELICIOUS AND
SUPREMELY NOURISHING

BOOK 3

Once Ramachandra said to his Guru, Vashishtha, "Lord, please tell me something about God."

Vashishtha said, "God? He is all greatness. My son, meditate on this."

Ramachandra meditated on God's Greatness for a few seconds. Then Vashishtha said, "I am so glad that you have seen and felt God's Greatness."

Ramachandra then said, "Lord, please say something more about God."

Vashishtha said, "God is all goodness. Meditate on God's Goodness."

Ramachandra meditated for a few seconds on God's Goodness. Vashishtha said, "Excellent! I am so glad that you have seen and felt God's Goodness."

Again Ramachandra asked his Master to tell him something more about God.

"God is all kindness, all compassion and all concern. Meditate on this."

Ramachandra meditated on God's Kindness, Compassion and Concern for a few seconds. Vashishtha said, "Excellent, excellent, my son."

Ramachandra then said, "Lord, please tell me something more about God."

His Guru replied, "God is all justice. Meditate on this."

Ramachandra meditated on God's Justice and Vashishtha said, "Marvellous! You have seen and felt God's Justice."

"Lord, something more I want to hear about God."

"God is all power. Meditate on this, my son."

Ramachandra meditated on God's Power, and Vashishtha said, "I knew, I knew that you would see and feel God's Power in a very short time."

"Something else I wish to hear from you, my Lord, about God."

Vashishtha remained silent.

"Why are you silent, my Lord?" Ramachandra asked. Still Vashishtha remained silent.

"Lord, why are you silent? I wish to learn more from you about God."

Vashishtha still remained silent.

"Why don't you want to teach me, my Lord?" asked Ramachandra. "If you do not teach me, how can I learn more about God? I want to learn everything about God from you."

Again, silence!

Ramachandra asked, "Have I offended you in any way? Consciously I know that I have not offended you. And if I have offended you unconsciously, please forgive me. Only I want you to teach me more about God."

But Vashishtha only remained silent. "Lord, Lord, if you do not teach me more about God, then I will definitely remain ignorant. If this is your will, if this is the Will of God, then I must remain silent, too."

Vashishtha blessed Ramachandra and said, "My son, you have got the answer. When all earthly questions are asked and all the answers are given, then question-life and sound-life come to an end. At that time, real answer-life and real silence-life begin. So silence is the answer. Silence is the unparalleled God. Silence unites the many and makes the many one. You and I are two. We are playing the role of teacher and student, Master and disciple. But you have learned everything that I know about God; therefore I remain silent. Silence is perfect oneness and oneness is God-perfection."

Ramachandra touched Vashishtha's feet and said, "Your name is silence, my Lord, Eternity's silence; and my name is gratitude,

Infinity's gratitude. In silence and in gratitude we shall forever and forever remain inseparably one."

GIM 42. *When argument ceases, illumination dawns*§

Once the great spiritual Master Kavir said to his son Kamal, "Kamal, please bring me a few flowers and a small quantity of milk for my worship."

Kamal said, "Father, why do you want flowers and why do you want milk? Flowers are polluted."

Kavir could not believe his ears. "What, flowers are polluted?"

"Yes," said Kamal, "flowers are polluted because the bees sit on the flowers and drink their honey. So they are polluted."

"And what about milk?" Kavir asked.

"Milk is also polluted," said Kamal, "because the calf has already tasted and drunk some milk from the mother before we get it."

Kavir became angry. "Son, this is what you have learned from your studies? You find fault with your father's request, and you argue with your father."

"No, father," said Kamal, "I am not arguing, I am just telling you a mere fact. You are asking me for flowers and milk. I am saying that you have to give God something that is totally fresh. I will go and bring flowers whose honey has been tasted by bees, and I will bring milk which has already been drunk by the calf. But if you really want to please God, you have to give Him something that is absolutely pure."

"Stop!" said Kavir. "Stop, stop your philosophy. O God, you have cursed me with such an argumentative son. He does not know who I am. The whole world worships me, and here my son gives me his proud wisdom."

"No, father, I am not offering you my wisdom. I am only telling you a mere fact."

Kavir said, "Enough of your insolence. In this world, when God creates something, everybody may not be able to eat it at the same time. In God's own Vision, somebody will have it first and others will have it afterwards. But that doesn't mean that the first one who tastes a particular thing is polluting it for others. A flower has been seen or touched or used a little by a bee, and milk has been touched by the calf, who is dearer than the dearest to the mother cow. Do you think that just because of that I won't be able to worship my Lord Supreme with flowers and milk? No, God created the flower, and before it was time for me to use the flower, it was time for the bee to taste its honey. And the time came for the calf to taste the cow's milk before the time came for me to use the milk.

"It is like two people going towards the same destination. I saw the Goal, the eternal Goal, long before you and I have already reached it whereas you are still traveling towards it. But does that mean you will say, 'What is the use of going to the Goal which has been seen and touched by somebody else?' No! In the spiritual world, when someone uses something for the first time, that doesn't mean that this particular thing cannot be touched or utilised by somebody else. You are traveling along the same path that I traveled, and going to the same Goal which I have already reached. Similarly, the flower that has been appreciated by the bee can and should be appreciated by those who see the flower later on. And milk that has been appreciated by the little calf should also be appreciated by others. So, my son, never argue with me."

"Father," said Kamal, "I shall never, never argue with you. Today you have illumined me. No other teacher has ever taught me in this way and nobody else will ever be able to teach me in this way. You are my father. You asked me to go to other teachers, and I went and studied. But now I see that the possessor of all real knowledge is nobody other than you yourself. Therefore,

I ask you to make me, shape me and guide me into your own, very own. Already in the physical world I am your own. In the spiritual world also I wish you to make me your worthy son, your own, very own."

"Son," said Kavir, "I shall. In fact, I am doing that very thing which you are now crying for. When the noise of argument ceases, the voice of illumination dawns."

"Father," said Kamal, "I wish to add something. When Compassion-Light dawns, the darkness of centuries in no time immediately disappears."

"Son, I also wish to add something: Compassion-Light dawns only when the heart is ready to receive Light from Above, from the Beyond, from the Eternal Source."

GIM 43. *Conquer your enemies*[5]

One day, a young man went to see his spiritual Master. He was upset and disturbed. "Master, Master, I want to give up spirituality altogether," he said.

"Why, why?" asked the Master.

"Because it is simply useless. I am a constant victim to undivine thoughts, evil thoughts, and to emotional, lower vital problems. How long can I continue this way? I was quite happy before I entered into the spiritual life. I didn't have so many vital problems then. But now it is torture, real torture. Let me conquer these undivine thoughts and forces first, and then I shall return to the spiritual life. But now it is not meant for me."

The Master said nothing. Only he gave the disciple a broad smile.

"Master, I promise you," the disciple continued, "I promise you I will really pray and meditate once I have conquered all the problems that I have."

The Master smiled again.

"Master, why are you smiling? Do you not think that I am saying the right thing?"

"No, my son," said the Master, "I am smiling because you need real wisdom from me."

"Master, that is why I came to you. But I feel that no matter what you say it will not help me. You have been inundating me with wisdom every day with your spiritual talks, with your affection, with your kindness, with your meditation. But still I find it simply impossible to overcome my lower vital problems and evil thoughts."

The Master said, "My son, look. Right now you have a fever, you have a stomach upset, you have everything; so won't you take medicine? You will not say, 'I will take medicine afterwards. Let my fever, stomach pain and everything else that I am suffering from first go away from me. When these things leave me, then I will take medicine.' When you suffer from something, you get something that will cure it. If you are bitten by a snake, you immediately take the antidote. Then only you will be cured. Now you are suffering. If you don't take the medicine, which is prayer and meditation, then how are you going to cure yourself? Will the disease go away on its own? Once the enemy attacks you, it will stay with you until you throw it out. So you have to cure yourself. Prayer and meditation are the medicine."

The disciple said, "Master, what you are saying is true. But I have tried for such a long time. Now I am tired of fighting. I have no enthusiasm, no will power. I feel that if I surrender to these forces, one day they will show me compassion. Once they show their compassion and feel that I am useless, they will leave me. Then I will immediately run towards you and I will again pray and meditate."

The Master said, "Oh, no! These enemies are eternal enemies. They never allow their victims to go in their own way. Knowing perfectly well that you are at their mercy, for some time they may remain in a relaxed mood, and you will think that they are not keeping an eye on you, that they are not keeping a strict watch over you. But no, when they see that you are trying to leave their prison cell, immediately they will be more strict with you. They will keep you under greater supervision, under strict orders.

"So conquer these enemies at any cost. Then only you will be saved. Never think that your enemy will grant you freedom. It is you who have to conquer the enemy and get freedom for yourself."

The disciple touched his Master's feet. "I know, Master, your Compassion is my sword, your Compassion is my shield and your Compassion is my victory's crown, which I shall place at your feet divine. From now on, I shall please you — you, you, only you — in your own way."

GIM 44. *Have faith in Vishnu!*[§]

Once a great devotee of Vishnu went horseback riding. He was enjoying the ride, when he happened to come near the house of a washerman. The washerman had just washed some clothes and put them out to dry. Unfortunately, the devotee's horse ran over the newly washed clothes, leaving its footprints on them. The washerman got furious and ran after the devotee, pulling him down from the horse.

The devotee started screaming, "O Vishnu, Vishnu, save me, save me!"

At the time, Vishnu was having his feet massaged by his consort in Heaven. All of a sudden he ran away. His consort cried, "What are you doing? Where are you going? Did I do anything wrong?"

Vishnu replied, "Don't worry, I am coming back soon." He opened the door, walked only a few steps outside his house and then returned.

His consort said, "Well, what happened? You ran outside, but there was nobody there. What were you doing?"

Vishnu said, "You don't know what happened? On earth my greatest devotee was being chased by a washerman. First he ran away, afraid for his life, and prayed to me to save him. But as soon as I ran to save him, suddenly he decided that he had strength enough to fight the man himself, so he didn't pray to me anymore. He just threatened the washerman and frightened him. The washerman felt that my devotee was much stronger than he, so he stopped chasing him. My devotee got back on his horse and continued his morning ride to enjoy the beauty of nature."

The consort said, "Since he had invoked you, he should not have changed his mind. He could have got hurt!"

Vishnu said, "Either one has to have faith in me or faith in oneself. If one has faith in me, then he is always safe. But if one has faith in oneself, sometimes ego enters into the picture. If the seeker has very intense aspiration and if he can establish his oneness with me, then faith in me and faith in himself are the same thing. But if he has not established oneness with my Will and my Consciousness, then his faith in himself is only a parade of ego. That kind of seeker is one day bound to fall in his spiritual life, without fail."

GIM 45. *Spirituality is for those who are careful*[§]

Once there was a beautiful woman who was very spiritual. Her husband was also quite spiritual. Often they used to invite seekers to their home for spiritual discussions, prayer and meditation. The two were very generous, and after these meetings the wife would usually serve dinner to everyone.

Once the husband had to go out of town on business for a few months. The seekers who previously had been coming to her home asked if they could continue meeting there. But she said, "Oh, no! My husband wouldn't like the idea. Only when he is here can I invite you over." That was not the real reason, however. Several times in the past, when her husband had been out of town, the wife had continued meeting with seekers. But now, during her husband's absence, she had become very friendly with one of her servants and eventually fell in love with him. Because she was deeply interested in the servant, she found no need for spirituality in her life.

One day, a spiritual Master was walking near her house. He looked very sad. When the wife saw him, she asked, "Why are you so sad?" The Master said, "I am very sad because from my childhood I have always carried a special toy with me. The toy was my friend, my only friend. Whenever I did anything very private and intimate, I allowed only this toy to accompany me. Nobody else would ever know what I was doing. The toy was like my collaborator, and it always suffered whenever I did anything wrong. But now I have done something so bad that, out of shame, the toy has fallen down and broken its head."

The woman was very sympathetic. "Let me buy you another toy so that you forget about this one," she said.

But the Master said, "No, I can't do that. How can I have another toy? This toy represented my inner being. It was part and parcel of my nature, my character, my life. If I get a new one just because it has smashed its head, then it will have another consciousness."

The lady got the point. Here she was married to a good and spiritual man, and now she was in love with a servant, of all people. She cried and cried at the feet of the Master. "Oh, forgive me, forgive me," she said.

The Master said, "I will forgive you for what you have done. Even your husband will forgive you, immediately he will forgive you, for his love for you is boundless. But your soul — the only real reality inside you — may not forgive you at all, or for a long time. It may withdraw and not come to the fore again this whole incarnation.

"Once one accepts the spiritual life, once one becomes a real seeker, at that time if one falls and enters into the vital and emotional life, indulging in unthinkable things, then the punishment is unbearable. One is compelled to lead a miserable, miserable life, without forgiveness.

"So, be careful before you accept the spiritual life, and then, once you have accepted the spiritual life, be constantly careful. For if you fall at that time, darkness-life will not care for you and wisdom-light will not care for you either. Aspiration-life will not care for you if you do not aspire and desire-life will not care for you, for it will feel that it cannot trust you totally. It will say, 'Again he may go back to aspiration-life.' And aspiration-life will not trust you. It will say, 'Oh, he left me to go back to desire-life.'

"So, you will be caught in between aspiration-life and desire-life. You will not get joy from desire-life, for you have already told aspiration-life that you will be its eternal friend. And once you betray desire-life and go after a higher life, desire-life will only torture you. So be careful! Spirituality is only for those who are always careful in what they say, do and become."

GIM 46. *Chandra Gupta and the lion*[§]

There was once a king named Samudra Gupta who had two sons: Rama Gupta and Chandra Gupta. Everyone liked Chandra Gupta, the younger of the two, because of his bravery, sweetness, politeness and humility. Chandra Gupta had all the divine virtues, whereas Rama Gupta was very haughty and undivine in every possible way. Even their father couldn't help liking his younger son better. All the members of the royal family and the court favoured Chandra Gupta, except for one very bad minister. This minister was a rogue of the first water, and he liked Rama Gupta for his own undivine reasons.

The two princes had many friends among the sons of ministers and high officials. One day, Chandra Gupta came to his father and asked "Father, can we go out to the river and play?"

The father said, "Why not, my son. Go and enjoy yourself."

The two brothers and eight or nine of their friends went to play by the river. All of a sudden, a ferocious lion came and everybody became frightened and ran away. Only Chandra Gupta stayed. He started fighting the animal and finally killed him. Afterwards, all the other children started appreciating Chandra Gupta.

His brother became very jealous and said, "Oh, he just killed a lion. Anybody can do that."

The friends said, "Anybody can do it? Then why did you run away, you coward?"

The brother said, "I ran away only because everybody else was running away. They would have pulled me with them, and would not have allowed me to stay."

"You liar!" everybody shouted. "Your brother didn't run away. He challenged the strength of the lion and killed it!"

Rama Gupta became furious. "I hate my brother! Everybody appreciates him and admires him. It isn't fair. I am also the

King's son, the prince of this kingdom, but nobody appreciates me."

Everyone said, "You are a coward, like us; that is why we can't appreciate you. But your brother set his strength against that of the wild beast and came out victorious. Indeed, he is destined to be King one day."

Rama Gupta said, "How? I am the older brother. It is my kingdom. It is I who will get the throne." Everyone continued to argue with him.

By now it was getting late, and still the children had not returned to the palace. The King became worried, and he sent a messenger to see if they were all right. When the messenger reached the river, he told the princes, "Your father is very worried. You must come back to the palace now." "We were enjoying the death of this lion," the children said.

When the King came to hear of the story, he couldn't believe his ears. He personally came to the river with his whole entourage of ministers and important people. "Chandra Gupta, you have done this?" he said. "This is beyond my imagination. I have had many dreams about how powerful and great you will be, and this only makes me more certain."

Everybody was shouting with joy that Chandra Gupta had killed the lion, but the rogue minister was very sarcastic. "At last Chandra Gupta has done something great," he said.

"Shut up, Minister," everyone said. "Why are you mocking him? Chandra Gupta has performed such a great feat, almost a miracle. He is the great hero in the family."

The minister became afraid he would be fired. He said, "I am sorry. I don't know why I said that. I really meant to say that you should give him a reward."

"What kind of reward should I give him?" asked the King. "Whatever I give him will be inadequate. On the one hand, I am so proud of him. On the other hand, I feel that he will get his reward for his virtuous life when the day comes for him to take care of the kingdom."

"What?" Rama Gupta cried out. "How is that possible? I am the older brother. The throne belongs to me."

The King answered, "No doubt, Rama Chandra, you will become King after my death. But I feel that somehow, someday, Chandra Gupta is destined to rule."

"Father," cried Rama Gupta, "you always speak well of Chandra Gupta. In your eyes I am nobody, just a speck of dust."

The King said, "Don't be a fool. You are also my son. Only be grateful that your brother has saved your life."

"I hate him!" screamed Rama Gupta. "I can save myself."

"Look, I am the King," the father said firmly. "Come back home peacefully. Otherwise, I will throw you out of my kingdom."

Rama Gupta became frightened and returned to the palace. Because his older brother felt so miserable, Chandra Gupta said to him, "O brother, I have killed a lion. But you and I are brothers, so easily you can feel that it is you who have killed it."

"You fool!" said Rama Gupta. "You killed the beast, and I will say that I did it?" He became furious.

"But what is the difference?" asked Chandra Gupta. "We are members of one family. Our parents, our relatives, even our father's subjects are all one. When you do something great and good, at that time I feel that it is I who have done it."

"What have I ever done?" asked Rama Gupta.

"You will do very great things," Chandra Gupta consoled him. "And I will claim them as my very own. Although I have killed this lion today, please feel that it is you who have done it. And one day when you do something significant, I will claim your achievement as my own."

GIM 47. *Rama Gupta's capture*[§]

When King Samudra Gupta died, he left two sons: Rama Gupta and Chandra Gupta. Rama Gupta was supposed to become King, since he was the eldest. But everybody spoke ill of him because of all his undivine qualities. Some said that the King would have really wanted Chandra Gupta to succeed him. The subjects also wished that Chandra Gupta could take the throne but, according to law, Rama Gupta was meant to become King.

There was an evil minister in the royal court. Rama Gupta took this evil minister into his confidence: "Immediately I have to become King, before it is too late. Otherwise, I fear that my brother will somehow win the throne."

The minister said, "You will become King without fail, but why don't we wait a few days. People are still mourning your father's death."

In his heart of hearts, the minister was very happy that Rama Gupta was anxious to take the throne. "The sooner the better for him," he said to himself. But outwardly he did not want to appear disrespectful to the King.

A few days later Rama Gupta came to the minister and gave him a very large amount of money as a bribe. The minister said, "Money I need, and also I am one with you. I don't like Chandra Gupta either. Everybody always appreciates him, whereas nobody even cares for my own son. When I think of the way you are treated, I am reminded of my own son. Let me make you King."

The minister called in the priest and told him to perform the ceremony making Rama Gupta King. Chandra Gupta did not feel sorry because, after all, he was the younger brother and was not supposed to be King. He was sincerely happy that his brother was becoming King, and he participated in the ceremony, giving everybody joy.

In a few years' time Rama Gupta married a most beautiful girl named Dhruva Devi. They had an intimate friend named Madhavi, who used to tell the Queen that Chandra Gupta was so great whereas her husband was not so great. Dhruva Devi all the time heard stories about Chandra Gupta's goodness and her husband's undivine qualities.

One day Dhruva Devi said to her husband, "I have heard so much about your younger brother's greatness. Is it all true?"

Rama Gupta became furious: "Everything you have heard from that Madhavi. I shall kill her! You shouldn't believe that stupid woman. What she says is not true. It is I who am great, greater, greatest. That's why I have become the King. I will banish Chandra Gupta from my kingdom."

The Queen said, "No, don't do that. I will not speak of him anymore. And even if you wanted to throw him out of the kingdom, do you really think you would be able to? The whole kingdom likes and admires him. Wait and see. You can't throw him out."

When Madhavi heard about this, she said to the Queen "Without Chandra Gupta, would there even be a kingdom? Rama Gupta is only King by name. The strength and power of the kingdom come from Chandra Gupta."

Rama Gupta was furious when he heard what Madhavi had said. "I need some rest," he said. "I am tired of always arguing with these rogues. They stay in my kingdom, eat my food and then speak ill of me. I don't need this kind of subject. I am going away for some time. O Queen if you want to come and enjoy some rest with me, you are most welcome. We shall take a few soldiers with us in case anything happens."

So with a small army, the King and Queen set out for a short vacation, wandering here and there. Alas, one day they came near the border of King Shaka's kingdom. Shaka's soldiers thought that they were coming to do battle. Since they knew the area so well, they circled around Rama Gupta's soldiers and caught them by surprise. Then they drove them across the border into Shaka's territory proper. As soon as they crossed the border, another army of Shaka attacked them from the front. Rama Gupta's men, caught off guard, were defeated and the King and Queen were held captive.

GIM 48. *The queen's plight* [§]

While King Rama Gupta and his Queen, Dhruva Devi, were out on a holiday, accompanied by a few of their soldiers, they were captured by the army of King Shaka.

King Shaka sent the captured King a message: "I will allow you to go back to your kingdom only if you give up your wife and allow her to marry me. Dhruva Devi rightfully belongs to me, because originally I was supposed to marry her."

Rama Gupta was surprised. "Dhruva Devi, is this true?" he asked. His wife admitted, "It is true. My father arranged for me to marry King Shaka, but at the eleventh hour he changed his mind. Shaka is such a bad man; he is undivine in every way. And I was so beautiful, so good and divine, that my father decided not to allow me to marry him."

Rama Gupta said, "Indeed, you are so beautiful that I will never part with you. I will fight Shaka."

When Shaka heard this, he laughed and laughed. "Already you are conquered," he told Rama Gupta. "What kind of fight will this be? You are practically dead. How are you going to fight if you are half dead? Now you are going to see your wife for the last time. I will force her to come and marry me. But for a few days let me allow you and your wife to stay with your conquered army. I am enjoying your imprisonment and mistreatment."

Afterwards, Rama Gupta said, "O Queen, if I don't give you to King Shaka, I will lose my entire kingdom. Again, if I give you away, I will feel miserable. But to be very, very frank with you, I want to remain king. So I am going to send you to this brute. When you get married, I will feel sorry, for I will miss you, but I want to go back to my kingdom."

The Queen was horror-struck: "I knew it, I knew it!" she cried. "What a rogue you are! Your brother would not have done this kind of thing."

Then Rama Gupta became furious: "Don't bring Chandra Gupta into the picture. Why has he not come to help us, if he is such a great hero?"

"He does not even know what happened to us," said the Queen. "If I could only send a message to him!"

"How will you send a message? Our army is now in chains, and many people have been killed," the king said.

But it happened that Chandra Gupta was wondering why his brother had not yet come back: "He left the palace for only a few days' rest; now he has been gone two weeks. What is delaying him?"

So Chandra Gupta decided to go searching for his brother and the Queen. He asked some of his friends and soldiers from his brother's army to accompany him. It was not long before Chandra Gupta heard that his brother was being held captive by King Shaka, and he went looking for him. When Shaka's soldiers saw Chandra Gupta coming, they laughed and laughed. "They have so few people. Let them go and see how badly we are treating their royal king and queen."

When Chandra Gupta came, Dhruva Devi started screaming and weeping. "Your brother is giving me away to King Shaka so that he can go back and rule his kingdom," she said.

Chandra Gupta was shocked. "How can you do this kind of thing? Think of how great our father was! For your kingdom you will give up such a kindhearted and beautiful woman?"

"Enough of your wisdom!" Rama Gupta said. "I need name and fame. I will get infinitely more by being King than by remaining with this wife."

Dhruva Devi was so horrified that she fell down on the ground. Chandra Gupta said to her, "Sister, I will not allow my brother to give you away. I will fight for you, and I will take you back."

So, with his very limited army he fought King Shaka's soldiers and won. Then he went to King Shaka, and also killed him. Afterwards he came and freed his brother and his wife and took them home.

GIM 49. *The death of the King*⁵

Chandra Gupta returned home after slaying the evil King Shaka, bringing with him his brother, King Rama Gupta, and the Queen, Dhruva Devi, who had been held captive for several weeks. Everybody was appreciating and admiring Chandra Gupta for his heroism. At the same time, they were criticising and cursing the King, for agreeing to give his own wife away in order to regain his kingdom. Everybody was filled with hatred for the undivine King.

The King felt miserable that everybody was appreciating his brother. "Something should be done," he said. "Why has this happened to me?"

His evil minister read the King's mind. "O King, you were a fool to expose your cowardice."

But Rama Gupta said, "Still I am the King. Yet nobody gives me any importance."

"What can you expect from your subjects?" the minister asked. "They all love and admire their Queen and they are angry that you wanted to give her away."

Rama Gupta became very agitated. "Even my own wife is more venerated than I am. This is my fate!" A friend of the undivine minister happened to overhear this conversation. He was extremely jealous of Chandra Gupta and had a clever idea.

"O King," he said, "I could not help overhearing your words. I fully sympathise with you. But I must tell you that you will never be happy as long as your brother stays on earth."

The King said, "Indeed, I fear you are right. I should banish him from the kingdom."

"He would only gather an army and return to challenge you. But," the friend continued, "O King, if your brother were dead, everybody would forget all about him. Then all the glory in this kingdom would be totally yours."

"I need glory, name and fame," agreed the King. "But alas, my brother will live on earth for many years."

"We can change his fate and our fate," said the minister. "What if poor Chandra Gupta were killed mysteriously in his sleep?"

"An excellent idea," said Rama Gupta.

"Tonight!" said the minister's friend. "You should kill him tonight, before another day passes and you lose more glory, name and fame."

"We shall help you rule the kingdom without him," said the minister. "Boundless will be our wealth and power!"

That night Chandra Gupta was sleeping when he heard a loud sound. "Who is there?" he demanded.

Someone was approaching him in the dark, sword in hand, and was about to stab him. "Villain!" Chandra Gupta cried out. "At this hour you have come to kill me?" With that, he pushed aside his assailant, grabbed the sword and stabbed the person.

When Chandra Gupta turned on the light, he saw it was his own brother that he had stabbed. "What can I do? Forgive me, forgive me. I didn't know it was you. If I had seen you, if I had known it was you, I would have allowed you to kill me and put an end to all your suffering. You should have asked me to leave the kingdom. I would have gladly gone away. I don't need name and fame. I am happy with what I have and what I am."

Chandra Gupta could do nothing to save his brother, who died in his arms. "What have I done, what have I done!" Chandra Gupta cried out. "I did not know it was my brother. Alas, my father was so great and good. Is this the fate of his sons and kingdom?" Chandra Gupta buried his head in his hands totally crushed and heartbroken.

GIM 50. *A father's dream becomes reality*[§]

With the death of Rama Gupta, his brother, Chandra Gupta, became King. The whole kingdom came to his inaugural ceremony. Everyone was crying with joy and relief, for they felt that he would be a just and kind King and that the land would flourish and prosper under his rule. The soldiers all pledged loyalty to their new King and said they were honoured to serve such a brave and heroic ruler.

After several days of festivities, the wife of Rama Gupta, Dhruva Devi, came to the new King. "Please," she said to him, "you have to marry me."

Chandra Gupta was surprised. "Dhruva Devi, your heart and soul are forever bound to my dear brother. Unfortunately, I took away his life, when I slew him without knowing who he was. I could never take away his Queen also. You will forever remain beloved to my kingdom as Rama Gupta's kind and beautiful Queen."

"No, Chandra Gupta," said Dhruva Devi. "You have saved me from that dreadful King Shaka. You have given me a new life. It is you who deserve my love and loyalty."

"But how could I ever marry my own brother's wife?" Chandra Gupta asked. Dhruva Devi fell at the King's feet: "Please, I have always admired your kindness and affection for humanity. I have always adored your valour and heroism. It is you who saved your brother when he was about to lose his kingdom and it is you who saved my prestige and honour."

"Speak no further," Chandra Gupta said. "My sense of loyalty to my brother would never allow me to accept your proposal. What would my subjects think of me?"

"Where was your brother's loyalty to me when he was ready to give me away to that King Shaka? He did not value me at all," Dhruva Devi cried. "Only you valued me enough to fight for my freedom and honour."

Chandra Gupta remained silent.

She continued, "In no way am I trying to exploit you or your new position. Because of your divine qualities, I have always appreciated you. I want to be as divine and spiritual as you are. Divine love is the only reality. You have to marry me."

The King said, "Dhruva Devi, my heart is deeply moved by your words. You shall again be Queen."

At that moment the undivine minister who had always supported Rama Gupta against his brother rushed into the room: "You are fulfilling your father's wish. Your father wanted you to become King, but I opposed it. I wanted Rama Gupta to be King because of my weakness for him. He reminded me of my own son. Forgive me."

Chandra Gupta said, "My father was not only great and good, but he was also all forgiveness. I want to become like my father. Whether or not I have got his greatness or goodness, God alone knows. But I have prayed to God to give me the power of forgiveness, and this He has given me. That is why I am forgiving you.

"I also pray that God will forgive me for having killed my brother, for I did not do it intentionally. I would have allowed him to kill me had I known that he was my attacker. I always tried to make him happy. His happiness was my happiness. God gave me capacity and I want always to use this for a good, divine purpose. Alas, this capacity has caused so much trouble for me. My own brother wanted to destroy me. O God, capacity is a boon; again, capacity is a great problem."

Then the minister said, "You will rule the kingdom peacefully and gloriously. I could not help overhearing your conversation with Dhruva Devi. She loves you, and it is you who deserve her. You should marry her. This is what all your subjects want. They are all hoping that she will again be Queen."

"They shall get their wish, O Minister, and you shall get my forgiveness."

Dhruva Devi said, "And your father is finally getting his wish. His dream has become a reality, now that your greatness and goodness will rule the land."

GIM 51. *Bhudep Mukherjee's examination*[§]

One day an examination was being held in a college classroom. The most brilliant student in the class was Bhudep Mukherjee. Bhudep Mukherjee was deeply engrossed in writing his exam when all of a sudden his fountain pen slipped from his hand and dropped to the floor. His English professor, who was standing nearby, picked up the pen and gave it back to the student. Bhudep Mukherjee took it from the teacher and, without saying anything, started writing again.

The professor was a little surprised. "Why didn't you say 'Thank you' to me?" he asked. Bhudep Mukherjee remained silent.

"Why don't you answer?" the professor said. "You Indians have no courtesy?" The student still remained silent.

"This is what I have taught you over the years?" the professor asked. "It seems that you are not feeling well, or perhaps you have a difficult question that is occupying all your attention. Otherwise, you are always respectful."

The student said, "No, nothing is wrong with me, I am perfectly all right and the questions are not difficult at all. It is true that I was deeply absorbed in answering a question. But that is not the reason I did not answer you. Sir, you always taught us to do our duty. Whenever we get an opportunity to help someone or to serve someone, we should do it without being asked. Today, when my pen slipped from my hand and dropped, you got the opportunity to help me and serve me. So why do I have to thank you? If you expect my gratitude, then it is not real self-offering. So it is better to help the needy with no expectation. This is what you have taught us, and I am only obeying you. I have not done anything wrong. At the time of my need you helped me, and whenever you are in need I will definitely help you."

The professor's anger by this time had changed into joy and gratitude. He said to the student, "I am so proud of you. I am so proud of you. Indeed you are right. When you are in need, others should come and help and not ask any reward for it. If someone is in need, we should go immediately to help the person. And if we expect a 'Thank you' or gratitude, it is a mistake. It is our duty at every moment to help others and even to sacrifice our lives for others."

Bhudep Mukherjee eventually became a very, very great scholar. He was a great son of Mother Bengal who did much for the intellectual and social development of his nation.

GIM 52. *Tagore sings*[s]

There was once a little boy who was very beautiful to look at and very smart, with many talents. He was talented even at a tender age. His father was very rich and well-respected; he owned vast plots of land and had many, many servants. The little boy used to spend most of his time with the servants. He was the youngest in the family and they all adored him.

One day, the boy was singing a song that he had composed himself. The song expressed the idea that, "The eye cannot see You, although You are inside the eye. The heart cannot know You, although You are inside the heart." He was singing it most soulfully, and the tune was simply excellent.

The father heard him singing from another room and was deeply moved. He asked his servants to go and bring the little boy to him. Then the father said to his youngest son, "Can you sing the song for me again?"

The boy didn't often get the opportunity to come to his father, because the father was so great and very busy. He could not approach his father any time he wanted to. So although it was a great honour that his father had called him, he was also afraid of his father and he felt shy. The father said, "I am your father. Please don't feel shy. Just sing the song that you were singing before, my child."

The boy sang a few times and the father was so deeply moved that he entered into trance. When his trance ended, the father entered his office and wrote the boy a cheque for 500 rupees. In those days, 500 rupees for a child was really something. When he gave it to the boy he said, "In the past, the Mogul Emperors used to honour talented people with great gifts. Now the Mogul Emperors are no more. But your talent is so remarkable that I know you rightfully deserve honour from the king. Unfortunately there is no king here to honour you. But I am your father, and I am giving you 500 rupees."

The son was so excited and delighted. He ran with the cheque and showed it to his servants. The servants lifted him up into the air. They were so proud that their little hero had become such a great poet.

Indeed, this heroic soul became the poet of poets. He became India's greatest poet ever and won the Nobel Prize. Many people have got the Nobel Prize and many poets have been honoured, but in India he remains matchless. He composed about 1800 songs, many of which are sung all over India, including India's national anthem, *Jana Gana*. Truly, Rabindranath Tagore was a creative genius who excelled in every field of the arts. In the latter part of his life he even took up painting. As poet, singer and playwright, he won love and respect not only in India but all over the world. He remains in the vanguard of poets for his lyrics, songs, plays and stories. India's Tagore will eternally remain unique. In 1961, on his birthday, the whole world observed his centenary.

GIM 53. *The train journey*[8]

There was once a very great man who came from a very rich family. He was a great seeker, a seeker of the highest order, and to the whole of Bengal he was the very embodiment of truth. Countless people admired him, loved him and adored him, and felt he was a saint.

One day he took his youngest son with him on a train ride from Calcutta to Bombay. He bought a full-price ticket for himself and a half-price ticket for his son, who was eleven years old.

After the train had been going for some time, the ticket collector entered into their compartment and asked for their tickets. When he saw the half-price ticket for the boy, he was a little bit hesitant, for the boy was very tall for his age, and he looked much older than eleven years old. But the ticket collector didn't say anything. He just marked the ticket and left.

After two hours another ticket collector came. He also hesitated because he too thought that the boy was over twelve years old, since he was so tall and smart looking. But he didn't say anything either.

After some time, these two ticket collectors brought the station master to the man's compartment, and the station master asked to see the tickets. The station master was so ignorant. He did not realise that this man was well known for his greatness and goodness.

By this time the man was very mad. So many times these ticket people were bothering him! "All right, see the tickets!" he said angrily.

The station master said, "This boy is a minor? How old is he?"

The man said, "Eleven." The station master said, "No. You are telling me a lie."

The man, whom all of Bengal worshipped as the embodiment of truth, said to himself, "What will you do with these ignorant people? It is useless to argue with them." So he paid the difference in the fare to the station master, saying, "Take it!"

The station master gave him a full ticket for his son, and returned his change. When the station master gave the great man his few rupees of change, the man became so furious that he threw the money on the floor and it all scattered.

Then the station master felt very embarrassed. "What a scene I created for one ticket for a young boy and a haughty old man!" he said to himself.

Because of the commotion, many people came running to see what had happened. What they saw was the great sage and saint of Bengal, Devendranath Tagore, Tagore's father. And the young boy was Tagore himself.

GIM 54. *Ishwar Chandra Vidyasagar*[§]

There was once a very great man who was knowledge incarnate. He was a professor of English at a college and was very, very brilliant. His eyes were full of light and in almost every way he was an ideal man. But unfortunately, on the physical plane he was not so handsome. He was very short, and his head was very big in comparison with the rest of his body

One day, an Englishman of higher authority wanted to see this Bengali scholar, so he sent for him. When the Bengali scholar came to the Englishman's office, he was shocked. The Englishman had his feet on the table and was smoking profusely, and he began talking to the scholar with an air of contempt.

The Indian, who was a principal of a particular Sanskrit college, could not believe what he saw. He said to himself, "How can Englishmen behave so badly? They have no courtesy. They have no etiquette."

When the meeting was over, he came back home mad and furious. "I shall one day pay that Englishman back in his own coin," he said.

A few months later this same Englishman needed a favour from the Sanskrit professor. So he personally came to the professor's office and knocked at the door. "Can I come in?" he said. But the professor did not answer. Only he asked his servant to bring his hookah.

The servant prepared the hookah and brought it to the professor. The professor placed his feet on the table, with his sandals on (he never wore shoes) and started smoking the Indian hookah. Then he asked the servant to let the Englishman in.

When the Englishman came in, he was so mad. He said, "I am an Englishman and I hold such a high post. Yet you are showing me such disrespect! What's wrong with you?"

The professor said, "Nothing is wrong with me. Only I happen to be a good student. I always learn everything from my teacher. The other day you taught me to act like this and I have to show you that I have learned everything you taught me. If I don't show you that I have learned what you have taught me, then you may not like me."

The Englishman was shocked and, at the same time, illumined by the learned man's remarks. This learned man became the ocean of compassion, the ocean of knowledge, whom all Bengal worshipped and adored. His name was Ishwar Chandra Vidyasagar.

GIM 55. *The gardener*[§]

There was a great leader who was very, very simple. From his appearance nobody could tell that he was a great leader. Only people who were around him and knew him well, or those who were in the political world, could recognise who he was. Otherwise, from his outer appearance he could fool anyone, since he was not tall and there was nothing about him that showed that he was bright or commanded respect and admiration from people. He always wore very simple clothes, and he was all simplicity and all sincerity.

One day he was working in his garden, digging and planting and doing everything all by himself. He was wearing very, very simple gardening clothes. A few middle-aged men came up to him and said, "Can you tell us where the chief is?"

He said, "Yes, I can. Just wait. I will call him." Then he went into the house, washed his hands, put on a panjabi and dhoti and came out and stood in front of them.

They said, "You! You have come again. You didn't tell the chief that we are here? We wanted to see the chief and not you."

This time the gardener was a little serious. He said, "Well, the chief is here. I am the chief."

"You are the Prime Minister of India?"

"Yes, I am!" Some of them bowed down, some were shocked. Some felt miserable. "Oh, we thought you were just the gardener," they said.

The Prime Minister said, "I am so glad that you didn't recognise me as the Prime Minister of India because I don't want the world to know me by my appearance, but by my actions. I want to remain always simple, always humble."

He was the second Prime Minister of India, after Nehru. Lal Bahadur Shastri: simplicity incarnate and heart's magnanimity incarnate. Lal Bahadur Shastri was without a single enemy. His own people admired him and the opposition party also admired him equally for his heart's nobility and his life's simplicity and purity.

GIM 56. *The blessings of Acharya Prafulla Chandra Ray*[§]

There was a very, very great scientist who was also a great patriot. Everyone adored him. He lived a very simple, austere and spiritual life and remained unmarried. He had a very long beard and moustache, and was very lean and thin. He believed that well-educated young men should not just accept the work of clerks and other unimportant work. He felt they should not act like slaves but should do something with their lives if they were well-educated. He came to realise that money gave one the opportunity to do quite a few things in life.

"Money properly used is a blessing, but money badly used is a curse," he used to always say. "If one has money and uses it properly, then one will have a decent life. And from this decent life one can try to aspire. But if one is pinched with hunger all the time and suffers from poverty, then how can one do anything great and good?"

He always used to advise everyone, especially the Bengalis, to enter into business and to make money, and then to use the money to try to do something great and good for mankind.

Just because he was great, after getting their degree young people used to come to him to get a recommendation from him for jobs as clerks. But instead of a recommendation, with all love and concern he would give them a smart slap. "Go away from here," he would say. "I will recommend you to become somebody's clerk and assistant? I don't want that! I want you people to enter into business and use the money you make to lead a decent life. Then only will you get the opportunity to do the right thing. But if you misuse the money you make, you will destroy your life."

One day, when the great scientist was an elderly man, a young man approached him and asked him to say a few words in favour of him so he would get a clerical appointment. As he usually did, with all love, affection and concern the great scientist gave the young man a smart slap. Then he said, "You deserve it! I always tell you people to enter into business."

The young man said, "Yes, I want to enter into business, but I have no money."

Then the scientist said, "You want to enter into business? How much do you need? I will give it to you."

He said, "I need ten thousand rupees."

The scientist said, "Ten thousand rupees you need for a business? Absurd! You don't need that much. I am giving you three thousand rupees. You people are under the impression that if you have a large amount of money to invest, then only will you be able to make money. It is not true! It is not the money you invest, but your will power.

"I am giving you three thousand rupees. You don't have to return this money to me, only promise me that you will enter into business. If you enter into business, I will be very happy. With this money you will start and, I tell you, you will be successful. With all my blessings I am giving you this money."

The young man bowed to him and said, "This money I am taking as your blessing."

The old man said, "Yes, it is my blessing. But you have to try to be successful. And even if you are not successful, I will be very happy and proud of you just because you have tried."

This man was India's most famous scientist-pioneer, P.C. Ray. He received his Ph.D. from Edinburgh University and, as a teacher of chemical science, had many pupils who later became great world chemists. When once asked if he had any children, he responded with a list of seventy-three of his dearest and brightest students. Such was his love and dedication for those who took him as their teacher-father.

GIM 57. *The Brahmin and the old woman*[§]

One day a high-class Brahmin went to the Ganges for a dip. On that particular day he was supposed to go to court, and he was late. So he could not spend as much time as usual bathing in the Ganges.

After hurriedly taking a dip, he was on his way back home when all of a sudden he heard someone say, "Hello, hello, can you spare a moment?" It was an elderly woman.

The Brahmin said, "Yes."

The woman said, "Today my house priest could not come and there is nobody to conduct our house puja today. Without a Brahmin, how can my daily house puja be performed? You are a Brahmin, so will you do me a favour? Will you come and do the puja? Our house deity will be displeased if he is not worshipped today. And I never eat without worshipping our presiding deity. So please come."

So the Brahmin said to the old lady, "Yes, I am coming." And he followed her to her house.

The Brahmin was well-educated. He was a great scholar who knew Sanskrit and even the scriptures well — far better than the Brahmin who usually conducted her pujas. He did everything. It took him an hour or so.

After he was finished, the lady said to him, "Now I wish to reward you. I would like to give you something from the puja. I will give you a fee, and also I wish you to take some coconuts and bananas. Please take."

The Brahmin said, "No, no. I cannot take this."

"No, you have to take this," the old lady said. "You have done me a favour, so you have to take money from me. You have to take fruits from the puja."

But the man said, "No, I cannot do it. I am very grateful that I was able to help you, but I cannot accept any fee." Then the Brahmin ran away.

The Brahmin happened to be the judge of the Calcutta High Court. He was a great scholar, a great pandit and a very great judge of the High Court. His name was Sri Gurudas Banerjee. The lady didn't know who he was, but he himself knew who he was and what he was. Even though he held such a high post, he still regarded his duty as duty.

GIM 58. *Chitta Ranjan Das*[§]

There was once a great leader whose heart was larger than the largest. In law he was extremely successful and as a national leader he was also quite successful. His real name was kindness, affection and compassion. He was always for the poor and the miserable and he used to help people far beyond their need.

The tips he gave to the police, for example, were ten times the amount that they usually got from others.

"These policemen work so hard," he said. "Just because they wear Indian dhotis and garments, we don't value them. But if the same work were done by Englishmen with trousers on, we would have to give them much more."

One day a man in the Congress who worked for the great leader came up to him crying. The great man said, "Why are you crying?"

He said, "I stay at your house, but just because I come from the lowest class, everyone goes away from me. I am given my food at the place where the dogs and the chickens stay. It is so dirty and filthy there. One of your servants brings my food and I eat there as if I were another dog or another chicken. Please do something for me."

Because of his low class, society did not permit him to sit with the members of the family. But still the great man felt very sad. He said to his wife, "All right, granted he cannot sit and eat with us, but can you not at least give him a nice place to eat? Why does he have to eat with the dogs and chickens? Can he not be given a better place?"

His wife said, "Yes, he should be given a better place. I shall see to it."

Although the wife told the servant to take his food to a nice place, a few days later the servant was careless and took the food to the same place. So once more the Congress worker came to the great man, crying and crying: "They have given me the food there again, just because I come of a low class. I am staying with you because of your affection and love for me. Otherwise, I would not stay. This kind of treatment I hate. Whenever your Brahmin cooks see me, they run away. They show tremendous contempt for me and literally hate me. Am I not a human being?"

The great leader felt miserable, and he burst into tears. He called his wife and said, "From now on this young man will eat not only inside the house, but actually in my room where I eat. He has to eat in my room whenever I am eating. If I happen to be elsewhere and it is time for him to eat, he has to eat in my room. I make it a law."

This great man was Chitta Ranjan Das. He was known as the most beloved friend of Mother Bengal. It was he who saved Sri Aurobindo from jail. When he died, Tagore said, "You came into the world with an immortal heart and you left it here on your way back."

GIM 59. *Sankaracharya becomes a sannyasi*[§]

There was once a great Sanskrit scholar who was also a matchless philosopher. When he was quite young he said to his mother, "Mother, I don't like this world. This world is not good. Here it is all bondage and illusion. I want to give up this world. I want to accept *sannyas*, renunciation."

The mother burst into tears, "My son, how can you accept *sannyas*? You know the entire creation is God's. How can you go out of God's creation? No, no, you cannot accept *sannyas*. You have to be with me. Without you I will not be able to live on earth. My whole life will be miserable and unbearable. Your absence will break my heart. I cannot allow you to accept *sannyas*."

The young man remained silent. He could not accept the life of a *sannyasi* without his mother's permission. According to the Scriptures, one has to take permission from one's parents or guardians. Then only will *sannyas* bear fruit. So he waited for his mother's permission devotedly, soulfully and helplessly.

One day he went swimming in a nearby river and there he was caught by a crocodile. He started screaming and his mother came running.

The crocodile said, "If you want to remain in ignorance, then I will eat you up, but if you don't want to remain in ignorance, then I will let you go."

Then the son said, "Mother this is the time to grant me my boon. If you don't allow me my wish, then the crocodile will kill me."

"I will give you my permission to accept *sannyas* if you feel that the crocodile will free you," the mother said.

Immediately the crocodile let him go, and he came up to his mother and said, "Now, Mother, you have to keep your promise!"

The mother said, "I will keep my promise, but my heart will break when you leave me. To lose you is to lose my all."

He said, "Mother, you will not lose me. Whenever you want me just think of me and meditate on me, and I shall come to you. Normally one does not see one's family for ten or twelve years after one has accepted *sannyas*. But in my case, whenever you want I will come. But I will not accept the worldly life and I will not get married. I will follow only the path of *sannyas*."

The mother blessed the son and said, "Go, go! You want to please God. Whether it is in God's Way or your own way, I do not know. But you do want to please God; that much I know. So I will be happy, because I know you are going for God. You feel He should be realised in a specific way. I won't stand in your way; I give you my full permission. But your absence will kill me. Now go. Go and be satisfied, for I am your dearest and you are my dearest. In your satisfaction I also will be satisfied."

The boy fell at his mother's feet for the last time and took her blessings. Then he left home.

This young man was none other than India's Sankaracharya, the peerless philosopher who introduced our Advaita philosophy, "One without a second."

GIM 60. *Netaji Subhas Chandra Bose and the hooligan chief*[5]

There was once a great patriot who conquered everyone's heart in India, especially the Bengalis. He was known as the leader of great leaders. When he was in college he was a most brilliant student. He had tremendous fondness for spiritual and religious people. Whenever he could be of any help to the poor, the sick or the needy, he would be the first person to go there.

Once when he was a young man, cholera broke out in Calcutta and all the rich people left the city. When the epidemic broke out, there was no medical treatment for the poor, so he used to go to the section of town where the very poor lived and treat them.

Now, in that part of town there were many hooligans. They used to threaten him and say, "Don't come to our section and don't bother us. We don't want to see you. You are well-educated and come from a rich family, whereas we are very poor and uneducated. We don't want you here." But although the hooligans didn't want him to come and help the poor, he didn't care. He said, "Do whatever you want. If you want to kill me, kill me. I have come into the world to help the poor and sickly. I shall continue coming with my money and my food to try to help as much as I can."

One day the only son of the leader of the hooligans was attacked by cholera. So the young man went to his house and started caring for the son, feeding him and giving him medical treatment. The hooligan leader was so moved! "I threatened you and warned you not to come to this area, and now when my own son is attacked by cholera you come to help him. You are so brave."

The young man said, "It is not a matter of bravery; it is my necessity. I see God in everybody. When I see somebody is suffering, when I see another human being in need, I feel it is my duty to help him. One must help one's brother when he is in need."

The hooligan chief bowed down to the young man and said, "You are not a human being. You are Divinity Incarnate."

This great leader and great patriot, this matchless leader and matchless patriot, was none other than Netaji Subhas Chandra Bose. The very mention of his name brings such a divine emotional feeling into the consciousness of India!

GIM 41. *(p. 249)* 13 January 1979
GIM 42. *(p. 251)* 13 January 1979
GIM 43. *(p. 253)* 13 January 1979
GIM 44. *(p. 255)* 14 January 1979
GIM 45. *(p. 257)* 14 January 1979
GIM 46. *(p. 259)* 14 January 1979
GIM 47. *(p. 262)* 14 January 1979
GIM 48. *(p. 264)* 14 January 1979
GIM 49. *(p. 266)* 14 January 1979
GIM 50. *(p. 268)* 14 January 1979
GIM 51. *(p. 270)* 15 January 1979
GIM 52. *(p. 272)* 15 January 1979
GIM 53. *(p. 273)* 15 January 1979
GIM 54. *(p. 275)* 15 January 1979
GIM 55. *(p. 276)* 15 January 1979
GIM 56. *(p. 277)* 15 January 1979
GIM 57. *(p. 279)* 15 January 1979
GIM 58. *(p. 280)* 15 January 1979
GIM 59. *(p. 282)* 16 January 1979
GIM 60. *(p. 284)* 15 January 1979

GREAT INDIAN MEALS:
DIVINELY DELICIOUS AND
SUPREMELY NOURISHING

BOOK 4

There was a great scientist named Dr. Satyendranath Bose. His was a truly immortal name in the scientific world, not only in India but also in various other countries as well. Some people are great, but they may not have enough goodness. In his case, however, he was not only great but also extremely good, kind and humble. His heart was the heart of a little child. He had a special fondness for children and used to play many games with them. One game that he liked particularly and used to play with them quite often was *Karam*. He himself was a fine player and, though he had distinguished himself as an eminent scientist, he used to enjoy playing with the children and they, for their part, accepted him as their hero.

Once he happened to be playing *Karam* with some children, and he was deeply absorbed in the game. A middle-aged man came by and for a long time was watching the game. After some time the scientist said to him, "What can I do for you?" The man replied, "I will be so grateful if you will preside over a meeting we are holding at our school. Tomorrow there will be a special meeting at our school, and I will be so grateful if you can be there to preside."

Very politely the scientist responded, "No, I cannot. I am sorry. Please find somebody else."

But again the visitor urged, "Oh, we need you badly. There is nobody as great as you are. We shall be deeply honoured if you come and preside over the meeting."

With utmost politeness the scientist repeated, "I cannot come tomorrow at that hour because I am supposed to play with my friends here. Nothing gives me greater joy than to play with children. I have presided over hundreds and hundreds of meetings, and there I don't get any joy.

"I want joy, you want joy, everybody wants joy. To me, this *Karam* is infinitely more meaningful than the opportunity you are giving me to preside over a meeting, for I know that intellectual people and argumentative people will come to that meeting, and they will bring their reasoning minds. I am fed up with the reasoning mind. I want only the heart, the sincere and pure heart, the oneness-heart. I get that kind of heart here, with my little friends.

"I have promised them that tomorrow I shall play with them, and I shall definitely do it. I only want to remain in the heart. I have played my role in the mind and now I am playing the role of my heart. Satisfaction is there, only there. Peace is there, only there."

GIM 62. *An ocean of kindness* [§]

Some people may be rich, but they may not give money to others. Some rich people, on the other hand, do give money to the poor and needy.

Kaji Mohammad Maharshin was a distinguished and highly learned man. At the same time he had a heart that cried all the time for the poor, the destitute and the needy. He was great, very great. Yet greatness itself was not enough for him. He became the living embodiment of goodness as well. Every night he used to go out and help the poverty stricken.

One particular winter night he saw a beggar woman in the street with her children. They had neither food nor clothing. There was nothing to protect them from the heavy rain, and they were crying bitterly. He became very sad and asked them whether they had eaten anything. They replied, "No, father. For the last three days we have had nothing."

Upon hearing this he felt extremely miserable and immediately offered them some money. "I am giving you money, true.

But tonight, at this hour, it will be so difficult for you to get food even with this money. So this money you can use tomorrow during the day. Tonight, I shall bring some food to you." Then he went out into the rain and walked alone for about two miles to where he was able to buy food from a store. He then offered this food to the mother.

This was a regular occurrence for the kind man. He opened himself wholeheartedly to the needs of the poor and helped them unreservedly. Each night he would walk along different streets of the city in order to find poor people to whom he might give money and other necessary help. During the day he had no time, because he worked extremely hard for his living. But in the evening he would turn to his own special work, which was service to mankind. In him the poor people of India found an ocean of kindness. His heart's magnanimity touched the whole of Bengal.

GIM 63. *Raja Rammohan Ray: emancipator of women*[§]

One day, a middle-aged man saw a group of people running after a young and beautiful girl. The people were playing on Indian drums, and they kept chasing the girl. The girl was running with all her might.

This middle-aged man happened to be one of India's pioneer pathfinders of the modern age. A great philanthropist and a very learned man, he had studied Eastern philosophy very thoroughly and was conversant in many languages. As his learning was varied and profound, even so his achievements were vast and wonderful. Right from his adolescence, he had sacrificed his life to bring to the fore the true gems of India's civilisation and to remove the obstacles that impeded her progress within and without. So when this great soul saw the girl running away, he said, "What is wrong? What is wrong? Why is she running and why are you following after her?"

A few of the people stopped to answer him. "Look, her husband has died. As you know, when the husband dies it is customary for the wife to jump into the burning pyre. This girl is afraid of death, but if she does not burn herself it will be a great evil, according to our custom. The wife has to sacrifice her life, but she does not want to. So we have to force her. We are running to catch her and then we shall throw her onto the pyre."

"Why, why, why?" said the man.

The people who were chasing her answered, "This is ultimately for her good. The Scriptures say that if the wife dies for the husband, her glory will increase."

At this the man said, "Forget about that kind of Scripture. If she does not feel love for her husband, why should she have to die? If she does not care for her husband and if she wants to live on earth to do good things for mankind, or if she feels that her own life is precious to her, then it is clearly wrong for her to sacrifice her life."

"There is no question of feeling in this case," the people insisted. "It is the law. She has to do it."

But the man was the spirit of freedom incarnate and he confronted the people, saying, "Wait! I will not allow you."

"Who are you?" they said. "Do you think you can stand against us?"

"All right," the man said, "take this girl. I am deeply sorry, but I am helpless to prevent you. One day, however, I shall succeed. One day I shall stop this evil practice of *sati*. If the wife has to die for the husband, why doesn't the husband have to sacrifice his life when the wife dies? Why does it not work both ways? This foolish and degrading practice I shall stop. I shall take help from the British Government and put an end to it. This is not mere stupidity; it is infinitely worse. It is a crime against the soul! If women don't want to die after their husbands have died, if they don't want to sacrifice their precious lives, then why should they? Each one is responsible to God for his or her own action, for his or her own life and death, so I don't think it is at all advisable for this practice to be forced on people. I shall stop it, I shall stop it!"

He pleaded with the British Government and since he was well known in British circles and greatly admired for his goodness, the British Government inclined to his point of view. They also found this practice absurd. So they passed a law banning *sati*.

Many people objected to this order. They thought that if people did not practice *sati* anymore, then God would be displeased. But again, there were countless millions of people who thought that this man had done the right thing. If a girl really loves her husband, she does not necessarily have to burn herself. If their oneness was very strong, she can pray to God to allow her to join her husband in the other world. And if her prayer is soulful, God will definitely listen to her prayer. But if the wife did not like the husband or hated him, then it is stupidity for her to burn herself just because it is the Indian practice.

The name of this great father of regenerate India was Raja Rammohan Ray. He was a great philosopher, a great worker, a great server, a great patriot, a great dreamer and a great fulfiller of his dream.

GIM 64. *The sannyasi in America*[§]

A great Indian hero, a great *sannyasi*, once came to America to preach Vedanta philosophy and also to bring India's message to that nation. After giving a special talk at a great religious gathering in Chicago, he became famous overnight.

This lofty spiritual figure had many friends and admirers. One day, some of these friends and admirers came to his house and asked him many questions about Vedanta and Indian philosophy and spirituality. They were very moved by his answers to their questions. By the time they departed, it was around midnight.

All of a sudden the man thought of India, his poor India, especially Mother Bengal. He said to himself, "Now I am going to bed. But there are thousands and thousands of people without beds, who will be lying in the street, poverty-stricken, tonight. Here I have got a cosy and most comfortable bed. But once upon a time, I was a sannyasi. Even now I am a sannyasi. I used to roam in the street with no food, nothing. Still, from time to time even today I have no food or clothes. I am in a destitute condition.

"Again, God blesses me with riches and my generous friends keep me at their homes. Right now some friends of mine have given me this beautiful apartment. Indeed, I am in great luxury. In a few minutes, I will go to sleep in a most comfortable bed. And yet so many of my fellow brothers and sisters in Bengal will be lying in the street.

"My heart bleeds for them. I have still not fulfilled my task. I have to help my poor Indian brothers. I have to save their lives, I have to illumine them, I have to awaken their consciousness. There is so much to do, so much to do! Alas, what am I doing here? Anyway, I need rest, but I will not sleep on the couch. I will sleep on the floor."

So he took off his turban and placed it on the floor, and passed the night lying down on his long turban. Early the following morning, when the owner of the apartment, who was his friend, came to invite him to breakfast, he saw this great Indian saint, this great Indian hero, lying on the floor. He said, "What is the matter?"

The Indian replied, "Thousands and thousands of my brothers and sisters spend the night in the streets. So how can I dream of staying the night in this most comfortable bed? I can't, I can't, unless and until I have done something for them. It is my bounden duty to serve God in the poor and the needy. So the life of comfort is not for me. The life of selfless service, the life of dedicated, devoted service, is for me. Service is my goal, service is my perfection in life."

This great Indian sannyasi was Swami Vivekananda. He was the pioneer sannyasi who came with India's age-old message of Vedanta to the West. His name inspired millions of Americans to lead a better life, a higher and more illumining life — to lead, in a sense, the God-life. Swami Vivekananda was Ramakrishna's peerless disciple-son.

GIM 65. *A citadel of strength*[§]

There was a time when hooligans used to torture the people of Bengal like anything. What they did was to inform the residents of certain houses that they were going to rob them, and then they did in fact come and rob them. They used to molest the women, torture the maids, steal what money they could and cause tremendous damage. As a consequence, many rich people left the city, while many others remained in a state of constant anxiety.

One day, the hooligans informed a particular house that they were going to come and plunder. The maids of the house were all frightened to death. Some of them immediately decided to leave the house, whereas others could not make up their minds. Finally, they all came to the decision that they would leave and allow the hooligans to take whatever they wanted. But at that moment, a young boy in the family, who was only twelve years old, said, "No! I shall not go. You can go. They will not be able to take anything, I assure you."

His uncle was thoroughly surprised. He exclaimed, "Oh, so you are the greatest hero! You will stay and they will kill you!"

The boy said, "I will not be killed. But you go. I have some older friends who are experts in stick arts and they can fight the hooligans."

The uncle said, "Don't be a fool."

"No, uncle," the boy pleaded, "give me a chance. I will not be harmed and, I assure you, nothing shall be stolen."

"All right, my child, then you do it," replied the uncle.

So the boy went and brought his friends, who knew the art of self-defence as well as how to attack people with their sticks.

When the hooligans came, there was a terrible fight. Many people were severely injured, but nobody was killed. In the end the hooligans were badly defeated, all because of the tremendous inner strength that this young boy possessed.

Eventually this young boy became the literary emperor of Bengal: Bankim Chandra Chatterji. His remarkable courage and manliness were allied with a patriotic fervour, a seer-vision and an inspiration-flood that aroused the great sub-continent of India. It was he who composed India's national song, *Bande Mataram,* which came from his famous novel *Ananda Math.*

Bankim Chandra demands our candid admiration. As a child, he mastered the Bengali alphabet at one sitting and, as he grew older, he revealed his true genius as a great patriot and a great lover of Mother India and of mankind.

GIM 66. *Bankim Chandra's only medicine*[§]

After he crossed the barrier of fifty, Bankim Chandra Chatterji did not remain well. He wanted to write quite a few books but, alas, his health was failing rapidly. The members of his family became alarmed that he was not taking the medicine that his doctor had prescribed for him.

One day, the doctor came to him and said, "What can I do? You don't take the medicine I give you. Do you not want to live? So many people will cry and miss you if you die. You are such a great man, the hero-leader of Bengal. Now, if you don't take medicine, how will they fare? How will they live on earth? You are the father of the nation, and if you leave, many will feel fatherless. Granted, you have a frail constitution, but in that frail constitution India has seen a reservoir of stupendous possibility materialised."

Bankim Chandra said, "Who said I don't take medicine?"

"Where is your medicine? Please show me," said the doctor.

Bankim Chandra picked up a copy of the Bhagavad-Gita from the table and showed it to the doctor. "This is my medicine, this is my only medicine. Your medicine may cure my body, but this will cure my body, vital, mind, heart and soul. This medicine has the message of Immortality. This medicine will make me immortal and there is no other medicine that can do that. So I must take only this medicine."

The doctor remained silent.

GIM 67. *Sri Ramakrishna and Bankim Chandra*§

Sri Ramakrishna and Bankim Chandra met with each other a few times and they liked each other very much. Bankim's name has two meanings. It means "the brightest side of the moon" and, at the same time, it means "a little bent." Sri Ramakrishna used to enjoy jokes with him and Bankim Chandra also used to cut jokes. One day, Sri Ramakrishna said to Bankim, "Bankim! What is it that has bent you?"

"Ah, Thakur, don't you know what has bent me? It is the kick of the Englishman's shoe!" Bankim replied.

Ramakrishna laughed and laughed, and everybody around also laughed. The reason is that, in those days, Englishmen used to torture the Indians like anything, and Bankim Chandra was a great lover of India. He constantly protested against English rule and wrote many patriotic novels. His novels are extremely inspiring, energising, illumining and fulfilling. He was a matchless novelist and also a man of indomitable will. The literary people of Bengal all bowed to him with their heart's devotion and life's gratitude.

His song *Bande Mataram* was the mantric incantation-fire of Mother India. It was the battle cry of freedom-fighters. Thousands of people sacrificed their lives while singing this song. To them, it was not a mere sound, but a living force; not words, but a fiery inspiration; nay, the vision of an apocalypse. Thousands and thousands of people received inspiration from this source of patriotism. Many people had to go to jail just because they sang this particular song, and all of them went happily and cheerfully. It was not an ordinary song but the mantra of mantras, which inspired them to fight against the English.

GIM 68. *No self-respect, no progress*[§]

Bankim Chandra was always for justice and self-respect. He said, "If there is no justice, the world will collapse; and if there is no self-respect, no one will make any progress."

The wild arrogance of the British could never frighten Bankim Chandra. When he served as a deputy-magistrate, his superior was an Englishman named Monroe. Monroe always demanded a disproportionate amount of respect, not only in the office but also elsewhere, even in the street. But Bankim used to tell him that he might be superior in the office, but he was not superior elsewhere.

"While in the office, I will show you respect and call you my superior. But if I see you elsewhere, then you are simply another human being like me. I cannot show you great respect, for I know who you are and what I am. Moreover, I know what I value. I appreciate inner strength and inner values. And in those things I far surpass you."

But the arrogant Commissioner would not listen to this. One day, Bankim Chandra happened to meet Monroe in the Eden Garden in Calcutta. He neither said hello to him nor showed him any respect. The following day, Monroe came to the office and began shouting at Bankim Chandra and berating him like anything.

In response, Bankim Chandra said, "I told you before. Here in the office, I will show you respect. Here you are my superior. But in the street, in the garden, I will have nothing to do with you English."

At this, Monroe grew really furious: "All right, I am transferring you," he shouted.

Bankim replied calmly, "So much the better. You don't like me and I don't like you. You don't need me and I don't need you.

You shall be satisfied by transferring me and I shall be satisfied by remaining away from you."

The British Commissioner remained silent, but he transferred Bankim Chandra nonetheless.

GIM 69. *Two genius friends*[§]

Even as a child, Satyen Bose was remarkable. Once he got 110 out of 100 in mathematics. Some of the students laughed; even some of the parents laughed. "How can someone get 110 out of 100?" they asked.

But Bose's teacher defended himself. He said, "In the examination this boy solved the mathematical problem in various ways. I am his teacher, yet I could only solve it in one way. But he has solved it in three ways. If he does not deserve 110 out of 100, then who does deserve it? I am his teacher, but I have learned from him."

At that time Satyen was only eleven years old. When he grew up and entered the university, he was so happy to have Jagadish Chandra Bose and Prafulla Chandra Ray, two very well-known Indian scientists, as his teachers. J. C. Bose taught him physics and Prafulla Ray taught him chemistry.

Satyen's guru was Einstein. Once, when he was teaching at Dacca University, he wrote an article on physics which he sent to Einstein. Einstein was so deeply impressed that he translated it into German. The University of Calcutta and other universities were so pleased to hear this that they sent Satyen to various places to gather more scientific knowledge. He went to work with Einstein and other great German scientists.

It happened that the position of head Professor of Science fell vacant at Calcutta University, so Satyen's friends asked him to apply for it.

But Satyen said, "I am not a Professor and I don't have a doctorate. They will never give me this."

His friends said, "Well, you don't need those qualifications. You have more knowledge than most of the scientists."

But still Satyen hesitated. "No, I can't ask for it."

Then his friends said, "Well, go and ask Einstein. Please ask him. Then we shall see. If Einstein puts in a few words for you, definitely you will get the job."

"How can I exploit his affection and love?" Satyen replied. "He appreciates me and loves me. Is this the time for me to take advantage of him? No! I won't take that course!"

His friends urged him further: "Go and ask, go and ask. It will help you and also it will help your Motherland."

At last, with tremendous hesitation, Satyen went to Einstein and explained the situation, concluding, "This is what my friends told me to do. Also I am a little tempted myself. Now, what will you do?"

Einstein immediately picked up his pen and wrote, "Can there be any equal to Satyen Bose? He deserves that post. Please give him the post if you can."

When the university authorities saw Einstein's letter they were so deeply moved that they did give Satyen the post. Then Satyen wrote another article on physics and sent it to Einstein. Einstein appreciated it so greatly that he translated it into German also. Satyen then wrote a further article, which he actually dedicated to Einstein. He thought of giving it to him personally and was ready to come to visit him when Einstein suddenly died. Einstein's death was a terrible shock to Satyen.

The scientific world remembers this immortal friendship in a most significant way. Satyen once wrote something which Einstein improved upon. Thereafter, it was known as "Bose-Einstein statistics."

GIM 70. *Satyen Bose solves the problem*[§]

Once a great scientist and well-known lecturer by the name of Niels Bohr was delivering a lecture on science to students at Calcutta University. Professor Satyen Bose was presiding at the lecture and he gave the speaker a glowing introduction. Then, to the students' wide surprise, Satyen Bose sat down and proceeded to close his eyes, and he appeared to fall asleep.

Niels Bohr's talk was extremely brilliant and everyone found it deeply interesting and illumining. Unfortunately, at a certain stage of the lecture, the visiting scientist found it extremely difficult to explain a particular point. Again and again he tried to solve the problem, rewriting it on the blackboard several times, but he could not solve it. Finally Bohr stopped and turned to Bose: "If Professor Bose helps me, I will be very grateful to him."

Professor Bose still had his eyes closed and the students thought that the Professor was sleeping, so they burst into laughter. Bohr asked them, "Why are you laughing?"

Most of the students hesitated, but one young man said, "We are laughing because it seems that Professor Bose has been asleep the whole time."

Upon hearing this, Professor Bose opened his eyes and said to the students: "Perhaps you are right. Now, what is the problem, O lecturer?"

Niels Bohr told him he was in trouble and asked for help. On hearing the nature of the problem Professor Bose said, "Ah! Is it a problem?" In a minute he solved it, to everybody's utter astonishment. Then he sat down and closed his eyes and said, "Yes, now I am going back to sleep once again."

The student who had accused Professor Bose of sleeping said, "Forgive me, Professor, it seems that your sleep world is more illumined than our wisdom world!"

Professor Bose kept his eyes closed for the rest of the lecture.

GIM 71. *Satyen Bose wants to resign*[§]

The eminent scientist and professor Satyen Bose was dearly loved by his students at Calcutta University and indeed by everyone, young and old. In Satyen Bose everyone found not only the wisdom of the mind, but also the love and affection of the heart. Bose was not only fond of children; he was also fond of animals, especially cats. In the evening of his life he used to spend a large amount of time playing with his cats. This unusual hobby only endeared him more to his students and friends. They were so delighted that such a great and eminent scientist was so fond of cats!

Once his students at the University wanted to postpone a certain examination. They felt that since Bose was so affectionate and kind to them, they could easily get the professor to delay it. But Bose told them, "No. Give me some valid reasons at least."

The students admitted, "We have no valid reasons; only we were not able to prepare for this examination."

"That is not a valid reason," said Bose. "You had enough time. Was there any special problem?"

"There was no real problem," said the students, "except that we fooled around and then we found that time had become very short."

Bose remained firm in his decision. "I am sorry. I will not postpone the examination. How can such a great university operate in this way? It is impossible."

Some of the students became angry and said: "You have to give us an extension of time; otherwise, we shall go on a hunger strike."

Bose finally said, "All right, here is the only solution that will please me. I cannot postpone the examination. I will simply resign."

On hearing this the students became very alarmed. "We are so fond of you," they cried. "We shall never allow you to resign, Baba. We shall study in the time that is left and if we do not secure high marks, we will know that this is what we deserve. But we can't bear for you to leave us. We need your affection, we need your blessings."

In this way Bose taught his students the power of conviction and determination, and the necessity for more sincere and serious attention to their studies.

GIM 72. *Satyen Bose and the Bengal Tiger*[§]

Ashutosh Mukherji was India's very, very great son and also Bengal's devoted child. Because of his heroism, Ashutosh was known as the "Bengal Tiger," and he did many brave and courageous things for his Mother India. As the head of Calcutta University, Ashutosh sacrificed his all so that the University could stand on the same footing as the highest ranking schools in the country.

Once, he wished a particular question to appear for three consecutive years on the final examination for one of the science courses. To please him, the professors posed the question, but not one student was able to answer it correctly.

After the third year Ashutosh asked to review the examination papers himself. Then he called all the professors into his office and said, "Why is it that nobody can answer this question? Do you not teach your students well?"

All the professors remained silent; either they could not or did not dare to answer the president's question. But Satyen Bose stood up and said, "What can we do? It is the question itself that is causing the problem. How can our students answer it when the question is not correct?"

Then Satyen Bose demonstrated to Ashutosh what was wrong with the question. The other professors were embarrassed and afraid that Ashutosh Mukherji would be angry with Bose. But instead, the president appreciated and admired him like anything: "Oh, I am so glad that you have found the mistake. I need brave people. I need correction from every side. Then only can Calcutta University remain in the vanguard of India's top-ranking universities. You are very great; again, you are very good. I bless you, for you are truly a great son of our Mother Bengal."

GIM 73. *Satyen Bose and the biographer*[§]

Once a young man came up to Satyen Bose and said, "Please, please, I want to write your biography."

Bose replied, "My biography? No, I am not a great man and I will never be a great man. So the answer is no, no, no!"

But the young man persisted: "This is the sign of your greatness. He who is truly great will never declare so to the world. His life is great, but his goodness covers his greatness. In your case, your goodness has far surpassed your greatness. But we want your greatness also to be appreciated, for if people do not show proper admiration for one who is really great, then how can they themselves ever become great? Your goodness is beyond our comprehension, but we treasure your goodness in the depths of our gratitude-hearts."

"Stop, stop!" Bose cried out. "How am I going to assimilate your Himalayan appreciation? For God's sake, or at least for my sake, don't waste your precious time writing my biography. Do something which will be of great help to you and also to Mother India. Otherwise, you will be wasting your time. Besides, I don't deserve to be honoured in this way."

The young man interrupted him, "Please, how can anyone judge his own importance in the eyes and hearts of his country-men? India loves you, Bengal loves you. It will be of great help not only to India but to the entire world if your great and good deeds are captured forever in a biography."

But Bose just shook his head, "I am not great enough or good enough to have a biography written about me. Please, don't waste your precious time, my boy. Do something else which will bring glory to Mother India."

The young man was deeply moved. "Your words have inspired and illumined me, and I shall indeed strive to follow in your footsteps and serve Mother India in a way that will be worthy of your life. But still, I shall cherish the hope that one day you will change your mind and allow me to write your biography, so that others may receive this same unparalleled inspiration and aspiration from your life and work."

GIM 74. *Depend only on God's Will*[5]

There was once a great spiritual Master who used to all the time tell his disciples, "Always depend on God's Will, always have complete faith in God's Will. Let God's Will be done." This was his motto.

One night he was about to go to sleep when he saw a snake near his bed. He said, "If I call my disciples they will come and immediately kill you. Again, if I do nothing, then you may kill me. Since I do not want you to be killed, the best thing is for me to leave the matter in God's Hands. If my time has come, then naturally you will kill me. If my time has not come, you will leave of your own accord."

The following day when one of the Master's attendants came in to see the Master, he saw the snake and was simply shocked: "Perhaps the snake stayed near the Master's bed throughout the night," he said.

The Master said, "Yes. He remained here all night."

The attendant asked, "Then how is it that you didn't call us?"

"Shall I depend on you, you weaklings," the Master asked, "or shall I depend on the Will of the Almighty, my Beloved Supreme? I depended on the Beloved Supreme, and He wanted me to stay on earth. Therefore, the snake did not bite me."

"But what is the snake doing here now?" asked the attendant.

"Call the others. Let all the disciples see the snake," the Master said. "The snake remains here to show human beings that when one has faith in God, God takes care of that person. I had perfect faith in God's dispensation; therefore, the snake did not bite me. It is through the snake that God is giving you people a lesson. Have perfect faith in the Master, have perfect faith in God. Then, no ignorance can touch you. On the one hand, the snake symbolises ignorance. On the other hand, it is carrying the message of the Supreme. If one has faith in the Will of the Supreme, one knows that whatever happens is for the best."

GIM 75. *Replace desire with aspiration*[§]

One day a disciple came up to his Master and said, "Master, this mind is horrible, horrible, horrible. I can't take it anymore. It is all meanness, jealousy, hypocrisy and lower vital thoughts."

The Master said, "My son, why do you speak ill of your mind? The mind is not bad; it is only that desire is entering into your mind and agitating it. The mind is not torturing you; it is you who are torturing the mind. Desire comes and wants to play with the mind or strike the mind to get some sound from it. Therefore, the mind starts defending itself and tries to kill you. A snake usually remains peaceful, but if you go and bite the snake, then naturally the snake will come and bite you or kill you. Very rarely will the snake bother you otherwise. So do not blame the mind. Blame your desire that strikes the mind."

The disciple said, "Then how can I get rid of desire?"

The Master said, "Desire has to be replaced, and this is possible only through aspiration. Empty the vessel of desire and fill it with aspiration. It is like emptying a vessel of dirty, filthy water and filling it with clean, pure water."

"How can I do that, Master?" asked the disciple.

The Master answered, "You can do it only by seeing what happens to those who have not emptied their vessels. They suffer unbearably, beyond their imagination. And those who empty desire-ignorance from their inner vessel and fill the vessel with aspiration-wisdom not only make themselves happy, but also make the Beloved Supreme happy. Not only are they fulfilled, but God Himself is fulfilled in and through them.

"So do not blame the mind. Blame desire that comes to torture the mind. Truth to tell, blaming desire is also not the correct way. One should bring into one's system something that will slowly, steadily and unerringly remove desire-life and replace it with its own reality. And that is aspiration. Replace desire with aspiration. Then you will have a heart of illumination and a life of perfection."

GIM 76. *The life of action*[§]

One day, a young man came to his Master with a problem. He had to make a decision, but he was not sure which course to take, and he was all the time changing his mind. "What should I do, Master?" he asked.

The Master said, "This moment you want to do something and the next moment you don't want to do that very thing. But I wish to tell you that by doing a particular thing or not doing it you are not going to solve your problems. If you say that you won't do something, you are creating problems for yourself; and if you say that you will do it, you are again creating problems for yourself."

The disciple asked, "Then what should I do? Either I have to do a particular thing or not do that thing."

The Master replied, "If you are doing something, then feel that God is doing it in and through you. If you decide not to do something, then feel that it is God who is not doing that thing. Always feel that, while you are going forward, God is working in and through you, and while you are going backward, He is also doing the same."

"But Master," the disciple said, "sometimes when I do something, I feel that instead of going forward and upward, I am going backward and downward. And since I don't know what is the right thing to do, I don't do anything."

The Master said, "You have to feel that you are like a carpenter's saw. When it goes forward, it cuts; and when it returns to the starting point, again it cuts. In your spiritual life also, when you go upward, feel that you are going up to realise God; and when you come down, feel that you are coming down to manifest God. At every moment feel that you are standing in front of a tree. When you climb up, feel that you are going to realise; and when you climb down, feel that you are going to manifest. So whether you are going up or going down, you are always acting.

"But you have to know if it is the Will of God for you to go up or down. And even if you do not know what is the Will of God, it is better that you act than not act, for action is infinitely superior to non-action. If you act, you will get the capacity for more action. If you do something wrong today, then tomorrow or the day after tomorrow you will have the capacity to do the right thing. But if you don't act at all because you are afraid of making a mistake, then you won't do anything either today, tomorrow or the day after tomorrow, and you will lose the strength ever to act.

"So if you don't know what is right, the second best thing is to use your inspiration and aspiration to do what you feel is best. If it is not the right thing, God will sympathise with you and show His Compassion because you tried, although you didn't know what the right thing was. Just because you tried to do the right thing according to your own understanding, God will give you more opportunity and more capacity to do the right thing eventually.

"So, my son, always act! The life of action is infinitely better than the life of non-action. You may not walk along the right road, but if you do not want to walk along any road at all, what can God do? My theory is to be like a carpenter's saw, going forward and backward. Go forward to realise and come back to manifest. Climb up the tree, get the fruits and bring them down to share with fellow seekers. That is the right way to please God in God's own Way."

GIM 77. *The King's favour*[§]

One day the ruler of the kingdom came to his spiritual Master and said, "Master, you have been helping me in my spiritual life unreservedly. May I do something for you?"

The Master said, "I have everything from God. What can you give me? What do I need?"

The King insisted, "Please, please, I will be so grateful if I can do something to please you. I will be so happy if I can be of some service to you or if you ask me to do something for you."

The Master said, "I will be really happy and grateful if you can chase away the flies that bother me so often."

"This is the thing that you are asking me to do?" said the King. "Such an easy task!"

"Then try, try," said the Master.

So the King started chasing away the flies. O God, each time he chased them away, they kept coming back. There was no end to the flies' mischief.

Then pride entered into the King: "I am the King. I am so obliged to the Master because he has given me some inner peace, which is so difficult to get from anybody. I wanted to do him a favour in return. I thought he would ask me for money or a vast plot of land, because I am such a kind-hearted and rich King. Now I feel really ashamed that I can't do even this kind of job for the Master. It is such an easy task, yet I can't do it."

The Master said, "O King, your heart wanted to please me, but your mind did not want to. Your heart thought that by pleasing me it would make progress. But your mind had a kind of pride in it. Your mind thought that by pleasing me it would do me a great favour. Therefore, I wanted you to go through this experience — not of humiliation, but of humility. I want humility from you. That is why I have given you this job.

"The spiritual Master does not need anything from the disciples. He entirely depends on God's Compassion. But again, God's Compassion can work in and through his disciples. His earthly and material needs will always be supplied by the Supreme in and through his disciples.

"In my case, I needed nothing. But because you wanted to help me, I gave you the easiest job of chasing flies. If even the easiest job you cannot do, how will you do the most difficult job, which is to please God in God's own Way? So give up your pride, give up your sense of humiliation. Only feel that in the spiritual life humility is of paramount importance. And of all the virtues, the most important is to offer gratitude to God for what you have and what you are.

"Then, if you want to help someone, feel that what you are offering is not actually help as such; it is an opportunity for you to be of service to your Beloved Supreme in and through the other individual. And if you go one step higher than this realisation, you will feel that the Supreme is fulfilling Himself in and through you. Do what the Supreme tells you to do, but on your own do not try to help mankind. Only try to serve the Supreme inside mankind. Then only you will please the Supreme in the Supreme's own Way."

GIM 78. *Gandhi Buri's supreme sacrifice*[§]

There was an extremely patriotic old lady who was 73 years old. She was the greatest admirer of Mahatma Gandhi; his very name used to give her a sea of inspiration. She wanted the British government to leave India, and she did many patriotic things that were extremely inspiring to the women of India. Because of this lady's extreme admiration for Mahatma Gandhi, everyone used to call her Gandhi Buri, "buri" meaning "old lady."

In 1942, Gandhi was arrested, and all of India became furious. In many places people held processions, using the slogan "Quit India," which was Mahatma Gandhi's offering to his brothers and sisters of India. The day after Gandhi's arrest, Gandhi Buri was involved in a march to a police station. The people in the procession wanted to take down the British flag, the Union Jack, from over the police station and hoist up the Indian flag.

The police stood in the way and warned the protesters that if they came forward one more step, they would shoot.

All the marchers stopped except Gandhi Buri. She snatched India's flag from one of the young boys in the procession and ran towards the police station. The police first laughed at her. "Enough, enough! No more! Go away from here, old woman. We don't want to kill you," they shouted.

But Gandhi Buri cried, "Kill me. I am not afraid of you. I want to free my Mother India."

She ran towards the staircase that led to the top of the police station. Before she reached the stairs the police shot her. With her right hand she was still holding the flag as she chanted a few times, "Bande Mataram, Bande Mataram, Bande Mataram: 'Mother, I bow to Thee.'" Then she left the body.

This old lady of 73 years was so courageous that she gave her life for her beloved country. There were some young boys in the procession who were shouting and screaming things against the British, but when the time came for them to sacrifice their lives, they hesitated. But Gandhi Buri devotedly and proudly gave her life. From that day on, people who were in that procession became more inspired to dedicate their lives totally to the freedom of India.

GIM 79. *The fire of freedom burns all-where*[§]

Thousands and thousands of people died for the freedom of India. They wanted freedom so badly that their lives were nothing for them, absolutely nothing. In 1928, patriots marched in Lahore in a big procession under the leadership of Lala Lajpat Rai, an old patriot of supreme height who was adored by all India.

The police charged the procession with big sticks, and Lala Lajpat Rai was beaten and killed. The whole nation became extremely angry, and everyone wanted to kill the person who was responsible for his death. They came to know that the British police officer, Mr. Scott, was the culprit.

Someone made an attempt on Scott's life. Alas, this person killed the wrong police officer, a Mr. Saunders, instead. As a result, many patriots were arrested, for the British didn't know who the actual culprit was.

In 1929 one of the great patriots, Jatin Das, was arrested. He was deeply shocked that a leader such as Lala Lajpat Rai had been killed, so he took a vow that he would not eat unless the British asked for forgiveness. "Something has to be done," he said. "I shall fast unto death unless they apologize. They have to apologize!"

At first the British mocked at Jatin Das, but then they became afraid that if he died, the Indian patriots would become more furious. So they tried in so many ways to get him to eat. At first they were kind and polite; then they became rude and threatening and tried to force him to eat.

He kept on saying, "I will not eat!"

After sixty-three days he died, and the members of his family and his fellow patriots were thrown into a sea of tears. They were so sad that such a great hero had passed away. Then they became infinitely more determined to throw off the British rule in India.

The members of Jatin Das's family received a telegram from Ireland. It was from the family of Terence MacSwiney, a young man who had died while fighting for the freedom of Ireland. His wife sent a telegram to the parents of Jatin Das saying, "We the members of MacSwiney's family are deeply grieved at your loss. At the same time we are extremely proud of your son's death. You will get your independence without fail."

The fire of freedom — where it burns! It burns everywhere. Where is Calcutta and where is Ireland? Here this letter shows the oneness-song that is sung all over the world where freedom is denied. Freedom is of paramount importance. Every country should be independent, each soul should be free. Then only nations and individuals will make the fastest progress.

GIM 80. *Only to please you, Mother*[§]

Raja Rammohan Ray was one who had indomitable faith in his own will power. Everywhere he was hailed as a hero supreme. He always used his heroic qualities in a divine way; he never misused his heroic qualities.

One day, when he was a young boy, something most significant happened in his life. His family, which was very, very rich, was having a Durga Puja. India's Durga Puja is a most inspiring time when devotees worship Mother Durga most soulfully.

It happened that Rammohan saw a man making the Durga idol out of straw and clay, and he helped the man build it. In a few days' time, the idol was placed inside the temple and everyone came to worship it as the supreme goddess, Mother Durga. Everybody was bowing down to the Mother Durga, but this little boy wouldn't bow down.

The priest could not believe his eyes: "Why are you not bowing down, my boy?" he asked.

Rammohan replied, "Why do I have to bow down to an idol made of straw and clay?"

This was nothing short of blasphemy! The boy's father was so furious: "I have this kind of son! He is an atheist!"

Rammohan's mother was afraid that some serious calamity would take place in the family if the boy did not bow to the idol. She ran to her son, pleading, "For God's sake, bow down! Otherwise, something will happen to us."

But Rammohan only said, "I know this idol is made of straw, clay and mud. I can't bow down before mud and clay."

Then the mother started crying helplessly before her son. "If you don't bow down to the statue, then I will stay here and cry all day and night," she said.

Rammohan said, "Mother, I can tolerate anything, but I will not be able to take your tears. Since you are begging me, I will bow down to the statue of Durga. But remember, I am bowing down to your goddess, since you see something in this idol. I am doing this only to please you, but not with the hope that I will get something from it. I am bowing down only to please you."

Rammohan soulfully bowed down to Mother Durga, and his family left the temple extremely moved by the young boy's words.

GIM 61. *(p. 289)* 18 January 1979
GIM 62. *(p. 290)* 18 January 1979
GIM 63. *(p. 291)* 18 January 1979
GIM 64. *(p. 294)* 18 January 1979
GIM 65. *(p. 295)* 18 January 1979
GIM 66. *(p. 297)* 18 January 1979
GIM 67. *(p. 298)* 18 January 1979
GIM 68. *(p. 299)* 18 January 1979
GIM 69. *(p. 300)* 18 January 1979
GIM 70. *(p. 302)* 18 January 1979
GIM 71. *(p. 303)* 18 January 1979
GIM 72. *(p. 304)* 18 January 1979
GIM 73. *(p. 305)* 18 January 1979
GIM 74. *(p. 306)* 18 January 1979
GIM 75. *(p. 307)* 18 January 1979
GIM 76. *(p. 309)* 18 January 1979
GIM 77. *(p. 311)* 18 January 1979
GIM 78. *(p. 312)* 21 January 1979
GIM 79. *(p. 314)* 21 January 1979
GIM 80. *(p. 315)* 21 January 1979

GREAT INDIAN MEALS:
DIVINELY DELICIOUS AND
SUPREMELY NOURISHING

BOOK 5

The Governor-General of India was an Englishman named Lord Bentinck. He was very strict and everybody was frightened to death at the very mention of his name.

Raj Rammohun Ray at this time was very well known as a man of knowledge and a great patriot. He was also a linguist who knew many languages.

One day, the Governor-General sent a messenger to Rammohun with the message: "The Governor-General wants to see you immediately."

Rammohun said to the messenger: "I know he is the Governor-General of India, but that does not mean that I have to listen to him and come immediately."

The messenger was shocked. "What do you mean?" he said.

"I will come if I have to, but in my own time," said Rammohun.

"I cannot believe this," said the messenger. "Even in my dreams I would not be able to believe this kind of thing. You Indians are at our feet, and yet you are acting so proud and haughty. You will see what kind of punishment you will get from Lord Bentinck."

Rammohun only said, "I am fully prepared. I know what kind of punishment I shall get, but also I know what I have to do with a foreign boss."

On hearing the story, Lord Bentinck became furious. But he said to himself, "By becoming furious, what am I going to accomplish. I need some help from Raj Rammohun Ray, so let me be wise. Since I am the needy one, I have to be very careful."

He wrote a very polite letter to Rammohun: "I am ready to see you at any time that is convenient for you. I will send my car to bring you here. Please let me know when you can come. I will be extremely happy and honoured to receive you."

The messenger came with the letter, and as soon as Rammohun read it, he said, "I am ready to see the Governor-General."

Rammohun explained to Bentinck when he saw him, "My skin may be dark, but I do have my own sense of prestige. You asked for me to come to see you immediately, but I did not come because my pride and prestige were hurt. When you wrote me a polite letter, then I felt sympathy for you. You may feel that the Indians are inferior, but you cannot treat us in that way."

The Governor-General shook hands with Rammohun and agreed, "I know it is absolutely necessary to preserve one's prestige. It was wrong on my part to address you in that way."

Rammohun said, "Your nobility has touched the very depths of my heart."

Wherever Rammohun went, he played the role of a leader most successfully. Everybody admired and adored him. The great poet Tagore wrote of him, "He is the traveller of India."

Indeed, Rammohun was the traveller who spread India's love-message, wisdom-message and oneness-message all over the world.

GIM 82. *Surya Sen of Chittagong*[5]

Surya Sen was a great patriot, a great revolutionary and a great martyr. Far beyond human imagination were the number of hours he worked to liberate his Mother India. The people of Chittagong adored this great hero. His very name used to give them tremendous joy, tremendous inspiration, tremendous encouragement and a tremendous sense of fulfilment. They called him *Master-da*. *Master* means teacher; *da* is the elder brother. He was everybody's elder brother; even people who weren't much younger than he called him Master-da.

He was a teacher. To him belonged the duty of transforming the British schools into Indian national schools. He used to teach in one of these national schools, and he conquered his students' hearts with his affection, love and concern.

He was not rich, nor handsome, nor striking in any way, but his inner strength was indomitable. His eyes used to shine brighter than the brightest. His inner personality conquered everybody's heart. *Bande Mataram* — "Mother, I bow to Thee" — was his sole mantra.

On February 18, 1930, the revolutionaries of Chittagong, led by Surya Sen, broke into the British armoury and stole a large quantity of guns and ammunition. Chittagong was thrown into the vortex of revolution. Previously, the military used to torture any revolutionaries whom they caught. Torture is an understatement! But after the armoury was robbed, the British Government resolved to put an end to their problems by capturing Surya Sen. So they offered a 10,000-rupee reward to anyone who could tell them about Surya Sen. Whether he was brought to them alive or dead, the British Government would pay 10,000 rupees.

But who among the people would do this kind of thing? Everybody loved Surya Sen dearly and adored him highly. But alas, God's creation is very peculiar. One of Surya Sen's relatives became jealous of this great hero and reached the height of meanness and treachery. His name was Netra Sen.

Surya Sen was always in hiding, moving from one place to another. Sometimes he used to take a job as a workman; sometimes he would take a job as a farmer, or milkman, or priest, or houseworker. This is how he used to avoid being captured.

Either because of money, or out of jealousy, or because of both, Netra Sen told the British Government that Surya Sen was at his house. As a result, the police came and captured him. This is how India's supreme hero was arrested. But before Netra

Sen was able to get his 10,000-rupee reward, he was sent to God.

This is how it happened. Netra Sen's wife was all for Surya Sen, and she was horrified by her husband's deed. She felt mortified by her husband's betrayal of Surya Sen. She couldn't believe her eyes; she couldn't believe her ears.

One evening she was serving her husband food when a great admirer of Surya Sen came into the house. He was carrying a very big knife, which is called a *dal*. With one stroke of the dal he chopped off the head of Netra Sen in the presence of his wife. Then slowly and stealthily he went away.

When the police arrived to investigate, they asked Netra Sen's wife if she had seen who the murderer was. She said, "I saw with my own eyes, but my heart will not permit me to tell you his name. I am sorry. I feel miserable that I was the wife of such a treacherous man, such an undivine man as Netra Sen. My husband betrayed the greatest hero of Chittagong. My husband betrayed a great son of Mother India. My husband cast a slur on the face of India. Therefore, I cannot tell the name of the person who took his life. He has definitely done the right thing.

"You can do anything with me. You can punish me, you can even kill me, but I shall never tell the name of the person who killed my husband. Our Master-da will be hanged, I know, but his name will forever be synonymous with India's immortal freedom-cry. Everybody loves him. Everybody adores him. I, too, love him and adore him, for he is the brightest sun in the firmament of Chittagong. Surya means sun and he is truly our sun."

On 12 January 1934, before the sun rose, Chittagong's sun, India's sun, was hanged. Before he was hanged, this great lover of India, this supreme lover of India, uttered his heart's mantra once: *Bande Mataram* — "Mother, I bow to Thee".

GIM 83. *Khudhiram*[§]

In 1905 Bengal was divided in two by Lord Curzon. Bengal's great political leaders were dead against it, but they were helpless. So there was a great revolt in Bengal. The political leaders and the adorers of Mother India were all fighting against the British. But the British were ruthless. Whenever they heard people chanting *Bande Mataram,* they used to arrest them. For the Indian patriots, Bande Mataram was the slogan. Bande Mataram was their mantra; Bande Mataram was their life-breath. By uttering Bande Mataram, thousands and thousands of people embraced death.

Of all the English, Judge Kingsford was the worst. He used to torture the revolutionaries mercilessly; his activities were atrocious. This led the revolutionaries to decide that Kingsford must be killed.

Two young men, two great revolutionaries, were chosen to execute this task. One was Peraphulla Chaki, the other was Khudhiram. They were young, they were spirited, they were devoted and they were sincere. They were two jewels of Mother Bengal. Their leaders were all appreciation for them and their friends were all admiration for them. So they took up the challenge; they would kill Kingsford.

Every evening, it was Kingsford's custom to go out in his carriage for a short ride. One evening, they hid near Kingsford's bungalow and when the carriage pulled away from the bungalow, the two young men attacked it. They threw a bomb into the vehicle and completely destroyed it. Alas, on that particular day Kingsford was not inside. Instead, his friend, Mrs. Kennedy, and her daughter were in the carriage, and both of them were killed.

Peraphulla Chaki was arrested but Khudhiram somehow managed to escape. Before the British Government could punish

Peraphulla Chaki, this hero of heroes committed suicide. In a few days' time Khudhiram was also arrested. He was caught in a railway station.

There was only one way in which the British Government dealt with such cases: on 11 August 1908, Khudhiram was hanged. But before he was hanged he sang a particular line from a song with all his heart's soulfulness:

"Mother, farewell! I am going out just for a short while. Mother, farewell! Do give me the permission to go out and come back."

This particular line he sang a few times, and then he was hanged.

Yes, Khudhiram did come back to Mother Bengal. He came back in different bodies, in different names, in different shapes — with new determination, new boldness and a heart of supreme sacrifice from Heaven.

GIM 84. *The child Narendranath*[§]

Swami Vivekananda's earlier name was Narendranath and his nickname was Bile. During his childhood and even in his adolescent years, he was extremely mischievous. This did not diminish his divinity. But his parents, especially his mother, sometimes would get puzzled and worry about him.

She used to say, "O Lord Shiva, I prayed to you to grant me a son like you. But instead of coming into my life, you have sent me your ghost. He is nothing but a ghost, my Bile, always breaking things and creating problems for me. How long can I tolerate his endless mischief?"

But there were quite a few good qualities that his mother also saw in him, so inwardly she was satisfied. But outwardly she always told everyone, "My Bile is so notorious!"

One day, when he was only five years old, Vivekananda saw in the living room a few Indian hookahs or smoking pipes. One was for the Brahmins, one for the Kshatriyas and one for the Muslims. He tasted each one, and to his surprise discovered that all the hookahs tasted the same.

Alas, he was caught by his own father. "What are you doing, Bile?" he asked.

Vivekananda replied, "Father, I was just examining the smoking pipes. I thought that the one for Brahmins would be better than the one for Kshatriyas, because Brahmins are so great. And the Muslims are so heroic and spirited, so I thought that the Muslim pipe would be special. But they are all the same. I wish to tell you, Father, that they are all the same. No one pipe is superior to another."

Vivekananda's parents were simply shocked. "How is it that you have started smoking at such a tender age?" they asked. "And what kind of things is a small boy like you saying?"

Then his mother said, "My son, you are too spoiled. You have become too smart. Come here." The child came to the mother and she took him upstairs to his room and closed the door from outside.

In two hours' time the maid came running to the mother, screaming: "Bile is throwing away all his clothes. Everything he has in his room he is throwing out through the window! There are a few beggars below who are grabbing his garments as they fall. And he himself is so happy!"

At this the mother ran upstairs and demanded, "What is the matter with you, Bile? Such expensive clothes you are throwing away!"

Vivekananda replied, "Mother, we are so rich. We can have whatever we want, whenever we want. But these are poor people. They have nothing, nothing. If we do not give to them, then who will give to them? We have enough, more than enough;

so my heart wants to give these things away. They need them more than I do."

His mother's heart was full of joy and delight. She embraced her son and shed tears of delight that his heart was so sympathetic, so vast and so all-giving, and that he had so much oneness with the poor and with the Supreme Pilot in all.

GIM 85. *Swami Vivekananda smokes with an untouchable*⁵

Swami Vivekananda enjoyed smoking. In the days of his pilgrimage, when he used to walk along the streets of India, here, there and elsewhere, smoking was his great avocation.

One evening, as Vivekananda was walking along a village street in northern India, he came to a small cottage where an old man was smoking an Indian hookah. Vivekananda had a tremendous desire to smoke, and he asked the old man if he would give him his pipe.

The man said, "Oh, Swami, I am a scavenger, I am an untouchable. How can I give you my hookah? How will you smoke from the hookah of an untouchable? I am so happy to see you. You are so handsome, so spirited. I am so fortunate to see you. But, alas, I come from an untouchable family."

Vivekananda felt sorry that the old man was an untouchable. He said to him, "I am sorry, I am sorry. Alas, I won't be able to smoke." Vivekananda left him and continued walking.

In a few minutes he felt miserable. He said to himself, "What am I doing? What am I doing? What have I done? What have I done? Did not Thakur teach me that wherever there is a human being, there also is Lord Shiva? Each human being embodies God. This is what I have learned from my Master, Sri Ramakrishna.

"I have given up everything; I am a sannyasin. So I am one with the rest of the world by virtue of my renunciation. Yet although I have renounced everything, still I have preserved this sense of discrimination. Here is a cobbler, here is a scavenger, here is a Brahmin, here is a Shudra. Low caste, high caste! How can I have the heart to distinguish? Are they not all God's children? The sense of separativity, the sense of superiority and inferiority: How can I have that kind of feeling?"

Vivekananda then went running back to the old man and said, "Please, please, give me your hookah. Each man is God Himself."

The old man fearfully and, at the same time, happily gave the hookah to Swami Vivekananda. Swami Vivekananda smoked to his heart's content and then said to the old man, "I am divinely happy, supremely happy, for two reasons. My human desire is fulfilled; I am able to smoke. And my divine desire is fulfilled, because I have been able to realise my inner vision of universal oneness. My Supreme Lord abides in all. This vision of mine I have been able to manifest today by smoking here from your hookah at your house.

"God is for all. He is not only for me, but He is for all. In each individual Him to see, Him to please unconditionally, is my only goal. I shall remain ever grateful to you, for it is through you that my Lord has taught me the supreme lesson: that we are all one, we are all equal, we are all children of our Absolute Lord Supreme."

GIM 86. *Vidyasagar: the ocean of compassion*[§]

Vidyasagar was the ocean of knowledge and also the ocean of compassion. There were people who used to think of him early in the morning and pray to God to make them as kind and as great as Vidyasagar. He was loved by everyone and adored by everyone.

Vidyasagar was one of those who helped to elevate the consciousness of the Bengalis tremendously, and in hundreds of ways he served the people of Bengal. He helped the Bengalis infinitely more than anyone can imagine in social activities and in fighting for the education of women and the early remarriage of widows. He also helped the poor and the needy, not only unreservedly, but also unconditionally.

Once he went to a particular district that was not well-known and where the people were not well-educated. He happened to be sitting at a railway station, watching the trains coming and going. In a short while a particular train stopped and a few passengers began to step down from it.

It was a very small railway station and there were very few coolies, so the passengers had to carry their own luggage. One young man began shouting, "Coolie! Coolie! Coolie!" He had only a small briefcase, but he was shouting for a coolie and nobody was there to come.

Vidyasagar stood up and went over to the young man. "I will carry it," he said. The young man did not know that Vidyasagar was a great man. He always wore the most modest clothes. And perhaps the young man had never even heard of Vidyasagar. God knows. Anyway, Vidyasagar took his briefcase and pretended to be a coolie because he was so modest and humble.

Carrying the briefcase, Vidyasagar followed the gentleman to the house of his parents-in-law. It was to be their first meeting since he had married their daughter. Vidyasagar and the young man arrived at their house and the hosts came out to greet them. Although they were simply delighted to see their new son-in-law, they were shocked to death to see Vidyasagar carrying his briefcase.

They fell at Vidyasagar's feet and said, "How can you do this? How can you do this? Will God not curse us? In knowledge, in compassion and in love, you are the greatest man in Bengal, and yet you carry this briefcase for our son-in-law! He is such a stupid fellow. He did not know who you are. Even now there is no remorse on his part!"

All the members of the household were so shocked, and they begged Vidyasagar to forgive the young man. Gradually, gradually, the son-in-law began to realise what he had unconsciously done.

Then Vidyasagar said to him, "It is because of you that Bengal is not progressing. You will never do your duty. It is such a tiny briefcase, and so light, but still you cannot carry it yourself. You have to wait for a coolie. Yes, when it is heavy, I understand; but when it is something that you can do yourself, that is incomprehensible to me. I am desperately trying to encourage people to be active, dynamic and self-sufficient. It is because people like you don't do your duty, which is so easy to do, that today Mother Bengal is so inferior to other parts of the world. You are all a disgrace to our country."

In this way Vidyasagar scolded them. The members of the family gladly accepted his scolding. "We deserve it. We deserve it. But we are very glad and grateful that you have come to our house. We could not have brought you to our house otherwise."

Vidyasagar replied, "No, you are wrong. I go to everybody's house. You people have made me great. You people have made me good. But I want everybody to be great and good. Then only my sister and brother Bengalis will really make progress. If you are not self-sufficient, if you are not active, if you are not dynamic, then you can never become good instruments for God and good instruments to achieve something great for Mother Bengal."

At this point the young man also fell at Vidyasagar's feet and said, "Vidyasagar, in addition to being the ocean of knowledge, you are also the ocean of compassion. Forgive me. From now on I will be a totally different person."

Vidyasagar blessed him, saying, "I need young people like you who will really work very hard, who will offer their heart and soul to raise the standard of Mother Bengal. I offer you my blessings unreservedly."

GIM 87. *Love is love*[5]

There was once a Muslim king who had a most beautiful daughter. Unfortunately or fortunately, his daughter had tremendous admiration for a Hindu king. This Hindu king was unmarried and the Muslim king's daughter wanted to marry him. But the Muslim king said, "Impossible! I will not allow you to marry a Hindu!"

The Muslim princess protested in the strongest terms. She said, "No, you have to allow me to marry him, because love is love. I admire him and love him. I must have him."

What could the Muslim king do? His daughter's happiness was dear to his heart. So he sent a messenger to the Hindu king seeking his views on the matter. As it happened, the Hindu king also loved this Muslim princess. So he replied, "If she loves me and I love her, then I don't see why we can't get married."

In due time, the two were married. The Muslim king tolerated the fact, whereas the parents of the Hindu King were very agreeable to the union. They said, "To please you, son, is our only desire." As this old couple had advanced in years, they had made their son the king and now, in their support of his marriage, they once more showed their tremendous love for him.

Over the years the Muslim king became terribly jealous of his son-in-law. Everybody appreciated and admired the Hindu king because of his courage, wisdom and sense of charity. Even the Muslim king's own subjects had tremendous appreciation for the Hindu king. The Muslim king could not tolerate this.

He wanted to conquer his son-in-law's kingdom, especially the capital, and throw his son-in-law in jail.

So, quite unexpectedly, he and his army attacked the Hindu king's palace. There was a terrible fight, but after a few days the palace was captured and the Hindu king was arrested. The Muslim king brought him to his palace and would not allow him to go back to his kingdom. He said, "You have to stay here in exile. Only on one condition shall I allow you to go back: if you send my daughter back to me and say that she is no longer your wife."

The Hindu king said, "I love your daughter; your daughter loves me. Our love for each other is tremendous. What will she think of me if I do this?"

The Muslim king said, "If you won't divorce my daughter, then I shall kill you."

What could the Hindu king do? He was helpless.

The wife of the Hindu king was furious that her father had attacked her husband without any advance warning. She put on her husband's uniform and started fighting against the Muslim king's army. Some of the soldiers laughed at her because she was so weak, although she was determined to fight and kill them. Some ran away out of fear that while defending themselves from her blows they might kill her, and they were extremely fond of her. Only a few completely took their king's side. "If you come near us," they said, "we will kill you."

In the meantime, a messenger came to the Hindu queen with a letter from her captured husband. When she read the message, she could not believe her eyes: "If I don't divorce you, your father will kill me. Therefore, I am divorcing you and returning you to your father. You go back to your father and let me come back to my kingdom. All I want to do is rule there peacefully."

The wife cried out, "Is this a Hindu heart? I loved a Hindu heart and against my father's will I married this man. I gave my all to him, I sacrificed everything for him. Now he has divorced me. And I am fighting to bring him back! I love my husband so dearly, but he loves his kingdom more than he loves me. His kingdom is more precious to him than my life's own sacrifice."

The wife grabbed a dagger. "You will get your kingdom back, but my father will not get his daughter back!" she said, and then she killed herself.

In a few days the Hindu king returned. At first he shed sincere tears over the loss of his wife, but then he became involved in ruling his kingdom peacefully and he began to forget her.

The Muslim king was struck with grief for what he had done. Instead of getting back his daughter, he lost her for good. The Muslim queen became mad at her husband and she said, "You should be hanged! Because of you we lost our dearest daughter. She loved her husband and he loved her. Is not love more important, infinitely more important, than your religion? Who is Hindu, who is Muslim? The dear ones will always remain dear. There is no Hindu, there is no Muslim; there is only oneness. Because of your stupidity, today I have lost my dearest daughter. Had I been in your place, I would have destroyed my life."

The Muslim king said, "Stop your philosophy! If I die, it is you who will be the sufferer. Already you have lost your daughter, and now you want to lose your husband as well? You will not be able to bear your suffering!"

The queen said, "No, I will be able to bear my suffering because I love justice. Because of you, I have lost my dearest daughter. If you die, I will feel that this is real justice."

The king said, "You may love justice, but I also have some sense of justice with regard to my subjects. If I die, they will be fatherless. I have made one serious blunder. So what? If I stay on earth I can still do many good things for my subjects. I want to stay on earth."

"Yes, stay on earth," the queen cried, "and I shall also stay on earth with a broken heart. But the whole world will hate you, and I will be the one to hate you most. I will stay on earth, not because I am needed, but in order to treasure the memory of my dearest, sweetest daughter. If I die, I do not know what will happen or where I will go, but if I stay on earth I will be able to repent. And my repentance is my consolation, my repentance is my illumination. For that purpose I will stay, whereas you can stay to lead a shameless life!"

GIM 88. *The tragedy of Dasharatha*[§]

There was once a great King named Dasharatha. He was the father of the great Ramachandra, one of India's Avatars. King Dasharatha was an expert in the art of archery and his teacher, Bhargava, was extremely pleased with his student. There was only one particular knowledge which Bhargava did not impart to his student. It was a special type of archery in which it is not necessary to even see the prey. By just hearing the sound of the animal, no matter where it is, the archer can shoot it. This secret knowledge Bhargava did not want to give Dasharatha because he was a Kshatriya. Although Kshatriyas are very spirited, courageous and determined, they have one weakness: they lack a disciplined life and sometimes they become a victim of restlessness. Therefore, Bhargava was unwilling to give Dasharatha the necessary skill.

But Dasharatha begged and begged his teacher. Repeatedly he declared, "I will not misuse it, I will not misuse it. I promise you."

Finally, Bhargava acceded to the King's entreaty. "All right," he said, "I will give it to you, since you are begging me. But I am afraid that one day you will bring a serious calamity to yourself and to the members of your family and also to some innocent victims through your unfortunate use of this knowledge. However, as you are begging me so earnestly, how can I displease you, my son?" So Bhargava gave the secret knowledge and secret capacity to his dearest student, Dasharatha.

Dasharatha was now extremely happy and delighted, for he knew that he had mastered all the strategies of archery.

A few years passed and one day a strong desire entered into Dasharatha's mind. He said, "Let me go into the deep forest and test the secret capacity that Bhargava has given me. Then I shall be able to discover whether I actually have learnt how to aim at animals without seeing them."

So Dasharatha went into the forest. When evening came, a sound reached his ears, which he was sure was the trumpeting of an elephant. Dasharatha immediately pulled back his bow and let the arrow fly. Then lo and behold, this time a human sound came back to him in the night: "Mother, Mother, I am finished."

Dasharatha followed the sound to its source and what did he see? He saw a little boy of nine who had come to fetch water from a pond. The little boy's father, a great sage, was blind. His mother was all affection and love for her only child, her darling son. Because his parents were old, the son helped them in many ways, even at this early age. This particular evening his parents had been thirsty, so he had come to draw water from a pond near their cottage. As he was approaching the pond, the arrow came flying towards his heart and struck him down.

When Dasharatha came and saw the scene, he felt intensely miserable at what he had done. He cried out piteously, "Oh, Guru Bhargava, you were right, you were right! I was not meant for this sacred, sacred knowledge, these extraordinary capacities."

The little boy turned his eyes to Dasharatha and said to him, "I am dying. No harm, I shall die. But do me a favour, will you?

Will you go and carry this pitcher to my parents? My parents are thirsty and they are expecting me at any moment. Please, please do me this last favour. Don't you worry about me. This is my fate, but please go and give water to my parents. They are thirsty, extremely thirsty." Then the little boy, Sindhu, turned his face to Heaven and died.

Dasharatha burst into tears. With one hand he took up the dead body of the little boy and with the other he carried the pitcher, full to the brim. Slowly, and with a heavy heart, he made his way to the cottage of Sindhu's parents.

When Sindhu's father heard the sound of footsteps he said, "Sindhu, Sindhu, my Sindhu, you have come! We are waiting for you. What happened to make you so late today, my child? Both your mother and I are pinched with thirst, and you have come to quench our thirst. You are our dearest child, our only darling. Please, please, always try to be on time. Do not waste any time when you go on errands that take you away from us. We need you badly at every moment."

Dasharatha could remain silent no longer. He said, "Oh sage, I am the wretched Dasharatha. Forgive me, forgive me. Your dearest, sweetest child, Sindhu, is no more. I have come and brought your son. But, alas, he is without life. Now, although I am the King, I am at your mercy entirely. Do anything you want with my life."

The father and mother could not believe their ears. As soon as the mother saw her son lying dead in Dasharatha's arms, she fainted and immediately her husband followed her. In an hour's time, when they had both recovered, they said to Dasharatha, "O King, please do us the kindness of arranging for a pyre to be made straight away. Our last request of you is this: As soon as the pyre is lit, we wish to join our son on it. As soon as the fire starts blazing, we shall place our son on it first and then we shall also enter into the climbing flames."

In great distress, the King said, "No, no, no! That cannot be done. One soul has died. Already I am responsible for one human being's losing his life, and at such a tender age! Now must I be responsible for two more? Oh no, no! Please forgive me, I am the King. I will do everything that is within my limited human capacity to console you, but this thing I cannot do."

With one voice the parents answered him. "No, King, stay we cannot. We cannot be dissuaded from joining our son. He was dearer than the dearest to us. Without him our life is meaningless and will always remain meaningless. Therefore, let us go with him."

"Then," Dasharatha said, "what will be my punishment?"

"No punishment," the mother replied. "Why should we blame you? This is our fate. We forgive you. Our son forgave you and we also forgive you."

Her husband, the sage, said, "Wait! My son has forgiven him, you can forgive him, but I cannot. Although I have done yoga and practised austerities all my life — infinitely more than my son and you — I cannot forgive him. I simply cannot!

"Dasharatha, you are responsible, totally responsible, for our son's death and I am compelled to curse you. You too, will one day miss your son the way I am missing mine. You will be obliged to send your son into the forest because of your foolish fondness for one of your wives and, through this unthinkable behaviour, you will lose your dearest, eldest son."

At the time of these events, Dasharatha didn't have a son. But when he heard the curse he cried out, "O God, O God, don't give me a son, don't give me a son. I don't need one, I don't need one. It is better not to have a son and not to miss the son than to send the son into the forest to be killed. But I cannot conceive how this death could take place. How could it happen? Why would it happen? Who among my wives would be so unkind as to compel me to send my son into the forest? Impossible,

impossible! Yet the curse of the sage may come true. O God, I beg You either to give me a son who will escape this curse or to give me no son at all. For to lose a son and enjoy the kingdom would be simply impossible for me. O Lord Supreme, forgive me, forgive my misdeed. Let this curse remain unfulfilled, I pray."

But, alas, how can the curse of a great sage pass unfulfilled? There came a time when Dasharatha was indeed compelled by his second wife, Kaikeyi, to send his son, who was dearer than the dearest to him, into the forest and there the inevitable happened. It was simply impossible for Dasharatha to bear the shock of his son's death and, lamenting the loss, he died.

GIM 89. *The defeat of Britrasur§*

God alone knows when this particular story took place. As you know, the gods and asuras always fight. They fight over Heaven, since they both want to possess it. Sometimes the asuras possess Heaven, and sometimes the gods do.

Why does it happen so? The gods lose Heaven when they misuse their freedom and enter into the enjoyment-life. At that time they are driven out by the asuras, or undivine forces. Then, when the asuras misuse their capacities and become extremely wicked, they are driven out by the cosmic gods. While we can expect this kind of undivine behaviour from the asuras, it is really painful when the cosmic gods also enter into the life of undivine enjoyment and are compelled to lose Heaven.

Now, each time the gods are driven from Heaven, they pray like anything in order to win back Heaven. They pray and pray and meditate and meditate, and gradually they regain their power. Then they drive out the asuras, who have been losing their capacities because of the undivine life they have been leading in Heaven. Then everything is reversed. The asuras pray and meditate and become stronger, while the gods become weaker because they have entered into the enjoyment life. Then finally the asuras drive out the cosmic gods. It has been going on like this from time immemorial.

Thousands of years ago there was a most powerful asura named Britrasur, who was the King of the asuras. Britrasur was able to drive the gods out of Heaven, and then he ruled Heaven mercilessly. Gradually, his subjects became very undivine and cruel, and they lived a very undivine life.

It happened that the King's wife developed a strong desire. She wanted to bring Indra's wife, Sachi, to her palace and make Sachi her maid. Indra was the King of the cosmic gods, but he had been driven away by Britrasur along with the other gods.

Britrasur said to his wife, "It is an excellent idea, my dear. I am sending my soldiers to arrest Sachi, and she will definitely become your maid. Your happiness is my happiness."

When news of this reached Indra, he became furious. He said, "What an insult! My wife, my Queen to become the maid of Britrasur's wife! True, I have been driven away by him. True, he is stronger than I am right now; he is stronger than any of the cosmic gods. But how does he dare to even think of taking my wife away from me? Such an insult I will not brook!"

So saying, Indra went to Brahma, the Creator. "O Brahma," he pleaded, "save me, save me. Look at the audacity of Britrasur! He wants to take my wife away from me and make her his own wife's slave."

Brahma replied, "Indra, when you suffer from a disease, you need medicine to cure yourself. You have all enjoyed life in a way that was beyond all proportion. Now you have to pay the penalty."

"That is true," Indra admitted. "But Lord Brahma, how long can they torture us? And this kind of audacity — to take my wife, of all people! How can I tolerate it?"

Brahma said, "When you suffer, you come to realise others' suffering. I am not saying that your wife should be taken away by Britrasur; far from it. But I am telling you, you must not enter and remain in the world of restless, base enjoyment. I tell you, Indra, you can get back Heaven only if a great sage offers you his boon."

"Who will do this kind of thing?" Indra asked. "Is there anyone who can offer me such a boon?"

"Yes, yes, there is such a person," said Brahma. "Dadichi, the son of Chyaban, can and will do it. This great son of Chyaban will offer you his boon. Your wife and your friends should go and take shelter at Dadichi's and Chyaban's house."

So Indra immediately went with his wife and army to their house and related all that had passed to Dadichi. Dadichi assured him, "Do not worry, I shall do the needful."

Upon hearing that Indra and his wife had taken shelter at Dadichi's house, Britrasur sent his soldiers there to arrest Indra's wife. If necessity demanded, they would arrest Indra too. But it was not so easy to arrest Indra's wife. Since the task was proving so difficult, Britrasur himself, the leader and King of the asuras, decided to personally come to seize her. Dadichi was waiting for Britrasur when he came and said to him, "Let us see whether you can take Indra's wife away from here. Let us see whether you can contend with my occult and spiritual power. Let us see who can destroy whom. I warn you, Britrasur, if you don't give up this foul and base desire of yours, I shall destroy you and all your friends and soldiers with my third eye — completely and utterly."

Britrasur remained silent but his wife said, "Oh no, I have come to take Sachi. She will massage my feet; she will become my slave, my perfect slave. What a perfect slave she will make!"

Calmly and quietly and with a broad smile, the sage Dadichi said to them, "All right, I am going to bathe in the lake and then

SRI CHINMOY

I will return. But I tell you, before I come back if you take away Indra's wife, then I shall destroy you all immediately. Yonder is the lake in which I shall bathe. When I return, I shall do the needful."

So Dadichi went to the lake. An hour, two hours, a day, two days went by, and still Dadichi did not return from the lake. The days ran into weeks, with still no sign of him. Finally, Indra and his army went to the lake to see what was going on. When he did not find Dadichi, he jumped into the lake to see whether Dadichi had given up his life and was at the bottom. It was true. Dadichi had taken away his life-breath while in trance. Indra found the body of Dadichi and brought it to the surface. But although it was dead, it was full of power; it emanated power. On seeing the dead body, Britrasur took fright and ran away. Indra at first chased him. But then Brahma himself intervened and asked Indra to take a particular bone from Dadichi's body and make a special mace, which was then known as Vajra. After the mace was completed, it flew up high into the air and from there it descended upon Britrasur's head, destroying him at the spot where he was standing.

This is how the cosmic gods regained Heaven and were spared the loss of Indra's wife, Sachi Devi. Indra and his soldiers and Sachi Devi all bowed down to Brahma, the Creator, with gratitude-hearts everlasting.

GIM 90. *Arjuna inspires Ekalavya*[§]

The young Pandavas and the young Kauravas used to learn archery from Dronacharya. Dronacharya was the supreme archer and everybody admired him not only for his skill but also for his lofty spiritual height. He taught the young Pandavas and the young Kauravas with utmost concern and love and instilled into them character, strength and manly vigour.

342

There came a time when the young Pandavas and Kauravas had to sit for an examination. In actuality, it was more a display of prowess than an examination and everybody was given the opportunity to show his capacity.

The grand winner was the third Pandava, Arjuna. All the people who had come to watch the events appreciated and admired Arjuna's matchless precision and expertise. Among the spectators were an old man and his son. The son was so deeply moved by Arjuna's capacity that he said to his father, "Father, I want to become an archer like Arjuna. I admire him so much."

His father answered, "Ekalavya, there is nothing wrong in that, my son. You practise hard and you will also be a fine archer."

"But how can I practise archery? I have to learn it first," reasoned the son.

"Agreed. You have to learn."

"But who will be my teacher? I wish to have Dronacharya as my teacher!"

"No son," the father said. "He will not become your teacher. We come of a low caste, so how will he become your teacher?"

But his son insisted, "What is low caste, what is high caste? I see he is a very kindhearted man."

The father said, "Yes, he is kind-hearted, but when it is a matter of teaching low caste people, he won't do it. He will only teach the Brahmins and Kshatriyas. I tell you, we are Sudras, so he cannot teach you."

The young man was very sad that he would not get Dronacharya as his teacher. On the way back home, he suddenly said to his father, "No, I am going to ask Dronacharya all the same. Who knows, perhaps he will teach me. So Father, you go home. I will come back alone."

His father said, "All right, you go if you must, but let me wait for you here. You go and see."

After his son had left, the father said, "How inspired my dear Ekalavya has been by the matchless Arjuna! I can clearly see that because of his aspiration and determination, my son is destined to become a great archer, whether Dronacharya agrees to teach him or not. It is only a matter of time."

GIM 91. *God will teach you*[8]

Inspired by Arjuna's peerless archery skill at a royal competition, Ekalavya approached Arjuna's archery teacher, Dronacharya. "Sir, sir, venerable sir, will you please teach me archery? I want to become just like Arjuna. I have such tremendous admiration for Arjuna. Will you teach me archery?"

Dronacharya replied, "Yes, I will teach you. But please tell me who you are."

The young man said, "My name is Ekalavya and my father is the chief caretaker."

Dronacharya looked disturbed. "Oh, you come of a very low family. I am sorry, but you have to forgive me, I cannot teach you."

The young man protested, "High caste, low caste! You are such a learned man, such a man of wisdom, and yet you are saying things like this. I was born in a low family, but if I do good things — great and mighty things — will it not compensate my birth?"

"You are speaking like a true philosopher, and let me say that I admire your philosophy. It is not your fault that you came into a low caste family. And if you have aspiration and determination, then naturally you are bound to succeed."

The young man said, "That is what I am saying. It was my fate. What can I do if I was destined to take birth in a low caste family? But if, with my aspiration and determination, I do something great and good, will it not please the world? Will it not please God?"

"Yes, certainly it will. I appreciate your philosophy. I see eye to eye with you. But I cannot fulfil your desire. I cannot teach you. You try! With your heart's aspiration and your unfaltering determination, you try. You will succeed one day, my boy. Of that, I assure you. If I do it, the Brahmins and my friends will all hate me. They will throw me out of society. I am an old man. At this age I don't want to be thrown out of society. So, make no mistake, I fully agree with your philosophy, but I am telling you that I am unable to fulfil your desire. You can call it my weakness or anything you want, but society is made like that. It has its own way of thinking. I do not want to be the one to justify it. I don't want to go into the reasons why the Kshatriyas and the Brahmins should not and must not mix with lower caste people. That will be a very long story, and it will be a painful one for you. So I don't want to tell it. You please go, and with your own aspiration and determination you will succeed."

Sorrowfully, the young man turned towards home. When he came upon his father, who had been waiting for him, he said, "Father, you were right. This old man will not teach me. Caste, caste, caste! Father, why were you born in a low caste?"

"What could I do," his father said. "My parents brought me into the world as I brought you into the world. Did I know I was going to take birth in a low caste family? Son, if we love God, then God will always please us and fulfil us. So if you want to learn the skills of archery, pray to God. God Himself will teach you."

"Yes, Father," Ekalavya said, "You are right. I have faith that because of my devotion to Dronacharya, God will definitely teach me."

GIM 92. *Ekalavya worships Drona*[§]

The young Ekalavya was determined to become a great archer. Although the master-archer Dronacharya could not teach him because he was of a low caste, the young man was adamant.

"I will pray to God," he said to his father. "Day and night I will pray. Drona's heart is good, but his mind was not good when I approached him. His heart sympathised with me, but his mind was afraid of what society would say if he taught a Sudra. But I want to have him as my teacher.

"So I have resolved to make a statue of Drona out of mud and clay, and I shall worship that statue as my teacher, my only teacher. From this statue I will get inspiration and be able to learn."

His father said, "That is a wonderful idea. If you retain that kind of faith in your teacher, my son, I am sure you will succeed."

So the young man made a statue that looked exactly like Drona. Constantly he used to pray to Drona and receive inspiration from him through the statue. In this way the young man was able not only to acquire the skills of archery, but to so master them that he became absolutely unique. He even learned how to stop the barking of dogs in such a way that his arrow pierced the dog's mouth and stuck there. He had that kind of capacity. He was an unparalleled archer and the feat that he could perform with dogs not even Arjuna himself could dream of doing.

One day Ekalavya was meditating in the forest. A dog started barking and it was disturbing his meditation. So he picked up his bow and shot some arrows into the dog's mouth. The dog, silenced, but not bleeding, ran away.

It so happened that Arjuna and the Pandava brothers were also in the forest, amusing themselves. When they saw the dog passing by, no one paid any attention to it. But Arjuna noticed to his astonishment that the dog had arrows inside its mouth but was not bleeding. He said, "Who can be such a great archer?" Overcome by curiosity, he followed the dog, which took him directly to Ekalavya, who was in a meditative consciousness.

Arjuna approached Ekalavya and, pointing at the dog, inquired, "Who has done this?"

"I have done it," Ekalavya said.

"You! You have such capacity? Who taught you?"

"My Guru."

"Who is your Guru?"

"My Guru is Drona," said Ekalavya.

"Drona is your Guru in archery!" Arjuna exclaimed. "He is my Guru!"

"Yes, Drona is also my Guru."

"When did he teach you, then? He is always with us in the kingdom."

"Oh no," said Ekalavya. "Here he is. Look, I have made a statue of him and I worship him in this statue. It was he who gave me the inspiration and the capacity to do this." Arjuna said quickly, "Thank you. I am very happy, very happy. I am very proud of you."

Although Arjuna felt sad that Ekalavya had far surpassed him in skill, he was very moved by the devotion and faith that the young man had for Dronacharya.

GIM 93. *For his dearest disciple the Master will do everything*[§]

When Prince Arjuna discovered that the untouchable, Ekalavya, who lived in the forest, was more skilled in archery than he was, he was very disturbed. He left the forest and ran home, furious. He went straight to Dronacharya and said to him, "You have deceived me."

"Remain calm and quiet, my son," said Dronacharya. "Why are you shouting and screaming?"

"You have deceived me! I have just seen someone who knows archery far better than I do. You told me that I was the best archer and now, look, you have deceived me, you have fooled me!"

Dronacharya affirmed, "No, I can never deceive you; I can never fool you."

"But you have done it," declared Arjuna. "In the forest there is a young man by the name of Ekalavya. He has made a statue of you which he worships. From the statue he has derived such a unique capacity. With his arrows he can stop the barking of a dog, which I can't do. And then, something else! He is able to shoot arrows through the mouth of a dog without making the dog bleed. Look at his capacity! I don't have that capacity. You told me I was the best! Now what can I do? I feel miserable, miserable."

Then Drona said, "Come with me, my son." And he took Arjuna into the forest to where Ekalavya lived. Drona went up to Ekalavya and said, "You have such capacity in archery. Who taught you? I have heard from Arjuna that you have stopped the barking of a dog."

"Yes," replied Ekalavya. "I was meditating most soulfully on you and the dog was bothering me. Therefore, I got annoyed with the dog and punished it so that it could not bark. But, in all sincerity, I did not know that the dog would not bleed. I was also surprised when I saw that there was no blood. So, this is all your grace, Dronacharya. I give all credit to you."

Drona said, "I am so proud of you, my boy. Now tell me, if it is true that I have done everything for you, then will you not give me a sacerdotal fee? You know that when you learn from a teacher, the teacher gives everything to the student. So it is customary for the student to give the teacher a reward."

"Yes, yes, I will give, I will give," Ekalavya replied earnestly. "Anything you want you may have. I am so grateful to you, so grateful to you."

"Are you sure that you will give me anything I want?"

"Yes, without any difficulty whatsoever. Unreservedly and unconditionally I shall give."

"Then give me, my son, your right thumb," said Dronacharya.

"My right thumb!" cried Ekalavya. "If I give you my right thumb, then what am I going to do? Will I remain an archer anymore? No, I must keep my promise. You take my right thumb. You be happy. I am so grateful to you. You gave me the capacity to become an excellent archer and I will be so proud that I am able to fulfil your desire. So please, please, take my right thumb. I am giving you my right thumb."

With these words he cut off his right thumb and gave it to Dronacharya. Then he said, "As an archer I could have been known the world over. Everybody would have come to know of me. But now I will be known as a devotee of yours. I am sure that to be a devotee is infinitely more meaningful and fruitful in my life than to be an archer."

Arjuna felt miserable that this took place because of him. He said to Ekalavya, "Please forgive me, I am the culprit, I am the culprit."

But Drona interrupted him, "No, you are not the culprit. I want to tell you one thing, I want to tell both of you. Arjuna, my son, today I wanted to show you that you have always been my dearest disciple — dearer to me than my own soul. In order to prove to the world that I can do everything to please my dearest disciple, I transformed you into an archer without equal in this land. But here also I wish to say that, in the inner worlds, Ekalavya will forever remain immortal because of his supreme sacrifice. No other human being could have made this kind of sacrifice."

GIM 94. *Patience illumines*[§]

There were two sisters, Kadru and Binate, who were both married to the sage Kashyapa. The sisters were extremely fond of each other. Kashyapa used to spend most of his time in meditation while his wives did the housework. Everything they sacrificed gladly, and Kashyapa was very pleased to have them as his wives.

Once, Kashyapa left for a few days of serious meditation. While he was away, the two sisters were talking, when unfortunately they entered into a serious dispute over the colour of Indra's elephant, Oirabat. Binate said it was white while Kadru said it was black. Each was so certain of being right that both agreed that whoever was wrong would become the slave of the other. This was the agreement they came to.

Kadru, who had three sons, asked them about that particular elephant. "You have seen Indra's Oirabat so many times. Can you tell me the colour of that elephant?"

The sons said, "Yes, Mother, it is white, pure white, like the moon."

Kadru cried out, "O God, what have I done? Now I have to become the slave of my sister. Save me, save me!"

"How can we save you?" they asked. "Why did you make that kind of promise? We are extremely sorry, and we will feel very miserable when you become Mother Binate's maid, but we are helpless."

"You are not helpless," Kadru said. "Do me a favour. Tomorrow morning Indra's elephant will come to the lake. You and a few friends must wear black garments and carry black pieces of cloth with you. Then, when the elephant starts approaching, cover it with the black. When Binate and I come to see it, I will say, 'Look, it is definitely black.' We will hear the sound of the elephant, but from a distance it will look black."

Early in the morning while it was still somewhat dark, the elephant came to the lake. Binate saw the pieces of cloth in front of the elephant. "Yes, it is black," she cried out. "I have lost!"

Kadru said, "Now you have to be my slave, my maidservant, for life."

When Kashyapa returned from his few days of meditation, he saw that Binate had become Kadru's slave and was sad and miserable. Kashyapa himself felt so sad. "How can this kind of thing happen?" he asked.

When Kashyapa heard all about it, he said to Binate, "Kadru's sons have deceived you. Actually, the elephant is white."

Binate could not believe her ears. "I am so sad to hear that my dear sister Kadru and her sons have deceived me. But now it is too late. I have committed myself to being her slave. A promise is a promise."

Kashyapa said, "Binate, you should have had more patience and waited for the elephant to come nearer. Then you would have discovered their trick and not committed yourself to be her slave forever."

Binate cried, "What shall I do now?"

"Wait for the hour," Kashyapa consoled her. "Although it is unfair, be patient. One day you will also have one or two sons. Your children will either take revenge or do something to illumine Kadru and her sons and make the family happy again."

In three or four years Binate was blessed with a child, but the birth was premature. Binate became very upset: "This is the result of my patience?" she cried. "How can I have a premature child? This child is supposed to save me. It is impossible." In her anger she kicked the child and the child became deformed.

"What have I done? What have I done?" she screamed.

Again Kashyapa consoled her. "You should have had more faith in my prophecy. Still my prophecy will one day prove true. Have patience: wait and see. Your sons will save you."

"I don't need any more children," she said. "I am ready to remain all the time a slave to my sister."

When her son was still very young, he said to Binate, "Mother, I fully understand that the reason you kicked me was because you were mad with grief. Torture yourself no longer about what you have done, and do not feel sad that you have become your own sister's slave. First Kadru and you were sisters, then you were married to the same sage. You were very happy, and now your life is all suffering and misery. But a time will come when you will be free from this bondage."

Two years later, Binate was blessed with another son, Arun, who was extremely bright spiritually. Binate was very happy to have this son.

Kashyapa said, "This son will really help you."

Indeed, the brightness of the child frightened and tortured Kadru and her children and they were terribly jealous of him. As Arun grew older, his illumination compelled the stepbrothers to surrender, and they began leading a divine life.

One day Binate said to her son, "Arun, I know you have the power to compel my sister to free me from my promise. But please, let your older brother be cured by you instead. I am ready to remain a slave forever."

But his older brother said to Arun, "No, I am ready to remain deformed. Let my mother be freed. You must not save me; save my mother."

Arun replied, "There is no reason why you, Mother, have to remain a slave. My stepbrothers have become divine. Kadru, too, is ready to receive illumination."

Very soon, Kadru freed Binate from her old promise, and again the two sisters became very close. The stepbrothers and brothers also became very fond of each other, and in a short time the oldest son of Binate was cured.

Kashyapa said, "Because of your patience, Binate, one of your sons has freed you, as I predicted. He has transformed and illumined Kadru and her sons. You lost the feeling of oneness over an elephant. But the past is dust. Now let us again enjoy the happiness of a oneness-family."

Immediately Indra's elephant Oirabat appeared outside Kashyapa's home, and his two wives bowed down at the sage's feet: "O Kashyapa, O great sage, we clearly see now that in spite of our ignorance you have illumined us. You have shown us that patience illumines and oneness ever lives in the heart of God's creation."

GIM 95. *The Goddess Ganga descends to earth*[§]

The greatest of all sacrificial rites is Ashwamedha, the horse sacrifice. In performing Ashwamedha, the owner of a horse will meditate most soulfully and offer some mantras to the horse. Then he will allow the horse to leave his home and roam all over the countryside. The owner has to fight with whoever captures the horse and bring him back. Then only the sacrifice can take place.

Once a great king named Sagar wanted to perform this rite. Already King Sagar had performed Ashwamedha ninety-nine times and this was to be his hundredth time. Indra, the King of the Gods, had only been able to perform this particular sacrifice one hundred times, and he became terribly jealous of the King.

Since Indra wanted to ruin the King's sacrifice, he stole the horse. Sagar sent his son, with a large army, to find the culprit and Indra was afraid he would be caught. So he entered into the nether world, first tying up the horse near a great sage who was meditating. After some time, Sagar's soldiers saw the animal near the sage, and they thought it was the sage who had stolen the horse.

The soldiers said, "This sage is so unwise to keep the horse tied so close to him. He should have at least let the horse go away. Now it is obvious who the thief is." So they started beating the sage most mercilessly. Suddenly the sage opened up his third eye and in a fleeting minute he killed Sagar's son and the entire army of six thousand soldiers.

When his son and the army did not return, King Sagar sent his grandson to find out where they were. The grandson looked for the horse and finally found the animal near the sage. The sage told him what had happened.

"Please, you have to return the horse," the boy said.

"No," said the sage. "Tell your grandfather, the King, that I won't tolerate this kind of thing. His soldiers struck me mercilessly, thinking I was the thief."

The boy asked, "O sage, what is to be done now? So many good men have died."

The sage replied, "Only if the river Ganga comes down from Heaven and touches these dead bodies with its water will they be revived. But for that you will have to pray and meditate for years."

The grandson returned to the King with the sad news. King Sagar immediately agreed to pray and meditate to please the Goddess Ganga. He began praying and meditating intensely, but in a few years' time he died.

Then the grandson, Angshuman, began meditating, but in a few years he also died. His son, Dilip, prayed and meditated for a few years and also died. Then his son, Bhagirath, also began praying and meditating most earnestly, and finally his prayer was heard by the Goddess Ganga.

Ganga appeared before him and said, "Before you, your father's father and also his grandfather all prayed to me. Their accumulated prayer and your prayer have touched the very depth of my heart; therefore, I am going to come down. But if I descend to earth with my tremendous speed, I will destroy the world. There has to be someone who is spiritually very great to hold back my speed and power, and that can only be Shiva."

Bhagirath then went and prayed to Shiva: "When Ganga descends most powerfully to rescue my family's army, please restrain the flow of her waters. Only you are powerful enough to perform this feat."

Shiva was very pleased with Bhagirath's prayer and he agreed. "I will hold her back with my matted hair."

When the Goddess Ganga began descending most powerfully, Shiva held her back with his matted hair. But his hair was so thick that Ganga's waters could not flow down to earth at all, and the dead bodies were not being revived.

So Shiva took out one of the hairs from his head so that the water could flow through. The flow was not as powerful as it would have been if Shiva had not interfered, but it was still very powerful. It descended and passed near a cottage of a sage named Jahnu, and began washing away his cottage.

The sage got mad and started drinking the water, until he had drunk the entire amount that had descended. So all the water entered into Jahnu and none of it touched the soldiers. Bhagirath begged Jahnu to release the water. So Jahnu emptied the water through his mouth and the river continued flowing. Finally it touched the spot where the dead bodies were.

As soon as the water touched them, all the soldiers revived. They were exactly the same age as when they had died.

Because of this story, other names of the Ganga are Jahnabi and Bhagirathi.

GIM 96. *The future grows in the present*[5]

There was a very rich man who had a slave. One day the slave saved the rich man's only son from drowning. His master was extremely pleased with him and set him free. Not only that, but he also gave him lots of gifts and money plus a large sailing boat.

Now that the ex-slave had money, he hired some people to work his boat and set out on a voyage across the ocean.

Alas, one day there was a terrible cyclone. The boat sank and everybody drowned, except this former slave. He began swimming towards a nearby island. When he reached it, he saw that many people were waiting for him, crying with delight, "The King has come! The King has come!"

The man said, "Why are you calling me King? I have lost everything except this loin cloth that I am wearing."

Everyone said, "This year you will be King. Every year we have a new king. You are King for this year."

"But I don't understand," said the man.

"We appoint a new king every year and now it is your turn," they said.

"Why are you so kind to me?" he asked. Then he said to himself, "Perhaps God, out of His infinite Bounty, is doing this since I have lost my boat."

So he turned to the crowd and asked, "Tell me only one thing. Is it only for a year?"

"Yes," came the reply.

"Then what will happen?" he asked.

They said, "Well, we shall throw you off of the island."

He asked, "Then where shall I go?"

They answered, "We only know that the King rules for one year. Then he must leave the kingdom."

The ex-slave asked, "Please, send me the wisest man in the kingdom." When the man came, the new King asked, "Is it true that each king rules only for a year and then must leave the island? Then God alone knows what happens to him. Is there any advice you can give me so that at the end of a year I don't become a beggar again?"

"Yes," said the wise man. "Now that you are King, try to make yourself another kingdom on a nearby island. Transform another island into a kingdom by sending your people to make roads, gardens, houses and so forth. Do everything in this one year. When you have established another kingdom, why do you have to worry? At the end of the year you can go there."

"How is it that my predecessors did not do this?" the man asked.

The wise man explained, "I told them, but they did not listen to me. They kept saying, 'In a few weeks we shall do it.' Then, two months before their reign was up, I used to tell them again, but they didn't think of their future."

The King said, "I will definitely listen to you. People will go find a new place where they will build another kingdom like this." The wise man said, "Will you do it, or will you have the same fate as your predecessors?"

"No," said the King, "I won't allow myself to have the same fate. I will start from today to send people to do the needful.

"Always we have to think of the future. Always we have to remember that the future grows in the present. If there is a gap between the present and the future, if we do not think of the future, then some calamity will always take place."

So the King sent out his subjects to build a new kingdom, and at the end of a year, the King went there and started ruling it.

GIM 97. *The poet and the King*[§]

There was once a King who used to appreciate poets and learned men in his kingdom. He would always shower gifts upon them and hold various contests in which he would give them awards.

There happened to be a poor poet who was poor not only in his outer life but also in his poetry. Everybody used to go to the palace and recite poems they had written about the King, and appreciate and flatter the King. But this particular poet would not or could not go.

His wife was very upset over this, and she kept telling him, "One day you have to go. How long can we remain poor? We have children, and we cannot meet with our expenses. You must go!"

The poet did not want to anger his wife because she had a bad temper and he was afraid she might do something drastic. So he went to the King and said, "I have written an excellent poem on you."

The King said, "All right, leave it here and come back tomorrow."

"Tomorrow?" the poet asked. "You won't read it today?"

"No, tomorrow," the King said.

The following day, when the poet returned to the palace, the King was giving away alms to the poor. Many people were standing in line, and each one came up and received something from the King. Then the King started calling the poets to come to him. But the King did not call out the name of this particular poet. The poet was puzzled and surprised, but he did not know what to do.

At long last the King turned to this particular poet and said, "I have given my alms for today. It is all over. We have had a wonderful meeting and everything is all over. You go home and take a shower and have something to eat."

The poet said, "When shall I come again?"

The King said, "Why will you have to come again? Don't you have a copy of the poem which you have left me? When I have time, I just read the poems. I have already read your poem. It is not necessary for you to come back."

The poet said, "Lord, Lord, I am very poor."

The King said, "I know you are very poor. You told me some sweet words in your poem, and I am also telling you some sweet words: please go home, take a shower and eat."

The poet said, "I have come here not to have appreciation for my poems, O great and rich man. I have come for something else."

"O poet," the King said, "your poem was beautiful, the metre was perfect, everything that a good poem needs your poem had in every way. Your poem about me was perfect. You have tremendous capacity, but you should not waste your capacity in writing such beautiful poems about a human being. You must write about God. He is the Creator, the Almighty. You have got divine capacity so you have to utilise it only for God. This kind of flattery I don't deserve. If it is sincere then I don't deserve it. If it is flattery, I don't need it. Only God deserves this kind of praise, and infinitely more. Since you have the capacity, you write about God; write about the Supreme Poet Himself. By writing about Him, you will get more capacity and you will write infinitely better poems." The King then threw away the poem which the poet had written about him.

The poor poet said to himself, "Alas, alas what am I going to tell my wife? To please her I came. To make her rich, I came. Now I have not got a rupee from the King. O God, bad luck is everywhere. He who is cursed with bad luck will have the same fate everywhere, for bad luck knows how to dog a human's fate."

GIM 98. *The golden swan*⁵

The Buddha told this story as something that took place in one of his previous incarnations. At that time, he was a simple man with a wife and three daughters. He was always kind to people and was dearly loved by his family. Unfortunately, he died before he could marry his daughters so he felt very sad. When he entered into the soul's world, he observed what was happening on earth, and saw that his family was almost poverty-stricken.

So he returned to his family as a beautiful golden swan and said to his wife, "I have come to you in this form. Once a month I shall come and leave one of my gold feathers for you to sell. In this way you will easily be able to meet with all your expenses."

So every month he used to come and leave a golden feather.

The wife was very happy, and the daughters also were so delighted when they saw their father. The swan used to stay for a few minutes and then leave.

One day an idea entered into the wife's mind: "My husband may not come regularly, or he may change his mind and stop coming, or he may grow old and die. The best thing is for me to catch him and strangle him the next time he comes, so that I can take away all his feathers."

The daughters were simply shocked: "How can you do this kind of thing, Mother?"

The wife said, "All right, I won't strangle him. But I will take away all his feathers. If he cannot fly anymore, no harm. You will take care of your father."

The daughters pleaded with their mother, "Please, we love our father so deeply. He is so kind to us. He could have stayed in the soul's world, but he comes in the form of a swan to help. Look at his love for us."

But the mother would not listen. The next time the bird came, she caught hold of him by the neck and took away all his feathers, one by one.

It was most painful to the swan and he cried and screamed most pitifully: "What are you doing? I have been so kind to you."

When she was finished, the bird was suffering like anything and it could not fly anymore. Then all of a sudden all the golden feathers turned into ordinary white feathers: they no longer were made of gold.

The greedy wife felt miserable and the daughters were smitten with grief. But what could the daughters do? Their mother was so cruel. Then the mother went inside her room and opened a box where she had been keeping the gold feathers that she had accumulated but had not yet sold. She knew that she still had many gold feathers, enough to meet her family's expenses for at least six months. But as soon as she opened the box, she found that these feathers, too, had turned into ordinary white feathers; they were no longer gold.

The three daughters, with great love and affection, each day fed the poor swan and showed him tremendous concern. The mother was now helpless; she hated her fate. "This is what happened because of my greed," she said to herself.

The daughters said to her, "This is what you have done! Even if our father had not come for six months or one year, we could have lived comfortably on the golden feathers that you had saved in your box. Now father does not have golden feathers anymore."

The father said, "This is your fate, my fate."

Slowly and steadily the feathers of the swan grew back again, but this time they were pure white, so the wife did not bother to take them from the bird. Finally the bird was able to fly away. The children were very happy that the bird was released. Now their father would be happy. They said, "He will be able to do everything in his own way."

The mother felt miserable, not because the bird had gone away, but because of her stupidity. She was not going to get any more golden feathers and once again she was poor.

GIM 99. *King Amar and God's inscrutable ways*[§]

There was once a king named Amar. One day he said to his commander, "Take ten thousand soldiers and go attack King Jaghen. Seize him and bring him to me."

The commander said, "Would you allow me to ask you one question?"

The King said, "No, I have no time. Go immediately! Everybody appreciates him and admires him. His very name torments me. I won't kill him, but I will keep him in prison for life. Life-imprisonment he will get in my palace."

The commander was sad to hear the King's request, but he had to follow his orders. He took ten thousand soldiers and went to the other king's kingdom. For seven days he fought with the soldiers of King Jaghen and finally he defeated them. As the commander was about to bring the captured King back to King Amar, all of a sudden the Queen approached him. She placed her right hand on the commander's shoulder and said, "My son." She said it with such affection that the commander's heart melted.

"What would you like?" the commander asked.

The Queen replied, "My son, please do me a favour. Just release your father. Take him to the King, but not in chains. You are such a brave hero. You have defeated us and now we are at your mercy. But please treat us well. Take us to your palace, and we shall definitely abide by your King's will since we have surrendered to him. My son, I do not want your father to go to King Amar in chains."

The words, "My son," conquered the commander's heart. "You have called me your son. How can a son do this kind of thing? You are my mother. I am leaving your husband, my father, here. Whatever happens to me, my fate I will gladly accept."

So he came back to the King alone, without King Jaghen. King Amar got furious: "Where is he? Where is King Jaghen? How did you come back without him? I was told that you had won the battle."

The commander replied, "Yes, I have won, but I could not bring the King because the Queen called me her son. There was such sincere affection and love in her voice. I didn't have the heart to bring her husband, who is now my father."

King Amar mocked at the commander, "Oh, I see. You have a new father, a new mother. All right, let your parents take care of you. You shall be imprisoned for seven days, and on the eighth day I shall kill you. Let me see how your mother, who has conquered your heart, can save you now."

The commander said, "If my mother cannot save me, no harm. She has such affection for me and I have such affection for her."

One of the soldiers, who was extremely fond of the commander, became sad and mad. He was sad because his chief was going to be killed and mad because that old lady, the Queen had come with such affection that the commander did not arrest King Jaghen. So the soldier went to King Jaghen's palace and said to the Queen, "Look what you have done. The commander will be hanged on the eighth day because he could not take your husband."

The Queen said, "I wanted him to take my husband, but not in chains. I said we would gladly abide by his King's decision. But he did not take us. We shall eternally remain grateful to him and we shall pray to God for his safety."

The soldier said, "Yes, yes, you will pray."

"Yes, we shall pray," the Queen assured him. "Believe me."

The soldier said, "All right, then, I will believe you," and he returned to his kingdom without saying anything to the commander.

The Queen of Jaghen was extremely sad. "Because of me, this commander is going to die. Love is so good; again, love can create such problems. Because of his love for me, the commander did not arrest my husband. I have to do something."

The Queen went to the palace of another King who happened to be their friend. This King was infinitely more powerful than King Amar, and his Queen was her good friend. The Queen of Jaghen said to her friend, the other Queen, "Sister, save me, save me! Save my life!"

The Queen said, "I shall do anything you want me to."

The Queen of Jaghen said, "I want you to save my son."

"Your son? asked her friend. "What has happened to him?"

"I have adopted a son," the Queen of Jaghen explained. "He was so kind to me. He came and attacked our Kingdom and arrested my husband and was going to take him to King Amar. I asked the commander to remove the chains and I told him that we would abide by King Amar's wishes. But because I called him 'son' with such affection, he not only listened to me, but he would not take my husband back to Amar. Now King Amar is angry and wants to kill him. He will be hanged in a few days' time. Please help me. I really want to save him."

"Don't worry," her friend said. "I will be able to help you. Your commander-son will be saved. King Amar is deeply in love with my daughter, but my husband and I do not like him at all. Therefore, we have not given permission to our daughter to marry him. My daughter loves him also, but she does not want to displease us for we are so fond of her. But now we will give our daughter permission to marry him on condition that he set the commander free."

"We are not afraid of him at all because we are much more powerful than he is; that's why he did not dare attack us when we refused to give him our daughter. Now we will tell him we will give him our daughter provided he release his commander. If the commander wants to continue to serve him, that is up to the commander; but King Amar must set him free."

At the Queen's request, the King sent a messenger to King Amar saying, "We are prepared to give our daughter to you, but on one condition: you have to set your commander free."

As soon as King Amar read the letter, he was so delighted and excited that he ran into the room where the commander was and personally released him. "Now my desire is finally going to be fulfilled. In comparison to what I am getting, setting you free is nothing. Now you go your own way. If you want to go to the other Queen who called you her son, you can go and be her commander. Or if you want to stay here, you are totally free to do so. For me to get this princess as my wife is to get everything. She is so beautiful, inwardly and outwardly. I didn't dare to fight her father knowing I was no match for him in courage, valour, strength and power. But now, on his own, he is giving me his daughter, and I am so grateful to him. I am also so grateful to you. It is because of God's inscrutable ways that I am getting my heart's desire fulfilled."

GIM 100. *King Fatul*[§]

There was a pious king named Fatul, who ruled his kingdom with utmost concern and compassion. His very name was a source of inspiration to his subjects. He had almost no enemies; everybody was his friend.

But alas, there was one individual who was dead against him, and that was his own younger brother, Kabu. Kabu was terribly jealous of his elder brother, because he had the throne. "Everybody admires him and nobody cares for me," Kabu said. "If I could become King, I would rule the kingdom more wisely, more affectionately and more divinely than my brother. If only I could be given a chance!"

King Fatul's subjects, however, felt that Kabu was useless. They said to him, "Your brother keeps you in the palace; that is more than enough for you. We will never accept you as our king. There is no comparison between you two."

At this Kabu was very sad and mad, but what could he do? He was helpless. He could never become King, even by dethroning his brother, for the subjects would not tolerate it. The best thing, he thought, would be for him to kill his brother.

King Fatul came to hear about his brother's feelings. He felt sorry for Kabu and one day said to him, "Kabu, don't kill me. It will be a disgrace to the royal family. My brother, I have tried my best to be of service to my subjects. But now I have had enough of name and fame. Since you have the desire to rule the kingdom, rule it. My only request is that you rule it wisely. I am giving up the throne and going into the forest to pray and meditate the rest of my life. The rest of my life I will give all to God."

The younger brother was so moved and he touched his brother's feet. "I will do my best. I really wanted to become King, and I shall not exploit my subjects. They are most precious to me. I am so grateful to you for your tremendous sacrifice."

When the older brother left the palace, all the people mourned and cried. They suffered beyond any human imagination. Thousands of his subjects followed him to the edge of the forest and then they returned with heavy hearts.

Once Kabu started ruling the kingdom, he began to fear what might happen when Fatul's son, Gokul, became mature. Kabu said, "Now he is a little boy, but in a few years' time, when he grows up, he may decide to fight for the throne, and everybody may take his side." Therefore, Kabu ordered Gokul and Gokul's mother into exile.

No matter how hard Kabu tried to be a good King, nobody appreciated him. Whenever he did something good, people felt it was all deception and ascribed some motive to it. They felt that he was not doing it sincerely, or that there was something behind it. Nobody listened to him and everybody hated him. This made Kabu very sad and angry.

King Kabu tried for a few years more, but still he failed to please his subjects. Finally he said, "I have had enough. If people don't like me, why do I have to rule the kingdom? I don't need these subjects. I can live all by myself and be happy."

He thought of his brother and said, "My brother was happy when he was the King, but now he has become infinitely happier. He prays and meditates in the forest and lives on fruits and nuts. He is so happy in the forest. I wanted happiness; that was my only desire. I thought that by becoming King I would become happy, but now I see I will never be happy as King."

So Kabu went to the forest and begged his brother to come back and rule the kingdom. But Fatul refused. "No, the joy that I am getting is real joy. Previously the joy was not complete. I was all the time afraid that another King would come and attack my kingdom, or that a minister of mine would create problems for me, or that my subjects wouldn't listen to me. All kinds of fears, worries and anxieties used to torment me, and my happiness was negligible. But now I have found peace and joy, and this joy nobody can steal. So I am not going back to the kingdom."

Kabu pleaded and pleaded with Fatul, "Please, I have tried in every possible way to be a good King, but my subjects don't believe that I am sincere."

Fatul said, "That is because your journey's start was not divine. Everybody loved me and adored me. You were the only one who was jealous of me. God brought me into the world a few years before you. That is why I became King. Our father was always most kind and affectionate to both of us. Do you not think that he felt sad in the other world that you were so jealous of me that I had to give you the throne?"

Some of the ministers who had come with King Kabu said, "King Kabu, let us go back to the palace. Somebody must be King."

The younger brother said, "I am not going back to the palace. I will also pray and meditate."

There was a chorus of laughter from the ministers, and Kabu got mad: "You are my subjects and still you mock at me? Do you think that I don't have the capacity to pray and meditate like my brother?"

They said, "Certainly you have, but this capacity is not yet manifested. In a few incarnations you will start to pray and meditate."

Kabu was very disturbed: "I am not going to leave this forest. Here I will pray and meditate with my brother."

Fatul said, "I have no objection, but you need more purity."

"What do you mean?" asked Kabu.

Fatul explained, "Purity means the sincere and soulful expansion of the heart. If your heart does not expand, you will not be able to enjoy the joy I am having. My heart expanded; I became one with all my subjects. Again my heart expanded and I gave you the kingdom. Therefore I was happy, I am happy and I shall always remain happy. It is because of my purity-heart that I am all the time getting joy."

Kabu said, "I don't know anything about purity and I don't want to know. But I know that if you remain my guide, my pole star, I will be happy. If you are my pilot, I am destined to be happy and peace will definitely follow me. Therefore, I am staying here; and I am not going back to the kingdom. It was your kingdom and I am giving it back to you."

But Fatul refused, "I won't take it."

Kabu insisted, "I shall soulfully remain with you."

At this point one of the ministers said, "If both brothers stay here, who will rule the kingdom? You two are not doing justice to your kingdom. One of you must come back; it is your duty. If Fatul does not want to return because he has already become a sannyasi, then Kabu should return. It is too soon for him to give up name and fame, since he so desired them."

Kabu said, "Anything that I find to be good, I always do immediately. So I will stay with my brother and, in serving him, I shall get the greatest joy."

Another minister who was very old said, "You will be happy, your older brother will be happy and my mind will be happy if we do one thing. You have a daughter and your brother has a son. Look at your meanness! When you became King, you put your older brother's son and wife in exile, even though your brother relinquished his throne for you. You should have kept his son and wife in your palace and given them your due affection and love. Where is your sense of duty?"

Kabu said, "Please, please, do not bring the past to the fore. I am miserable for all my misdeeds. Only tell me what you want me to do. I will do everything to please my nephew — I am setting him free immediately. O forgive me, I have done everything wrong and undivine because of fear. I thought that when he became mature everybody would take his side and dethrone me. That's why I put him into exile. Now I myself do not want the kingdom. I want a higher Kingdom, a divinely pure Kingdom, a divinely illumining Kingdom."

The older minister said, "Then your daughter and your brother's son should get married and rule as King and Queen. Both of them are extremely good in every way. If they become King and Queen, then your kingdom will once more shine bright, brighter, brightest. Your brother is happy because he has become a sannyasi and renounced the world. He is getting God as his only friend. You will be happy from now on, for you are getting your brother as your pole star to guide you. You will be happy because you are entering into the spiritual life which is the real life. So naturally you will get real happiness from it.

"And we will be happy only when we have a good King and Queen. Your daughter and your brother's son will be a good match, and we shall devotedly listen to them. We shall be happy, extremely happy, when they rule us and guide us."

Kabu said, "Definitely we shall do that. But you go and arrange it, O Minister. I won't go back. I will remain here for the rest of my life together with my brother. You can release my nephew and tell him that I implore his forgiveness. Also tell my sister-in-law that I implore her forgiveness ten times. Now let my daughter and nephew get married and let them peacefully rule the kingdom. Let everyone enjoy peace in his own way, for peace is satisfaction and satisfaction is all."

GIM 81. *(p.321)* 21 January 1979
GIM 82. *(p.322)* 22 January 1979
GIM 83. *(p.325)* 22 January 1979
GIM 84. *(p.326)* 22 January 1979
GIM 85. *(p.328)* 22 January 1979
GIM 86. *(p.329)* 22 January 1979
GIM 87. *(p.332)* 22 January 1979
GIM 88. *(p.335)* 23 January 1979
GIM 89. *(p.339)* 23 January 1979
GIM 90. *(p.342)* 23 January 1979
GIM 91. *(p.344)* 23 January 1979
GIM 92. *(p.346)* 23 January 1979
GIM 93. *(p.347)* 23 January 1979
GIM 94. *(p.350)* 23 January 1979
GIM 95. *(p.353)* 23 January 1979
GIM 96. *(p.356)* 24 January 1979
GIM 97. *(p.358)* 24 January 1979
GIM 98. *(p.360)* 24 January 1979
GIM 99. *(p.362)* 24 January 1979
GIM 100. *(p.365)* 24 January 1979

GREAT INDIAN MEALS:
DIVINELY DELICIOUS AND
SUPREMELY NOURISHING

BOOK 6

There was a good king named Yayati. He ruled his kingdom for a long time and then he gave his kingdom to his son, Puru, and went into the forest. There he practised austerities for a long time. When he died, he went to the highest Heaven.

When he arrived in Heaven, Lord Indra asked him, "How did you come to Heaven?"

King Yayati replied, "Why, I have practised austerities more than anybody else. By virtue of my austerities I have come here."

Lord Indra became furious. "You are too proud. This kind of pride I can't tolerate. Only I am entitled to have such pride, because of my boundless power."

The King was shocked at Indra's behaviour. He could not believe his ears. Indra continued, "You have to return to earth. I won't allow you to stay here."

Poor Yayati was about to return to earth because Indra was forcing him when suddenly Ashtaka, his grandson, appeared. Ashtaka was accompanied by two of his friends, Vasuman and Shaivi. Ashtaka said to his grandfather, "Please stay in the highest Heaven with us. Here I will give you shelter. Our region perhaps is not as great as you deserve, but please accept our heart's humble offering."

Vasuman and Shaivi also said the same: "We would be honoured to be able to give you shelter here, O Yayati. Do stay."

On hearing this, Indra got furious. "What right do you have to say that to this shamelessly proud human being? Heaven is all mine; each part belongs to me. I forbid you to give him shelter in my Heaven."

"Please, Indra," the three friends pleaded, "we beg you to allow Yayati to stay with us."

"All right!" cried Indra. "For this disobedience, all four of you must descend into the world."

"Impossible!" the three friends replied.

But Indra forced them to return to earth, along with King Yayati. When they descended to earth, they started praying and meditating very soulfully. After a few years, again Yayati was in a position to go to Heaven. Just through his meditation power he had developed the capacity to leave his body and go back to Heaven.

But Ashtaka, Vasuman and Shaivi hadn't yet acquired that kind of power, so Yayati said to them, "I have the power to go to Heaven, but I shall not go. Because you three were very kind to me when we were in Heaven, now I shall wait for you."

All three friends immediately said, "No, you should go. When our time comes, when we have acquired this power, when we are illumined like you, then we shall also ascend to Heaven."

But Yayati said, "No, I can't do that. I shall wait."

So the King waited and eventually the others also were in a position to go to Heaven. This time Indra again asked Yayati, "How did you come?"

Yayati said wisely, "Oh, I have practiced a little austerities, but it is all due to your Grace. The very fact that I practised those austerities was also due to your Grace."

Indra was extremely pleased with Yayati's answer. "Yayati, this kind of humility is good. Now you can stay in Heaven as long as you want to. You can stay because you have learned the true meaning of humility," he said.

GIM 102. *Why the sun shines in England*[§]

Once an English officer came to an Indian village. This particular village was fortunate to have a few well-educated people, some of whom knew English quite well. One day, when the English officer had come to visit the village chief, two men came to the chief to make complaints against each other.

The first man said, "Sir, I bought a plot of land from this man, and I was cultivating it to grow paddies. While digging, I came across some gold coins buried in the ground."

The chief asked, "So what is the problem, then?"

The man continued, "I am telling him to take the gold coins, because they don't belong to me. I bought the land only, but I didn't buy the gold coins."

The second man spoke up. "Sir, how can I take the gold coins. When I sold him the land, whatever was inside it became his. The gold coins belong to him, so I can't take them. If I take them, it will be all deception."

The first one said the same. "If I take the coins, sir, it will be all deception on my part, since I didn't pay for the gold coins."

In this way both of them were arguing in front of the chief. The chief finally said, "Your argument will never come to an end."

Both of the parties asked, "Chief, then do you have a solution?"

"Yes," replied the chief. To the first man the chief said, "Do you have a son?"

"Yes," replied the man.

"And do you have a daughter?" the chief asked the second man.

"Yes, I do," answered the second one.

"Then," declared the chief, "it is very easy. I am giving the gold coins to you for your daughter. Your daughter and his son will get married. Then, as a dowry your daughter will bring the money to her husband's home. There very happily they will live."

Both men thanked the chief deeply, "O Chief, your wisdom has saved us. We shall definitely listen to your advice."

The Englishman was observing the whole scene. When the two men left, he said to the chief, "I am so surprised to find these kinds of people on earth, especially in India. How can such saintly people live in India?"

The chief said, "It is quite possible. Here people are sincere. They don't know any other way to act; for them, this kind of nobility and sincerity is the only way. What would you have done if this had happened in England?"

The Englishman replied, "I would have given them each a smart slap and taken away the gold coins, saying that they belonged to the government."

The chief was silent for a moment. Then he asked the Englishman: "Does the sun shine in England?"

"Certainly," answered the Englishman.

"Do you have the moon?" the chief asked.

"Certainly," the Englishman replied again.

"Do you have stars?"

"Certainly."

"Do you have rain and water?"

"Certainly."

"Do you have animals and birds?"

"Yes, of course."

The chief jumped to his feet. "Ah, now I understand! God has given England the sun, moon, stars and water, not for Englishmen, but for the innocent birds and animals that live there. God certainly would not have given the sun, moon, stars and water to you people."

The Englishman got the point.

GIM 103. *The Emperor's three dolls*⁵

There was once a king who had a very, very wise minister.

Everybody used to admire the minister's wisdom. This king was good friends with a particular emperor. One day the emperor gave three dolls to the king and said to him, "I will be very happy if either your minister or anybody else can tell me which is the first class doll, which is second class and which is third class."

The king thanked the emperor profusely, "O Emperor, I am all gratitude for your gifts. I shall always cherish our friendship, and I shall gladly ask the members of my court and my kingdom to look at these dolls."

The following day the king invited all his very intelligent friends and members of the court to see the dolls. All of them looked at the three dolls, and some of them held them and examined them in every possible way. But most of them said, "O King, we are sorry. All three dolls look exactly the same to us. Either they are all first class, or all second class or all third class; it is hard to tell. But we can only say that whatever class they belong to, they all belong to the same one."

"This answer is not satisfactory," said the king. Then he turned to his wise minister and asked, "Why are you remaining silent? You are the wisest of all. Why are you not saying anything about these dolls?"

"What do I know about dolls?" replied the minister.

"Please," pleaded the king, "you must help me. If you do not come up with a satisfactory answer, what will the Emperor say about my kingdom? He will think that we have no intelligent people here."

The minister finally agreed to look at the dolls. "Let me take them home and examine them."

The king said, "Take them and keep them for several days so that you can find the answer. Otherwise, I will be really embarrassed."

The minister took home the dolls. He noticed that although the dolls looked exactly alike, there were some small differences. One doll had one hole in one of its ears. Another had two holes, one in each ear. And the third doll had one hole in one of its ears and another hole in its mouth.

"Now I know the answer," cried the minister. "The first class doll is the one that has only one hole in its ear. This doll hears with a sympathetic ear, and then keeps whatever it hears to itself. There is no way for what it hears to come out. This doll represents very good people. When these kinds of people hear something, they keep it to themselves. This world is full of corruption and they don't want to spread gossip.

"The second doll is also silent, but whatever it hears goes in one ear and out the other. It does not keep any information to itself. Regardless of whether it hears good and soulful things or undivine things, the information just passes through one ear and out the other. These people are indifferent to the world situation.

"The third one has the hole in one ear and another hole in the mouth. As soon as it hears anything, immediately through its foul mouth it tells the whole world.

"So, the first doll remains silent, because it knows that the world is full of corruption and it does not want to add to the world's ignorance. The second doll is indifferent. Whatever it hears immediately goes out the other ear. And the third doll immediately tells the whole world everything with its foul tongue. This is the answer that my King needs for his Emperor friend."

The following day the minister told the king his answer, and this answer was sent to the emperor. The emperor said, "The minister is absolutely right. Now I see that the King indeed has some intelligent people in his kingdom." And the king gave the minister a very good reward for his divine wisdom.

GIM 104. *The ministers' demise*[5]

In India there was a particular kingdom where the ministers were very bad — absolutely wicked to the backbone. They killed one king after another, after each had ruled only about a year or so. They would not allow any king to rule for more than a year. The ministers were very deceptive and cruel, and they got great joy in killing the kings.

Once a new king named Lara came to the throne. He thought that since he had become King, his days were numbered. "What can I do?" he asked. "How can I fight with the ministers when they are so cruel and powerful? Let me resign myself to my fate."

But all his subjects loved King Lara dearly and they felt miserable that he too would soon be killed like his predecessors. The King's wife, Jayanati, came to know that the ministers were indeed plotting to kill her husband. She was determined to save him, but she cried bitterly because she did not know how to go about it.

One day she said to her husband, "You go and live in the forest. My son and I can stay here, because we are not important and the ministers will not bother to kill us. Your life is much more precious to me than the kingdom. Please go live peacefully in the forest. This is the only way that we can be assured that the ministers will not kill you."

King Lara refused, "No, that I cannot do. If I go I will have to take you and our child. I must take care of you. Without you I cannot go."

But the Queen insisted on his going. Finally the King said, "All right, if you insist I will go into the forest. But I am afraid they will harm you."

"No," she said. "They know that my child and I are helpless without you. They won't bother us after you leave, because we are useless people. The ministers won't do anything to us."

King Lara went into the forest and the ministers no longer felt threatened by him. But alas, they started torturing the Queen. They put her into prison and did not allow her to eat. Finally, they made up their minds to kill her.

Through all this, the Queen didn't say a word. Even when she was about to be hanged, she remained silent to the last moment. But there were people in the kingdom who loved the King deeply and who loved the Queen deeply. They got furious with the ministers. "There is a limit to one's patience. We shall destroy the ministers," they said.

So they went into the forest and told the King, and they brought him back to fight against the ministers.

Although his subjects were for him, unfortunately the military was under the control of the ministers. The King said, "It is useless to fight against the military. Now I am helpless, my wife is helpless, our child is helpless. Only I can cry and lament for my Queen. And I know that they will kill me as well, after they kill my wife. I resign my fate to God's Will."

As soon as the King said, "God's Will," something happened. All of a sudden the soldiers felt that they were doing something undivine by listening to the ministers. The soldiers were very tricky, and their commander said to the ministers, "We should also kill the subjects who are still cherishing good memories of the King and Queen."

"That is a good idea," said the ministers.

"Then let us go and destroy them," cried the soldiers. "We shall leave immediately to destroy the whole area surrounding the kingdom."

But as soon as the soldiers encountered the people who appreciated the King and Queen they told them, "We are your followers. We also are admirers of the King and Queen and we shall follow your instructions. Whatever you want, we shall do."

All the subjects said, "Kill the ministers!" and the ministers were killed. Then the King and Queen and their subjects lived happily and peacefully.

GIM 105. *Money corrupts*[§]

There were two friends who were extremely good to each other, kind to each other and fond of each other. One of them decided to go out on a pilgrimage. His name was Rakhal. Now, Rakhal happened to be quite rich. So he took all the money that was necessary for the pilgrimage. He found that he had a large amount of money left over. So he said, "Since it is not good for me to take a very large amount on my pilgrimage the best thing is to leave the rest with my best friend, Ribhu. On my return I will take it back."

So Rakhal took ten thousand rupees in a small box and he went to his friend's house. Ribhu was meditating at the foot of a tree near his house. So Rakhal went to the foot of the tree and said to his friend, "Please do me a favour."

The friend said, "Of course, we are such intimate friends. Is there anything I will not do for you?"

Rakhal said, "Here is my money. Please keep it for me. I am going tomorrow to Benares and many other sacred places. When I return, you will give me back the money."

Ribhu said, "Certainly! I will keep it for you. So Ribhu found a piece of paper and wrote out a receipt. "Here is a receipt," he said.

"What an insult to our friendship!" Rakhal exclaimed. "If I can't trust you, then who will trust whom in God's world. I will not dare to distrust you. To keep my money with you is as good as keeping it in my own safe."

Ribhu thanked him deeply. "I am so glad that you have such faith in me."

His friend said, "I am so glad that I have such a good intimate friend in you."

So both of them were very happy. Ribhu invited Rakhal to eat dinner at his house. "You are going away tomorrow. Have a good and safe journey. I will be very happy to see you and am looking forward to your telling me stories about all the sacred places. It will help me so much in my spiritual life."

So Ribhu took Rakhal's money while his friend left on the pilgrimage.

Two months later Rakhal came back from his pilgrimage. He came to Ribhu and his friend was very polite and hospitable. They talked for a while and then Rakhal said, "I would like to have my money back."

"What money?" asked Ribhu. "Where is it?"

Rakhal could not believe his ears. "I gave you money on the eve of my departure on my pilgrimage."

"Don't tell me a lie," Ribhu said.

"Don't you remember?" Rakhal said. "You were meditating at the foot of a tree."

"Then show me the receipt," the friend demanded.

"I didn't take any receipt," said Rakhal. "You wanted to give me one, but I said it would hurt our friendship. We were so close to each other. It would have proved that we were not so close."

"No," insisted Ribhu. "It is all lies. You didn't give me any money. Only you came to my house and ate and then left."

The man said, "All right. I am going to the village chief."

So he went to the village chief, who was also the judge, and reported the incident. The village chief summoned Ribhu, and the two stood in front of him in the courtroom.

The village chief asked Ribhu: "Did you take money to keep safe for him until his return?"

"No," Ribhu said. "He is telling lies. We are such good friends. If he had given me money, I would certainly be happy to give it back to him. Perhaps he lost it when he went on his pilgrimage. We were best of friends once upon a time, but since he came back from his pilgrimage, he is acting insane."

At this point Rakhal started crying. "Look at this friendship! I will never have any more friends in this life. My best friend has betrayed me."

The chief said to Rakhal, "Are you sure that you gave him the money?"

"I gave him the money," said Rakhal. "Otherwise, I wouldn't say things against him, since he was such a good friend of mine."

"Were there any witnesses?" asked the village chief."

"No," said the man. "It was evening and there was no one around."

"Not even children playing at the foot of the tree?" asked the judge.

"No," said the man.

"Then what can I do?" asked the chief.

"You have to trust me," said Rakhal.

"How can I trust you? It is just your word against his. The best thing is for you to ask that particular tree to come here and tell me what happened."

Everybody in the court roared with laughter.

"How can the tree come?" asked the man.

"No, go ask the tree to come," insisted the judge. "The tree will definitely come. All the trees are obedient to me because of my divine justice and fondness for everything in God's creation. The tree will come without fail."

The man thought that the judge was making fun of him. "O God, I have lost my friend and I have lost my money. Now what am I to do?" he said to himself. "Now the judge is also making fun of me." So he went home very sad and depressed.

Meanwhile, five minutes, ten minutes, a half hour and finally two hours passed, and the judge was becoming impatient. It would not have taken Rakhal more than fifteen minutes to bring a message from the tree. So the judge was about to send someone to find Rakhal. "He has to bring us some news," the chief said. "He must bring a message from the tree."

Now the friend said, "I know where the tree is, and it is quite far. I think he has not even gone there, since it is such a long trip."

"You know where the tree is?" said the judge. "And you don't know where the money has gone? If he did not give you money under that tree, how is it that you know which tree it is?"

"That much I know," Ribhu said.

"This shows that he definitely gave you the money," said the chief. "Money corrupts. Once you got the ten thousand rupees, you became totally corrupted. You have to return his money; otherwise, I will not allow you to leave the court."

"I don't have the money here," said the man. "It is at my house."

The judge sent two guards with the man to get the money and bring it back. When Ribhu returned, the judge said, "For telling lies and harassing that man, and for wasting my precious time, I am fining you 200 rupees."

"O God, I am returning the money. It is I who should get some money for keeping it safe for my friend."

"No," said the chief. "To tell lies and deceive an intimate friend is the worst crime. You have to give 200 rupees."

The man said, "All right. But can I have my friendship back, at least?"

The chief said, "It is up to you, but you are such a scoundrel that I will advise him not to take you again as his friend."

In the meantime, Rakhal returned to the court, and the chief gave him back the money. Immediately Rakhal wanted to give half of it to his friend. "He kept the money safe for me. Now, since he has told the truth at long last, I want to give him some of it."

"I compelled him to tell the truth with my wisdom so that you could get your money back, " said the chief.

"Then I should give you some money," said the man.

The chief said, "I don't take any fee. For me, my service to mankind is unconditional. I am rich enough that I don't have to work. So don't give me money. All I want is justice in my village. Now, both of you go home. I advise you not to be friends with someone who will deceive and desert you. It is not good to have that kind of friend!"

GIM 106. *The woodcutter and the barber*[s]

Once there was a woodcutter and a barber. One day, the barber went to the woodcutter and said, "I want to buy some fuel."

The woodcutter had the wood on the back of his donkey. "That is wonderful," he said. "How much do you want?"

"Everything that you have," the barber replied.

So the woodcutter gave him all the wood and said, "Now, please give me the money."

"No," said the barber. "First you have to give me everything; otherwise, I won't give you any money."

The woodcutter explained, "I can't give you that last piece of wood. It is tied to the donkey's back and it always remains there as the foundation for the wood pile."

The barber insisted, "You have to give me everything."

"I can't," the woodcutter said again. "That one always remains on the donkey."

"Then I won't give you money," said the barber. "I told you that you have to give everything. Since you are not giving everything and because you have wasted my time, I am taking away some of this wood without paying."

The woodcutter tried to stop him, but the barber was so strong that the woodcutter had no choice but to allow the barber to take the wood.

"That barber is such a rogue!" cried the woodcutter, and he went immediately to the village chief and made a complaint against him.

The village chief said to him, "You also do the same kind of thing to him. Then everything will be all right."

In a few weeks the woodcutter went to the barber's shop and said, "O barber, I am so glad to see you after such a long time. I also have my friend with me. First you cut my hair and give me a shave, and then I will go bring my friend."

The barber was delighted to have two customers. "Wonderful," he said, and he shaved the woodcutter and cut his hair.

"Excellent," said the woodcutter. "Now I am going to bring my friend. Once you have shaved him, I will give you money for both of us."

The woodcutter went out and brought his donkey into the barber shop. "After you shave my friend, then only I will pay you."

"You rascal!" shouted the barber. "How can I shave a donkey?"

"Please," said the woodcutter, "you can see that he has got a beard, and his moustache looks so awful. If you don't shave him,

I am not going to pay for my shave and haircut. This is my only friend, my best friend. You saw my friend a few weeks ago. I have no more intimate friend on earth than this donkey. He is my only friend."

The barber got furious. "You have to pay."

The woodcutter said calmly, "The last time you took wood from me, you wanted me to give you everything. I could not, so you got mad and took away my precious wood without paying me. Now, before I came to you, I told you that I had a friend who also needs a shave. Since you have not shaved my friend, why should I give you any money, dear barber?"

The woodcutter took his donkey and left. The barber was so angry that he went immediately to see the village chief. The chief remembered the complaint that he had received from the woodcutter against the barber. So the chief simply said, "Tit for tat."

GIM 107. *Dream, you have opened my eyes, but broken my heart*[§]

There was a good and great king whom everybody loved. The King had a son whom the subjects also loved. One day the King had a dream that his son was killed in a battle. So he said, "Because of my dream, I will never allow my son to fight. I shall keep him in the palace. He is now of age. Let me get the most beautiful girl in my kingdom for him to marry."

So the King found the most beautiful girl in his kingdom and asked her to marry the prince. She was so delighted and proud to be asked to marry the prince and she happily agreed.

She and her husband lived in the palace and were very happy together. One day, a subject came to the King very disturbed. "O King," he said, "our village is on the verge of destruction. Everybody is frightened to death. There is a wild boar that is chasing everybody. We cannot go to work, we cannot eat, we cannot do anything because this boar is so destructive. It destroys everything in its way. Please send your son; our prince can kill that boar."

The King said, "Oh no, I can't send my son. I will send the commander of my army to kill the boar."

The commander immediately agreed, but the prince said, "No, father, I am ashamed of myself. Everybody thinks that I am useless. All the subjects see that I do not fight, but spend all my time with my wife. I want to prove that I know archery. I can easily kill the boar."

The father said, "No, I had a dream that you were killed in battle. I cannot let you go."

"It is all your mental hallucination," said the prince. "I was not killed. And anyway, this is not a battle. It is just a wild boar. Easily I can kill it."

But the King would not agree.

"Father, if you don't allow me to go, then I will leave the palace for good."

The King became alarmed, "Son, don't do that. Go and kill the boar then."

The prince was about to go when the King stopped him. He said, "Wait for a few minutes. You know, your friend is here visiting. He is the son of another king who is a good friend of mine. I will be happy if this prince goes with you."

"I don't need any help," insisted the prince. "Everybody knows he is a great fighter, but this time I want to prove that I am also a great fighter."

"Since he is your friend," said the King, "you should take him."

"All right," said the prince. "I will take him so that he can see my capacity. I have never proven my capacity."

"Yes, yes, son," said the King. "You show your capacity."

So the other prince went with him. When they saw the boar, the prince aimed at it from a distance and shot his arrow, and immediately the boar fell down. The prince ran up to the beast, delighted that he had killed it.

His friend, who was watching from far away, was so thrilled that the prince had been successful. But suddenly the friend saw that the boar was moving a little. He said, "O my God, that means the boar is still alive. At any moment it may get up and kill my friend."

"Everybody thinks that my friend has killed it, and he has already received all the credit. So if I shoot it again, people will think that I am only fooling around, shooting a dead boar."

So the other prince aimed at the boar from where he was standing.

Alas, instead of hitting the boar, the arrow went into his friend and killed him.

The prince was horrified. "I am always such a great aim. What have I done?" he cried.

Many people in the village had observed all this, and they brought the dead prince and the other prince back to the palace. The father began weeping bitterly. "I wanted to avoid this, but I failed. I knew my son was destined to be killed. This prince should go free. I am suffering from the loss of my own son. It will serve no purpose to punish the son of my dear friend. My friend's son is also dear to me. It is I who requested him to go, knowing that my own son was not a good fighter and didn't have good aim."

They made a funeral pyre for the dead prince. The father, mother, friends and relatives were crying and weeping, creating a great scene. In a few hours' time the Queen, who had been so beautiful, had become ugly — pale with anxieties, worries and frustrations about what had happened. She was miserable and everybody in the whole place was miserable.

Just when the burning flames reached their height, all of a sudden the other prince jumped into the pyre and was quickly burned to death.

"What am I going to tell his father?" the King lamented.

The Queen said, "What will he say? His son killed our son."

"But it was I who sent my friend's son with my son to kill the boar."

The King was silent for a moment. Then he said, "My dream, my dream. Always believe in dreams. I told my son, 'Whenever you have a dream, believe it.' The dream warned me, but I did not pay attention to my dream. That is why today I have lost my only son and also my friend's son, who were dearer than the dearest to me. The dream warned me that I should be careful, but my son did not believe in it and I did not heed it. O dream, dream, you have opened my eyes, but broken my heart."

GIM 108. *God wanted to preserve your lives* §

There once was a big temple in one of the cities of India. Inside the temple there were quite a few statues, relating to Indian pujas, made of gold and covered with jewels. Therefore, three guards were posted in front of each of the doors of the temple. And in front of each door there also stood a statue of Lord Shiva.

One day, a famous archer and his son from another city happened to pass by. One of the guards said to them, "Here it is customary to bow down if you come near the statue of Lord Shiva."

The archer said, "Oh, I am sorry, I didn't know," and he bowed down to the statue.

But his son wouldn't bow down. "Who is Shiva, anyway?" he asked.

The father said, "He is one of the cosmic gods who is very powerful, very kind, very great and very good. So please bow down to him."

The guards said, "If you want to stand near the statue, bow down. Otherwise, go away from here."

But the boy said, "No, I won't go away and I won't bow down to your Lord Shiva."

So the father and son were arrested and brought before the head priest, who took them inside the temple. When they saw all the beautiful statues and expensive items in the temple, they were amazed at the splendour and riches.

The head priest said, "Since you wouldn't bow down to Lord Shiva, you will have to receive punishment. But we shall give you another chance. We can't blame the son entirely, although it was he who wouldn't bow down, for it is the father's fault for not teaching him spirituality right from the beginning.

"Now, you have to pass an examination. We will place a coconut on the top of your son's head. Since you are a most famous archer, you will have to shoot the coconut off his head. If you succeed, we shall free you and your son. If you fail, we will put you in our jail for a few months."

"Am I such a fool?" said the father. "If I miss my target, my son's eyes, nose or head will be badly injured. Although I am very skilled, I don't want to take that kind of risk. My son is dearer than the dearest."

The son said, "Father, don't worry. I know your capacity. I know you will succeed."

"If you don't do it," the priest said, "we will not allow you to go back home."

The father finally agreed, although extremely reluctantly. With fear and anger he aimed at the coconut and released his arrow. As soon as he shot the arrow, the boy screamed with joy because the father was successful. But the father thought that the boy screamed with pain, so he fell unconscious.

The son came running to him. "Father, you have been successful! You have done it! Why have you fainted?"

When the father got his senses back, the priest said, "We will let you go now. It is a good thing that your aim was perfect. In that way you were able to save your son."

"Yes," said the father, "and I am so glad that you were able to save your own life also."

"My life?" asked the priest.

"Yes," said the archer. "If I had hurt or killed my son, if my aim had not been perfect, I have other arrows here. I would have used them all on you. So God wanted to preserve both my son's life and your life as well."

GIM 109. *Krishna's outer blessing is his inner gratitude*[§]

There was once a terrible King named Kangsa. Kangsa was the worst possible human being, the worst hostile force, an evil force incarnate. He had killed so many people mercilessly. There was no human being as undivine as he was. His very name used to create unimaginable fear in his subjects.

One day Kangsa and his minister had a secret meeting. "Everybody is appreciating Krishna," Kangsa said. "We must kill Krishna immediately, and also his brother Balarama."

"How can we kill them?" asked the minister.

"Only by inviting both of them here. Otherwise, we will not be able to kill them," said Kangsa.

"But under what pretext should we send for them?" asked the minister.

"We will say that we wish to honour them because they are so great and good," Kangsa said, "and we will ask Krishna's uncle, Akrura, to bring them."

Akrura was in the palace at that time, and he happened to overhear their conversation. So when Kangsa told him to invite Krishna and Balarama to the palace, Akrura said, "Yes, certainly I will go and invite Krishna and his brother to come here." But when Akrura went to visit Krishna he said, "I have come to invite you to the palace, but I must warn you that Kangsa and his minister will arrest you and kill you if you go. I know that your spiritual power can easily destroy people. You are the Lord incarnate. But it is my heart's desire to tell you what they are going to try to do. If you are prepared, it will be easier for you. I am so glad that I have been able to be of service to you."

Krishna was very pleased with Akrura. "We are all gratitude for your loyalty and truthfulness. Since you have come to invite us, we shall come. I will be prepared and Balarama will also be prepared. As you know, he is a great warrior; he is an expert in the use of the mace. He taught the head of the Pandava brothers, Duryodhana, how to use the mace."

When Krishna and Balarama went to the King's palace, they were ready for the attack and successfully destroyed Kangsa, the evil force incarnate.

GIM 110. *The great sage Agastya*[§]

Agastya's mother was the most beautiful nymph, Urvasi, and his father was the cosmic god, Varuna. Agastya himself was very short, almost a dwarf and his skin was dark. Before he became a great sage, he used to be extremely good in sorcery and witchcraft.

Once a great many sages and seers assembled in the Himalayas. Because of their vast wisdom, they were very heavy. It was not their physical bodies, but their wisdom that was heavy. So many sages had gathered together with their wisdom that the earth began to sink.

Because Agastya's wisdom was the heaviest, the other sages requested that he leave the Himalayas, which are in the North, and go to the South. Agastya agreed and with his boundless knowledge and wisdom he went to the South.

On the way he took some water from the Ganges to put in the Kaveri River, which is in the South. He also brought with him a few of the seers' sons and daughters, and also strong young men. He took with him to the South everything he would need to make a good civilisation.

Everybody appreciated Agastya. The sages appreciated him because he listened to their request. The people whom he brought with him to the South appreciated him very much, and the people who were already living in the South also appreciated him. He became truly an object of adoration. Because of his knowledge, because of his wisdom, because of the advice he offered people in every way, he became the sage of sages in the South.

Agastya is very well known in south India. It was he who brought science and literature into that part of India. It was he who introduced Tamil grammar. He was good in astrology, magic, sorcery and many things.

GIM III. *Agastya and the Vindhya mountains*[§]

Once the Vindhya mountains were causing serious problems for the cosmic gods. They were growing up high, higher, highest each day. They were growing so tall that they were becoming taller than the Himalayas. They were becoming so powerful that they threatened to block the sun as it progressed across the sky. But the cosmic gods could do nothing, since the mountains would not surrender or bow down to anybody, or listen to anybody's requests. They were growing up tall, taller and tallest, and the gods were very concerned.

Agastya was the Guru of the Vindhyas. The Vindhya mountains worshipped him. So the cosmic gods begged Agastya to do something to stop the mountains' growth.

One day Agastya came and stood before the Vindhyas. As soon as they saw him they bowed down out of admiration and reverence. Agastya said to the mountains, "I am very pleased with you."

The mountains said, "We are so happy that you have come. Please tell us what we can do for you. Anything you ask us we will do."

Agastya said, "Nothing. I am very appreciative of your respect, love and devotion for me. Now, if you want to please me, remain bowed down until I come back. I am now going out on a pilgrimage. Until I return to you, please remain in this condition. I will deeply appreciate your devotion and your love for me."

Agastya went out on a pilgrimage and he never came back. Ever since, the Vindhya range has remained bowed.

GIM 112. *Agastya swallows the ocean*[§]

Many times wars would break out between the cosmic gods and the demons.

Once, after fighting with the gods, the demons concealed themselves in the depths of the ocean. At that time, the demons were extremely powerful, so they were able to hide in the depths of the ocean. The cosmic gods could not do anything; they could not even trace them.

Agastya, the great sage, saw what had happened, and he became mad at the ocean. He said, "Why did you allow the demons to enter into you and why do you allow them to remain in your very depths?"

Agastya was so angry that he went to the shore and began drinking up all the waters of the ocean.

The cosmic gods came and begged him to stop. "No, no, you cannot do that! If you do that, the earth will be in terrible danger of drying up and God's creation will be destroyed. Please give the ocean back its water."

Agastya said, "If that is what you want, I will give back the water. I wanted to punish the demons and I wanted to punish the ocean for helping the demons. But you are wise, and what you are asking me to do is a good thing. I don't want God's creation to be destroyed. Therefore, I am restoring the water." And with that he disgorged all the water.

GIM 113. *Agastya has a son*[8]

Once Agastya saw in a vision that his ancestors were being held suspended by their heels over a deep chasm. They begged him to help them. He was told that they could be saved only by his son. But he didn't have a son. He was not even married.

So he said, "I shall listen to their request, but I have to get married. I don't want to marry just anybody. I want to marry only the world's most beautiful girl. I will collect the most beautiful, most soulful and most fulfilling attributes from everything that I can see in God's creation — from birds, animals, flowers and everything. Then I will know what qualities I want my wife to have."

So he looked for a girl and finally found one. Her name was Lopamudra. She was the daughter of King Bidarbha. Although King Bidarbha did not like Agastya because he was not handsome, he was afraid of the sage's power, so he gave his daughter to him.

The girl was full of vital desires, so they soon had a son. The son became great in every way, spiritually and otherwise, and eventually he did free Agastya's ancestors. Agastya was very happy that he could save his ancestors by having a son.

GIM 114. *Ilvala the demon*[5]

Agastya was living in a cottage in the forest. The particular place where Agastya lived was full of demons, or raksasas. These raksasas used to terrorise all the people in that forest, but they did not dare to attack Agastya because he was so powerful.

There was a particular raksasa, Ilvala, who was especially fearsome, and everybody in the forest was frightened to death of him. Ilvala had a younger brother, Vatapi, who had the ability to change himself into a ram. People would then unwittingly take him for sacrifice. After killing the ram, they would cook it and offer it as food to their family, guests and themselves. When the meal was over, Ilvala used to summon his brother with his occult power. As soon as he called, Vatapi would burst forth from the stomachs of all the people who had eaten the ram, and thus they were killed. Then Vatapi became a ram again.

This went on for quite a few years. A large number of people were killed in this way, but nobody could do anything about it.

Once the two brothers tried this trick on Agastya and Agastya ate the ram. But when Ilvala cried to Vatapi to come forth, Agastya just laughed and laughed. He said in a thunderous laughter, "Where is your brother now, Ilvala? I have digested him. He is all gone. I have digested him very nicely so you can't have him. And you have to remain my slave for the rest of your life. If you resist, I will destroy you with my occult power."

Ilvala said, "O sage, O sage, do not destroy me. I shall be your slave. I shall eternally remain your slave. I will do everything possible and impossible for you. Only do not destroy me. I know you can easily destroy me. I am at your feet. Give me protection. Show your compassion to me. This is what I need, although I do not deserve it. I am sure you will grant it, for you are not only the most powerful, but also the most benevolent sage. Forgive me. Forgive me."

Agastya said, "I am forgiving you. Remain my slave, and from now on try to become spiritual and divine."

GIM 115. *Balarama and the apple orchard*[§]

Krishna was very dark, but his brother, Balarama, was light-complexioned. Some Puranas are of the opinion that Balarama was the incarnation of Lord Vishnu, while others believe that he was the incarnation of the cosmic serpent, Shesha. Again, still others feel that he was the incarnation of Lakshmana, Sri Ramachandra's younger brother.

Balarama and Krishna were always adventurous. In their boyhood, both brothers were extremely, extremely fond of each other. Krishna always enjoyed doing mischievous pranks, but Balarama was not inclined that way. Still, he used to love Krishna for his cute mischief.

On one occasion, when they were in their teens, they were passing an orchard, when they saw some apples. Naturally they picked some and ate them, as is quite natural for young boys to do.

The orchard was owned by a demon named Dhenuka. Dhenuka was an admirer of Kangsa, the hostile force incarnate, who was ruling the kingdom at that time. Dhenuka hated Krishna and Balarama. Since he had the capacity to take the form of an ass, he immediately did so and started kicking the two boys very hard. But Balarama and Krishna ate to their heart's content, not paying any attention to the ass.

When they had eaten as much as they wanted, Balarama said, "Now that we have eaten your apples, we are strong; so we are ready to fight with you." Then he caught the ass by its heels and whirled him around his head until the ass died. Then Balarama flung its carcass onto a nearby palm tree. Many came to see the deplorable incident and they also fought with Balarama and Krishna. But alas, it was all in vain. They too met with the same fate, and the palm tree was soon festooned with the carcasses of asses.

Children often do a little mischief. If older ones punish them beyond their due, this is what happens. Children have strength indomitable and the older ones, because of their lack of wisdom, suffer what they rightfully deserve. But if they forgive the children when they do something wrong, or if they illumine them, then all the catastrophes and hurtful incidents that children can create for grownups can easily be avoided.

GIM 116. *Balarama conquers Pralamba*⁵

Once there was an athletic competition that many athletes participated in. Kangsa, the hostile force incarnate, sent the asura Pralamba to join in the competition against Krishna and Balarama. Kangsa told Pralamba, "Please defeat these two brothers. If you can defeat them, I shall gladly and unreservedly give you anything that you want. I would hate to see them become victorious. You must defeat them."

Pralamba said, "Do not worry, my Lord. I shall defeat them badly. I give you my word of honour."

Kangsa said, "Nothing will please me more. If you defeat them, you will offer me a world of happiness. Certainly you can and you will."

"I can and I will," said the demon Pralamba.

The athletic competition commenced, and everyone was showing their prowess. It was said that the winner of each event would be carried on the shoulders of the loser. Pralamba deliberately lost in one of the games so he would get the chance to carry Balarama on his back. When Balarama got on his back, the demon suddenly expanded his form, becoming very huge, and he ran away with Balarama.

Krishna was surprised and shocked. He cried out, "What are you doing? What are you doing?" Krishna was about to fight Pralamba, but instead he said to Balarama, "Brother, Brother, bring your immortal nature to the fore. Why are you allowing yourself to be carried away? If you do not listen to my request, I shall have to fight this demon and kill him."

Balarama laughed and laughed. "Krishna, my brother, you know who I am. Why are you worrying? Let him carry me as far as he wants to."

Krishna said, "No, no. I do not want him to carry you any further. Please, please use your powers and destroy this demon. Otherwise, I shall."

Balarama gave a hearty laugh, summoned his divine strength and became infinitely, infinitely more powerful than the demon, squeezing Pralamba to death.

Balarama was strength incarnate and indomitable courage incarnate. When necessity demanded, he acted. But he never misused his strength, never!

GIM 117. *The river Yamuna*[§]

Balarama had many, many good qualities: kindness, compassion, affection, love, forgiveness and so forth. But he also had one bad quality. He enjoyed drinking wine profusely. Then, when he was in a state of intoxication, he did not know what was going on and he was not fully conscious of outer happenings.

Once, after drinking wine, he asked the river Yamuna to come to him so that he could bathe. Yamuna laughed and laughed, "Look at the audacity of this mortal. How dare he summon me! I shall not go."

Balarama waited and waited. Then he became furious and said, "Yamuna, you are not coming to me? Then I shall punish you badly." He took his primary weapon, the ploughshare, into the river and dragged all of Yamuna's water out of the river.

Yamuna was shocked; he never thought that a human being could do this. He begged for forgiveness. "I will never, never disobey you. I will always listen to your command. Please give me back my water," he pleaded.

Balarama returned the river's water.

Yamuna said, "Balarama, you are not only powerful, but also merciful. If you had not forgiven me, I would have remained empty, totally empty. I admire your power. I worship your forgiveness."

GIM 118. *The imprisonment of Krishna's son*[§]

Eternally mischievous, the Kauravas once got an opportunity to imprison Krishna's son, Shamba.

Krishna sent some of his representatives to arrange for Shamba's release, but they came back saying, "They refuse to reason. They will not let Shamba go."

Balarama, Krishna's brother, became furious that his nephew was imprisoned. Balarama went to Asanapada, the Kaurava palace, and thrust his ploughshare under its ramparts. Then he said to Duryodhana, the chief Kaurava, "If you do not surrender Shamba now, I will destroy this palace!"

Duryodhana knew Balarama's strength and immediately surrendered Shamba. "We know you are all strength. Again, you are all forgiveness. We have committed an unpardonable crime. Now we realise it and we are releasing Krishna's son. Forgive us, Balarama."

Balarama said, "Do not act like a fool. Your power is nothing but the exhilaration of your stupidity. Whom are you challenging? Krishna? He is the Lord Himself! Whom are you challenging? Me? I am the one who holds measureless strength. O mortals, never dare to create anger either in my brother Krishna or in me, for immediate death will come and shake hands with you. Be careful!"

GIM 119. *Divida*[§]

There was a great man whose name was Divida. Once upon a time he was nice to Balarama. But alas, it is difficult to always remain a kind, good and nice human being, and slowly he developed arrogance and tyrannous qualities. He did many, many undivine things, and people could not bear his arrogance or his tyranny.

The worst incident occurred when he was tempted to steal Balarama's ploughshare. He entered into Balarama's house in the middle of the night and stole the ploughshare.

When Balarama discovered his loss, he challenged Divida to mortal combat, in a few seconds cutting off the thief's head.

He told Divida's friends and others, "Never, never dare to steal my main instrument, the ploughshare. That is my life-breath. If you create any problems for me, ignorance will befriend you. I do not want ignorance to befriend you. When you allow ignorance to befriend you, eventually death comes to befriend you. So be wise. Don't try to make a fool of me and don't try to make a fool of my brother, Krishna. Do not make a fool of anyone, or eventually yours shall be the unimaginable punishment!"

GIM 120. *Balarama marries*[§]

In those days it was socially acceptable and almost customary for people to marry more than one wife. Sri Krishna was married more than twice. But his brother, Balarama, married only once. He married a most beautiful girl named Revati.

Raivata, Revati's father, at first did not want his beautiful daughter to marry Balarama because he was so short, whereas she was so tall. He also thought that it was beneath his dignity to offer his daughter to Balarama.

But Brahma knew that Balarama loved Revati dearly, even before his marriage. He told Raivata, "If you do not please Balarama when he asks for your daughter, and if you do not give her to him, then you will be sent to death immediately. So be wise. I am not asking because of his power, but because he is very kind-hearted. He is not only great and powerful, but also kind and good. He is the right person."

So, at Brahma's advice, Raivata went to Balarama and begged him to marry his daughter. Balarama smiled and agreed, saying, "You are fulfilling my heart's desire."

On the wedding day Balarama was shocked to see his wife's height. He told Revati, "What will people think of me if I marry you? You are so tall. Let me shorten you. I assure you, it will not harm you. With my divine ploughshare I shall shorten you and you will not be affected."

So he shortened his wife and they became the same height.

GIM 101. *(p.375)* 27 January 1979
GIM 102. *(p.377)* 27 January 1979
GIM 103. *(p.379)* 27 January 1979
GIM 104. *(p.381)* 27 January 1979
GIM 105. *(p.383)* 27 January 1979
GIM 106. *(p.387)* 27 January 1979
GIM 107. *(p.389)* 27 January 1979
GIM 108. *(p.392)* 27 January 1979
GIM 109. *(p.394)* 27 January 1979
GIM 110. *(p.395)* 29 January 1979
GIM 111. *(p.396)* 29 January 1979
GIM 112. *(p.397)* 29 January 1979
GIM 113. *(p.398)* 29 January 1979
GIM 114. *(p.399)* 29 January 1979
GIM 115. *(p.400)* 29 January 1979
GIM 116. *(p.401)* 29 January 1979
GIM 117. *(p.402)* 29 January 1979
GIM 118. *(p.403)* 29 January 1979
GIM 119. *(p.404)* 29 January 1979
GIM 120. *(p.405)* 29 January 1979

GREAT INDIAN MEALS:
DIVINELY DELICIOUS AND
SUPREMELY NOURISHING

BOOK 7

Balarama and his wife had two sons, Nisatha and Ulmuka. Like her husband, Revati was indulgent in wine. They used to drink together, but they never lost their senses.

One day Revati asked her husband, "Do you love me more than wine?"

Balarama said, "Yes, I love you more than wine. Otherwise, I would not have married you. I would have remained satisfied with my wine, my first wife. You are my second wife."

Revati said, "Oh no, if you were married to your wine before me, I will go back to my parents' house. I won't stay with you."

Balarama said, "Where are your parents? Am I not your all?"

"Certainly you are my all," Revati replied.

"Stay with your parents here. I shall never hurt you. You are my only wife — my first, last and only wife."

"My Lord, let us be wise. We must not allow our sons to drink."

"That is an excellent idea. We must not allow them to drink. When they grow up like us, at that time they can drink if they wish. Now, let them study and become wise. Let them practise sports and become strong. Let them pray and meditate. Let them be physically, mentally and spiritually strong. Our children will be strong in every way," said Balarama.

"Yes, my Lord, I am sure your wish will be fulfilled. What you envision is coming from your third eye and I have implicit faith in what you say."

Balarama said, "Our children will be good and they will please us. For that I will give you all credit, for it is you who will do everything for them. Because of you, they will become great and good. I know what I am. I am always preoccupied in my own world, so I know I will do next to nothing for them. It is you who will do everything for them. And for that I am and I shall always remain grateful to you."

"No, my Lord," said Revati, "your inner blessings and inner guidance will guide the three of us always."

GIM 122. *Akampan the hero*[8]

King Ravana was the greatest hostile force. His Commander-in-chief was Akampan, his uncle. Akampan's mother, Ketumali, and father, Sumali, were so proud that their son was Commander-in-chief of the great monarch Ravana.

In the Dandakaranye forest, Rama killed thousands of *raksasas* [demons]. When Akampan brought this sad news to Ravana, the King became furious. He scolded and insulted his Commander badly. "You are useless!" he said to him. "That is why your soldiers could not fight!"

Akampan said, "What can I do? Rama is so powerful, so unimaginably powerful."

Ravana said, "Powerful? Powerful? You are useless, useless, my Commander!"

Akampan said, "My Lord, you want us to seize Ramachandra's wife Sita for you. But I tell you, by fighting you won't get her. You have to play some trick. In some tricky way you have to steal her. In a fair way we will never, never get her."

Ravana became furious again. "We won't get her because you have no strength: no physical strength, no vital strength, no mental strength, no soul strength!"

"Soul strength? What is it? I am hearing this word 'soul' for the first time from you. What is soul?"

Ravana said, "Forget about it. Forget about it. Physical strength you need. Physical strength!"

"With physical strength we will not be able to get Sita. I am sorry," said Akampan. "It is only by trickery that we will get her."

Indeed, it was by playing a trick that Ravana eventually did take Sita away from Rama. But when the fight took place between Ravana and Hanuman, the greatest devotee of Rama, Hanuman threw a huge tree at Akampan and killed him. When Akampan was killed, Ravana's mother, who was also Akampan's sister, cried bitterly for the loss of her dearest brother.

Ravana said to her, "My dearest mother, your brother was a great hero. To be a great hero is infinitely more valuable than to remain alive. Akampan is mortal, but his valour, his strength, his capacities — these are immortal. Who cares for his death? Death comes to everyone, but he has fought like a real hero. Therefore, Akampan remains immortal, especially in my life."

GIM 123. *Nahusha returns to earth*⁸

Once Indra, the King of the cosmic gods, did something very, very undivine. Because of this he was compelled to remain inside the sea for some time. In his place a very pious king named Nahusha was asked to rule Heaven.

Nahusha was not only a very pious king but also a very kind-hearted king. Everybody liked him when he was made King of Heaven. But alas, in a few months' time, some undivine forces entered into him and he wanted to have Indra's wife, Sachi. Poor Indra, meanwhile, was still in the sea.

When Sachi heard of this she was sad and mad. How could she go to Nahusha? She went to Brihaspati, the Guru of the cosmic gods, for advice.

He said, "Don't worry. Don't worry. Just send a message to King Nahusha that only if he can come for you with a chariot driven by seven sages will he get you."

When Nahusha received the message he said, "It is so easy, so easy." So he got seven sages to drive the chariot that was taking him to Sachi, Indra's wife. The great sage Agastya was one of the seven sages. Quite inadvertently, King Nahusha's feet touched Agastya's body. Agastya became furious. "How do you dare to touch my head with your feet?"

"Forgive me! Forgive me!" pleaded Nahusha. "I didn't do it intentionally!"

"Whether you did it intentionally or unintentionally, you did it. Your carelessness is unpardonable. I curse you! You will become a snake!"

King Nahusha cried and cried in front of the sages, but it was of no avail.

Agastya said, "No, I can't change my curse. You have to go to earth as a snake. You are never to stay in Heaven again."

So, instead of going to Sachi's house, Nahusha was compelled to go down to the world. After he was on earth for a long time, Agastya said, "I can now modify your curse, O Nahusha, since you are crying and weeping so bitterly. Yudhishthira, the most pious man on earth, will one day bless you. With his help you will be able to get back your human form and you will be able to return to Heaven."

Sachi, meanwhile, was so happy and delighted that she didn't have to go to King Nahusha.

GIM 124. *The origin of dice*[§]

We all know that the game of dice is a most deplorable and most tempting game. After playing for a while, people lose their brains and become senseless. People who are addicted to the game do not remain normal.

Even the most pious, generous and kindhearted people — men such as Yudhishthira — were fond of this game. So many kings lost their kingdoms and became poorer than the poorest because of dice. But they did not give up this game.

Now, who introduced this game? It was Lord Shiva, nobody else. He and his consort, Parvati, used to play this game. Shiva taught his wife how to play because it was her wish to become as good as he in as many ways as possible. She played extremely well, and they had wonderful games together.

In playing dice, Shiva's consciousness did not descend, as is the case with ordinary humans. Parvati too maintained her highest consciousness. They played dice for the sake of the game. But for ordinary human beings it has always been a dangerous game. One has to lose. One has to win. For ordinary humans who are nothing short of weaklings, naturally the intoxication of the game will prove to be their ruin. Kings would give away their kingdoms, even their wives who were dearer than the dearest to them, to keep their promises when they lost.

But Shiva and Parvati did not become losers. They played dice with innocent joy. So it is not what one plays but who plays that is of paramount importance. For ordinary humans, this kind of life ends in utter destruction.

GIM 125. *Gautama creates a new eye*[8]

There was a great sage and philosopher named Gautama. Gautama was able to conquer everything except his pride. Nevertheless, he was a great sage and philosopher.

Once, Vyasa, another sage, spoke contemptuously about a book Gautama had written on logic. He said the book was useless.

On hearing this, Gautama became very, very angry and said that he would never look at Vyasa's face again.

Vyasa came to realise he had made a deplorable mistake, so he pleaded with Gautama to forgive him. He begged, "I didn't mean it. I didn't mean it. It was a joke when I said that your book was useless. You are never useless, never. I appreciate you and admire you."

Gautama said, "If you criticise my book it is as good as criticising me. How can you separate my book, my creation, from me?"

Vyasa said, "I understand, I understand. Please forgive me. Please forgive me."

Gautama agreed to forgive him. But he said, "If I see you in a normal way with my eyes, then I will not be fulfilling my promise. In the sacred books, it is said that it is a great sin to break one's promise. I have promised that I will not look at you. How can I break my promise? All right, let me put my vision in my feet. Let me put a new eye on my foot, and with that eye I shall see you."

Vyasa said, "No matter where your eyes are, as long as you see me, I will be very happy."

So Gautama created a new eye and placed it on his right foot, and from there he looked at the sage, Vyasa. Vyasa was very, very happy that Gautama had forgiven him.

When the period of forgiveness was finished, Gautama removed the eye from his right foot and once more in a normal way he saw and talked with Vyasa.

GIM 126. *The death of Akshyoi*[§]

Ravana, the great hostile force, and his wife, Mandodari, had a few sons. Akshyoi was one of their very, very powerful sons, and his parents were very proud of him.

One day Hanuman, Rama's dearest devotee, was sent by Sri Ramachandra to find out where Sita was. He came to Sita with greatest difficulty and saw her and talked with her. On his way back to Rama, he destroyed Ashokvana, a most beautiful garden where Ravana and his people enjoyed themselves to their hearts' content. Hanuman destroyed it completely.

On hearing this, Ravana sent five of his captains and also his son Akshyoi to attack Hanuman. The captains and his son were all killed. His wife, Mandodari, got furious, and scolded him and insulted him, "Because of you, because of you, I have lost my son! He was dearer than the dearest in my life. Why did you send him? Those five captains were not enough?"

"They were not enough and here is the proof," replied Ravana. "They were also killed along with my son."

"You should have sent them only! So what if they are killed. Who cares for them? But because of you, my son was killed. I hate you! Never dare to send any of our other sons to fight. You are paying the soldiers in your army. You are paying the captains and the commanders. They have to work for their pay. For them it is either victory or defeat. Either they will take their enemies' lives or their enemies will take their lives. So let them play with life and death. I want my children to be with me. Let them be heroes with me."

Ravana asked, "How can they be heroes if they don't fight and kill?"

"One can become a great hero by developing strength. But one does not have to go into battle to show one's capacity. One can demonstrate it without killing or being killed," said Mandodari.

"O Mandodari, you are talking philosophy," Ravana said.

"My philosophy is if you are sure, then fight and kill. But if you are not sure, then don't go. Cleverness is also strength. Who wants to lose his life? Life is so precious. If my son is one hundred per cent sure of killing someone, then I will allow him to go. But if he is not sure, then I will not let him go. This son of ours, who was so close to my heart and soul, I lost. But before you send the rest of our sons to any other battle, you must ask me and I shall see."

Ravana said, "I am the monarch and you are ruling my life. But love is blind, and because of my love for you, I am surrendering to you."

Mandodari said, "I shall not exploit your love. My love for you shall give you wisdom always."

GIM 127. *Bhrigu's curse*⁵

There was a great sage named Bhrigu, who married a most beautiful girl named Puloma. Puloma was beauty incarnate. Alas, a *raksasa* [demon] had also admired her beauty and had also wanted to marry her. He was very much in love with her, but Puloma's father would not give her to a demon. He gladly gave her to Bhrigu, however, and they were happily married.

Puloma knew of the demon's secret love for her and she hated it. She did not care for the raksasa at all.

One day, when Puloma was walking along the street, the raksasa saw how beautiful she was, but he did not recognise her as Puloma. The raksasa asked a sage standing nearby who she was. The sage, Agni, told him that it was Puloma, the wife of Bhrigu.

The demon asked him, "Where can I see her and talk to her?"

Agni replied, "You are seeing her now. If you want to talk to her, you must go to Bhrigu's house and see if he will allow you."

A great desire entered into the raksasa, and he made up his mind to kidnap Puloma. At the time she was pregnant, and while being snatched away a child was born to her. As soon as the child was born, boundless light and boundless power emanated from his body, and the demon was killed.

The sage Bhrigu was extremely angry with Agni. "Why did you tell the raksasa who Puloma was?" He was so furious that he cursed Agni, "Now, Agni, you must eat everything in God's creation: the good, the bad, the divine, the undivine, everything. Let me see how your stomach can bear undivine things!"

Agni said, "Oh, I have to eat everything?"

"Yes, everything. From now on you cannot leave anything. Everything in God's creation you have to eat. This is my curse," said Bhrigu.

Agni was very, very disturbed. He pleaded, "No, no. I can't do that. I can't eat everything. Please forgive me!"

"No, you have to eat everything, since you were such a fool. You had to tell the raksasa who my dearest wife was. Yes, our son killed the raksasa, but the very fact that my wife was touched by the raksasa is most painful to me. So you deserve this curse."

"Will I ever be able, some day, to free myself from this curse?"

"Certainly," said Bhrigu. "When the hour arrives, you will see. But now you are compelled to suffer from my curse."

Agni was sad and Bhrigu was happy. Happiness in one's life, in a sense, produces sadness in somebody else's life and vice versa.

GIM 128. *Happiness reigns supreme*[§]

In the Mahabharata it is said that there was a king named Shwetaki. He was a very good king and a very great king. He performed religious rites devotedly.

One day Agni, the great sage, went to his palace and ate there. Because of the curse that the sage Bhrigu had placed upon him, Agni was forced to eat all things in God's creation, whether divine or undivine. This day at King Shwetaki's palace, Agni voraciously ate clarified butter and then he suffered from stomach upset. He tried so many ways to cure himself, but he was not able to free himself from the pain. It was unbearable.

Agni thought to himself, "Since I am suffering so much anyway, I may as well eat everything. I don't want to stop. How long can I go on suffering from this stomach pain?" So he started eating everything. He went into Indra's beautiful forest, Khandava, and began eating everything in sight. Indra tried to prevent Agni from eating the animals in the forest, but Agni was so powerful that Indra could not do anything.

Krishna and Arjuna happened to be walking in the forest, and Indra went to them and begged for help. "Look, Agni is destroying my beautiful forest. He won't allow anything here to remain. Everything is being killed and devoured by him. Now please, please help me. I cannot fight him. Agni is too powerful for me!"

Krishna and Arjuna agreed. "Give us some weapons," they said. "We have come with nothing. If you can give us some weapons to fight Agni, we shall do it."

Indra gave the *Sudarshan Chakra* — Krishna's famous disc — to Krishna. To Arjuna he gave the famous bow called *Gandhiva*. After getting these most powerful instruments from Indra, Lord Krishna and Arjuna fought against Agni and finally defeated him.

Indra became very happy and said, "I am so grateful to you two. Please keep your weapons. Krishna, with your disc you will be able to conquer the world. And, Arjuna, with your bow you will be able to conquer the world."

Indeed, in the time of the Mahabharata Arjuna used his Gandhiva, his most powerful bow, countless times. And with Sudarshan Chakra Krishna killed many undivine beings.

Agni also became happy, for the curse that he had received from Bhrigu was no longer in power. Now he could eat food that was only divine and he no longer had to eat undivine food.

So Indra was happy because his beautiful forest was not going to be disturbed any more. Arjuna and Krishna were very happy, because they received such divine weapons from Indra. And Agni was also happy that he had been defeated by them and freed from his curse. Happiness reigned supreme in everybody's life.

GIM 129. *Kahor's curse*[s]

There was a great sage named Uddalaka. He had a disciple named Kahor whom he was very fond of. Kahor was not only very spiritual but he also had a great knowledge of the Vedas and the Upanishads.

After Kahor had been studying spirituality for a long time, Uddalaka asked him to marry his daughter, Sujata. Kahor happily married his teacher's daughter, and they lived together quite happily.

Every day Kahor would recite from the Vedas. He was very conversant with the Vedas and everybody admired his Vedic knowledge.

One day, while he was reciting, he heard someone say to him, "You are wrong. You are wrong."

He looked around to see where the message was coming from. He found that it was coming from inside his wife. At this time his wife was pregnant, and a human voice was coming from the child that was inside her.

Kahor said, "Who dares to correct me? I know the Vedas extremely well. I am an authority! You fool, you are inside my wife, and yet you dare to correct me? Alright! I curse you! When you are born, you will not have a proper body! Your body will be twisted in eight places!"

Sujata was shocked and so sad. She cried, "What have you done? What have you done?"

Kahor said, "What have I done? How could anyone dare to correct me in the Vedas?"

Sujata said, "But is he not to be your son? What will people think of you and what will people think of me?"

"I am so sorry. Anger is such. I have knowledge. I have wisdom. Everything I have. But when the time comes, the undivine forces eclipse our vision. I am really sorry. But what can I do? I have already cursed the child."

Sujata said, "O God, You have given my husband the Vedic knowledge, but You have not given him the heart's wisdom. Now both of us will suffer."

In due course the child was born and, in accord with Kahor's curse, his limbs were twisted in eight different places. His name was Ashtabakra. When Ashtabakra was born his father was not at home. Sujata was very sad. She was swimming in the sea of tears.

For many years Ashtabakra did not meet his father, who had cursed him, as Kahor had left home while Sujata was still pregnant. He had gone to another kingdom to try to gain wealth by defeating another sage in a contest of Vedic knowledge. Kahor lost and was held there.

GIM 130. *Ashtabakra frees his father*[§]

Kahor, disciple of the great sage Uddalaka, was married to his teacher's daughter, Sujata. Kahor was an authority on the Vedas and the Upanishads and everybody admired him for his great knowledge.

While Sujata was pregnant, Kahor went to King Janaka to show his Vedic knowledge. He hoped that the King would appreciate him and give him lots of money and property.

In the palace Janaka had a great sage and scholar named Bandi. When Kahor arrived Janaka told him, "If you can defeat the palace sage in arguments, then only will I give you money and property. But whoever loses the debate will be thrown into the water and have to stay there. Do you agree?"

Bandi said, "Yes, I agree."

Kahor smiled and laughed. "I can easily defeat Bandi," he said. "So let us enter into argument."

From the Vedas and Upanishads they quoted. Each wanted to show his supremacy. At last it was finally proved that Kahor lost. Kahor was thrown into the water and there he had to remain for many years.

Meanwhile, Kahor's child was born. His name was Ashtabakra. He studied the Vedas and Upanishads like his father and became totally conversant with them. Even before he had been born, in fact, while still inside his mother's stomach, he had learned the Vedas and Upanishads. It was during this period that he had found fault with his father's Vedic knowledge and corrected him from inside his mother's womb. In his anger at being criticised, Kahor had cursed his son and Ashtabakra was born with his body twisted in eight places. Even so, he forgave his father, saying, "My father did the right thing. Why did I find fault with him? It was my fault."

One day Ashtabakra told Sujata, "Mother, I am now grown up. Please let me go and challenge the sage, Bandi. I will be able to defeat him and free my father."

Sujata said, "Your father also bragged and said he would defeat Bandi. Because he failed, he is no longer with us. He is inside the water. We can't see him and he can't see us. We can't go to him. He can't come to us. So, boasting is not good, my son. Let us stay peacefully here. Let us see what God does for us to bring your father back. Definitely one day we will be able to bring back your father."

Ashtabakra said, "Oh no, Mother. I shall not listen to you. I am going to King Janaka's place and I will defeat Bandi." So he travelled to Janaka's palace and like his father before him, he challenged Janaka's sage and philosopher, Bandi. Bandi accepted the challenge. But this time, it had been decided that if Ashtabakra defeated Bandi his father would be freed. Bandi would not have to go into the water, but Ashtabakra would be known as the greatest scholar and sage.

For quite a few days they argued, each one showing his capacities. Finally Bandi lost. Then Ashtabakra entered into the river and got his father. The moment Kahor came out of the river, Ashtabakra's body became totally normal. All his bends were gone. His father's happiness had changed his body.

So everybody was happy. Ashtabakra took his father home and they all lived together happily. This also made King Janaka happy. Even Bandi was happy to know that there was someone superior in knowledge to him.

Bandi was a great scholar and sage, and he also had abundant sincerity. He did not have any jealousy. Bandi said, "If there is someone really superior to me, I should be happy instead of becoming sad and miserable." So in his defeat Bandi was quite happy. He made up his mind to learn the Shastras, the scriptures, more thoroughly and to devote more time to spirituality. Everyone was swimming in the sea of delight.

GIM 131. *Ashtabakra is tested*§

There was a great sage named Badanya. Ashtabakra, a great scholar and authority on the Vedas, wanted to marry Badanya's daughter, Suprabha, who was extremely beautiful. Ashtabakra was enamoured of her beauty. But Badanya would not agree to this marriage.

Finally he said to Ashtabakra, "You go to the Himalayas. There you will see an elderly woman praying and meditating. If she is satisfied with you, then I will allow you to marry my daughter."

Ashtabakra went to the Himalayas and saw the elderly lady praying and meditating there. He became her guest. She watched his life to see whether he was good, kind, spiritual and so forth. She also wanted to see if he could be assailed by temptation, or if he had self-control. Although she was quite advanced in years, with her spiritual powers she had the ability to take the form of a very young and most attractive woman. Even when the elderly lady became young and very beautiful, he was not interested in her. He prayed and meditated beside her, all the time thinking of Suprabha, his future wife. Ashtabakra and the elderly lady were very good to each other.

One day she said, "Now you go back to Suprabha's father, Badanya. I will tell him that you are faithful only to Suprabha. Your sincerity has moved me. Therefore, you deserve her. You go."

He went to Badanya. Badanya said, "I am very pleased with your love for my daughter and your true sincere concern for her. Your interest and faithfulness have pleased me. I give Suprabha to you."

Ashtabakra and Suprabha went back to Ashtabakra's home. All were flooded with tremendous joy.

GIM 132. *Ahalya, beauty incarnate*[§]

Brahma, the Creator, had a mentally begotten daughter named Ahalya. She was beauty incarnate; nobody could equal her in beauty. She possessed a supreme beauty all the time.

One day Brahma took her to the great sage Gautama and asked him to take care of her for some time and teach her spiritual discipline and dedication. Gautama was very pleased with his disciple. She was also extremely pleased with her Master.

After some time Brahma came to Gautama to take his daughter back. Gautama returned her, saying, "I was so happy to teach your daughter."

Brahma said, "I am so grateful to you."

A few months later Brahma came back to Gautama and said, "You have to marry my daughter, for you have been very kind to her and she is all admiration and adoration for you. I will be so proud to have you as my son-in-law. So please marry my daughter."

"If that is what you want, O Lord Brahma, then I am willing to have your daughter as my wife. Previously she was my spiritual daughter. Now, if she wants me to be her husband, I am more than willing. She is not only extremely beautiful, but also extremely good and kindhearted. I will be very pleased to have her, and I will happily marry her."

Gautama and Ahalya were married, and they were exceedingly happy. One day Ahalya told Gautama, "On my return home, my father was all appreciation for you. He was seeing my good qualities and he couldn't believe his eyes that I had become so spiritual."

Gautama said, "I am so glad to have taught you. I have had many disciples, but none of them could learn things as fast as you did. In every way you surpassed your spiritual brothers and sisters. So I am very proud of you. Now the time has come for you to teach others."

Ahalya said, "How can I teach others? I have just learned from you!"

"There will be many newcomers. You will teach them, and once they have learned basic things from you, they can come to me for further spiritual knowledge."

Ahalya devotedly said, "My Lord, I shall do it. To please you in your own way is my life."

GIM 133. *Ahalya is disgraced*[§]

Gautama, the great sage and philosopher, and his wife, Ahalya, were living together very peacefully, very happily and very fruitfully. But alas, Indra, king of the cosmic gods, became terribly jealous of them.

He said to himself, "Ahalya was the most beautiful woman. It was I who deserved her. How could it be possible for Gautama to marry her? I wanted to marry her. No, I cannot tolerate this! I must do something. I must punish both of them. It is I, the King of the gods, who deserved her and not that silly Gautama."

So one day he took Gautama's form and went to Ahalya while her husband was bathing in the river. He appeared before her in an absolutely vital and emotional consciousness.

Ahalya knew it was not her real husband and said, "I know, I know, Indra. You have come and taken the form of my husband. You are not my husband Gautama, but still I love you. I have tremendous love for you. You are so handsome, so beautiful, so powerful. I have tremendous love for you."

Indra said, "Really I wanted you long before you were married. I always treasured you inside my heart. I have tremendous, tremendous love for you. Your very name, your very beauty, thrill my heart. Certainly we are meant for each other."

"It seems so," said Ahalya.

At that very moment Gautama came. As soon as Gautama saw both of them, he used his third eye of destruction. "I am using this, Indra, to punish you. How can you fall in love with my wife? I curse you! With my third eye I am making you impotent."

Indra said, "Forgive me. Forgive me."

"No forgiveness. No forgiveness. You impossible, unthinkable character!"

To Ahalya he said, "Unthinkable! Unbelievable! You are my best disciple! You I married because of your father's request. You surpassed everyone in spirituality. Now this is what you have done with your life? Falling in love with this worst possible scoundrel, Indra! You also I am cursing. You will live here unseen by people. You will eat only wind. You will never have any proper food. You will lie down here practically dead. Nobody will care for you. Everyone will despise you for your unfaithfulness.

"You were the most beautiful woman, but now there will be many who will be more beautiful. Now that I am withdrawing my blessing-power, you will be a disgrace and everyone will hate you. But I tell you, after many, many years, Sri Ramachandra will pass by here and walk over your body. He will forgive you. When he does, you will be relieved of your sin and you will regain your spirituality and beauty. In the meantime, my curse and your life will go together. I gave you my aspiration, my realisation, my occult power, everything! And you became unfaithful. Impossible creature!"

Gautama's rage cursed both Indra and Ahalya. Indra assumed his own form and was cursed with impotency while Ahalya lost all her physical beauty and withered away to mingle with the dust of Gautama's palace grounds.

GIM 134. *Ahalya is freed*[§]

Sri Ramachandra was walking past the palace of the ancient sage and philosopher, Gautama, when he heard a cry from the earth beneath his feet. Looking down he saw the frail frame of a woman in the dust. As he helped her up her body became alive and she cried, burying her tears in his feet. "O Rama!"

Rama said, "What have I done? Please tell me what I can do for you. Forgive me!"

The woman said, "I am Ahalya. I was the wife of Gautama, the sage. My body has lain here for hundreds of years because of the curse Gautama put on me. I was unfaithful to him when Indra tempted me. I was left here to feast on the wind, and all my beauty was taken from me."

Rama said, "What can I do for you?"

"You have already done it, my Lord. You have touched me. Now I am pure. Now I am pure. You have saved my life. Now please tell me what I can do for you?"

Rama said, "What you will do for me? You are free from your sin. That is what gives me most joy. So from now on, remain in your beauty. Never be unfaithful. Lead a life of purity, as you lived before you were married. Please go back and regain your purity, regain your spirituality, regain everything that you had.

"Physical beauty should be an expression of inner beauty. Physical beauty must not attract others. On the contrary, physical beauty should only inspire others to become friends with their own inner beauty, which is all light. Physical beauty must not be a hindrance. Physical beauty must not lord itself over others. Physical beauty should be an added thing to the inner beauty. It should be a true expression of the inner beauty, which reflects the Divinity and Immortality within us. Inner beauty and outer beauty must go together, fulfilling each other. Inner beauty is self-giving. Outer beauty is Light-spreading."

Ahalya fell down at Rama's feet and offered her heart of gratitude to him. Rama blessed her and said, "I accept your gratitude-heart. Take my blessingful joy and pride."

GIM 135. *Ashwasen tries to avenge his father*[§]

There was a snake-like man named Takshaka. Agni begged Arjuna and Krishna to destroy the forest, Khandava, where Takshaka happened to live. They listened to his request and destroyed whoever and whatever was living in the forest.

Takshaka and his wife were killed, but their son Ashwasen, who was just a little baby at the time, escaped. Indra, who was guarding the forest when Krishna and Arjuna began their destruction, created a great gust of wind which compelled Arjuna to swoon for a few seconds. In this brief time, Indra helped Ashwasen to escape.

Ashwasen grew into a mature boy. In the battle, when Karna, the great hero of the Kauravas, was fighting against Arjuna, Ashwasen entered into Karna's arrow in the form of a snake. Karna, however, was not aware of this. Even as the arrow was being aimed at Arjuna, Krishna could see that it was a most dangerous arrow. When Karna shot the arrow, Krishna pressed Arjuna's chariot one foot down into the earth. The arrow pierced Arjuna's golden crown, totally destroying it, but Arjuna was quite safe.

Ashwasen, the snake, came to Karna and said, "It was I who entered into your arrow to kill Arjuna. Now please use me once again."

"It is beneath my dignity to use the same kind of arrow twice for Arjuna," said Karna. "I will not use it."

"If you don't want to use my help inside your arrow, then let me go and kill Arjuna myself," pleaded Ashwasen. So Ashwasen went and tried to kill Arjuna, but he was killed by Arjuna instead; for Arjuna was an infinitely superior archer.

This is what Krishna, the Knower of everything, the Knower of all, can do. Had Krishna not been in Arjuna's chariot, Arjuna's head would have been cut to pieces by Karna's arrow. So the Lord will always take care of His dear ones.

GIM 136. *Sangya's marriage to the Sun God*[5]

Vishwakarma was a great sage. He asked his daughter, Sangya, to marry the sun, Surya. She was very happy and very proud to marry him. But alas, a very short time after their marriage, she became frightened to death whenever she saw her husband. He was extremely luminous and powerful. His brilliance and power tortured her, and she was unable to go near him.

So she created a lady exactly like herself and called her Chhaya. Then she left the lady with Surya and went back to her parents' house. Her father was extremely annoyed with her. He said, "How can you do this? How can you deceive your husband? He is so kind, so good, so great."

"But Father, what can I do? He is too powerful. His heat kills me. As soon as he comes near me, I die from his excessive heat."

Vishwakarma said, "You should be very proud of him. You should ask him if there is a way to keep his heat from torturing you. He is so powerful. You must go. I don't want you to come back to stay with me. After getting married, it is absurd to leave one's husband and come back to one's parents. Now you must go. I will not keep you with me."

So Sangya left her father, but she did not go back to Surya. She took the form of a female horse and roamed around the earth.

In the meantime, Surya looked everywhere for his wife. He knew that Chhaya was not his real wife, so he searched for Sangya. Finally he came to know that she had taken the form of a horse and was roaming around. Surya also took the form of a horse and found her. He said, "I am so sorry that my heat tortured you. I am taking human form again. You also please take human form again. Let us remain happily married. I will not hurt you with my heat. I will reduce my heat and power to keep you. You were so beautiful, so kind to me once upon a time. I want you to be happy. Let us go home."

Sangya went home with Surya. He kept his promise to her and reduced his heat and power, and they lived together peacefully and happily.

GIM 137. *Ashwini and Rebant*[§]

Surya, the sun god, and his wife, Sangya, had twin sons. Their names were Ashwini and Rebant, but everyone called them by one name — Ashwinikumar. They were extremely beautiful and looked very much alike. They became great physicians and were known as heavenly physicians. They could cure incurable diseases. Some people said they were not actually human beings, but were really Indra and Varuna. Others said that one was earth and the other Heaven. They were also called day and night, and the sun and the moon.

Three times a day they would leave Heaven and go to earth to watch what was happening there. They would shower earth with their love, concern and compassion. All this they would do secretly in their glowing white chariots.

In many cases the human physicians on earth would not be able to cure their patients. Medical science often fails. The two brothers would hear the crying families and secretly descend to earth to save the sick person. The doctors would sometimes be pronouncing the patients dead when the brothers would save them. No one could understand what had happened, but the families would dance with joy that a miracle had taken place to save their loved ones.

GIM 138. *Alakshmi gets married*[s]

Lakshmi, the cosmic goddess, was very divine, but her older sister, Alakshmi, was totally undivine. The ocean was turned and emptied and from its floor came the undivine Alakshmi, wearing a garland full of blood. Her clothes also were stained with blood. Every part of her was covered with blood.

No one dared to marry the dark, ugly-looking woman; not the cosmic gods, not the demons, not even the asuras. Because she could not find a husband she was very sad and mad. She wondered, "Who will marry me?"

But the great sage, Duhsha, who devotedly practised austerities said, "It is my will that I do everything that nobody else can do. So, if no one wants to marry Alakshmi, then I will marry her. Not because I love her, but because nobody dares to marry her. If necessity demands, I will love her too. Right now I am only marrying her because no one else will, but if I feel like loving her, I will love her too. But let me first marry her, at least."

So Duhsha married Alakshmi and she was extremely happy. She wore dirty, filthy garments and adorned herself with jewels made of iron. She was the cause of all unfortunate things that happened in the family and always caused calamities. She smeared her entire body with a sandal paste made of pebbles and stones, and always carried a broom in one hand. She was ugliness incarnate and unkindness incarnate. Her very face was destruction. Her eyes and every part of her were destruction incarnate.

Duhsha said, "Well, I have passed my first examination; I married her, which no one else could do. But I don't even want to sit for my second examination. I don't want to love her. I don't want to love her."

He lived with her for a few years and then prayed, "O God, save me. It is not always advisable to go against the current. When most people do things in one way, it is advisable to follow their way and not try to do things differently in order to win appreciation and admiration from them. No, if others are doing the right thing, I should also do the right thing. I did not do the right thing by marrying this undivine woman, to say the least. So let me get rid of her and return to my spiritual, austere life. I shall enjoy only divinity in its purest form."

So Duhsha threw Alakshmi out of his house. She cursed him saying, "You will be destroyed."

Duhsha said, "Good. But I will be destroyed by someone else other than you. I am ready to be destroyed, but not by you. And if I have spiritual power, occult power, yogic power, then let us see who can destroy me. Needless to say, you cannot."

"No, I cannot destroy you, true, but there will be someone to destroy you someday, somewhere, somehow."

He said, "Let us wait and see who that person will be. But for now at least let me get some joy in my life. You get out of my life and let me get joy, joy, joy. I need joy in my life."

So Alakshmi had to leave her husband.

GIM 139. *Ashwatthwama and Krishna's disc*[§]

Dronacharya was the archery teacher for the Kauravas and Pandavas. In those days, Dronacharya was matchless in archery. Dronacharya had a son named Ashwatthwama. He was named Ashwatthwama because as soon as he was born he started neighing like a horse, and *Ashwa* means horse. Dronacharya was extremely fond of his son. Ashwatthwama learned archery from his father and became a great hero.

Ashwatthwama's mother was the sister of another great archer, Kripacharya. Kripacharya also helped Ashwatthwama, as well as the Kauravas and Pandavas, in archery. It was also Kripacharya who had requested Dronacharya to teach the Pandavas and Kauravas after him. They were very close relatives.

Ashwatthwama learned many secret ways to use the bow and arrow and soon became an expert.

The Pandavas were in the forest because of Arjuna's and Yudhishthira's defeat in a game of dice with Duryodhana and the Kauravas. Ashwatthwama knew that Krishna was very fond of the Pandavas, especially Arjuna. So he thought, "This is the time for me to go to Krishna and get something from him."

He went to Krishna and said, "I am giving you my most powerful weapon, the *Brahmashira*. It can kill anyone when it is used against them. Will you not give me your *Sudharshan Chakra* disc in return? Will you not trade with me? I would be so grateful."

Krishna said, "Wonderful! I am ready to exchange. Please take it."

Ashwatthwama tried to lift the Chakra disc up, but it was impossible for him to lift it.

Krishna said, "Young man, you cannot even lift my weapon. How are you going to use it?"

Ashwatthwama was embarrassed and ashamed. Krishna smiled at him saying, "Be satisfied with what you have and fight against others with the help of your weapon. My weapon is too heavy for you."

GIM 140. *Ashwatthwama's treachery*[5]

In the battle of Kurukshetra, Ashwatthwama and his father, Dronacharya, took the side of the Kauravas. When the Pandavas killed Dronacharya, Ashwatthwama was enraged. He was smitten with grief and anger and wanted to kill all of the Pandavas immediately. He begged Duryodhana to give him a chance to be the commander of the Kaurava army. Duryodhana gave him the chance.

It had been agreed that at night they would not fight. But Ashwatthwama, his maternal uncle, Kripacharya, and a few others that night entered the tent of the sleeping Pandavas. Ashwatthwama killed Draupadi's five sons. Then he and the others quickly ran away.

What they did was unthinkable. At night they were not supposed to fight; yet Ashwatthwama and his soldiers came like cowards and killed five innocent human beings.

Ashwatthwama went back to the Kauravas' tent and bragged like anything. Kripacharya and the soldiers who had secretly accompanied him also bragged. They said, "It does not matter how we kill, but that we kill. Who cares whether we use divine means or undivine means? Our objective is to kill. These are our enemies and although we promised that we would not fight at night, in war who cares for rules or promises? Our main promise is to kill our enemies. So we have fulfilled our main promise. Who cares to keep the other promise about only fighting during the day?"

All of those who went into the Kauravas' tent danced with joy because of their victory.

GIM 121. *(p.409)* 29 January 1979
GIM 122. *(p.410)* 3 February 1979
GIM 123. *(p.411)* 3 February 1979
GIM 124. *(p.412)* 3 February 1979
GIM 125. *(p.413)* 3 February 1979
GIM 126. *(p.414)* 3 February 1979
GIM 127. *(p.416)* 3 February 1979
GIM 128. *(p.417)* 3 February 1979
GIM 129. *(p.419)* 3 February 1979
GIM 130. *(p.420)* 3 February 1979
GIM 131. *(p.422)* 3 February 1979
GIM 132. *(p.423)* 3 February 1979
GIM 133. *(p.425)* 3 February 1979
GIM 134. *(p.426)* 3 February 1979
GIM 135. *(p.428)* 4 February 1979
GIM 136. *(p.429)* 4 February 1979
GIM 137. *(p.430)* 4 February 1979
GIM 138. *(p.431)* 4 February 1979
GIM 139. *(p.432)* 4 February 1979
GIM 140. *(p.433)* 4 February 1979

GREAT INDIAN MEALS: DIVINELY DELICIOUS AND SUPREMELY NOURISHING

BOOK 8

In the battle of Kurukshetra, the Pandavas and Kauravas had a rule that they would fight only during the day. Unfortunately, one night the Kauravas broke this rule. After the death of his father Dronacharya, Ashwatthwama entered into the tent of the Pandavas and killed the five sons of Draupadi.

When Draupadi found that her sons had been killed, she cried and cried bitterly. She told Bhima, "Bhima, I am not going to eat anymore until you kill Ashwatthwama and bring his crown to me. If you cannot do this, then I will starve. I will sit here and do nothing until you do my bidding."

Bhima ran out to kill Ashwatthwama, with Yudhishthira and Arjuna following closely. They heard that Ashwatthwama was hiding on the bank of the Ganges, pretending to meditate amongst the sages there. He had taken the disguise of a sage and sat near Vyasa.

With great difficulty Bhima, Arjuna and Yudhishthira found him. As they approached, Ashwatthwama took out his most dangerous arrow, the *Brahmashira*. Arjuna also had this same arrow. Before Ashwatthwama and Arjuna began battle with these dangerous arrows, the great sages Narada and Vyasa, as well as many others, stood up and said, "Stop! Stop! Withdraw those arrows! Otherwise, thousands of people will be killed! You can't do that. You must have some compassion for innocent mankind."

Arjuna said, "I am ready to withdraw, because I don't want to kill unnecessarily, especially not innocent people."

Ashwatthwama said, "I will also withdraw."

Arjuna was able to withdraw his arrow because of his spirituality. He had practised spirituality for so many years and had become good in hundreds of ways.

But Ashwatthwama could not withdraw his arrow and it killed Arjuna's grandson. Every one cried. They were in a sea of tears.

But Sri Krishna smiled and, with his yogic power, revived Arjuna's grandson.

Bhima had not forgotten Draupadi's request and said, "You are the loser. Arjuna defeated you by bringing back his arrow. You are now at our mercy. Give us your crown. If you do not do this, we shall kill you here and now."

Poor Ashwatthwama, what could he do? So he gave his crown to Bhima and Bhima took it to Draupadi.

Draupadi's grief diminished a small amount because she saw that the pride and glory of Ashwatthwama had fallen. She placed the crown on Yudhishthira's head saying, "You deserve this. You are the head of the Pandava family. If I see this crown on you, I will be happy because it means we have conquered him and he has surrendered to us."

Yudhishthira said, "If that makes you happy, I will wear it. But remember that it is painful for me to wear his crown because he is wicked to the backbone. He cruelly killed our children at night."

Draupadi said, "You are right. You are right. Now that Bhima has brought us the crown, let us throw it out. We don't need it. His pride is at our feet. Let us throw the crown away."

GIM 142. *Ashwini's receptivity*§

Ashwini is the name of a star. This particular star looks like the head of a horse. Therefore, it is called Ashwini because *Ashwa* means horse.

The moon has twenty-seven wives, and Ashwini is one of them. Ashwini is very, very close to the moon. It is also the first star that became visible near the moon. Some of the stars were terribly jealous of Ashwini because she had tremendous beauty and because the moon had special fondness for her.

One day the moon said to all his wives, "For two reasons I have special fondness for my Ashwini. First, she came into my life long before all of you. Secondly, the beauty that Ashwini has pleases me most. Everybody has a special beauty, but Ashwini's beauty gives me the most joy. For these two reasons she has become closest to me."

"My Lord," said Ashwini, "I am beautiful, I am close to you, I came first to you, not because I deserve to, but because your compassion allowed me to. It is because you pour your own beauty into me that everyone sees beauty in me. If you take away your beauty, then I will be uglier than the ugliest. Your compassion is unparalleled. It will always remain so."

The moon said, "Yes, my compassion is unparalleled and, something more, unconditional. But I would like my other wives to become receptive like you. Then I will be very happy. Otherwise, my unconditional, unfathomable love-beauty will be of no avail. There should be others to receive it like you. Receptivity is of paramount importance. Otherwise, we remain where we always have been."

GIM 143. *Arundhati*⁵

Arundhati, the wife of the sage Vashishtha, was extremely learned and extremely spiritual. She developed occult and spiritual powers by the grace of her husband. She was extremely devoted to Vashishtha.

In the Mahabharata it is said that if one becomes virtuous and totally devoted to her husband like Arundhati, then one can easily go to Heaven and there she will be worshipped.

In the sky there is a special star called Arundhati. It shines most beautifully beside Vashishtha. It is said that whoever can-

441

not see Arundhati in the sky will have a very short life. Those who cannot see Arundhati are unfortunate people. How can these people accomplish anything when they have such short lives?

In India when a marriage takes place, at night the village priest shows the Arundhati star to the bride so that she can become as beautiful, as learned and as spiritual as Arundhati. Arundhati is the ideal of the young girls and also of married women. To all women Arundhati represents woman's aspiration, woman's realisation, woman's beauty and woman's devotedness to the husband, plus spiritual power and occult power in infinite measure.

GIM 144. *Arishtanemi*[§]

In the time of the Mahabharata there was a great sage named Arishtanemi. He had a beautiful young son who was conversant with the Vedas. The father was extremely proud of his son.

One day Arishtanemi's son was playing in the forest. It happened that a prince was hunting in the forest at the same time. Alas, he mistook the boy for a deer and killed him.

When the prince found out that he had slain the son of Arishtanemi, he was smitten with sorrow. He went to see Arishtanemi and beg for forgiveness. He did not know where Arishtanemi's home was, so he had to make inquiries. Finally, he came to the cottage of the boy's father and said, "Forgive me, forgive me."

"What have you done wrong that I have to forgive you?"

"Oh, your son!"

"My son? Do you need my son?"

"Arishtanemi, your son is no more."

"Who says my son is no more? My son is resting in his room."

The prince asked, "Are you sure your son is in his room?"

"Yes, he is."

"Then...." said the prince, bewildered.

"Then, what?"

"That means I have killed somebody else's son, not your son."

"Do you want to see my son?"

"Yes, can I see him?"

Arishtanemi called out, "Son! Come out, my son!" The son came out of his room.

"Oh! This is the boy! This is the boy that I killed!" said the prince. "How can he be alive? I saw him lying in the forest!"

Arishtanemi smiled and said, "O prince, how can my son be dead? You thought he was a deer and you aimed your arrow at him by mistake. You thought you killed him, but the soul of my son came to me and asked me to revive him. For me, this is like drinking water. I have occult power. I have spiritual power. As soon as his soul came, I revived him."

"But what about the wound? He was bleeding."

"That is also nothing. You did not remove the arrow, but with my occult power I removed it."

Oh, forgive me! I did not even remove the arrow!"

"I easily removed it and you cannot even see any wound."

"No, I can't," marvelled the prince.

"When I revived him, my son came to his senses and ran home. He reached here long before you."

"How can anyone do this?" asked the prince.

"You have to practice spirituality. God's Power is infinitely stronger than man's power. If you can kill someone, then God can give new life to that person. Again, if God wants someone to die, you cannot keep that person alive. My will has become one with God's Will. God wanted my son to remain on earth. Therefore, I was able to revive him. But if God had wanted my son to die from your arrow, I would have accepted my fate cheerfully. When you have implicit oneness with God's Will, you can do the miracle of miracles. But at that time, there is no such thing as a miracle. It is all perfectly natural. God's Will is the only natural reality in God's entire creation."

"Will your son forgive me? You may forgive me, but will your young boy ever forgive me?"

The son said, "The question of forgiveness does not arise. I am so grateful to you."

"How can you be grateful to me? I hurt you."

"I am grateful to you because I always wanted people to know of my father's spiritual power. Today you were the instrument which permitted my father to show his spiritual power. You are the prince. Everybody knows you. You will go to the palace and tell your father. Then the entire world will come to know who my father is. He has such tremendous occult and spiritual power. So you have done me a favour unconsciously. Therefore, I am most grateful to you."

The prince said, "O God, good people do live on earth. I thought that there were no good human beings on earth, for I always see people around me of my own standard. Now I see that there is another standard, in which people can be as nice as you. We shall always walk in the footsteps of good people like you two. Forgiveness is your choice. Oneness is your choice. You forgive mankind because you are one with God's Will. Again, because you are always one with God's Will, God does everything in and through you in His own Way. How I wish I could accept spirituality. But, unfortunately, my life is full of desire."

Arishtanemi said, "Prince, I am very pleased with you. There is an hour for everything. When your hour strikes, you will enter into spirituality. At that time I will be of real help to you. One day you will become as spiritually great as you are now physically great. The hour will definitely arrive for you to become spiritually great, too. Just wait! Have patience and I assure you that I will help you far, far beyond your imagination, for to help you at that time will be to fulfil once again my Beloved Supreme's Will. In His own Way I shall fulfil Him at His chosen hour.

"There is nothing divine you cannot do when you become one with God's Will. He is omniscient. He is omnipotent. He is omnipresent. He does not want to maintain His omniscience, omnipotence and omnipresence only for Himself. He wants to give them away to all those who truly care for Him as their own, very own. Love Him, adore Him and fulfil Him in His own Way, for He is everything. Try to please Him in every way and do not hanker for your own fulfilment. At that time, whatever you will automatically becomes God's Will too.

"Now we are crying to fulfil God in God's own Way. A day will come when, by virtue of our own constant oneness with God's Will, whatever we will shall automatically become God's Will, for our will and God's Will can never be separate. The drop knows what the Source wants and the Source always knows what the drop wants. In pleasing the Source continuously, the drop becomes fully aware of the Source's Will. Again, if the drop does something spontaneously, even without being aware of God's Will, the drop will carry the Will of the Source."

GIM 145. *A Brahmin's inner fire*§

Dangsha was a great demon who was very, very undivine. One day he stole the wife of the great sage Brighu. When Brighu discovered this, he cursed Dangsha, turning him into an insect. "You will be a most powerful insect. You will no longer be a demon," he said.

The demon became a most destructive insect and his name was Alarka. This insect used to bite people and cause them tremendous, tremendous suffering.

Parashuram, the great hero, taught his student Karna how to fight. One day, after instructing Karna for a long time, Parashuram was resting on the ground. Karna placed his teacher's head on his lap and said, "You should have some comfort. You are so kind to me. It is a great honour for me to place your head on my lap."

Parashuram was resting peacefully on Karna's lap when suddenly this insect, Alarka, bit Karna most powerfully. His thigh began to bleed profusely, but he remained silent because he did not want to disturb his master's peace. Still, the bite was very painful.

After some time Parashuram awakened and saw that Karna's thigh was bleeding profusely. He said, "What happened? What happened, my boy?"

"Master, while you were sleeping an insect bit me. But it is nothing. It doesn't matter at all. I am so happy that you were able to take rest for as long as you wanted to. You are always so kind to me. It gives me so much joy when I am able to serve you. You are teaching me to become a great hero, so I am so grateful to you. This small insect bite doesn't bother me at all."

"Karna, you are so good and divine. I will destroy this insect."

In a fleeting second Parashuram destroyed Alarka. Then he said, "I am grateful to you because you are really kind to me, but I am mad at you because you have deceived me."

"How? How have I deceived you?"

"Karna, you cannot be a Brahmin. You came to me as a Brahmin and that is why I taught you. But if you had been a Brahmin, you would not have tolerated this. A Brahmin's inner fire comes to the fore whenever there is any injustice. A Brahmin will not attack anybody, but when there is an injustice, a Brahmin will not tolerate it. When this insect bit you, it was a terrible injustice; yet you tolerated it. A Kshatriya can tolerate many things. Although Kshatriyas are heroes of the highest order, they have the slave mentality and, when necessary, they can tolerate anything. In your case, you have tolerated this. So from today I will not keep you as my student. You have to leave my house."

After some time, Karna did become a very great hero who played a significant role in the Mahabharata.

GIM 146. *Vyasa becomes freed of depression*[§]

Vyasa was the great sage who wrote the Mahabharata. One day he was terribly depressed. He thought, "What am I going to do with my life? I am all depression, depression, depression. I have read the Vedas. I am an authority on the Vedas. Everyone comes to me for knowledge. I am the greatest of all the sages, but today I am so depressed. What am I going to do? In the Mahabharata I have written so many stories to console people when they are depressed. And now I myself am dying of depression."

Narada appeared before him. Narada was a great sage who sang the glories of Vishnu everywhere. He was a great seeker, the greatest singer and the greatest devotee, but sometimes he would act very undivine. He would become jealous of people who were very happy and would then create problems for them. For this reason, people called him a problem-maker.

When Narada appeared, Vyasa said, "O Narada, save me, save me! I am in trouble!"

"You are in trouble? Everybody says that I am the problem-maker," said Narada. "I can only make more problems for you. What kind of help do you need?"

"Narada, please tell me how I can have peace of mind. I am so depressed today."

"You are depressed? You have given consolation to thousands of people. Who will believe that you are depressed?"

"You must believe me and you must save me!"

"But you always call me the problem-maker!"

"Yes, but at the same time you are closest to Vishnu. Vishnu can console anyone. So can you not ask Vishnu to console me?"

"I cannot ask Vishnu that. He will laugh at me if I tell him that you, of all people, need consolation. He says that you are the wisest person on earth. He won't believe that you have become a victim of depression."

"But I am suffering. Please tell Vishnu. He will cure me."

"I can tell Vishnu, but it is not necessary. I myself can tell you how to be cured."

"Then please tell me. I have faith in you."

"You have written the Mahabharata. You know everything that is in the Vedas, but are you doing the right thing?"

"What have I done wrong?"

"Have you written one book that is only about Lord Krishna?"

"Oh no."

"Then start writing! Write the Bhagavatam, which will be all about Krishna from beginning to end. Then there will be no depression in your life. Your soul wants you to write a new book only about Krishna."

"All right, I am starting," he said. As soon as he started writing, his depression was transformed into delight, delight, delight.

GIM 147. *The theft of the Syamantak diamond*§

Krishna had many wives. One of his wives was named Satyabhama. Satyabhama's father had a special diamond named *Syamantak*. Whenever anyone touched the diamond, immediately it produced hundreds of gold coins. Because of that diamond. Satyabhama's family was quite well-to-do, and her father was very fond of the Syamantak diamond.

There was a very greedy man named Shatdhanwa who became envious of Satyabhama's father, so he killed him and stole the diamond. When Satyabhama heard of this, she cried bitterly and said to Krishna, "You have to get this diamond back and kill Shatdhanwa."

"Definitely I shall do so," said Krishna. "How could Shatdhanwa do this kind of thing!"

So Krishna began searching for Shatdhanwa, but Shatdhanwa kept running away from him. Then, quite unexpectedly, Krishna suddenly found the diamond. His uncle, Akrura, had been meditating when all of a sudden somebody had dropped this diamond on his lap. When Krishna came, he found the diamond on Akrura's lap while Akrura was still in deep meditation.

"How did you get this?" Krishna asked.

"I don't know. My eyes were closed," answered Akrura. "You know I have not stolen it. Somebody put it in my lap and ran away very fast."

"Are you going to keep it?" Krishna asked.

"Never, never!" said Akrura. "I don't want this. Since you have been looking for it, you take it. It belongs to Satyabhama's father and Satyabhama and you are one, so please take it."

Krishna said to him, "Once you came to me and warned me of a plot against my life. You came and told me that Kangsa was going to kill me. At that time you proved to be my best friend. And here again you have done something most significant. When you got the diamond, you could have easily hidden it. But you conquered your greed and for that I am most proud of you. You have been on God's side from the very beginning. So for these two reasons I am giving you a boon."

"Please," said Akrura, "I do not want a boon. It is enough that I have been able to serve you twice in this incarnation of mine. For that I am so grateful to you. It is you who are working inside me. Otherwise, I would not have happened to overhear King Kangsa's plan to kill you. And now, because of you I have this diamond. You have been searching for it, and because it was put in my lap I am again in a position to serve you."

Akrura bowed down to Krishna. "You give me the inspiration to conquer greed. It is all your inner doing. Outwardly I am doing things and the world is giving me credit. But I know that you don't need me to save you and you don't need this diamond as your property. I know that you have been inspiring me to help you. I am so grateful that you have utilised me on these two occasions. They will remain immortal in my life."

Krishna said, "Friends I have, admirers I have, dear ones I have. But how I wish to have people like you. You have proven yourself to be one of my dearest ones. My outer blessing is my inner gratitude, and my inner gratitude is my soul's only satisfaction."

Akrura said, "You are right, you are absolutely right, Krishna, my Krishna."

GIM 148. *Saturn defeats Indra*⁸

Once Indra and Saturn (Shani) had a serious argument over who was greater. Indra said he was the greater of the two. Saturn said, "No, I am greater. Prove your supremacy."

Indra said, "No. It is beneath my dignity to prove it. Everybody knows that I am the King of the cosmic gods. Therefore, am I not greater than you, you fool?"

"Say whatever you want to," said Saturn. "I feel that I am greater."

"Greater in what respect?"

"I can do anything I want to," said Saturn.

Indra laughed and laughed.

"Tomorrow I shall take hold of you," said Saturn. "Let me see how you can save yourself."

"All right," said Indra. "You will see what I can do."

The following day Indra went into a forest and hid. He said, "Let me see how Saturn will catch me." He did not come out of the forest the whole day. The next day Indra went to Saturn and said, "Look, Saturn, you could not keep your promise, so how can you be greater than I?"

Saturn said, "Can't you see? You were afraid of me. That is why you hid the entire day. If you were brave, you would have come and stood in front of me. From this can you not see that I am greater and more powerful than you?"

Indra accepted defeat and felt deeply embarrassed.

GIM 149. *She lends money with wisdom*[8]

There was a very rich man who was extremely cruel and miserly. His wife was very kind-hearted and affectionate, and full of sympathy for everyone. Nobody liked the husband, but everybody liked the wife. However, she said, "God gave me this bad husband, so what can I do? Nobody likes him, so at least I have to like him. Somebody has to like him." She was very kind and affectionate to him and served him day and night.

Once a famine struck the region where they lived, and many villagers came to them for help. The wife gave money to everyone and showered all the people with affection and sympathy. Her husband did not mind her generosity, even though he was so miserly. He said, "As long as I don't have to personally give, I am satisfied." His wife was very grateful for this.

When she gave money to the people, they said, "We are only borrowing this money. We will pay you back."

She said, "No, no. You don't have to pay it back. This is a gift. You just take it."

They said, "No, no. We shall repay you when the famine is over."

She said, "If you really want to repay me, then give me the money the day my husband dies."

Some of the people were shocked to hear the wife talk like this. Others thought that when her husband died, she would have many expenses for the funeral and so forth, so that was why she said this.

One of their sons happened to be present when his mother said this. The son loved both parents dearly, but upon hearing this he was very displeased, disappointed and angry. He went to his father and said, "Mother is asking people to repay the money she is giving them after your death."

The father could not believe this. "How can she say this? She always gives money freely, so why is she now asking them to return the money and why does it have to be on my death?"

The husband went to the wife and asked her, "Please tell me why you are saying this to these people?"

She said, "You don't understand. You see, people don't like you. They hate you. Everybody wants you to die today. But many people have taken lots of money from me, and by nature people don't want to return money. Although they say they are taking it as a loan, they don't want to return it. So, from now on, instead of thinking of your death, they will pray to God to keep you alive so that they don't have to return the money. I want you to live on earth for many, many years. Who knows? One day you may also become very affectionate, kind-hearted and sympathetic.

"So, I played a trick. I want them to pray to God every day that you live. Previously they prayed to God for your death. Now they will pray to God for you to live on earth. This will make me very happy. Who cares for the money? I want you to live for a very long time."

The husband was extremely moved by his wife's wisdom. The son was also very pleased with his mother.

GIM 150. *Viksha's boon*[§]

There was a King Viksha, who was very cruel and unkind. No-body liked him. He wanted to conquer everybody. He said, "There are many ways to conquer people — with weapons, or deception, or other means. But in my case I want to conquer in a different way. I will conquer by touch. Whomever I want to kill, I will touch the head of the person and he will die immediately. How can I do this? I am undivine, but I do have faith in God. Among the cosmic gods I know Shiva is very easy to please. So I will pray to him."

He prayed for many, many years. One day Shiva came and said, "You have been calling, calling and calling. What do you want? I will give you whatever you want."

"Yes, I want something, but you can't give it to me."

"I can't give it to you? Then why are you praying?"

"Yes, I have been praying to you, but I don't remember when I started."

Shiva said, "Many, many years ago."

"Oh! I have been praying for many, many years? I didn't know? I was in trance. So now you have come! I am so glad and grateful. O Lord Shiva, give me the boon that whenever I touch somebody's head, that person will die immediately. With my touch I wish to be able to turn that person's entire body to ashes."

Shiva said, "Wonderful. Wonderful. I am pleased with your prayer so I am giving you this boon. Whomever you touch on the head will die immediately."

The King said, "I am so grateful to you, so grateful! Now, may I use it on you to see if you are telling the truth?"

Shiva said, "You want to use it on me?"

"Yes! How else will I know if you are telling the truth?"

Shiva started running away. "O God, what have I done?" he thought. He ran to Vishnu's place, and Viksha was chasing him. With his third eye Vishnu had seen all that had happened and said to the King, "Why are you running? Why are you running? Great King, you are running after Shiva. What has he done? If you ask him to come to you, he will come. Why do you have to chase him? You are the King. We all run after you. You don't have to run after us."

This flattery satisfied King Viksha to a great extent. He said to Vishnu, "Look at this liar! I prayed to Shiva for so many years. He came to give me the boon, but he doesn't want me to test the boon to see if it is real or not."

"What kind of boon?" asked Vishnu.

"I asked him for the power to burn somebody to ashes just by touching his head. He gave me the boon, but when I tried to place my hands on his head, he ran away."

"Does it take such a long time for you to prove it?" asked Vishnu. "Just touch your own head and see if it is true or not."

"But if I touch my head will I not burn to ashes?"

"Oh no. As soon as you are about to be burned, take your hands away. Then you will know if it is true."

"You are right. Let me just touch my head." As soon as he did so, he was burned to ashes.

Shiva said to Vishnu, "Oh, you saved me!"

Vishnu said, "You have saved me many times. We are inseparable friends. We shall eternally remain one. When either one of us is in danger, the other will come to his rescue."

GIM 151. *Outer beauty, but inner ugliness*[s]

Once a great sage named Eurba was walking along the street with his daughter, Kundala. She was very, very beautiful. As they were walking, another sage, Durbasha, saw them. Durbasha practiced austerities most soulfully, but his temper was of the quickest. He cursed people constantly and everyone knew of his temper.

When Durbasha saw Kundala, he immediately fell in love with her. He asked Eurba, "Please tell me who she is."

"She is my daughter."

"Your daughter?"

"Yes."

"Is she married?"

"No. She is not married."

"She is so beautiful."

"Yes, she is beautiful, but only physically is she beautiful. Inside she is always quarreling and fighting with the members of the family. Inside she is ugly, ugly, ugly. She is jealousy incarnate."

"I do not know about her inner bad qualities and I do not care to hear about them. I am so full of admiration for her physical beauty. Please, please, please give me your daughter."

Eurba said, "No, I won't give her to you. I don't trust you. Once you see how quarrelsome and jealous she can become, you may throw her out after you are married. Although she is very undivine, I have that much sympathy for my daughter that I do not want her to suffer this kind of fate."

"I promise that no matter what she does, I will not use my occult power. I will never destroy her, because I am so fond of her physical beauty."

Eurba said, "Are you sure you will not destroy her one day when you get angry with her?"

"No, no, no. I promise you, I will give her everything and try only to please her. If she wants me to give up prayer and meditation, I will do so. I will give up everything for her. I won't even meditate on Lord Krishna, who is dearer than the dearest to me, if that is her wish. Once I get her, she will become my dearer than the dearest. She will be my all."

Eurba said, "I can't believe it."

"Please! Love is blind. I love this girl more than my life. She is so beautiful. Please give her to me."

Eurba finally agreed and in due course, Kundala and Durbasha were married. Durbasha totally forgot about spirituality. He did nothing spiritual at all. He was always with his beautiful wife, bound by her physical beauty. Kundala was constantly complaining, scolding Durbasha for everything. Even when he had not done anything wrong she scolded him. Durbasha said, "I gave up everything for you. My prayer, my meditation, my Krishna, my Beloved Lord — all I gave up for you, and still you are always scolding me."

"Who asked you to give up Krishna and spirituality, you fool? Nobody would have married you, but I agreed to marry you."

Durbasha said, "And nobody would have married you! You are so ugly inwardly. Your father was so right. In spite of knowing how bad you were, I married you."

"Who asked you to marry me?"

"My love for your physical beauty."

"Physical beauty? Look what you have done! You have ruined my physical beauty. You said if you married me, you would please me. Are you pleasing me in any way? I am asking you to do many things, but you are not pleasing me. I am asking you to make me very rich."

"How can I make you rich?"

"You have spiritual power, occult power. Make me very rich. I want to have many servants. I want to have a beautiful palace.

If you can't give me these things, I will go on scolding and insulting you."

Durbasha said, "Enough! Enough! I cannot tolerate you anymore. I am destroying you with my third eye."

As soon as Durbasha opened up his third eye, Eurba came and said, "My boy, my boy, I told you that my daughter was so undivine. In spite of knowing that, you wanted to marry her, so I gave her to you. But don't destroy her, don't destroy her. Give me back my daughter. Since I brought her into the world I will bear the burden the rest of my life. I don't want her destroyed."

Durbasha said, "Either take her away, Eurba, or I am going to destroy her immediately."

Eurba took back his daughter and said, "God gave you to me, my daughter, and God wants me to marry patience. My name will be patience and nothing else. As long as I stay on earth, I will show you my infinite compassion and infinite forgiveness. What else can I do? If God blessed me with you, I shall pay the penalty for the rest of my life."

GIM 152. *Krishna's supreme love*[§]

Kangsa was the hostile force incarnate. He was wicked to the backbone. He tortured each and every person in his kingdom. His worst enemy was Lord Krishna. He wanted to destroy Lord Krishna right from the very beginning, even before Krishna was mature enough to fight against him. He wanted to destroy Krishna even when Krishna was only an infant.

Kangsa had a friend who was a great admirer. He was also wicked to the backbone. One day, this friend came to Kangsa and said, "Your worst enemy is Krishna. I want to destroy him and make you happy."

"If you do this, you will make me the world's happiest person," Kangsa said.

"Yes, I will do it."

One day Kangsa's friend went to Brindavan where Krishna was playing games with the *gopis*. The gopis were extremely happy, for they were playing with their beloved Krishna. When this particular hostile force entered Brindavan, the gopis were frightened to death, because his face was so frightening. Krishna remained silent for some time.

The undivine being said to Krishna, "You remain silent because you are doing something wrong. It is undivine and immoral to play with these people. Everybody thinks that you are very spiritual and divine, but you do nothing but play with these gopis."

Krishna still remained silent.

"Yes, you remain silent because you are not doing the right thing. Had you been doing the right thing, you would have spoken."

Krishna said, "The right thing is always compassion and forgiveness. I have always been doing the right thing by consoling and listening to you people. But this time I have to withdraw my Compassion aspect. My Justice-Light, my destruction aspect, I have to adopt."

In a twinkling, in front of all the gopis, Krishna destroyed this evil force. Then he said to the gopis, "My love for you people, the world will not understand. I don't care if the world understands. Your devoted hearts will always be appreciated by me. Remain devoted to me and I shall always take care of you. Here on earth and there in Heaven, I shall always take care of you, my devoted friends.

"Animal love, human love, divine love and supreme love. Animal love does not know what human love is. Human love does not know what divine love is. Divine love does not know what supreme love is. Animal love is ultimate destruction. Human love is ultimate frustration. Divine love is ultimate illumination.

Supreme love is ultimate illumination, ultimate perfection and ultimate satisfaction.

"This supreme love I am offering to you, my earthly friends. If you accept my supreme love in my own supreme way, you will all be nearest and closest to me."

The gopis offered their gratitude-hearts through their soulful smiles.

GIM 153. *Balarama forgives Bhima*[§]

Balarama, Sri Krishna's brother, was a great fighter. He had three principal weapons. Of the three, his favourite was the ploughshare. The other two were the mace and the club.

Bhima, of the Pandavas, and Duryodhana, of the Kauravas, learned how to use the mace from him. When the Pandavas and Kauravas fought, Balarama remained neutral. Once, Bhima adopted foul means while fighting with Duryodhana. This offended Balarama's sense of fair play terribly. So he immediately seized his club to punish Bhima.

But Sri Krishna restrained him. Sri Krishna said, "True, this time Bhima was wrong, but Brother, many, many times Bhima was innocent when Duryodhana showed tremendous hostility towards him and his brothers. You know, Brother, right from his boyhood, Duryodhana treated Bhima badly. So please forgive Bhima for this misdeed. It is only once he has done this, whereas he has been treated mercilessly so many times by Duryodhana."

So Balarama forgave Bhima.

GIM 154. *The aftermath of Kurukshetra*

When the battle of Kurukshetra was over, countless people were killed. Sri Krishna's family, relatives and dear ones were all killed in the great, unthinkable turmoil and confusion. Even Sri Krishna himself left the body.

When it was Balarama's time, he sat down under a tree and went to sleep. Soon his soul, in the form of the cosmic serpent, Shesha, whose incarnation he was, came out from his mouth and laughed at Balarama's lifeless body. He was found on a rock, under a tree.

Poor Arjuna, his dear Balarama and his dearer than the dearest Krishna were no more. Arjuna had to do the final obsequies for these two and also for many, many more. His heart broke, but alas, this is life. Happiness is followed by sorrow. This is an undeniable fact.

GIM 155. *Lord Shiva is above humanity's curse*

Bhrigu was a supreme sage who was found in many Indian legends and Hindu mythology. Once a terrible quarrel arose between Shiva and Daksha, Shiva's father-in-law. Bhrigu took Daksha's side and officiated at Daksha's sacrifice. Shiva became terribly angry with Bhrigu and said, "How dare you take Daksha's side!"

Bhrigu said, "I can take whichever side I want to. It is my business, not yours."

Shiva pulled Bhrigu's beard off, and poor Bhrigu suffered a lot from the pain.

Bhrigu was married to one of Daksha's daughters, Khyati. She was extremely devoted to her husband and pleased him in every way. Bhrigu was extremely proud of her.

She was extremely angry with Shiva for pulling off Bhrigu's beard and cursed him. The curse was that Shiva would become ugly. But Lord Shiva is above humanity's curse. If he had wanted to be cursed, he could have easily suffered from the curse. But Shiva's beauty remained unparalleled.

GIM 156. *The greatest of the deities*[§]

Once the sages wanted to know who among the great deities — Brahma, Vishnu and Shiva — was the greatest. They debated and debated. Finally they appointed Bhrigu to settle the matter. Bhrigu visited Shiva's place, but he was not allowed to enter because Shiva and his consort were having a serious discussion. Bhrigu got mad and said, "Shiva, you are always like this. Your very nature is to be disrespectful. You do not honour anybody. You are careless and callous. I curse you. No good person will ever love you or adore you, not to speak of worship you. You are so bad."

Then Bhrigu went to visit Brahma. Brahma was listening to the discourses of the great intellectuals. The intellectuals were appreciating and admiring Brahma's capacities. He was so engulfed in his own importance that he paid no attention to Bhrigu's presence. Bhrigu became furious and said, "Brahma, I never knew that you were so undivine. You don't care for guests. A guest is nothing short of God Himself. I curse you! Now nobody desiring salvation will come to you. You are so undivine. Only bad people, intellectual people, clever people, will come to you. Sincere seekers will not come to you."

Then Bhrigu went to Vishnu. Vishnu was fast asleep. He heard the sound of Bhrigu's arrival, but did not pay any attention. He continued to enjoy his sleep. Bhrigu said to himself, "Here is the worst!" and he kicked Vishnu very hard. Vishnu did not become annoyed at all. In fact, he apologized at once for not being ready to receive the sage. He said, "O sage, I am sorry, I am sorry. Forgive me. I am sure you are deeply hurt because you have kicked me. I feel sorry, extremely sorry, sincerely sorry. Please forgive me. I hope that you are not injured. I am so proud that a holy man has kicked me. You are really a holy man and I deserved your kick."

Bhrigu said, "You are truly virtuous and humble. Because of your humility, not only will all human beings worship you, but the cosmic gods will also worship you. You are great, greater, greatest. Undoubtedly, you are greater than Shiva and Brahma."

GIM 157. *Bhrigu's method of casting horoscopes*⁵

Bhrigu was better than anyone else in astrology. He was greatly versed in the mysterious workings of human destiny. He compiled astrological charts giving the horoscope of every person who was born or yet to be born. His charts were infallible. It was he who introduced the use of fire.

There was a young boy in India who was amused to hear of all the astrological capacities of Bhrigu. He almost doubted Bhrigu's capacities. His elder brother was extremely fond of astrology and was also well versed in it.

He said, "You don't believe Bhrigu. You think that his method of casting horoscopes is all hallucination. But you are wrong, my dear brother. Let me cast your horoscope according to Bhrigu."

A few days later the young boy read his horoscope. There it was written that at the age of eleven he would go to a spiritual ashram to stay permanently under the guidance of a very, very great spiritual master. Then, after twenty years, he would start offering his own light to the world.

At that time, the young boy was in Bengal. When the hour came, the boy was taken by the elder members of his family to a great spiritual institute in south India, and there he stayed for twenty years. Then he became a spiritual Master and offered his own light to the world. So Bhrigu's way of casting horoscopes was infallible.

Another incident which the young boy never forgot was Bhrigu's explanation of why his maternal uncle had no children. According to Bhrigu's book, his maternal uncle's horoscope said that in his previous incarnation he was a great hunter. While hunting one day, he killed a pregnant deer. The pregnant deer cursed him saying, "I would not have cared if you had killed me alone, but I am pregnant and you have killed the child inside me. Therefore, I am cursing you. In your next incarnation you will not have one child. You will see the pain of not having a child in your next incarnation."

Alas, the curse fell absolutely true, and the boy's maternal uncle remained childless.

GIM 158. *Vishma's birth*[§]

There was a great king named Shantanu. His father's name was Pratip and his mother's name was Sunanda. Shantanu's elder brother was Devapi. Devapi became a sannyasi and did not care for earthly name and fame. He did not care for anything. He left the palace and Shantanu had to ascend the throne when King Pratip, his father, died.

Shantanu had a special capacity which nobody else had. When he touched a human being, no matter how old the person was, by his mere touch he could transform that person into a strong and vigorous youth. He did it many times and was always successful.

Shantanu was very beautiful and also pious, truthful, hard-working and dynamic. He was very fond of hunting and was a great hunter. He especially loved hunting deer.

One day, he saw at the bank of the Ganges a most beautiful woman. He became enamoured of her beauty and ran to her saying, "Please tell me who you are. In fact, you don't have to tell me who you are. Just marry me. I wish to marry you. I am the King. I will give you everything you want just for the asking."

The beautiful girl, Gangadevi, said, "Are you sure you will be able to fulfil me in every way?"

"Yes, I can and I shall. Your beauty has captured my heart."

"All right then, I will marry you on one condition."

"Any condition I shall fulfil."

"No matter what I do, you will not stand in my way. No matter what I say, you will not stand in my way."

"Never, never! I shall not stand in your way. Just be my wife. I will be at your beck and call. Indeed, you are beauty incarnate."

They were married and both King and Queen were happy. Alas, when they had their first child, the mother threw the child into the Ganges. They had seven children, and as soon as each child was born she threw the infant into the Ganges.

The King knew that if he scolded her or stood in her way, she would leave him because that was the condition she made. His love for her was boundless, and for fear of losing her, he remained silent.

But when the eighth child was born, he was sad, disturbed and mad. He said, "How can you do this? Are you not a human being? You are the child's mother. How can a mother do this? The mother is supposed to be flooded with love and compassion for her children. You are so cruel, so undivine. How can I keep you as my wife?"

The wife smiled and smiled, "So! You have failed to keep your promise. I can't stay with you anymore. I am going and I am taking my son with me. When this child grows into a youth, I shall bring him back to you — I promise you. Now, I have to take care of him, because it is the mother only who can take care of a small baby. But when he grows up, I shall bring him to you."

She did keep her promise. The name of that eighth child was Vishma, the unparalleled hero of the Mahabharata.

GIM 159. *Rich people, open up your eyes and hearts*[§]

Four or five young boys belonged to a special club. Each day they went from door to door to collect material objects and money from people. They were taking up this collection so they could do things that would inspire the villagers to lead a better life and fight against the British Government. They put everything in a big bag and, at the end of the day, they brought the bag to their leader.

One day, a young lame boy came and joined them. At first they didn't want to have a lame boy with them. They were singing songs to Krishna, saying, "O Krishna, you took the Pandavas' side against the Kauravas and the Pandavas won. The British people are the Kauravas. Please take our side. With your help only will we be able to conquer the British rule." They were singing this while walking along the street. The poor lame boy also joined them. Since he was singing so soulfully, they allowed him to follow them.

By the end of the day they had gone to many places. They were about to give the bag to the leader without looking inside to see what they had got. The young lame boy said, "I wish to see how much you have got."

All the boys mocked at him, "You are such a greedy fellow. We never look to see how much we got. We just give the bag to the leader."

The leader said, "Since the fellow is asking and he is lame, let us show him."

Still the boys were laughing at him: "This is his sincere love for his country!"

While they were emptying the bag, the lame boy emptied his small bag and said, "Now I don't have to see. I have seen everything."

The boys saw that the lame boy had given what he had got from begging door to door for two or three days.

The leader said, "Look, he gave everything that he had and is. We go door to door, but sometimes people won't give us anything. They are suffering so much from British rule, but even rich people give us next to nothing. If all India had a heart like this beggar, by today India would have been free."

The leader ran and grabbed the lame boy and embraced him. "You have opened our eyes."

The lame boy said, "Your heart, your eyes, everything are open. It is we who have to go from door to door now and open up the eyes and hearts of rich people."

GIM 160. *Tagore and Gandhi: both are right*[§]

Tagore and Gandhi are two immortals. They were extremely good friends and they had tremendous appreciation and admiration for each other. Tagore used to call Gandhi "Mahatma," which means great soul, and Gandhi used to call Tagore "Gurudev" — spiritual teacher, Master of inner wisdom and light.

Once, in front of many people, they were having a simple discussion. Unfortunately, the discussion became very heated. Some people took Tagore's side, while others took Gandhi's side. A great artist named Nandalal Bose happened to be there, so people asked him which side he was on.

"We are taking sides," they said, "so you must take one side."

"I am sorry," the artist replied. "Please do not ask me to take sides."

Still, everyone wanted to hear his opinion. "You must be in agreement with either Gandhi or Tagore. We are curious to know what you are thinking," they said.

Again Nandalal Bose said, "I can't take any side."

"What do you mean?" they asked him. "Don't you have a mind of your own?" Finally Nandalal Bose said, "I am an artist. If you ask me which colour I like most, I have to say that I feel that all colours are good; to me they are all excellent. Here, I have great admiration for these two, so for me both of them are right. I won't take either side. Both Tagore and Gandhi are right."

GIM 141. *(p. 439)* 4 February 1979
GIM 142. *(p. 440)* 5 February 1979
GIM 143. *(p. 441)* 5 February 1979
GIM 144. *(p. 442)* 5 February 1979
GIM 145. *(p. 445)* 5 February 1979
GIM 146. *(p. 447)* 5 February 1979
GIM 147. *(p. 448)* 5 February 1979
GIM 148. *(p. 450)* 6 February 1979
GIM 149. *(p. 451)* 6 February 1979
GIM 150. *(p. 453)* 6 February 1979
GIM 151. *(p. 455)* 6 February 1979
GIM 152. *(p. 457)* 6 February 1979
GIM 153. *(p. 459)* 8 February 1979
GIM 154. *(p. 460)* 8 February 1979
GIM 155. *(p. 460)* 8 February 1979
GIM 156. *(p. 461)* 8 February 1979
GIM 157. *(p. 462)* 8 February 1979
GIM 158. *(p. 463)* 8 February 1979
GIM 159. *(p. 465)* 14 February 1979
GIM 160. *(p. 466)* 14 February 1979

GREAT INDIAN MEALS:
DIVINELY DELICIOUS AND
SUPREMELY NOURISHING

BOOK 9

Gandhi would never tell a lie. Once the inspector visited his school class and gave a few words of dictation. The third word was 'kettle'. Gandhi's friends were able to spell the word properly, but unfortunately Gandhi did not know how.

The inspector began going around to each and every student to check the papers. The teacher saw that Gandhi's spelling was wrong, so with his foot he touched Gandhi's leg to draw Gandhi's attention. With his eyes he was telling Gandhi to look at somebody else's paper. But Gandhi did not want to copy from anyone.

When the inspector came to Gandhi, he said, "Here I have found a mistake. This boy does not know how to spell 'kettle'. He has written it 'ketle'."

The inspector didn't get angry, but he was sad that one person did not know the answer. Finally, the inspector left.

The teacher was very angry with Gandhi. "I told you to look at your friend's paper, but you didn't listen to me. You are a disgrace to my class."

Gandhi said, "I may be a disgrace, but I can't tell a lie and I can't say anything that is false."

Gandhi was sad that he had made a mistake and had not been able to please his teacher, but he was happy that he had at least pleased himself by being honest.

The teacher was silent.

GIM 162. *Gandhi's matchless sincerity*§

A friend of Gandhi's once needed money and asked Gandhi if he could help him. Gandhi first said, "I have no money." Then he conceded, "All right, I will try my best."

Gandhi stole a piece of gold from his brother and sold it. He then gave the money to his friend. Afterwards, he felt miserable that he had stolen something.

He used to always tell his father everything. He did not keep any secrets from him. Although his father was very sick and bedridden, Gandhi wrote him a note, saying, "I stole a piece of gold and I feel very sad and miserable. Please forgive me."

As soon as his father read the note, he immediately got up from his bed. Gandhi was afraid he was going to strike him. But there were tears in his father's eyes. Then Gandhi thought that his father was very sad that his son had stolen something from his own brother. So he felt even more miserable. Finally, his father tore up the note and there were more tears in his eyes.

Gandhi assured his father, "Father, I will never steal anymore. This is my first and last time. Please do not cry."

His father was so moved that he cried and cried. "I am crying, son, not because you have stolen something but because of your sincerity. You are always so truthful. I have never seen anybody as sincere as you. I am crying because of your sincerity, not because you have committed a theft. I am so proud of your sincerity and honesty."

GIM 163. *Gandhi and the goat's meat*

When he was thirteen, Gandhi got married to a girl of the same age. The two were extremely fond of each other. When Gandhi was about eighteen, he wanted to go to Europe to continue his college studies. By that time, his father had died and his mother was in charge of his life. Gandhi's relatives also wanted Gandhi to go to Europe and they requested his mother to send her son. But she was very worried. She said, "No, no. If I send him to Europe, he will be ruined. Now he is so close to me. There he will start drinking, eating meat and mixing with women."

Gandhi promised his mother that he would not drink, eat meat or mix with women, and he did keep his promise. After getting his degree in law, he came home. On his return he found that his mother had died.

Gandhi had a Muslim friend who always tried to persuade him to eat meat. "No," Gandhi would answer him, "Hindus don't eat meat, especially my caste. My ancestors never ate meat."

But the friend insisted. "If you don't eat meat, you will remain weak. You have to eat meat if you want to be physically strong."

Gandhi very much wanted to be physically strong. "Are you sure it will make me strong?" he asked.

"Yes," replied his Muslim friend.

Since Gandhi was very weak, one evening he tried some goat's meat. That night Gandhi saw that the goat was crying inside his stomach. The goat was so miserable.

Gandhi cried, "I can't eat meat anymore! I have seen the goat crying inside me." And he gave up eating meat forever.

But he was fond of goat's milk, and he used to drink it. "One can take goat's milk," he used to say, "but not goat's meat."

GIM 164. *The emperor's watermelon*⁸

There was a great Muslim emperor who was very kind. He used to fulfil the desires of his subjects unconditionally. One day, while the emperor was walking along the street, he saw a mendicant singing a song. The song went thus: "Even if Allah does not give us anything, no harm; for our Emperor will give us everything."

The mendicant did not know that it was the emperor who was walking by, since the emperor was wearing ordinary clothes. The emperor said to him, "You come to my palace tomorrow."

"Palace?" asked the mendicant.

"Yes," replied the emperor. "I am the Emperor. You come to my palace."

The mendicant was moved and, at the same time, a little frightened, but he came to the palace the following day. The emperor said, "Yesterday you were singing a song. I am pleased with you. I am giving you this watermelon as a gift from me."

Outwardly the man thanked him, but inwardly he said to himself, "I thought that he would make me very rich. Now he is only giving me a watermelon. All right, let me accept this gift, since he is giving it to me."

On the way back to his house, somebody asked the mendicant if he was going to sell the watermelon. The mendicant thought, "The best thing is to get rid of this watermelon. Who wants to carry such a heavy thing anyway?"

So he sold it for a very nominal price. With that money he bought some cookies and ate them. O God. A few days later he was walking along the street and whom did he see? The emperor. The emperor said, "So, are you happy now?"

The mendicant confessed, "No, I am not. You were so kind to me and you invited me to come to your palace. But you gave me just a watermelon, instead of giving me something valuable. I feel that I have missed my chance."

The emperor said, "You are such a fool! You should have examined the watermelon. Inside I had put a few gold coins. I had cut out a piece and put it back, adding four gold coins."

On hearing this, the man started striking his forehead. "Now the man I sold the watermelon to — I am sure he has got these gold coins. I do not even know who the man was."

The emperor said, "You deserve this fate. When I saw you the first time, you were flattering me to such an extent. It is impossible for me to be more kind-hearted to humanity than Allah Himself. Out of His Compassion, Allah has given me a little wealth and a little kindness. Yet you have to flatter me to such an extent, saying that I am more compassionate than God! Is it possible? Because of your unthinkable flattery, you deserve this punishment. How can a human being have more Compassion than Allah Himself? Be sincere. Then only will you be given everything. If you promise to me that you will be sincere, then I will give you a little money. I will give you ten gold coins, but from now on, be sincere. The world doesn't need flattery. It needs sincerity. If you sincerely pray to God, God will give you everything."

GIM 165. *You have far surpassed me*[5]

One day a little boy went to a great man and he bowed down to him with folded hands. The great man asked, "My boy, what is your name?"

When the boy told him, the great man immediately became annoyed. "My name? How do you dare to have my name?"

"I don't know," replied the boy. "My parents gave it to me."

"Your parents?" said the man. "How did they dare to give you my name?"

"I do not know," answered the little boy, "but my grandfather says one day I will become as great as you are. That's why they gave me this name."

The great man became furious. "How dare you say this to me? How dare your grandfather tell you this!"

The little boy said, "I do not know. Only my parents and grandfather have told me that I will be as great as you. That's why they have sent me to you."

"Have you come for my compassion and protection, or have you come to bless me?" the man asked.

"I have not come to bless you," said the boy. "I am touching your feet. I have need for your blessings."

"What kind of blessings do you want? Little candies, cookies or a few rupees? What is in the back of your mind?"

The boy said, "No, I have not come to get anything, only to be blessed by you. If you could only touch my head and say that you are blessing me."

"Why do I have to touch your head with my hand? You can touch my feet with your head."

So the little boy touched the great man's feet with his head. The man had remained seated in a chair during the conversation, but at that moment he stood up and lifted the child on his shoulder and said, "My boy, you have far surpassed me. You don't have to surpass me in the future; you have surpassed me already with your patience. I have become great, but I have not conquered anger and pride. You have conquered both anger and pride at such a young age. You deserve this name more than I do, so I am giving you a little money as my blessing."

The man gave the little boy 500 rupees, and the young boy returned home to his family.

GIM 166. *Gandhi's ashram*[§]

After he left Africa and returned to India, Mahatma Gandhi opened up an ashram at the request of his close friends. The immediate members of his family and a few friends went to live in the ashram. There they led a very simple, pious life and they prayed and meditated.

The ashram was supported by rich merchants who used to come on many occasions. So the ashram was doing well, and everybody was happy that such a good ashram existed.

One day, Gandhi received a letter from a schoolteacher. "I will be so glad and grateful if you allow me to stay at your ashram with my wife and child. I will do anything you want me to do." At the end of the letter the teacher wrote, "Only one thing I hesitate to tell you, but I must be sincere with you. I am an untouchable."

When Gandhi read this, he buried his head in his hands. "O God, I love the untouchables. for they are God's children. But now my family will be furious. How can I allow this man at the ashram? On the other hand, how can I refuse him? He has written such a soulful letter. My heart breaks."

Gandhi spoke to the members of his family about the matter. They were so nice. "If you want to have this man here, definitely invite him to join us," they said.

Still Gandhi hesitated. "The merchants who support the ashram are very fanatic. They belong to society, and they will worry about what society will think of them." Then Gandhi said, "No, I will allow this teacher to work and live here at the ashram."

The untouchable came to the ashram. As soon as the merchants heard about this, they stopped giving money to Gandhi. They said, "You are ruining society. You come from a good family, a good caste. How can you do this kind of thing? We will not give you money in support of such an unthinkable thing."

Gandhi told them, "All right, do not give us money. But if somebody sincerely and soulfully wants to serve this ashram, I will allow him. Untouchables are God's children also."

Soon Gandhi ran into financial difficulty. One day, while walking along the street, he saw a merchant with a carriage. The merchant approached him and said, "I am a rich merchant who used to help support your ashram. Since you let an untouchable into your ashram, I have been unable to help you, because I am afraid of what my friends might say. My heart is one with you, but I have to live in society. You are above society, so you can welcome an untouchable into your community. But I want to give you money secretly. Please promise me that you will not tell anyone about this."

Gandhi promised him, "I won't tell a soul about this."

The merchant said, "Then tomorrow come here and I will give you a very large amount of money."

Gandhi believed the merchant and the following day he returned to the same place. The merchant did come and he gave him a very large amount of money. Gandhi did not even know the man's name, since many merchants had helped his ashram, and he did not know all of them personally. Gandhi asked him his name, but the merchant wouldn't tell him. "Please," the merchant said, "I can't give you my name. Yours is a noble cause and I fully agree with you. But I have to live in society, so this must remain a secret. You are doing the right thing; therefore, I am supporting your cause. But it is not necessary for you to know my name."

On that day, Gandhi's fate changed.

GIM 167. *You have proved to be my real wife*[5]

Gandhi was returning to India from South Africa. Many friends and many lawyers came to his farewell party to say goodbye to him and his family. The family received very expensive gifts and Gandhi's wife and sons were especially delighted.

Gandhi was always renouncing things, so he said, "Why are they giving me these things? They only bind me, and I want to be free. I really want to give away most of these things; I want to give away anything that I don't need."

The wife and sons said, "We do need some things. Please do not give away everything."

Then Gandhi saw that someone had given some very expensive and beautiful jewellery to his wife. "I can't keep this," he told her.

"This jewellery was given to me," she said, "not to you."

But Gandhi said, "It is because of me that they know you. Otherwise, they would not have given you this."

The wife said, "Why did I come into your life? There are so many people on earth, but it is I who was chosen to be your wife. This kind of argument will never end. I won't give up this jewellery."

The children took the side of their father. "Because of Father you got the jewellery. Now you have to give it up."

The wife became furious. "I won't give it away."

But Gandhi said, "Tomorrow I will take this expensive jewellery and sell it, and put the money in the bank. The money will be only for those who love their country and serve their country. They will take money from that bank and spend it to liberate their country, but not for anything else."

The children again took their father's side. "It is an excellent idea, Father! Let us do it!"

The wife said, "You fools! You are siding with your father, but I need this jewellery for you, for your wives. Your father gives away everything. What are you going to have for your own families?"

The children laughed and laughed. "We don't have to think of that right now. It is too early."

Finally Gandhi's wife said, "All right, I don't need it either. Since your father has renounced everything, I do not need this either."

Gandhi said, "At last you have proved to be my real wife."

GIM 168. *Your compassionate words have solved my problems*⁸

There was a king who was very good, kind and just. Everybody admired him and loved him. One day, as the king was about to get up from his throne after having finished his day's routine work, an old lady came up to him. "I have something to tell you, O King," she said.

The king said, "Please, I am tired. Tomorrow please come and speak to me."

But the old lady said, "No, you have to hear what I want to say today."

"I am tired," the king said again, "but all right, tell me."

"If you don't listen to me today, if you don't give me fifteen minutes' time without any interruptions, I will pray to God to give us another King. I thought you were very kind-hearted, but since you are proving yourself otherwise, I will pray to God to replace you."

Everybody laughed and laughed, but the king said, "Don't laugh at her. I am going to listen to her. It is not because I am afraid of her scolding or curse. God, out of His infinite Compassion, has made me King. Tomorrow He can easily replace me, not because of her request, but if in any way I am not being divine. He will do what He wants to do with me. If I am really compassionate, I can spend fifteen minutes listening to her, no matter how tired and exhausted I am. It is not because I may lose my throne, but because this is the compassionate thing to do. How many unimportant things I have done today! Who knows, this poor woman probably has serious problems. That's why she has come to me. When I have problems, I know how I suffer. So let me listen and see if I can be of some help to her."

The old lady said, "O King, your compassionate words have taken away all my worries and anxieties. You are really great. You are greater than any other king in God's creation. Your compassionate words in silence have solved all my problems."

GIM 169. *You too can be free*

One day a young boy of twelve was playing all by himself under a tree. Suddenly he saw a policeman waving a revolver and chasing a young man. Since the young man was running very fast and the policeman could not keep up, he asked the boy, "Can you help me? If you run with me, I will definitely appreciate you and also I will give you some money." The policeman was a little bit older than the young man who was running away.

The boy asked, "Why are you chasing him?"

The policeman replied, "Because I was asked by higher authorities to arrest him."

"For what?" the boy asked.

"Because this young man belongs to a club that wants to overthrow the British rule."

"But are you not an Indian?" asked the young boy.

"Yes," answered the policeman, "I am an Indian."

"Then why are you doing this? Are you not ashamed of your conduct? A young man wants to free his country. I am only twelve years old, but I know how good it is to be free."

The policeman said, "A little boy has to teach me about freedom? I can shoot you, kill you."

"Let me see you shoot me," said the boy.

The policeman said, "I am very pleased with you. But I have to support my family, my children. Do you think I like my job? I have to arrest him so I will get a good reward. Then my children will be able to lead a comfortable life. Forget about comfort; even to give them basic, ordinary lessons I need this money. Otherwise, I also don't like the British Government. I hate it, I hate it."

"If you really don't like the British, if you really want to work somewhere else, you don't have to work under the British Government directly," said the boy.

The policeman said, "Who will take care of me? Who will take care of my family?"

"God," said the boy.

The policeman started laughing. "Oh, your philosophy! God will take care of everybody." And the policeman mocked at him.

At this point the boy's father appeared. The father had been looking for his son, who had gone out alone to play. "Come home, my boy," he said, "it is time to eat."

"Father," said the boy, "the policeman was laughing at me because I said God will take care of him. He does not want to work for the British Government, but because of his wife and children he has to take this job. Now I am telling him that if he gives up this job, God will take care of him. He was chasing a young man who is trying to free his country and he asked me to help him arrest this man."

The father said, "God spoke through you. I am ready to give this man a job in my office if he is really sincere."

The policeman said, "Definitely I will work there."

The gentleman said, "I have so many things to do at my office. I will promise to you a higher salary. I want to prove to you that my son was right when he said, 'God takes care of us if we really want to do the right thing'. To liberate us from the British Government is absolutely the right thing. Not to help them in any way is the right thing. God spoke through my son's mouth and now God is speaking again through my action. You come and work with me."

GIM 170. *The king's choice*[5]

There was a time in India when kings used to honour poets. Once, many poets came to the palace for a poetry contest. The king was to select the best poet. Finally he selected two poets who had written extremely good poems: one young man and one old man.

The king said, "Now the time has come for me to make the final decision between these two. In both cases, the poems are so good that it is difficult for me to say which one is the better of the two." The king said to the young man, "Please read your poem again."

The young man read out his most soulful and spiritual poem. The aspiration of the poem moved everyone deeply. The king said, "I am so pleased," and he gave the young man his own necklace. The young poet was so moved, and everybody gave him thunderous applause.

As soon as the old man came up to read his poem, some people giggled, others laughed; everything went on. The king said, "Stop, stop! I am also an old man, almost this poet's age. Do not make fun of him because of his age."

The old man read out his poem. It was about the passing of Dasharatha, the father of Ramachandra, in the absence of his son. The king cried, "Oh, it is a most pathetic story. This is also most beautiful. I am giving you my golden ring. Even now I won't be able to make the choice. The young man's poem is more spiritual and full of dedication, and your poem is about the passing of Sri Ramachandra's father."

Most of the people in the court said the young man's poem was nicer than the other poet's, but the king said, "You are prejudiced because all of you are young. One day all of you will become old. I may not appear old, but I am almost the same age as this poet. I wish to tell you, do not mock at old age. Your time also will come. Always be nice and kind to people. You see that I am having real difficulty in making the choice. For me, both are equal. Both are supremely great. Even though I am unable to make the choice, I am so happy that I am able to appreciate their merits. They deserve all my appreciation and admiration, in addition to the humble little gifts I have given them."

GIM 171. *My Motherland comes first*[8]

There was a great political leader named Vallabh Bhai Patel. He was one of the right-hand men of Gandhi and everybody admired him. He had tremendous will and was known as the iron man of India. He encouraged and inspired millions of people to fight against the British rule.

Once he was giving a talk about the freedom of India. He spoke of how India could have freedom and liberate itself from the British. In the middle of the talk a mailman came to Vallabh Bhai Patel and gave him a telegram. He opened it only to learn of the quite unexpected death of his wife. But Vallabh Bhai Patel didn't say a word to anyone. He continued lecturing for an hour or so. Then he answered everyone's questions with utmost calm and quiet.

Afterwards, tears were flowing from his eyes. Everybody came up to him, asking, "What happened? What is the matter?"

He showed them the telegram.

"How could you answer questions so calmly and quietly, and how could you finish such an inspiring lecture?"

The great political leader replied, "Duty comes first. My Motherland comes first. My wife was dear to me, but my Motherland is infinitely dearer. Therefore, I have done my duty to my Motherland first. This is infinitely more important than to think of one's wife. I have done my first and foremost duty. Now I am performing my next duty: I am crying for my wife."

GIM 172. *The wise villager*[8]

There was a very old villager whom everybody appreciated and admired. She had tremendous wisdom, and many people, even from other villages, used to come to her for advice. She was quite poor, but she was very reluctant to take money from people.

One day it was raining very heavily. About ten guests were at her house. She felt that if her guests, plus her own children and grandchildren, stayed inside her one room, they would all suffocate. So she asked her relatives to remain outside the house. "I beg of you to go outside in the rain," she said.

They listened to her and went outside, where they got totally drenched.

Then she saw that her one-room house was not big enough even for the guests. She asked them, "Would you kindly remain standing while I give you food."

After she served her guests she said, "I have to be one with everyone. I am one with you because you are my guests. Guests are like gods. I have to honour, worship and adore you. The members of my family, I asked to remain outside. Now I am going outside to feed them. I have to be one with everybody. This is how God wants me to live on earth — to be one with everybody. You deserve one treatment and they deserve another treatment. Their suffering is my suffering. Again, I don't want you to go outside in the rain because you will suffer. It is I who should serve my family in this way."

Everybody was deeply moved by the old woman's words, and they appreciated and admired her great wisdom.

GIM 173. *The prince's illumination*[§]

There was a prince who was very handsome. He was extremely proud of his beauty. Everybody appreciated his beauty, and he himself used to admire his own beauty. One day, when he was walking along the street, he saw a religious mendicant carrying a skull. The prince said, "What are you doing? Such an ugly thing you are carrying!"

The mendicant said, "Ugly? In my life, I have never seen anything so beautiful as this skull. Therefore, I am carrying it and I keep it with me twenty-four hours a day."

"That is beautiful?" mocked the prince. "It is so ugly!"

"No," said the mendicant, "it is beautiful. Only I want to know whose skull it is — whether it was a king's or prince's. I am trying to find out, but if I don't get the answer, no harm."

The prince asked, "You can't see any beauty in me?"

"You are beautiful?" laughed the mendicant. "You are nothing in comparison to my skull."

"Are you telling me the truth?" the prince said. "I am the prince."

"If you want to know the truth," said the religious man, "I am telling you the truth. But if you want to hear flattery, I will say that you are more beautiful than my skull."

"Are you saying that everybody is flattering me?" asked the prince.

"That I don't know," said the mendicant, "but I want to say that my skull is infinitely more beautiful than any part of your body."

The prince was still bewildered. "How?"

The mendicant explained, "Beauty we see with our inner heart. You may see beauty in something, and I may see beauty in something else. It is our own inner development that determines what we consider beautiful. I can clearly see from my yogic practice, from my spiritual experience, that this skull belonged to a person who practised spirituality. To me, whoever practises spirituality is beautiful. You do not practise spirituality, so you are ugly according to my inner understanding. Whoever practises spirituality is beautiful and whoever does not practise spirituality is ugly."

The prince was at once humiliated and illumined.

GIM 174. *God will take care of us*[§]

There was a very spiritual man who was also extremely interested in reading. He used to read voraciously. He had a wife and two sons. Since he did not work at a regular job, it was difficult for him to meet with the expenses of his family. He had only a small plot of land, which his sons used to plough and grow rice on. This was their main source of income.

The spiritual seeker used to buy books like anything. His wife was dead against it. She would say to him, "You buy books, and we can't even eat properly."

On one particular day he bought a book for twenty rupees. His wife was furious. "Now we won't be able to eat for two days!"

Her husband said, "No, God will take care of us. Since he has given us mouths, he will bring us food also."

His wife was very skeptical. "This is your spirituality! You read and you talk."

On the following day the seeker received a registered letter. He opened it to find that somebody had sent him forty rupees. The letter said, "Here are forty rupees. Last night I had a dream. I don't know who you are, but in my dream a most luminous person came and told me to send you forty rupees. The luminous being gave me your name and address and said that you were close to him. Since you are very spiritual, he wanted me to send you this money right away. I am sending it registered, in case my dream was not true."

The seeker accepted the letter and his son said, "See, my father is right."

"Your father is right?" said the wife. "It is my worries which made everything all right."

The husband said, "At least there should be something to keep everything all right. It may be your worries, or my prayers, or God's Compassion for us, or my children's luck. But as for me, I feel I know who is responsible and who alone will always be responsible, and that is my Beloved Lord."

GIM 175. *The unconditional gift*[§]

Once a spiritual Master was enjoying his morning walk. It was a very, very cold winter day. One of his disciples came running up to him and gave him an expensive, beautiful shawl. Then he went back inside and left the Master. The Master was walking in a meditative mood when he saw a poor old man near him. The old man was also in a meditative mood, so the Master asked him, "Can I interrupt you?"

The spiritual man said, "Yes, certainly, you can. You are a spiritual Master. You have every right to speak to me. How I wish to become as great as you are."

"Yes, I am a spiritual Master," he replied, "but I have a little more money-power than you do. How I wish you would take this shawl from me."

"I need only God," the old man said.

"Yes," said the Master, "but God is speaking through me. If you have this shawl, you will be able to meditate better."

"Is it so?" asked the man.

"Yes," the Master said, "if you don't suffer from cold so much, you will be able to meditate better. I have finished my meditation and I am going home. Please take this shawl."

The poor man finally accepted the shawl and thanked the spiritual Master. He continued praying and meditating.

When the Master returned home, the disciple asked, "Where is the shawl? Such an expensive, beautiful shawl I gave to you!"

The Master said, "Make up your mind. Did you give it to me to carry for you or to have as my own?"

The disciple said, "I gave it to you to have as your own."

"Then, if you give me something as a gift," said the Master, "how do you dare to ask me for it?"

"I am not asking for it for myself," said the disciple, "but for you, so the next time you go out you will be able to use it."

"Did you give me this to please me or to please yourself? If it was to please yourself, I have the money. I am sending someone to get a more expensive, beautiful shawl and I will give it to you. But if you did it just to please me, for my sake, then keep silent."

The disciple got the point. " I gave it to please you, Master."

The Master blessed the disciple. "Whenever you give something to the Master, you can't ask the Master to use it in your own way. He will always use it in his own way. That is the right way."

GIM 176. *Gandhi's tie*[§]

Gandhi was once working as a lawyer in South Africa. He wanted to be economical, since everything was very expensive there. Since the washermen used to charge very high amounts, Gandhi thought of washing his clothes himself. He read a few books about how to wash clothes properly, how to iron and so forth.

One day, while he was washing his clothes, he used too much starch on a particular tie. Then he did not press it properly. That day, when he went to court, his friends noticed something funny about his tie and began laughing.

"What is wrong with you?" they asked. "Why is starch falling from your tie?"

Gandhi said, "You are making fun of me. I am giving you joy. It is not an easy task to give people joy. Right now I am learning to wash clothes. I badly want to save money and washermen are charging very high prices. Soon I will become an expert, but now I am giving you joy, so I am very happy. It is a difficult thing to give others joy, but I am doing it. Therefore, I am proud of myself."

GIM 177. *Gandhi's self-sufficiency*[§]

One day Gandhi went to an English barber to have his hair cut. But the barber said to him, "You black man, I won't cut your hair! Go away."

Gandhi was unhappy, but he was, as always, forgiving. So he said, "He is right. If he cuts my hair, who knows what will happen. We are all the time fighting against the British. They feel we are inferior people. Perhaps his boss will fire him if he cuts my hair. After all, our barbers will not cut the hair of someone of a low caste. According to the British, we are inferior.

That's why the British barber is not cutting my hair. What can I do? I shall not go to another barber for more insults."

So Gandhi cut his own hair. He stood in front of a mirror and started with the front The front came out well, but the back was not so good.

The next day, when Gandhi came to court, everybody laughed and laughed. "Why didn't you go to a barber?" they asked.

"One barber has already insulted me," Gandhi said. "He is absolutely right. Why should he cut my hair? All right, make fun of me. One day I will learn to cut hair and wash things also. I want to be self-sufficient. When I am self-sufficient, I will be really happy. I am sure you are happy now because you are making fun of me and I am happy that I can give you joy. But a day will come when you will be proud of me. I will learn how to cut hair by myself. I want to be self-sufficient in all ways. Today my incapacity is making you happy. Some day my capacity will make you happy.

GIM 178. *Greed pays the penalty*[§]

There was once a seeker living in an ashram who developed leprosy. Nobody with that kind of disease was allowed to remain in the ashram, so the head of the ashram asked him to leave. His wife and children were allowed to stay, but he was told that he had to leave. Poor fellow, what could he do?

So he bought a ticket and got on the train which would take him back to his home town. In the compartment he was sitting in there happened to be a few other passengers and also a huge trunk which was locked very tightly.

All the other passengers got off the train at their respective stops, but nobody took the trunk. This man was the only person left in the compartment, and still the trunk remained. Since he was all alone, a brilliant idea struck his mind. "Since nobody has claimed that box, let me take it home. Perhaps there will be something precious inside."

He could not carry the box, so he asked the taxi driver to help him take the box home. His house was empty, since his wife was in the ashram with his children. He was very excited and curious and he broke open the locks. When he opened the box he practically fainted. Inside was a dead body which was cut into four or five pieces. To see a dead body is bad enough. But what could he do with a dead body in his house? How could he bury it or cremate it all by himself? And if he asked anybody to help him, he would be arrested.

He decided to ask some of his relatives, but his relatives were frightened to death, and they refused to help him dispose of the body. "This is what you learn at the ashram — to steal somebody else's possession? Now you pay the penalty," they said, and they would not help him.

The man locked the box again and hired two strong men to take it to a nearby river. But the two men wanted to know what was inside. He said, "Just some rubbish, which I don't want to keep. These are all my wife's belongings. I want to get rid of them. She was so evil." Then he made up a story about how bad his wife was.

The two strong men were about to throw the box into the river when, O God, a policeman happened to pass by. The man told the same story about his wife, but the policeman was curious or perhaps he was just tempted to get the things which were in the box. So he ordered the man to open it. As a result, this man who had been in the ashram was arrested and put in jail. Even today, still he has not been released. So, for his greed he is paying the penalty!

This kind of story is instructive. If you have greed, you pay the penalty. And if you are not cautious, also you pay the penalty.

GIM 161. *(p. 471)* 14 February 1979
GIM 162. *(p. 472)* 14 February 1979
GIM 163. *(p. 473)* 14 February 1979
GIM 164. *(p. 474)* 20 February 1979
GIM 165. *(p. 475)* 20 February 1979
GIM 166. *(p. 477)* 20 February 1979
GIM 167. *(p. 479)* 20 February 1979
GIM 168. *(p. 480)* 20 February 1979
GIM 169. *(p. 481)* 20 February 1979
GIM 170. *(p. 483)* 20 February 1979
GIM 171. *(p. 484)* 20 February 1979
GIM 172. *(p. 485)* 20 February 1979
GIM 173. *(p. 486)* 20 February 1979
GIM 174. *(p. 487)* 20 February 1979
GIM 175. *(p. 488)* 20 February 1979
GIM 176. *(p. 490)* 20 February 1979
GIM 177. *(p. 490)* 20 February 1979
GIM 178. *(p. 491)* 12 May 1979

GREAT INDIAN MEALS:
DIVINELY DELICIOUS AND
SUPREMELY NOURISHING

BOOK 10

They say that all fools are not really fools; some only pretend to be fools. And again, all wise men are not really wise; some just pretend.

There was once a very poor Brahmin and Brahmini. The Brahmin was very, very idle and his wife used to insult him. One day she kicked him out of the house. "You are such a fool," she said. "Your idleness I can forgive, but not your stupidity." So the poor man was thrown out. He left his home and at the end of six months he came back.

On that day, his wife was making special cakes. Although he did not enter into the house, from outside he was secretly listening to the noise, and he could easily count how many cakes she was making.

Then he shouted aloud, "Are you at home?" In India husbands don't call their wives by name. It is just an Indian custom. His wife came outside and she was so happy to see her husband. "Now you can't call me a fool anymore," he said. " I have developed intuition-power. I can easily say how many cakes you have made."

"How many?" she asked.

"Twenty-one," he replied.

She was so astonished. How could he have known when he had not even entered into the room? She was so happy and proud that her husband had become so wise and full of intuitive knowledge. "Now that you know everything," she said, "let us beat the drum and tell all the villagers that you can save each and every one of them from their difficulties and dangers."

The husband agreed, "Certainly."

Many people came to see the poor Brahmin, and each time he told them, "Not today, not today. Today the Supreme Goddess is not pleased with me because I have done something wrong.

I will speak to you some other day." By this time his wife had learned that her husband had only tricked her into believing that he had intuition-power and she had taught him to say this to the villagers.

One day a man came who was very sad because he had lost his donkey. When the Brahmini heard the petition of the man, she instructed her husband, "Don't say you will speak to him today." Then on behalf of her husband she said, "Today the Goddess is not pleased with him. Please do not bother him. But if you come tomorrow, he will be able to help you. I can see that tomorrow the Goddess will be pleased with him." The man was so happy that perhaps tomorrow the Brahmin would do something for him.

That night, around midnight, the husband was sleeping, but not the wife. She heard a donkey braying and she followed the sound. The wife was very tricky. She found the donkey and tied it to one of the pillars of the house. When the man came the following morning to see the Brahmin, he found the donkey there. It happened to be the same one he had lost. He was so happy and pleased, and he gave the couple some money.

The Brahmin's fame spread all over the village. Finally the king came to know about the incident. The queen had recently lost her golden necklace and both the king and the queen were very upset about this. They summoned this poor man to the palace. His wife also came with him, for she knew that he wouldn't know how to find the necklace. The man was trembling all over because he was afraid that the king and queen would punish him if he failed to find it. The wife told the king, "He is trembling, not because he will not be able to tell you who has taken the necklace, but because you are so great. It is not because he does not have the capacity, but because we are so insignificant."

The king said, "You have to find the necklace. I have no idea whether it was stolen or misplaced."

"Please give me a few days," replied the Brahmin, "as this is a serious matter."

"Take as many days as you want," said the king, "but I have to get it back! When I get it back, I will reward you."

The Brahmin and Brahmini went home, and the Brahmin started crying to the goddess Jagadhambha, "Save me, save me, save me! I do not know who has taken the necklace. The King is no good. Perhaps the King will kill me. Are you so unkind? Please save me!" At night he cried in silence; during the day he cried aloud.

It happened that the next day one of the king's maidservants, whose namesake was the goddess Jagadhambha, happened to be passing by. She heard somebody crying because he was going to be killed, saying, "Goddess Jagadhambha, why are you so unkind? Where have you taken the necklace? You have to save me. Save me!"

The maidservant felt extremely sorry because she was the culprit; she had stolen the necklace. She said to herself, "I stole it and, because of me, this man is going to be hanged. He is crying so bitterly." She came and told the Brahmin and Brahmini that it was she who had stolen the necklace. "If you tell the King, the King will kill me," she said. "You have to do something so that the King will not punish either you or me."

The wife was so clever. She said, "You have saved us; now we will save you. Bring the necklace."

The maidservant went home and brought the necklace to the wife. Then the wife said, "We will save you. Don't worry, we will not betray you."

The maidservant said, "Oh, they will never suspect me. They are so fond of me."

The wife put the necklace into a box that could float on water and went to the king. "It will be good for my husband to concentrate at night," she said. "He can concentrate better in the dark. Tonight he will come to your palace and concentrate on the necklace and let you know where it is."

The king was very happy. "Do anything you want; only find the necklace," the king said.

That night, the husband and wife went to the palace. All the lights were extinguished and they threw the box containing the necklace into a small pond near the palace. Then they went to the king and said, "Now we would like to meditate, and definitely we will be able to tell you where the necklace is." They meditated for some time and vision dawned on them. At that time their vision was working powerfully; the day before they had had no vision.

"Please send someone to yonder pond," said the Brahmin. "There is a tiny box floating on the water, and the Queen's necklace is definitely inside it. My intuition is working today." The king's guards found the box and, indeed, inside was the necklace.

Then the king asked, "Who stole it? How did it get in the box?"

"You have the necklace," said the Brahmin. "My intuition goes only this far. You wanted to know where it was and we found it. We have fulfilled your request. Now it is up to you whether you will give us the reward or not."

The king said, "Why wouldn't I give it to you? You found the thing which had been lost. It is so precious to me, so invaluable."

So the king gave the Brahmin and his wife a very good fortune, and with that fortune they left their village. After all, if this kind of thing ever happened again, perhaps Jagadhambha the goddess would not save them, and, even now, perhaps Jagadhambha the maidservant was not satisfied!

GIM 180. *The farmer and the zamindar*

Once four farmers, idle talkers, were chatting. A young village man happened to pass by. One farmer said, "Where are you going?"

The young man replied, "Don't bother me. I am going to the home of the *zamindar,* the rich man in the village. I have some important business with him."

"You don't have to be proud," one of the idle talkers said. "I can go to visit the zamindar and eat with him anytime I want."

The young man became furious. He said, "Why do you cut jokes with me? Will it ever be possible for you to go to the zamindar's place? You are such an insignificant person."

The farmer in question said, "Don't brag; I can go whenever I want."

The young man said, "If you can eat with the zamindar, I will give you two absolutely new bullocks. And if you cannot eat with him, then for six months you have to plough my field with your own bullocks." The farmer agreed.

"Then let us see who wins," said the young man, continuing on to his destination.

The farmer took a short cut and reached the zamindar's house before the young man. He knew the way quite well because he lived in the same area as the zamindar, whereas the young man was from another village. The farmer entered and offered his pranam to the zamindar. "What are you here for?" the zamindar asked.

"I have something very special to ask you," replied the farmer. "I know you will forgive me."

"What is it?" the rich man said.

The farmer said, "I have found a piece of gold which is as big as an egg. You are very sincere and honest. Please tell me what its value is. I can't trust anybody but you, because you are the zamindar."

The rich man said, "Oh, I am so happy for you. First sit down and let me order food. You have brought such good news. I am so pleased and happy that you have found this piece of gold. Now you will be rich like me. You don't have to worry anymore; you won't have to beg or work at all. But first of all, eat. Later, I will tell you the exact price of the gold."

Immediately the servants brought food and both of them started eating. At that moment the young man came in. When the meal was over, the zamindar said to the farmer, "Now show me your gold."

The farmer answered, "I didn't tell you that I was going to show it to you; I wanted only to know the price. You told me to eat with you, so I did. But you didn't ask me to show it to you. I only came to know the price."

The zamindar got mad. He shouted, "Get out of here! Get out of here!"

The farmer left, but he was waiting outside the door when the young man came out later. The young man had lost.

So the farmer ate at the zamindar's house, plus he got two bullocks.

GIM 181. *Who carries bad luck?*

One day early in the morning the Emperor Akbar met with one of his subjects. Later that day something unfortunate happened. While the Emperor was having breakfast, he ate a strand of hair that was in his food. He said that just because he had seen that particular man, this had happened and he wanted the man to be punished. Some others in the Emperor's court agreed that this man carried very bad luck. Akbar said, "Then he should be hanged."

The poor man was supposed to be hanged the following day. He knew that the Emperor's court minister was aware of his plight. He went to the minister and begged him for help, but the minister said, "The Emperor wants to kill you. How can I dare to save you? Impossible!"

"No, you must save me, you must save me," begged the man.

"How?" said the court minister. "I can't." Then suddenly the minister whispered something in the man's ear.

The following day the time came for the man to be hanged. Akbar said, "Are you ready?"

The man said, "Lord, you are saying that because you saw me, your fate became most deplorable. Now, can I not also say that because I saw you, my fate has become even more deplorable? If I had not seen you, I would not be facing my death. I may have caused you some bad luck, but in my life you have caused me worse luck. You will stay on earth but I have to die. So who carries the worse luck?"

The Emperor said, "I have lost the case," and the man was set free.

GIM 182. *The prayers of Ramjan*

There was a very poor Muslim man who used to deal in donkeys, monkeys and dogs. One day he had not been able to sell either his donkeys, monkeys or dogs and he was returning from the village market. It was getting dark and night had set in. It was the month that the Muslims call *Ramjan*. For that month Muslims fast during the day and eat only at night. On a specific day of that month, when the stars become very favourable, they feel that no matter what one wishes for, he will get it.

One of the donkeys knew this and said, "How long shall I play the role of a donkey? O Allah, O God, make me the emperor of the world." Then the donkey said to one of the monkeys, "Our prayers will be fulfilled because this is a most auspicious day. I have prayed. Now you pray."

The monkey said, "I pray to be the strongest man in the world." The monkey also believed that his prayer would be fulfilled.

Then one of the dogs said, "I pray to become the commander-in-chief of the world." They all prayed, and they were fully convinced that their desires would be fulfilled.

Then these three animals said to the Muslim, "Now we have prayed. You will see that soon our desires will be fulfilled."

The poor man said, "Yes, I can also pray." Immediately he prayed to Allah, "O God, O God, O God, this is my only prayer. Before You grant their prayers, please make me blind. I don't want to be ruled by a donkey, a monkey and a dog. Please grant my prayer first. Let me be blind so that, if I have to be under their control, at least I don't have to see them."

GIM 183. *Trishanku*

There was once a very handsome King named Trishanku. He had a strong desire to go to Heaven with his physical body, so he went to his Master, Vashishtha, and told him about this desire. Trishanku begged Vashishtha to create for him a special mountain so that he could walk right up to Heaven.

Vashishtha said to him, "You fool, nobody can do that. With the physical body, you cannot go to Heaven. It is impossible. Give up this desire. It is the height of stupidity."

Trishanku felt sad and miserable. He left his kingdom on foot to look for another Master who would be kind enough to fulfil his desire. One day he came upon Vashishtha's sons. He said to them, "Your father could not help me, but I am sure you have more spiritual power. You are practising austerities, while your father is now old and does not practise spirituality anymore. I am not criticising your father, but please, please help me. Please grant me this boon: I want to go to Heaven with this physical body of mine."

Vashishtha's sons became angry at Trishanku. They said, "If our father discouraged you, if our father dissuaded you from this desire, we will never fulfil it! It is impossible! What the father says has to be carried out by the sons. We will not help you in any way, you fool. Now, allow us to meditate peacefully."

Then one of Vashishtha's sons cursed Trishanku. He made the King's face ugly and took away his royal stature.

Now Trishanku felt more miserable than ever. His Guru had not helped him. And his Guru's sons had not only failed to help him but had been rude and ruthless to him. He went on walking until he came to the cottage owned by the sage Vishwamitra. He told Vishwamitra his sad story and prayed to Vishwamitra to help him.

Since Vishwamitra and Vashishtha were always at daggers drawn, Vishwamitra was very kind to Trishanku when he heard his story. Vishwamitra said, "I shall definitely help you. I will use all my spiritual and occult power to enable you to go to Heaven with your physical body. But I do not want to waste my power in transforming your face once again."

So Vishwamitra used all his power and took Trishanku to Heaven bodily. But when Trishanku arrived in Heaven, some of the cosmic gods, especially Indra, became terribly jealous of him. "You are a mortal," they said. "How can you be here with your physical body? How can you break the cosmic law?" And they threw him out of Heaven.

When they threw Trishanku out, it took a little time for him to fall to earth again. While he was descending, midway between Heaven and earth he cried out, "Vishwamitra, you took me to Heaven, but the gods have thrown me out. What are you going to do?"

Vishwamitra said, "Wait, wait! I am coming to save you!" With his occult power Vishwamitra kept Trishanku suspended in mid-air between Heaven and earth. Vishwamitra was furious with the cosmic gods. He said, " I used all my occult power to take him to Heaven; now the cosmic gods are jealous of him. I will fight against Indra and all the cosmic gods. I shall meditate and get more occult power and spiritual power to fight against them."

Vishwamitra meditated for many, many years, and then he mustered all his occult power and spiritual power. He said, "All right, if Brahma could create the universe, then I too can create a universe." And he created another world with stars, a sun and planets, only for Trishanku to live in.

As soon as Vishwamitra created a new world for Trishanku, the cosmic gods again became jealous. They said to the sage, "Why have you made him another world? He doesn't have to have another world. You demolish it, and we shall allow him to remain in Heaven."

Vishwamitra said, "Even if you allow him to remain in Heaven peacefully, I shall keep my world safe. Now you are promising that you will allow him to stay in Heaven, but I know that as soon as I destroy my world, you will throw him out again. Then again I will have to meditate for many years to get occult power and spiritual power to help him."

The cosmic gods said, "All right, we agree that he can stay either in our world or in your world. But we have only one request: while he stays in your world, let him hang in midair with his head towards the earth and his legs towards Heaven." Vishwamitra said, "Oh, that is nothing to him. From now on his legs will remain upward and his head downward."

So poor Trishanku had to stay upside down in Vishwamitra's world to enjoy Vishwamitra's new creation.

Commentary: Nowadays we can go to the moon and to many distant places without using occult power or spiritual power. The power of modern science takes astronauts to these places and brings them back. Trishanku's world is not the world where souls go, but it is a vital region near the moon. We can go to the moon and come back through the power of our scientific knowledge. But poor Trishanku went with occult power, and he is still hanging there with his head down and his legs up.

We learn something very significant from this story. When the cosmic gods, whom we appreciate, admire and adore, see a mortal turn immortal or get tremendous occult or spiritual power, or any kind of power, in the beginning they do not want to allow him to surpass them. But if that mortal really surpasses them, in spite of their efforts, they reluctantly allow him to retain his achievement.

It is like a kite. In the beginning the man flying the kite holds the string, and the kite flies the way the man wants it to. He will not allow the kite to go beyond the reach of the string. The kite is his possession; it is under his jurisdiction. But sometimes the string breaks and the kite flies away. At first the owner feels sad that the kite has escaped from his control. But afterwards he gets tremendous joy when he sees that his kite has gone so high, into the universal Beyond, and he appreciates the capacity of the kite.

Similarly, the cosmic gods try to keep human beings always under their feet. But when a mortal human being does surpass them, the cosmic gods try to take the credit. At first they try to block the human beings, who are under them, from going beyond them. But then, like earthly parents who see that their children have gone far beyond them, they become happy and proud. As in the ordinary world, in the spiritual world also, meanness, jealousy and insecurity may come to an end if one sees that somebody has really surpassed him. When this happens in the case of the cosmic gods, instead of being jealous of a human being, the gods say, "Oh, I saw him, I helped him. It was with my help that he was able to become so great."

GIM 184. *I shall worship you only with my left hand*

In India there lived a merchant named Chand who was quite rich. He had six boats, and in these six boats he carried his merchandise. He also had six sons who all worked in their father's business.

Chand was a great devotee of Lord Shiva. Every day he used to pray to Lord Shiva most devotedly and soulfully. After many years Lord Shiva became extremely pleased with him and gave him a special boon, the boon of immortality on earth. Needless to say, Chand was delighted to get this boon.

One day Chand's wife went to the river Gangur to bathe. On her way back she saw many people enjoying a special festival at the house of one of her neighbours. She went inside the house and there she saw a small statue of Manasha, the snake-goddess. All the people were devotedly worshipping that particular goddess. When Chand's wife asked why they were so fond of this goddess, the mother of the family told her that they had become extremely rich by worshipping Manasha. The statue had come from the river Gangur, and her two sons had become rich by worshipping the goddess who was represented by this particular statue.

Chand's wife knew that her husband was not as rich as these two brothers, so she begged them to give her a statue of exactly the same type. In a few days they made a mould and gave her a statue just like theirs. She was so happy to get the statue, and she immediately brought it home and started worshipping the goddess Manasha so that her husband could become as rich as their neighbours. But when Chand saw what she was doing, instead of becoming happy, he got furious.

He said, "I have been praying to Lord Shiva for years and years! He has been kind enough to give me the boon of immortality. Now how can I worship somebody else? I don't need this goddess." Then he kicked the statue of Manasha, and it smashed to pieces. His wife was extremely shocked, and his six sons were very unhappy and frightened because their father had shown such disrespect to a goddess.

The goddess Manasha was so angry that she cursed Chand. Her curse was that she would take away all his children and all his possessions and make him an ordinary mortal again. In this way she would humble him and force him to bow down before her and worship her. One day Manasha took human form as a most beautiful woman. When Chand saw this beautiful woman, he was tempted. When earthly temptation entered into him, Manasha was able to take away the boon that Chand had received from Lord Shiva. Now he became mortal once again and could easily be killed by the goddess or by any human being.

In the course of time Manasha started fulfilling the rest of her curse. One day when Chand was sailing to a distant city, three of his boats capsized and sank. Three of Chand's sons who were on the boats died, along with the crew members. That was the first serious misfortune. A few months later, he went with his remaining sons on a business trip. This time there was a serious hurricane. In this terrible storm Chand's remaining three boats sank, his last three sons died and all the rest of his wealth was lost.

Chand himself was also about to drown, but the goddess Manasha, who was watching everything, said to herself, "If he dies now, then my objective will not be fulfilled. I want him to worship me. If he dies, then he will not be able to worship me. I have to keep him alive. But how am I going to do it?" Then she caused a lotus plant with a few blooms on it to appear right in front of him.

When Chand touched the lotus, he immediately thought of the goddess Manasha, because Manasha's other name is Lotus. But Chand was too angry with Manasha to take any help from her at all. He thought, "Manasha is the cause of all my suffering. I will not take help even from a lotus plant." But already the goddess had been able to give him strength through the lotus and, with greatest difficulty, he reached the shore and came out of the water.

For three days Chand could get nothing to eat. He became so weak that he could hardly walk. Finally, on the third day he came to a friend's house and his friend gave him something to eat. When he heard Chand's story he said, "Compromise. Pray to this goddess. Then she will not create any more suffering for you."

Chand said, "No, that I will not do."

It took Chand several months to return home on foot. There he saw his wife fondling a little baby. It was his own child, a seventh son. Chand said, "That means the curse is now removed. Otherwise, how could I have a son now? This child must be a sign of prosperity." So Chand gave the child the name of Laksmindar, which means "one who is blessed by the goddess of prosperity."

Some years passed, and Laksmindar attained maturity. Chand found a most beautiful wife for him. The girl's name was Behula. Chand was once again very happy with his little family.

Then, early one morning, Behula suddenly started screaming and crying. Chand and his wife ran to her and saw that their only son was dead. He had been bitten by a snake. After so many years the snake-goddess had taken the form of a snake and killed their last son.

According to Indian tradition, if somebody dies of a snake-bite, then he cannot be cremated. His body has to be thrown into the water or put on a raft or a small boat. Then the boat can carry his body wherever it will. Behula was so devoted to Laksmindar that she said, "I am not going to allow him to be thrown into the river. He is dead, true, but I cannot leave him. I don't need my parents or my father-in-law and mother-in-law. I need only my beloved husband." So, with Laksmindar's dead body, Behula entered into the boat and floated away to an unknown destination. Behula was praying constantly to Lord Shiva. She said, "Lord Shiva, my father-in-law has worshipped you so devotedly for years and years. Can you not do anything for his son? Will this be his fate?"

Lord Shiva heard her soulful prayer and came out of his long trance. He commanded the goddess Manasha to give back Chand's sons and all his wealth. The other cosmic gods also requested the same thing. But the goddess prayed to Lord Shiva to first grant her a boon. She wanted Chand to worship her at least once. Only then, she said, would she give back his wealth, his ships and all his children.

Lord Shiva said, "Only once? All right, I shall grant your boon." Then Lord Shiva said to Behula, "Go and beg your father-in-law to worship Manasha just once," and he took the boat which was carrying her back to where it had started from.

Behula went to Chand and said, "You are unbearably proud. That is why this has happened. You did not want to worship the snake-goddess; you only wanted to worship Lord Shiva. Now can you not worship her only once? Then you will get back all your beloved sons, your ships, your wealth — everything. Can you not worship her just once?"

Chand said, "No, I will never surrender."

Behula said, "Have you no affection for your sons? Did you never love your dear ones, your children, your wife?"

He said, "Yes, I did love my dear ones. I loved all my sons."

"Then where has your affection gone?" she asked.

"It still remains," said Chand, "but now some competition is going on between affection and pride."

"Your pride has won," said Behula. "You did not care as much for the members of your family as you cared for your own pride. Otherwise you would have surrendered to the goddess long ago and worshipped her to save your sons." Chand finally said, "You are right. Now let me surrender to affection. Let affection win. Let me first get back my children, my ships and my wealth. Then I will worship Manasha."

Behula was extremely happy. She spoke to Lord Shiva, and Lord Shiva spoke to Manasha. The goddess agreed to give back everything to Chand.

Now Chand had been forced to worship her, but his pride was still strong. He said to himself, "I used my right hand to worship Lord Shiva, so I will never use my right hand to worship this goddess. It will be a real insult to Lord Shiva, so I will never do it. I will use my left hand. I promised that I would worship her once, but I didn't say I would use my right hand."

Manasha became furious because, according to Indian tradition, the right hand or both hands are always used for worship. But Chand would worship her only with his left hand. In India seekers are very fastidious about using the right hand instead of the left hand for worship. When a seeker places a flower or a candle on the shrine, when he puts a sacred mark on his forehead, always it has to be done with the right hand. Everything sacred has to be touched with the right hand. Manasha said, "You promised that you would worship me. It was well understood that you would have to worship with your right hand, not with your left hand. Two hands are not necessary, but at least you should use your right hand."

But Chand had got back all his sons and all his possessions, and Lord Shiva was once again protecting him. So he worshipped Manasha with his left hand only. Lord Shiva again gave the boon of immortality not only to Chand but also to his daughter-in-law, Behula.

Even now it is said that if you want to worship the goddess Manasha you can do it with your left hand, whereas all other gods and goddesses have to be worshipped either with both hands or with the right hand.

GIM 185. *A father's oneness-heart*

An elderly gentleman named Ramesh went out early one winter morning to get some fresh air. It was extremely cold. When Gokul, a friend of his, happened to see him, he said, "Ramesh, what are you doing? You are not wearing winter clothes. You are wearing spring clothes. You will suffer badly from this cold! Why are you acting like a fool?"

Ramesh thanked Gokul and said, "Yes, you are right, you are right. I am going home."

He returned home and said to his son, who was a businessman and had amassed vast wealth, "Son, I went out this morning, but my friend Gokul asked me why I was acting like a fool and wearing spring clothes in winter."

The son said, "He was right, Father. Let me go and get you some warm winter clothes."

"Wait," said Ramesh. "You know that thousands of people who live right around our house are so poor that they cannot afford to have warm clothes and shoes. My heart will not permit me to wear winter clothes and shoes unless I see them also warmly clothed."

The son said, "Father, I know you have a big heart. Since I am your son, I shall without fail fulfil your desire."

Ramesh blessed his son, saying, "I am so proud of you."

The son went out and, in a few hours' time, brought home winter clothes and shoes for 25,000 people. He said to Ramesh, "Father, I don't think you will need more, but if you do, I will give them to you."

Then Ramesh said to his son, "Son, since I am a Brahmin, now you have to invite all the poor Brahmins."

But his son asked, "Why only Brahmins?"

Ramesh said, "You are right; I should not discriminate. It should be first come, first served."

Soon thousands of people belonging to different castes started pouring in — about 25,000 people in all. They were delighted and, at the same time, extremely grateful to receive this unexpected gift.

Ramesh blessed his son from the very depth of his heart for fulfilling his desire, and the son said to him, "I am so proud that I have a father who is so kind to the poor." In this way the father and son mutually appreciated each other. Finally, the son said to his father, "Now that I have fulfilled your desire, Father, will you now take your own winter clothes and shoes?"

Ramesh said, "My foolish son, am I not wearing winter clothes and shoes through these 25,000 people? Why do I need one extra? Do they not represent me, and do I not represent them? I do not need winter clothes or shoes. In their happiness is my happiness. In their comfort is my comfort. I assure you, I will not fall sick, for my oneness-heart with them will definitely keep my body warm."

His son shed profuse tears of gratitude and pride that he was blessed with such a divine father.

GIM 186. *Laosen does the impossible*

There was once a King named Karnasen who was a great hero. For many years he defeated all his enemies in battle, but eventually he lost to a most powerful King. King Karnasen lost his wife, his hero-sons and all his dear ones. He himself would have been killed by his opponent, but that King showed him compassion. He said, "You are an old man. I don't want to kill you. I have killed your wife and sons and all your relatives. I have destroyed your army. Now you can go peacefully on your way."

Karnasen felt miserable. Since nobody in his family was still alive, he went to another kingdom and took shelter there. The King of that particular kingdom, whose name was Gaur, was very kind to him and showed him great hospitality. He invited Karnasen to spend the rest of his life there. One day King Gaur said to Karnasen, "If you would like to marry, I will ask one of my sisters-in-law to marry you."

King Karnasen said, "I am an old man. At this age, why should I again enter into family life?"

But King Gaur replied, "No, no, you will be happy. It is good to have some near and dear ones."

King Karnasen finally agreed, and soon he married a sister-in-law of King Gaur named Ranjabati. At that time Kripan, Ranjabati's brother, was away from the kingdom. When he returned and heard that his sister had married without his knowledge, especially to someone who was now a true beggar, he became furious. Kripan also became jealous, since King Gaur was showing Karnasen considerable affection and love. Kripan had hoped that he would become the dearest to the King, but now he saw that somebody else was becoming the dearest. He could not insult King Gaur, but he wanted to punish Karnasen.

Karnasen and his wife lived together for a number of years, but unfortunately Ranjabati was not blessed with a child. According to Indian tradition, if you do not have children, then you are not a woman of good character. So one day, in public, Kripan said to her, "You are a useless woman. You are a barren field!"

Poor Ranjabati felt miserable. She prayed and prayed to the Sun god to grant her a child. Finally the Sun god listened to her prayer and she did have a child. Karnasen gave this son the name Laosen.

Laosen was extremely beautiful. Right from his childhood he showed tremendous physical strength, and he became a great wrestler in his youth. He could defeat three or four wrestlers at a time. Laosen even used to fight with tigers and whales. Now Kripan, Laosen's maternal uncle, once again became extremely jealous. First he had been jealous of Karnasen because he was getting so much affection from King Gaur. Now he was jealous of Karnasen's son because he had become so powerful.

Kripan tried in many ways to kill Laosen. Once he hired ruffians to kill him. Another time he cleverly invited his brother-in-law and nephew to visit him so that he could honour them, and then he put two mad elephants along the route to kill his so-called guests. In many ways he made their lives miserable and caused suffering for them.

One day Kripan became so desperately angry that he said to King Gaur, "I shall leave this kingdom if you do not banish Laosen."

King Gaur said, "How can I do it, and why should I do it? Laosen is unconquerable. I am so happy that he is a relative of mine. If anyone attacks our kingdom, he will be able to defeat the enemy."

Kripan said, "Do you think that he can defeat anybody?"

The King said, "He is unconquerable. Nobody can defeat him — nobody, nobody."

Kripan said, "Can he do the impossible?"

King Gaur said, "I will call nothing impossible. There is nothing on earth that Laosen cannot do."

"All right, I will believe it if he can compel the sun to rise in the West."

King Gaur said rashly, "Yes, he will be able to do even that."

Kripan was delighted to hear this. He knew that Laosen could never compel the sun to rise in the West.

When Laosen heard of this, he went immediately to the King. King Gaur was extremely fond of Laosen's father and extremely proud of Laosen. But now he was worried. On the one hand, he believed that Laosen could do the impossible because he had so much faith in the young man. On the other hand, he could not help feeling that it was truly impossible to make the sun rise in the West.

But Laosen said to the King, "Don't worry. If you have made a promise, I will fulfil it." Then Laosen started praying to the Sun god as his mother had done many years before. Soon the Sun god came to him and said, "Please continue to pray. I will see if it can be done. Just pray, pray, pray."

So Laosen prayed and prayed. Meanwhile, his maternal uncle was very happy. Kripan was sure that the sun would never rise in the West. One day he said to King Gaur, "Laosen is unable to fulfil your promise. Now you have to fulfil my desire. He has to leave the kingdom since he can't do the impossible."

King Gaur said, "Give him some more time. He has said that he will be able to do it. Just give him some time."

Laosen prayed and prayed. One day one of his maids said to him, "Don't worry. The sun will be pleased with you someday."

Laosen said, "I have been praying and praying for such a long time. I am afraid he will never grant me this boon."

Then the maid said, "Just cut off your head and he will be pleased with you."

Laosen said, "If I cut off my head, then I will only die, and if the sun still does not rise in the West, I will not be able to do anything more. But if the Sun god agrees to fulfil my desire, then I am ready to kill myself."

The maid said, "No, do it now. The Sun god will definitely be pleased with you."

So Laosen chopped off his head and immediately the Sun god appeared. He brought Laosen back to life and said, "Now I am truly pleased with you. I shall fulfil your desire. Tomorrow the world will see that instead of coming from the East I will appear in the West. You can go and tell King Gaur and your father."

Laosen was filled with joy. He ran to tell his father and King Gaur. Both of them, as always, believed him. Then King Gaur told Kripan, "Tomorrow morning you will see that Laosen has really done the impossible."

Kripan said, "Tomorrow morning! You yourself have given the time. If Laosen doesn't make the sun rise in the West tomorrow morning, then you have to throw him out of this kingdom."

King Gaur said, "Yes, but he will do it."

Kripan was the first person to disbelieve it, and the following morning he got up long before anybody else to see the sunrise. But to Kripan's amazement the sun did rise in the West. Then the Sun god appeared before everyone and said to Kripan, "You have caused so much suffering for Karnasen and his son Laosen. Laosen is my devotee, and you have tortured him for many years. Now you deserve some punishment. From now to the end of your life you will suffer from leprosy." This was the worst possible punishment that he could have given.

Then King Gaur asked the Sun god, "How could you do it? How could you rise in the West?"

The Sun god said, "Is there anything that I will not do for my true devotee? If somebody were to insult me and say, 'Sun, you always have to rise in the East. Obviously you can't appear in the West; you don't have the power,' immediately I would agree. I would say, 'You are right. I can't do it!' But my devotee is dearer to me than my life itself. When he accepts a challenge, I also have to accept it. Kripan could have challenged me personally, but if he had done it, I would not have taken the trouble of breaking the cosmic law. But he challenged my true devotee, who is so dear to me. And Laosen was ready to sacrifice his own life in order to keep his promise.

"You can defeat me, but not my devotee. A true devotee can always do the impossible. God Himself may not want to do a particular thing; there is no need for Him to show the world that for Him nothing is impossible. But God does want to show the world that there is someone else who can do everything, and that is His true devotee. So don't challenge a devotee. You will always lose."

GIM 187. *Sympathetic oneness*

A father and son were walking together, enjoying the early morning breeze. They had covered a good distance when all of a sudden the father said to the son, "Son, stop!"

The son said, "Father, has something happened? Is anything wrong?"

The father said, "Nothing in particular, but let us not walk any farther on this road."

"Why not, Father?" asked the son.

"Do you see that elderly man coming towards us?" the father asked, pointing down the road.

"Yes, I can see him," replied the son.

"That man is a friend of mine," said the father. "He has borrowed some money from me and now he is unable to pay it back. Each time he sees me he tells me that he will get the money from somebody else and, without fail, will give it to me. This has been happening again and again, so I don't want to embarrass him anymore."

The son said, "Father, if you don't want to embarrass him, why don't you tell him that you have given him the money and you will not take it back, that it is just a donation?"

"I have already told him that," said the father. "When I said, 'I don't want it back; it is an offering,' he got mad. He said, 'Am I a beggar? I am your friend. When I was in need, you gave me money, and when I am no longer in need, I will give it back. I want to remain your friend and not a beggar.' Now I don't want to embarrass him, and I don't want to be embarrassed myself. So let us quickly take another road and avoid him."

The son said, "Father, you are really good and great. I am so proud of you. It is usually the one who owes the money who tries to avoid the person from whom he has borrowed it. In your case you are desperately trying to avoid this man, although you are the giver. It is usually the receiver who is embarrassed, not the giver. But you want to spare him the embarrassment. I am truly grateful to you and proud of you, Father. What I have learned from you is sympathetic oneness."

GIM 188. *Purity: selfless oneness with God*

Once there lived a pious youth named Nagamuddin who came from a Muslim family. He used to study all day and night. His father died when he was still quite young, and suddenly Nagamuddin had to support his poor mother. He started looking for a job here, there and everywhere, but he did not succeed in getting one.

One day he went to a Muslim priest and begged him to give him a job in any line, although he said he would be very happy if he could also become a priest. The priest said, "I will give you a job, but I can't make you a priest, for you will far surpass me and every other priest on earth. You have no idea how great you are. One day everybody will come to know of you. Even the Emperor of Delhi will come to you to honour you."

A burning desire to realise God had long been consuming Nagamuddin. He had been looking for his Guru everywhere. Finally one day he went to a very spiritual man named Phariduddin and said to him, "Please become my Guru. I am tired of searching for a Guru."

Phariduddin accepted Nagamuddin as his devoted disciple, and Nagamuddin learned to cook so that he could prepare meals for his Master. He enjoyed the Master's deep affection for him. But the Master and the disciple were very, very poor. Sometimes for days on end they had no food to eat. They spent most of their time praying and meditating and totally neglected the demands of the body.

One day somebody gave Nagamuddin some flour so he could make bread. Nagamuddin did not have money, and he knew that his Master also had no money to buy one of the necessary ingredients to make bread — salt. So he went to the village market and borrowed some salt from a shop. The shopkeeper readily gave him the salt because he knew that Nagamuddin was a spiritual man, and that his Master was very great.

Nagamuddin brought the salt back and made delicious bread for his Master. But when he offered Phariduddin a few pieces of bread, something unusual happened. On other days when he would give something to his Master, the Master would eat it happily and bless Nagamuddin for the food. But that day Phariduddin said, "I shall not eat your food. There is tremendous impurity in it."

Neither the Master nor the disciple had eaten for three days, but because there was tremendous impurity in the food, the Master would not eat it. Nagamuddin felt miserable. He could not account for it.

Then his Master said, "I can clearly see that you have borrowed salt from a shopkeeper to make this bread. This is indeed a disgraceful act. Never borrow anything from anyone. If you borrow, your consciousness descends and you become impure. The man who gave you the salt is so proud that he has given you something, so he is treasuring impurity. And when you borrow something, you become a victim to worries and anxieties. Worries and anxieties are also a kind of impurity. If you do not have total purity in your system, in every cell of your body, then you will not be able to realise God. So from now on, don't borrow anything — money or material gifts. Worries and anxieties will assail you and purity will leave you.

"If you have purity, then you have everything. There are two ways to have purity. One is by seeing God inside everyone, consciously and constantly. The other is by imagining God and consciously repeating His Name as many times as possible. My son, if you have purity, you do not have to go to God. God Himself will make you see His infinite Divinity. What God is will be reflected in you. You will be an exact replica of God.

"Purity expedites God's Hour. Purity embodies God's Power. If you have purity, then there is nothing that you cannot accomplish. Purity is the harbinger of selfless oneness — Eternity's perfect, selfless oneness with God."

GIM 189. *I wish to be fair*

A Sanskrit scholar used to teach in a college. One day the principal of the school said to him, "I have a piece of good news for you: you have been promoted."

The scholar said, "How can it be? I don't deserve a promotion!"

"But we need a teacher for the higher course," said the principal.

The Sanskrit scholar said, "Oh, I can easily solve that problem. My own teacher is now out of employment. It is he who deserves this post. He knows Sanskrit far better than I do. Let me go and tell him that you have a post for him. He will be able to teach very well. I assure you that you will be satisfied with him."

The principal said, "Oh no, we can't take your teacher for the higher class when we do not know him at all. He can take your class, and you can teach the higher class."

The scholar said, "That is absurd. I can't allow that. My teacher knows much more than I do!"

The principal said, "You have served this college for several years, so we know your capacity. Without knowing your teacher's capacity, how can we give him that post?"

The scholar said, "You have faith in me, and I have faith in my teacher. I know his capacity."

The principal said, "If you do not accept this offer, you will stay where you are forever."

"You are trying to tempt me, but I am not tempted by you," said the scholar. "Just because you have tried to tempt me, you deserve punishment. Either you accept my teacher for the higher class, or I am leaving this school."

The following day the scholar did not come to the school. The principal was utterly amazed at this professor's love for his teacher. On the one hand, he was helpless. On the other hand, he was proud that he had such a self-giving man teaching in his college. So the principal informed the scholar to bring his teacher.

When they were both standing before him, the principal said to the scholar, "I have never seen and perhaps will never see a man like you."

"No, you will see many, many who will far surpass me," said the scholar. "But I wish to tell you that, in life, when I am fair to someone, then God is fair to me — only then, and not even one second before. So I always try to be fair."

Then the principal gave the higher post to the scholar's teacher, and the scholar resumed teaching his own class.

GIM 190. *A new kind of army*

Once a boy of sixteen inherited the throne when his father died. A neighbouring king who had been his father's enemy sent a letter to the young king, saying, "You are just a little boy. Surrender to me; otherwise, I shall come and capture your throne and kill you."

The elderly ministers of the young king advised him to be very cautious. They said that this king, his enemy, was very strong, so he would have to be very careful.

But the young king said, "No, I won't listen to you people. I will send my soldiers, but they will be different from regular soldiers. These soldiers will be sweepers and garbage collectors and so forth."

The sixteen-year-old king supplied the sweepers with weapons which they didn't even know how to use. The king's soldiers showed the sweepers only how to carry them. Nonetheless, these new soldiers went to the enemy, shouting and screaming that they would kill all the enemy soldiers. When the enemy saw the modern weapons of these ferocious-looking soldiers, they all surrendered without even a fight.

The young boy arrested the enemy king and asked him to beg for forgiveness. The old king immediately asked for forgiveness, and the boy returned his soldiers.

GIM 191. *The defeat of the Muslim ruler Pathan*

The sixteen-year-old king then wanted to conquer Chittagong. He felt that Chittagong was a beautiful place, but the Muslim ruler Pathan was no good. The young king knew that the soldiers of this ruler were extremely powerful. So he said, "We shall have to play some tricks."

He asked one of his men to go to Pathan's soldiers and ask why they were fighting for the Muslim ruler, since Pathan was so bad. If they were fighting just for money, then the young king would pay them more. Let them leave the Muslim king and be his soldiers.

The enemy soldiers said, "If you can give us a higher salary, we will leave King Pathan immediately." So the young king gave them a higher salary and took them away. Then he declared war against the ruler of Chittagong and easily won. He became the ruler of Chittagong and, for a long time, ruled Chittagong with utmost compassion and justice.

GIM 192. *Chaitanya wins over the Muslim soldiers*

Sri Chaitanya was one of India's greatest spiritual Masters. Once there was a Muslim leader who turned against him. In the beginning, the Muslim leader was very nice and was not against Chaitanya and his followers. "They are Hindus, great worshippers of Vishnu," he said. "There is nothing wrong in what they are doing. It is their faith. Why should we stand against their faith?"

But the leader's admirers and followers said, "They must not be allowed to dance and sing in the street. They are destroying our peace. Let us send our soldiers into the city. The next time these devotees start singing and dancing in the street, our soldiers will beat them black and blue, and they will stop."

After much persuasion, the Muslim leader finally agreed. But when his soldiers went to stop Chaitanya and his followers, the soldiers saw that thousands of people were singing and dancing with them. The soldiers felt utterly lost.

In a half hour's time, the soldiers got so intoxicated from watching Chaitanya dance that they also started dancing. When the Muslim leader came and saw that his soldiers had been very nicely converted and were dancing with the enemies, the leader came and fell at Chaitanya's feet and begged his forgiveness.

He said, "I didn't want to torture you, but my followers instigated me. Now my army has seen something divine in you and your devotees, and my men have joined you."

Chaitanya replied, "Whoever has faith in God and love of God has found the true religion."

GIM 193. *Shivaji*

There was a great King, a great hero of the highest order, named Shivaji. He was from Maharastra, so he was called the Maratha King. Once he wrote a letter to Tukara, a great seeker who had become a saint, inviting him to come to his palace. Shivaji had heard much about the saint and had developed highest admiration for him.

But Tukara declined his invitation. He wrote back: "O King, you have invited me to come to your palace, but I don't find any necessity to come. You will present me with gifts, but I do not need anything from you. If I want to eat, there are trees bearing fruits. When I walk along the street, I see that people have discarded their used, old clothes, and I can use them if I need clothes. If I want shelter, I already have a piece of metal, and also there are many caves all around where I can take shelter. What else do I need on earth? I cannot accept your invitation and I do not need anything from you."

Shivaji realised his mistake, and he came to Tukara's home, walking barefoot to honour him. India's greatest poet Tagore wrote a most beautiful, soulful and powerful poem about Shivaji. That poem stands as one of Tagore's greatest achievements.

GIM 194. *Babar and the cave*

The first Mogul Emperor's name was Babar. He was not as great as Akbar, who was the greatest of all the Mogul Emperors, but he still was a very great Emperor. Since he was the first, he had to fight and fight and fight to establish his kingdom.

Once, with a group of friends and admirers, he went to visit his relatives. On their way back it started pouring. It was raining cats and dogs, and there was no place for them to take shelter. Then, to their wide surprise, they discovered a tiny cave, so they begged the Emperor to enter into the cave while all of them remained outside. They were ready to be thoroughly drenched.

But the Emperor said, "How can I do that? You are my intimate friends and admirers. This protection is not enough for all of us. Since it is not adequate for all of us, I don't need it. I am more than happy to be outside with you."

So Babar didn't enter into the cave. The rain lasted for a long time and the following day they reached their destination. This was Babar's loving oneness with his friends and admirers.

GIM 195. *Solaman's one wish*

During his lifetime, the Mogul Emperor Shahjan built the famous Taj Mahal in memory of his beloved wife, Mamataj. Shahjan had four sons. When he died, the second son, Aurongajeb, wanted to get the throne. So he killed his older brother, Dara, arrested his two younger brothers and declared that he would rule the entire kingdom. The son of Dara, Solaman, went to Sri Naga for shelter. But the King of Sri Naga, instead of giving him shelter, arrested him and sent him to Aurongajeb, who was in his capital in Delhi.

When Aurongajeb saw his nephew, for a moment he felt sad that Solaman was in such a miserable state. He asked his nephew what he wanted. If Solaman wanted to leave, he would not kill him. But Solaman said, "If you want to fulfil my only desire, then kill me immediately. You have killed my father. Now I don't want to remain on earth."

Aurongajeb said, "What are you talking about? I shall not kill you. I shall allow you to go in your own way."

Solaman said, "I do not need that favour from you. Only one favour I want: kill me here and now."

This was Solaman's oneness with his father. Needless to say, Aurongajeb didn't kill him.

GIM 196. *Can you tell me where there is no God?*

Nanak was the founder of Sikhism. He was an excellent, excellent Guru. When he was young, Nanak paid very little attention to sports. Unlike most of his friends, he didn't care for games at all. Nanak always used to think of God and meditate on God. He only wanted to mix with spiritual people. In school he didn't do well because he was all the time in his own world.

Since he was not doing well, his father, who was a business-man, said, "The best thing is for him to go into business." So he opened up a shop for his son.

O God! Nanak was unlike other businessmen. He used to give away money to spiritual people, to saddhus. The father saw that he would soon go bankrupt if he kept his son in the shop. The father said, "In some way this boy has to become worldly-minded. If he remains all the time in the spiritual world, then he will be totally lost and our family will be disgraced." So he asked his son to get married, even though he was quite young. Nanak obeyed.

But again it was the same story. Nanak was praying and meditating all the time. Whenever he got the opportunity, he used to go to see religious people, spiritual mendicants. His wife used to cry and cry for her husband. But what could she do? He was a hopeless case. Finally one day, without any rhyme or reason, the wife died. Nanak was quite happy. He said, "Now I can become a mendicant and go wherever I want to." So he became a mendicant and went to many places to pray and meditate. He used to go to Hindu temples, Muslim mosques and Christian churches alike. He used to go wherever he could find a place to meditate.

One day Nanak decided to go on a pilgrimage to Mecca, which is the most holy place for Muslims. During his journey he happened to lie down for a while with his feet facing a mosque. A priest saw this and said to Nanak, "Look at your audacity! You are lying here with your feet pointing directly at the mosque. What are you doing?"

Nanak said, "Forgive me, I am very tired; I am simply ex-hausted. Please do me a favour. Will you kindly lift up my feet and point them in a direction where there is no God?"

The priest got the point. He said, "You have taught me that God is everywhere. I have been telling people that Allah is everywhere and in everything, and that the whole world is His creation. But today you have shown me that no matter which direction we face, God is there. So you have taught me a most significant lesson."

GIM 197. *Cremation or burial?*

Usually one spiritual Master is not liked by the disciples of other Masters — especially by those following different paths or religions. But both Muslims and Hindus liked Nanak very much, although he was a Sikh and had his own path. Everybody used to speak very highly of him. As a matter of fact, he had many disciples and admirers who were Hindus, Muslims and followers of other religions as well.

When Guru Nanak died, there was a terrible controversy between his Hindu and Muslim disciples. The Hindus said he had to be cremated and the Muslims said that he had to be buried. What could be done? The two parties were about to fight for the dead body.

In accordance with Indian tradition the dead body had been covered with a piece of cloth. All of a sudden, someone removed the cloth and everyone was amazed to see that the dead body had completely disappeared! In its place were hundreds of beautiful, fragrant flowers. So the Hindus and the Muslims each took half of the flowers.

Believe it or not, this is absolutely a true story. Real spiritual Masters can perform this kind of miracle. This story tells us that after the soul has left, you can discard the body in any manner you want. If you belong to the Hindu religion, then you will follow the Hindu system of cremation. If you belong to the Muslim religion, then you will follow the Muslim system of burial. But if you go beyond all religions, then you can do whatever you want to. When their life's journey is about to come to a close, some spiritual Masters just run into a river or an ocean, never to be found. Some leave the body through their *sahasrara* or crown chakra. Some set fire to themselves, while others use their spiritual power to invoke burning flames from above, and when the flames descend they are totally burnt. So this is a most significant story.

GIM 198. *The son of the Guru is to be worshipped like the Guru*

Nanak's successor was a very good spiritual Master, although he was not as great as Nanak. The successor of this Master was also very good. They were all good Masters.

Nanak's successor had two sons. They thought that when their father left the body, one of them would become the new Master. But the father knew well that neither of his sons was spiritual, so he did not appoint either of them to be his representative. Before he died, he appointed one of his disciples to become the Guru in his physical absence. This made the two sons very angry with their father as well as with his successor. They became very jealous of the new Master, and always they used to speak ill of him. In every way they tried to hurt him.

This new Master was compassion incarnate. He used to say that the Guru's sons have to be worshipped like the Guru himself, because the Indian system is like that. It is said that the son of the Guru is to be revered exactly like the father. But it has happened that the father has been a God-realised soul and the son nothing but a donkey.

One day this particular spiritual Master was giving a wonderful discourse. Many disciples were around him, listening with rapt attention.

Then the Master and the disciples meditated for some time with utmost sincerity. O God! All of a sudden the younger son of the previous Master came right up to the new Master and started beating him mercilessly. Finally he kicked the Master off his throne.

The disciples were shocked and horrified and ran up to save their Master. They wanted to kill the son of the previous Master then and there. But this Master said, "If you are my true disciples, then you must not touch him. I won't allow you even to touch him, let alone strike him!" So they all had to prove that they were their Master's loyal disciples.

The Master then said, "He is my Master's son. Therefore, I have to treat him as my own son. This is our tradition. God will take care of him, so I am asking you not to take revenge. If somebody does something wrong to me, I will remain silent. Let him do it a second time and a third time, and I will still remain silent. But if the culprit does something wrong, something really undivine more than three times, then God will have special Concern for the victim. If the victim is repeatedly harassed or mistreated, then God Himself will take care of the aggressor. In some way God will punish him.

"I assure you, I have forgiven this fellow. He is my Master's son. But if he goes on doing this kind of thing a few times more, then God Himself will punish him. As a matter of fact, he has done many undivine things. This is not the first incident. Soon he will start reaping the fruits of his misconduct. He will be severely punished in the very near future." The Master's prophecy proved to be true. This rogue did something very undivine to somebody else and that person punished the culprit so mercilessly that he was bedridden for months. Even then the spiritual Master said, "I feel really sorry for him. Although God Himself has punished him and he deserved this punishment, I feel sorry that my Master's son had to be punished so badly."

Look at the faith and love this Master had for his own Master! The previous Master's son was undivine, to say the least, but he was always ready to forgive him, just because he was his own Master's son.

PART IV

INDIA AND HER MIRACLE-FEAST:
COME AND ENJOY YOURSELF

I have decided to narrate a few traditional stories which are well-known in India. These stories are not my own creations; they are about spiritual Masters who used to show their occult power as easily and as often as we drink water. I am one of those who do not appreciate miracles, for quite often miracles only feed curiosity, and there is a yawning gulf between curiosity and aspiration. Again, there are some Masters who think that it is advisable for an individual to start his spiritual journey, even if he has to start with curiosity. Eventually the same person will enter into the world of true aspiration.

Sometimes occultists want to prove that modern science does not have the last word with regard to God's creation. They want to show that the infinite wealth of the inner world can easily silence all the achievements of mankind in the outer world. To be sure, what we call a miracle is nothing but a common occurrence in the world beyond our senses. Inwardly we can learn from these great Masters, from their fascinating miracles, from their soul-stirring lives. That is why I am interested in telling these stories.

— Sri Chinmoy

INDIA AND HER MIRACLE-FEAST:
COME AND ENJOY YOURSELF

BOOK 1:
TRADITIONAL INDIAN STORIES
ABOUT TROILANGA SWAMI

There was once a very great spiritual Master whose name was Troilanga Swami. He was the possessor of tremendous occult power and spiritual power. Sri Ramakrishna went to see him a few times. According to Sri Ramakrishna, he was the moving Lord Shiva. Once, Sri Ramakrishna asked him, through gestures, about God. Also through gestures, Troilanga Swami made it clear to Sri Ramakrishna that high above in Heaven, God is One, but when we are in the body, then the body becomes the only reality for us and God becomes many.

Commentary: When silence answers a question, the answer is most effective. Here, in silence one spiritual Master put the question, and in silence another Master answered. The giver and the receiver were extremely pleased with each other.

Indeed, the body sings the song of God's multiplicity and the soul sings the song of God's unity or God the transcendental Vision.

IMF 3. *The world-renouncer*

Troilanga Swami renounced everything. He always remained unclothed. He did not ask anybody for food. If others came and fed him, he ate, but he never cared for quality or quantity. Anything people gave, he ate, and he left the quantity up to his devotees and admirers. In one of his visits to Troilanga Swami, Sri Ramakrishna offered him a very large quantity of Indian sweets. Another time, some wicked people offered him a very, very large quantity of the chemical lime. He ate it and it caused him to vomit immediately. They were so shocked. But for their misbehaviour they touched his feet and cried, and he forgave them immediately.

Commentary: He who has renounced the world not only sees the universal Truth-Beauty but also sees the universe as the Truth-Beauty and as the illumining and fulfilling Reality.

IMF 4. *Lover and Beloved are one*

Troilanga Swami once went into a Kali temple. He was followed into the temple by a young, highly advanced seeker named Bijoykrishna Goswami. To Bijoykrishna's wide surprise, Troilanga Swami passed water and sprinkled the whole statue of Kali. Bijoykrishna was frightened and horrified that a man could do this. "What are you doing?" he demanded.

Troilanga Swami replied, "This is all Ganges water. I am worshipping the Mother Kali."

When the people who were in charge of the temple came in, Bijoykrishna told them what the Master had done. The people in charge were not at all shocked. "Oh, Troilanga Swami has done it," they said. "He is one with Lord Shiva. If it had been somebody else, we would have taken him to task. We would have been furious and we would have punished him. But Troilanga Swami is always in Lord Shiva-Consciousness. Shiva and Kali are one, so we don't have to worry at all."

Commentary: The Source is Existence-Consciousness-Bliss. It is Reality omnipresent, omniscient and omnipotent. The lover of the Source, the knower of the Source, the dweller in the Source and the possessor of the Source are all the same. Troilanga Swami as the lover of Kali and the beloved of Kali is the self-same reality.

IMF 5. *Initiation is purification*

One day Troilanga Swami said to the young seeker Bijoykrishna Goswami, "Look here, I shall have to initiate you."

Bijoykrishna said, "I don't want to be initiated by you. You are so undivine. What you did in the Kali temple was so shocking to me."

Troilanga Swami said, "No, I have received an inner command from Above. You have to be initiated by me. It is absolutely necessary for everyone to be initiated. If there is no initiation, then there can be no purification. You need purification in your life, and if you do not have this purification, there will be no God-realisation for you. I have got the command from within. Otherwise, I would be the last person to ask to initiate anybody."

When Bijoykrishna heard these words, he fell at the Swami's feet and got initiation. It helped him considerably in his purification and expedited his spiritual journey. Eventually, Bijoykrishna Goswami also became a very great spiritual Master.

Commentary: Initiation is of paramount importance. The Master can initiate the seeker either outwardly or inwardly. But the traditional outer way, as part of a religious rite, is far less effective than the silence-initiation. In the silence-initiation, the Master offers a portion of his life-breath to the seeker for his ignorance-illumination and his delight-realisation. Initiation is purification. No purification, no perfection. No perfection, no satisfaction either on earth or in Heaven.

IMF 6. *Body-reality and soul-reality*

Once Troilanga Swami was walking along the street near an Indian king's palace. This king was a great admirer of his. When the king heard that Troilanga Swami was nearby, he himself ran out and brought him into the palace. The Master was naked, so the king's attendants put very nice, expensive clothes on him and he looked extremely beautiful. Then they fed him most delicious food. The king and his party were blessed by the Master and they had a long conversation with him, although ordinarily he was a man of few words. Sometimes he would not talk at all for months.

When Troilanga Swami left the palace to go back to his cottage, some of the palace guards watched him from a distance. When he was practically out of sight, three hooligans attacked him and took away all the expensive robes that had been given to him by the king. The guards came running and arrested the hooligans. Then they begged Troilanga Swami to come to the king's palace once again, and he agreed.

When the king heard what had happened, he was about to punish the hooligans and put them in jail. But Troilanga Swami said, "No, don't do that. To me there is no difference whether I have the clothes or not. My soul is not affected at all when I don't have any clothes. Long before you gave me the clothes, I had my soul inside my body, and this is the only real thing. What shall I do with the things that do not fulfil any need of my soul?" So the hooligans were allowed to go free and the Master peacefully went on his way.

Commentary: The body-reality needs decoration, ornamentation and embellishment for its satisfaction. The soul-reality needs only its oneness with Infinity's Immortality for its eternal satisfaction.

IMF 7. *A saint beyond temptation-life*

Troilanga Swami weighed over three hundred pounds. He lived in Benares and used to spend most of his time bathing in the water of the Ganges. Once he was walking along the street naked, when he passed a new magistrate who had just come to the area. The magistrate became furious and ordered a policeman to arrest the Master and lock him in a small room. The following morning the magistrate saw Troilanga Swami walking outside the room. "How did you come out?" he demanded.

Troilanga Swami answered, "It was so easy. I came out because I felt like coming out. During the night I emptied myself and now it is smelling; therefore, I thought it would be better for me to come out of the room. So I came out."

This time the magistrate himself put the Master under lock and key, using a double lock. The following morning, the magistrate was working in his office when all of a sudden he saw Troilanga Swami in one corner of the office, smiling at him. The magistrate said, "How is it possible for you to be here?"

Troilanga Swami told him, "You should not disturb the innocent Hindu Yogis. They can do anything they want to. I am walking along the street naked, but I am not interested in any women. In the case of ordinary men, they are full of lust. They have all kinds of emotional problems, lower vital problems, sex problems. But I am not like that. Also, people who look at me see that my body is so heavy and odd. So who will be interested in me? I have renounced the whole world, and at the same time nobody is interested in me in an impure way. So why do you bother me? I am not creating temptation and I am not tempted by anyone. If you want to torture the Hindu Yogis, you will be embarrassed and at every moment you will fail, because we are far above human torture."

Commentary: A truly God-realised person is he who has the capacity not to be affected by others and, at the same time, not to affect others. He protects himself from the rest of the world and he protects the world from himself. This miraculous achievement of his is due to the inseparable oneness of his body's divinity with his soul's supreme universality. The body enjoys the soul's freedom. The soul enjoys the body's acceptance of the soul's reality.

IMF 8. *God's Compassion-Power*

A young woman was bitterly sobbing and weeping over the dead body of her husband, who had been bitten by a snake. According to Indian tradition, when somebody dies of a snake bite, he cannot be cremated; the dead body has to be thrown into the water. So the man's relatives had brought his body to the bank of the river, but the wife was weeping bitterly and did not want them to throw the body into the water. All of a sudden, Troilanga Swami appeared. Everybody knew that he was a great spiritual Master. He took some mud and clay from the Ganges, placed it on the spot where the man had been bitten by the snake and massaged it a little. Then Troilanga Swami jumped into the water. In a few minutes, the man opened his eyes, looked around and asked why they had brought him there. Then the man and his wife went their way.

Commentary: Indeed, death is powerful, but spiritual power is infinitely more powerful. It reminds death that death cannot mark the end of life, for it is God's Will that life will eternally flow in and through death. In this story, God's Compassion-Power overrules His Justice-Power.

IMF 9. *Insult brings retribution*

One day Troilanga Swami was walking along the street naked when a magistrate and his wife saw him. The wife was horrified and wanted to have him arrested. As the guards were about to arrest the Yogi, Troilanga Swami suddenly disappeared. There were many people surrounding him, so everyone was surprised that he could escape. After a short time, he appeared in the same spot, smiling. The magistrate got furious. "Why do you do this kind of thing?" he shouted. He insulted the Master mercilessly, saying, "You are such an odd-looking fellow! Why do you move around naked? Do you have no sense? You create so much nuisance for us!" But he let Troilanga Swami go.

That night the magistrate had a dream. In the dream he saw a sannyasi, wearing the skin of a tiger and holding a trident, running towards him to kill him. The sannyasi said to the magistrate, "How did you dare to insult Troilanga Swami? He is such a great spiritual Master. I shall not let you remain in this sanctified city of Benares." The magistrate was frightened to death. He shouted out loud in his sleep, and his attendants came to his rescue and woke him up.

The following day the magistrate himself went to Troilanga Swami, placed himself at his feet and begged for forgiveness, which was immediately granted.

Commentary: When one insults a God-realised Master, he incurs immediate retribution, not from the Master himself but from God, who loves the Master, His supreme instrument, more than He loves Himself. The Master forgives the culprits, for forgiveness is what he knows. But God, in spite of being His own Eternity's and Infinity's Forgiveness, does not allow His chosen instrument to be ridiculed and insulted, for His instrument is he who is of God and for God alone. After all, what God wants is always the constant manifestation of His own Truth-Light-Beauty.

IMF 10. *The king and the sword*

A great Indian king once went on a boat trip on the Ganges. He and his attendants saw a man swimming behind them. It was Troilanga Swami. It happened, in an hour or so, that Troilanga Swami swam near the boat smiling, so they helped him into the boat. He was naked as usual, but the people there did not mind because they all knew him, and had tremendous respect, love and veneration for him. The king was also pleased to see him, because he also admired him.

The king had a sword hanging around his waist. Troilanga Swami took it from him and examined it and played with it like a child. Then he suddenly threw it into the Ganges. The king was furious. He had received this sword for his valour and for his merit, so he felt miserable that he had lost such a precious thing. He wanted to punish the man but everybody protested: "Oh no, he is a saint; you can't do that. It will be a terrible thing if you touch him."

The king said, "If you people are not willing to punish him, then once we land I will get other people who will gladly listen to me and punish this man."

When they were about to reach the shore, Troilanga Swami, who was seated in the boat, placed his hand in the water. All of a sudden two shining swords appeared in his hand. They were identical, and both looked exactly like the one he had thrown into the Ganges. Everybody was astonished. The Master said to the king, "O King, now find the one that belonged to you."

The king was totally nonplussed. He did not know which one was actually his. Then Troilanga Swami said to him, "You fool, you don't know which one belongs to you? You don't know your own possession?" Then he threw away the one that was not the king's, and said, "In this world nothing will remain with you. When you die, everything you have will have to remain here. To the Real in you I say, 'Don't live in the world of enjoyment. Remain in the world of aspiration. Remain in the world of Light, Peace and Bliss. You are a king, but you are a fool as well. Be wise. Then only will you have true happiness in life. Be spiritually wise!'"

Commentary: Unless and until we become spiritually wise, we shall never know what our true possession is. Our true possession, our eternal possession, our only possession, is our love of God. There cannot be anything else here on earth or there in Heaven for us to claim as our own. Only our love of God — our constant, soulful and self-giving love of God — can be our eternal possession. This possession will always remain safe, and we ourselves will also be safe only when we claim this possession as our own, very own.

Once we know that we have love of God in abundant, boundless and infinite measure, then God's possession, which is His entire creation, immediately becomes our possession as well. Our love of God claims God, and the moment we offer our love to God, God's creation immediately becomes ours as well. His entire creation comes from His Vision, and He and His Vision are inseparable. When we claim God with our love, God's Concern and God's creation immediately claim us; for the sole possessor is God and nobody else.

Here on earth everything that we can see, we try to claim. Everything that is around us also wants to claim us. But we cannot claim others and they cannot claim us, for we see that something is missing in them and they see that the same thing is missing in us. What is missing is love of God. This is the seed, the possibility-seed, which eventually grows into the in-evitability-fruit.

IMF 11. *Discrimination abolished, equality's universality reigns*

A king, his queen and their dear ones were swimming in a private swimming pool. There were guards all around, so nobody knew how Troilanga Swami had managed to come in and stand right in front of the swimming pool. As he was naked and very fat, he was extremely odd-looking. When the king and queen saw that he was watching them swim, they were furious. The king wanted to punish Troilanga Swami, and there was a great uproar all around the pool.

Meanwhile, Troilanga Swami's devotees were looking for their Master. When they learned where he was, they ran and told the king how great the Master was. "He has a childlike nature; that is why he was watching you swim," they said. "Just like a child he has come here for innocent amusement. He has no lower vital problems. He is above all that. For him, sandalwood and waste matter are the same. Everything is the same to him."

The king said, "If everything is the same to him, then he has to eat what I eat: meat. Since he is a spiritual man, I am sure he does not eat meat. Let us see if everything is equal to him."

Troilanga Swami said, "Yes, I am ready to eat meat, but first, will you eat my food?" The king, knowing perfectly well that since he was a sadhu, he would eat only fruit and milk, said, "Certainly I will eat your food."

Then, in front of everyone, Troilanga Swami immediately emptied himself and started eating. Everyone was amazed and horrified. Then, he said to the king, "Now, eat what I have eaten." The king simply ran the other way. But the onlookers got a very good fragrance from this — like sandalwood — and they were surprised and moved.

Later the king said to Troilanga Swami, "I know your spiritual power. I know who you are, and I am issuing a message that nobody should bother you anymore, even if you walk naked."

Commentary: The beauty of a childlike, innocent flower-heart gives off a special fragrance everywhere, not only from what it has within itself, but also from the beauty that it sees all around.

It was not Troilanga Swami's so-called curiosity that compelled him to go to the swimming pool, but it was his equality-vision which wanted to show to the world the evenness of reality everywhere. Discrimination abolished, equality's universality reigns.

IMF 12. *The world-renunciation song*

One day Troilanga Swami was with his disciples when a nicely-dressed middle-aged Bengali gentleman wearing a new dhoti and perfumed with oil came to him. To the disciples' wide surprise, Troilanga Swami embraced the gentleman.

Everybody said: "How can you embrace someone who is so sophisticated and unspiritual? There is no spirituality in him."

Troilanga Swami said to them, "You fools, you don't recognise him. You people would have to give up everything in life, renounce everything, in order to come to his spiritual state of consciousness. In your highest state of consciousness you cannot equal him. For him to wear clean, new, ironed clothes or to use perfume is nothing. He has reached such a spiritual height that he will not be affected no matter what he wears or what he does. You can't judge people by their outer appearance. He is really a great seeker, an extraordinary soul."

Troilanga Swami's words proved true. The man's name was Shyama Charan Lahiri and he was later known to be a great spiritual Master.

Commentary: If one knows how to sing the world-renunciation song well, then one can never be tempted by the world-possession song, not to speak of the world-temptation dance. His divine realisation is not affected in the inner world, his human performance is not affected in the outer world. He is like a boat that is in the water and, at the same time, is not affected by the water.

IMF 13. *A heart of compassion*

Troilanga Swami and one of his dear disciples were meditating together on the bank of the Ganges. All of a sudden a terrible hurricane arose. The disciple said to the Master, "Let us go home. Let us hurry to our ashram."

The Master said, "How can I go home now? Look at the pitiful condition of the passengers in that boat on the river. The boat is about to sink."

The disciple said, "I also feel sorry for them, but what can we do?"

In a few minutes' time the disciple saw the boat sink. He felt miserable and started crying for the passengers. Then he looked around. To his wide surprise he saw that his Master was missing. Then he felt totally miserable. The hurricane was in its full fury, the boat had sunk and his Master was not visible. He began praying to the Master to come back from wherever he had gone.

After a short time he saw the boat that had sunk come up again right in front of him with all the passengers, and inside the boat was also a naked man, Troilanga Swami. Before that moment, nobody in the boat had seen the Master. He had gone unseen and brought the boat and the passengers back to shore unharmed and safe. This was another of Troilanga Swami's miracles.

Commentary: A God-representative is he who embodies Eternity's Compassion-Heart, Infinity's Protection-Light and Immortality's Illumination-Soul.

INDIA AND HER MIRACLE-FEAST:
COME AND ENJOY YOURSELF

BOOK 2:
TRADITIONAL INDIAN STORIES
ABOUT SHYAMA CHARAN LAHIRI

One evening, Shyama Charan Lahiri was roaming at the foot of the Himalayas while on a short visit to the area, when he heard a voice saying, "Shyama Charan, Shyama Charan." He was surprised to see a sadhu calling him from a distance. The sadhu approached him and said, "Can't you recognise me, my child, my son?" Then he uttered the name of Shyama Charan's father and grandfather. Even then Shyama Charan could not recognise him. The sadhu showed him abundant affection and led him into a cave and showed him a trident, a sacred water pot, a lion skin, a tiger skin and some beads. He said, "Can you recognise these? They are all yours," but Shyama Charan could not recognise them. The sadhu then placed his hand on Shyama Charan's spine. Immediately Shyama Charan came to realise that those were indeed his belongings.

The sadhu said to him, "My name is Babaji, my son. You were my dear disciple in your previous incarnation. You left the body at a very high stage of spiritual development. I want you to complete your spiritual life in this incarnation."

Shyama Charan bowed to his Master and cried and cried. He said that he would not go back to his wife and family, but Babaji said, "No, you have to return to them. God wants you to lead a family life and, at the same time, remain in your highest consciousness and guide householders in leading a better, higher and purer life. I shall initiate you in a few days' time. As long as you remain near the Himalayas, come and see me every day."

Shyama Charan was overjoyed that his Master was going to initiate him. With a heart full of gratitude and delight, he left.

A few days later Lahiri returned to the Master. Babaji said, "The time has come for me to initiate you, but before I do, you have to drink this liquid."

Shyama Charan drank a very large quantity of an oily liquid from an earthen jar. It caused him to vomit and empty himself many, many times. Then Babaji said, "Now you are purified, my son. I am giving you puri, halwa and other sweetmeats. Eat them to your heart's content." Shyama Charan ate them voraciously. Then the Master initiated him compassionately, unreservedly and unconditionally.

Commentary: To say that each soul is blessed with only one incarnation is to commit a Himalayan blunder. Each soul goes through many, many incarnations before it embodies, reveals and manifests the ultimate Truth. We start from one point and eventually there comes a time when we reach the goal. Each incarnation helps the soul go forward to the destined goal. If we start something in this incarnation and do not complete it, then in the next incarnation we shall have to complete it, for unless we do, we shall have no abiding satisfaction. Each incarnation means covering a few more steps while walking along Eternity's road. If we keep walking, marching and running forward, each incarnation is undoubtedly a movement forward to a more illumining and more fulfilling reality.

IMF 15. *Master saviour*

After initiating Shyama Charan, Master Babaji, the Lion Yogi, said to his disciple, "Initiation is of paramount importance; therefore, I have initiated you. But now, in three days' time, I want you to leave for your home. You have to go back to work. Your family needs you badly."

Shyama Charan cried and cried. He did not want to go. His Master consoled him and said, "No, you have to do something most special for God while staying with your family and leading the life of a householder. But I assure you, whenever you are in need of me, just invoke me, and I shall come to see you and bless you."

With a heavy heart, Shyama Charan left for home. On his way, he stayed for two or three days at the home of some of his friends. His friends said to him, "Do you believe in occult power or spiritual power? We don't believe in it. There was a time when Indian sadhus had occult power, but now those days are gone. People who claim that they have occult powers are all fakes."

Shyama Charan said, "What do you mean? I have just been initiated by a great spiritual Master. I know how much occult power he has."

His friends did not believe him, so he said, "If you don't believe me, I can prove it. You just leave this room, allow me to meditate for a few minutes and I assure you my Master will come here."

Lahiri's friends had no faith in occult power, but they were all curious, so they left. When his friends left the room, he invoked his Master most soulfully. In fifteen minutes' time Babaji came into the room in his subtle body, and then he assumed his physical body.

Shyama Charan was overjoyed to see his Master inside the room, but Babaji scolded and insulted him mercilessly. He said, "Look at your audacity! I came from such a great distance, only to please your curiosity and to challenge your atheist friends. I warn you, I will never, never do this kind of thing again. I told you that whenever you invoke me I shall come, but I am revoking my promise to you. Now I wish to say that whenever I want to see you, only then shall I come to you, wherever you are."

Shyama Charan cried and cried for forgiveness. Babaji said, "I have forgiven you, but never invoke me any more to display my occult power or to display your devotion. Only when I feel the need shall I come to see you. In the inner world you can invoke me, you can feel my presence, but I don't want to show my physical presence this way any more."

Shyama Charan bowed down to Babaji and said, "Now that you have come, O Master, out of your infinite Compassion, please, please give me a boon."

"What is your boon?" Babaji asked.

"I want my friends to come and see you," said Shyama Charan, "so that they will believe in your occult power."

The Master laughed at him, saying, "Yes, and also in your invocation-power. Go and tell them to come."

Shyama Charan opened the door and his friends came in. They were so surprised to see a sadhu with long hair and a long beard seated in a lotus position. Babaji did not talk to them, but he smiled at everyone and everybody bowed down to him. Shyama Charan brought some food for the Master and the Master ate in front of them. Then Babaji asked everyone to leave for a few minutes. When they returned, he had disappeared.

Commentary: The display of occult power or spiritual power in order to create aspiration is an indication of a lack of wisdom. Miracle-power does not and cannot change humanity's face. Humanity's face can be transformed only by inner awakening, inner cry, inner dedication and inner surrender to God. Curiosity is not spirituality. An inner cry is the only true spirituality which God appreciates lovingly, compassionately and unreservedly. For God's universal Oneness, universal Love, universal Light and universal Delight can be made manifest only in our heart's inner cry.

IMF 16. *The conqueror of time and space*

Shyama Charan used to work in an office. It happened that for a few days his boss, who was an Englishman, was very sad and disturbed. One day he asked his boss the reason for his sadness. The boss said that his wife was extremely ill in a hospital in England, and that he had not heard any recent news from her or from the family.

Shyama Charan said to him, "Let me enter into the adjacent room and meditate for some time. Then I will bring you some news." The boss smiled at the young clerk and inwardly appreciated his good will, but he did not have real faith in him. He felt that to do this kind of thing, one had to be a great spiritual Master with tremendous occult power.

In fifteen minutes, Shyama Charan came out of the room and said to his boss, "In two or three days' time you will receive a letter from your wife. She is doing well. I assure you, you don't have to worry about her at all." He even told his boss what was inside the letter.

In three days, a letter did arrive from his wife, and the contents of the letter were exactly what Shyama Charan had said. But the story does not end here. In a few months, the boss's wife came to India. One day she visited her husband's office. When she saw Shyama Charan, her eyes opened wide in surprise. She said to her husband, "How can this man be here? I saw him near my death bed in the hospital. He looked at me and smiled, and then I recovered." Her husband and all those who were working in the office were taken aback. But Shyama Charan continued his job as a clerk in that office for many, many years, for he had to support his family. Only after many years, when he had collected a few disciples, was he able to retire.

Commentary: A spiritual Master is he who has solved space problems, time problems and all other human problems. In his oneness-heart with God's Cosmic Will, the length and breadth of the world abides. He does not go anywhere; he is just there when necessity demands. Medical power is quite often uncertain. But spiritual power is uncertain only when it is not aware of the omniscient capacity of the Source. When spirituality is fully aware of the capacity of the Source, and its surrender gradually gains the capacity of the Source, lo and behold, it is blessed by the Source and grows into the all-powerful Source itself.

IMF 17. *The art of photography surrenders*

Shyama Charan Lahiri was dead against anyone's taking a photograph of him. But since his intimate disciples were repeatedly requesting permission to take his photograph, he once agreed. The disciples called in a photographer, and like a child the Master asked him questions. The photographer was deeply honoured, so he taught the Master the ABCs of photography.

But when it was time for the Master's picture to be taken, the photographer could not see him in the viewfinder. He aimed the camera at the Master, but the Master was not visible. When he focused on others, he saw them perfectly, but when he focused on Shyama Charan, there was nothing visible at all.

Finally the frustrated photographer said to the Master, "It is impossible. I can't take your picture. I don't know what you are doing."

The Master smiled and said, "All right, I shall behave myself. Now you can take it." This time when the photographer looked through the viewfinder, Shyama Charan Lahiri was clearly visible, so he snapped the picture. Then Shyama Charan Lahiri said to him, "Spirituality and spiritual power far surpass modern science. Just have faith in the Real, which is spirituality."

That particular picture is an immortal picture, the most authentic and the highest picture taken of the Master. His disciples now worship in front of that picture.

Commentary: Some spiritual Masters are not in favour of picture-taking. They feel that since the body-reality is so transient, why pay any attention to it? There are other Masters who are of the opinion that a photograph does not represent a mere object, but can serve as an inspirational force and an elevating and illumining experience. These Masters feel the supreme necessity of seeing the highest reality inside the body-reality first, and then transforming the body-reality into the soul's universal mission and transcendental vision. According to them, a photograph is not a mere piece of paper reflecting an outer face or appearance; it is an illumining revelation of what one inwardly is.

There are those who think the achievements of the world, in the world, are useless, and the world itself is useless, for it is unreal; therefore, they do not want to leave behind anything when they enter into the other world. But those who think of the world as the field of God-manifestation will strive to leave behind a transformed life and revelations of an immortal soul. Both parties are equally correct in their respective approaches to reality, according to the depth and height of their own realisation.

IMF 18. *Medical science cries, spiritual science smiles*

A disciple of Shyama Charan Lahiri, Chandra Mohan, had just got his medical degree. He went to his Master and placed himself at his feet. The Master blessed him and asked him quite a few questions about medical science. Then he said to his disciple, "Can you tell me if I am alive?" Immediately the

Master lay down and stopped his heartbeat. The young man who had just got his degree could not feel the Master's pulse or heartbeat. He was astonished. There were other men there and they also could not feel anything. Shyama Charan Lahiri was absolutely like a dead body.

This went on for ten or fifteen minutes. Then suddenly Shyama Charan Lahiri opened his eyes and said, "You people should always remember that far beyond medical science is spiritual science. The medical world will never be able to fathom the spiritual mysteries. But these spiritual mysteries are not mysteries as such. They are the real realities of normal people, and normal people are those who believe in God implicitly."

Commentary: Spirituality invents, medical science discovers. This invention of spirituality is in perfect harmony with God's omniscient Vision and omnipotent Reality. Spirituality is the foundation of the life-reality-building. This building has quite a few floors: science, art, philosophy, religion and so forth. If there is no foundation, there can be no edifice. It is the spirituality-foundation that supports all the floors and, at the same time, transcends the capacity of even the upper floors. It is consciously one with the root-reality of God's Existence-Consciousness-Bliss.

IMF 19. *Justice-light shines*

One of Shyama Charan Lahiri's disciples was named Kali Kumar. He worked in an office and used to visit the Master quite often. Unfortunately, Kali Kumar's boss did not like the idea of his being devoted to a spiritual Master. His boss was a middle-aged man, and he wanted to be Kali Kumar's only boss, so he literally hated the spiritual Master.

One day, the boss followed Kali Kumar to his Master's ashram with the idea of insulting the Master. He wanted to complain that Kali Kumar was not as obedient to him as he was to the Master. Before the boss could say anything, however, Shyama Charan Lahiri started speaking to Kali Kumar. "Today I wish to show you something which may please you. Turn off the light." Kali Kumar turned off the light and they meditated for a few minutes. Then the Master said, "Can you see anything?" Both Kali Kumar and his boss saw a most beautiful young girl. Then the Master said to the boss, "Do you recognise her?" The boss was so ashamed and embarrassed. "Is it not your lover?" Shyama Charan continued. "Your wife and children are so devoted and faithful to you. How is it that you have fallen desperately in love with this girl?"

Kali Kumar's boss cried and cried. "Please forgive me," he begged the Master, "I want to become your disciple. I want to be initiated by you."

Shyama Charan said, "I can't initiate you right now. You have to wait for six months. If you lead a pure life for six months and remain faithful to your wife, I will initiate you."

The boss remained faithful to his wife for only three months; then he went back to his girlfriend, and after four months he passed away.

Commentary: If you try to harass a real spiritual Master, then ruthless embarrassment will dog you. The spiritual Master will easily forgive you, but it will be most difficult, almost impossible, for your own soul to forgive you. Your soul knows that a true spiritual Master is not only your best friend but your only friend. When you harass a spiritual Master, you attempt to break the eternal friendship that shines between your soul and the spiritual Master; therefore, your soul does not approve of it at all. At that time, your soul invokes the cosmic Will or justice-light to play their role inside your unaspiring and unlit life.

IMF 20. *The thirsty person and the well*

A great aspirant named Kebalananda used to go to a spiritual Master named Bhaskarananda to study metaphysical subjects, but actually his real Guru was Shyama Charan Lahiri. One day Bhaskarananda asked Kebalananda to speak to Shyama Charan Lahiri on his behalf. He wanted to learn a few spiritual secrets from the Master.

But when Kebalananda mentioned the matter to his Guru, Lahiri said, "Why should I do this? Always if somebody is thirsty, that person goes to the well. Does the well go to the thirsty person?"

When Kebalananda took this message to Bhaskarananda, Bhaskarananda felt embarrassed and ashamed and he went to Shyama Charan Lahiri personally to learn the spiritual secrets.

Commentary: It is quite natural for the thirsty person to go to the well to quench his thirst, for usually there is and can be no other way. But again, we have to know who the thirsty person is. If the thirsty person is a helpless little child who lacks the outer capacity or strength to come to the Source, then the Source, out of its infinite Compassion, has to go to the child who is parched with thirst.

Often the role of the seeker is that of a little child and the role of the Master is that of the affectionate mother. The childlike seeker cries in one room of the building and the mother comes running to fulfil the child's needs. But if the seeker is mature in every human way, then he should come to the Master, the Source, wherever he is, for the seeker will get tremendous delight if he drinks Nectar-Bliss at the Source, and also he will have the opportunity to appreciate his own personal efforts to come to the Source.

IMF 21. *Awareness and wisdom-light*

Shyama Charan Lahiri's wife's name was Kashimani. Once she woke up in the middle of the night and was so surprised to see that her husband was not at his usual meditation spot. He was seated in a lotus position high up in the air, quite a few metres above the ground. Her husband said to her, "Kashimani, it is high time for you to wake up from your sleep. This time when you wake up, remain in that condition forever. Don't go back to ignorance-sleep. Get up and look for wisdom-light within."

Commentary: Human life is unconscious sleep. Divine life is conscious awareness. Unconscious sleep makes us feel that there are millions of things which we cannot do on earth. Conscious awareness shows us clearly that there is nothing here on earth or there in Heaven which we cannot do. As a matter of fact, it makes us feel unmistakably that everything has already been done; what we are doing now is only observing and appreciating it.

IMF 22. *The Master's spiritual power*

Sri Yukteshwar, who later became Swami Yogananda's Guru, was a very close disciple of Shyama Charan Lahiri. One day his dearest friend, Ram, was attacked by cholera. Two doctors tried to save his life, but it seemed that all their efforts were in vain. It was a matter of a few hours before Ram would die.

Yukteshwar ran to his Master, crying to him to save his friend's life. Shyama Charan Lahiri said to Yukteshwar, "You have doctors. Why do you need me? The doctors will save him. They will be able to do the needful. I don't have to be involved."

Yukteshwar went back, full of hope, but gradually his friend's condition became worse. When it was a matter of four or five minutes before he would die, Ram said to his dearest friend Yukteshwar, "I will be dead in a few minutes. Please tell the Master that I have a last wish. My last wish is that he come and touch my dead body and thus bless me. This will be my last plea to him." In a few minutes' time he passed away.

Crying, Yukteshwar went back again to Shyama Charan Lahiri in order to give him Ram's message. The Master said, "How is Ram?"

Yukteshwar replied, "Please go and see him yourself. This was his last prayer to you: that you would touch his dead body and bless him."

But Shyama Charan said, "Then why should I go? He is not dead."

"Yes," said Yukteshwar, "He is dead. The doctors have pronounced it."

Shyama Charan Lahiri took some oil from a lamp and said, "Go and put a little bit of this oil into his mouth."

His friend was dead, but this was the command of the Master, so what else could Yukteshwar do? He went and put a small quantity of the oil that his Master had given him into Ram's mouth. In a few minutes Ram came to life, saying that he had had a dream in which he saw Shyama Charan Lahiri in a most beautiful form. The Master had said to him, "Ram, why are you sleeping? Get up and come to me."

Then Ram stood up, put on his clothes and both the friends went to Shyama Charan's place. The Master said to Yukteshwar, "Now I have taught you how to conquer death. From now on if anybody dies, just take a small quantity of oil and put it into his mouth. I have given you the medicine to conquer death."

Everybody laughed and laughed, because they knew perfectly well that the oil was just an outer gesture, a token, a symbol, whereas the actual gift of life had come from Lahiri.

Commentary: It is only the omnipotent spirituality that can turn impossibility into facile possibility. But spirituality, out of its sheer magnanimity, tries to adopt outer earthly means so that it can convince the physical mind that the truth-principle can be accessible to the human in us. Otherwise, without the least possible hesitation, one can say that it is the spiritual force that in silence turns the impossible reality into clear and certain possibility. Not only that, but afterwards it turns possibility into practical and inevitable reality.

It was the Master's spiritual power that revived Ram. Otherwise, no matter what kind of oil one puts into a dying man's mouth, will he survive? It could have been anything. Only to convince the physical mind with a physical object did the Master tell his disciple to use oil. That is why spiritual Masters say, "Do this, do that," when somebody is sick. Actually, it is their spiritual power which cures, but they know that this will convince the physical mind, so the patient's physical mind can believe that the Master has true concern for him.

IMF 23. *The call from the world beyond*

On 26 December 1895, Shyama Charan Lahiri was extremely sick and was lying down. He was surrounded by his intimate disciples and was explaining to them some of his favourite verses from the Bhagavad Gita. All of a sudden he stood up and said, "What am I doing here? Why am I wasting time? It is high time for me to go home to my real home."

A few hours later, on the same day, three of his intimate disciples at different places saw his luminous spiritual body consoling them. They did not know of his passing; they knew only that he was extremely sick. But when they went to their Master's ashram, they found that he had died. His physical body was dead, but he had travelled to visit them in his spiritual body.

Commentary: When the soul-bird comes out of the body-cage, it can be easily visible to those who want to see it. At that time the limitations of the body disappear and the infinite expansion of the soul appears. When a sincere seeker enters into the ignorance-life, he says to himself, "What am I doing here?" When the same seeker enters into the aspiration-world, he says to himself, "Why do I not remain here all the time?" Our earthly home embodies the desire-life; our heavenly home embodies the illumination-life.

INDIA AND HER MIRACLE-FEAST:
COME AND ENJOY YOURSELF

BOOK 3:
TRADITIONAL INDIAN STORIES
ABOUT GAMBHIRANANDA

Gambhirananda was a great spiritual Master. While still in his youth, before he became known as a great Master with tremendous occult power, he happened one day to pass by a cottage owned by a great aspirant. He did not know anything about the owner, and when he entered into the cottage nobody was there. He stayed inside the cottage and meditated there for three days. Each night a snake appeared before him.

When the actual owner came back, he was surprised and happy to see a young seeker. Gambhirananda told the owner about the snake. The owner said, "I have been meditating here for twelve years in order to see that snake. It is not a mere snake. It is a great spiritual Master, a great liberator, who takes the form of a snake. Whoever sees the snake will, without fail, be liberated. I am so happy that you have seen the snake. I am so proud that you have taken shelter in my little cottage."

Commentary: The human in us will never know when the God-Hour will strike. It is the divine in us that knows when the God-Hour is about to strike for us. The human in us is always puzzled even when the God-Hour strikes. But the divine in us knows that it is a normal occurrence that takes place unseen by our human eyes and unnoticed by our human mind. God's Hour strikes when man is ready with his unconditional surrender-bell.

IMF 25. *Music: aspiration-bud and Realisation-flower*

Gambhirananda was a great musician. He used to play on the sitar most hauntingly. A spiritual Master named Bijoykrishna opened an Ashram with his own disciples near Gambhirananda's home. But in the middle of the night when Bijoykrishna would hear Gambhirananda playing on the sitar in the distance, Bijoykrishna would run through the forest, which was filled with dangerous and ferocious animals, without being afraid, only to place himself at Gambhirananda's feet.

Commentary: Gambhirananda's outer music helped even another Master's aspiration increase. His inner music accelerated the speed of God's March within Bijoykrishna. The outer music brings our soul to the fore. The inner music helps us to see God's Compassion-Eye, His Illumination-Feet and His Satisfaction-Delight.

IMF 26. *Master, you have and you are the man-saving power*

Gambhirananda had a very close attendant named Akki who served him for many years. One day Akki became extremely ill quite unexpectedly and died. His younger brother, Munni, came running to the Master, crying. He touched his Master's feet and said, "You have to save your favourite disciple, Akki. He has died."

Gambhirananda said, "I do not claim to have that kind of power."

Munni said, "You don't have to claim to have it. I am claiming it on your behalf. You do have that power."

Gambhirananda could not refuse Munni's loving emotional demand, so he went with Munni to see his disciple's dead body.

When the Master sprinkled a few drops of water from a sacred vessel on Akki's body, Akki came back to life.

Commentary: Death-power snatched Akki away, but his Master's Compassion-power brought him back. Death says to the body, "Look what I can do." The Master says to death, "I do not deny your capacity, but God has given me a higher capacity. You believe in God's cosmic Law. I, too, believe in God's cosmic Law, but at times God gets tremendous joy by breaking His own cosmic Law, if by doing so He can increase the aspiration for Light and Truth in a seeker."

IMF 27. *The soulful and blessingful tiger*

Gambhirananda used to play music far into the night for his disciples and admirers. One night, while he was playing, a tiger appeared before him. The members of the audience all began shouting and screaming, and they ran out of the room. But the Master remained calm and said to the tiger, "Come, let us go. Let me put you back in your den. These people are afraid of you."

After the Master had led the tiger back to his den, the disciples and admirers came back into the room. Then Gambhirananda told them that this tiger was not a real tiger. He said, "A Master of the highest order has taken the form of this tiger, and moves from place to place to bless seekers. He did not come to devour us, he came to bless us."

Commentary: When one realises God, the ferocious qualities of the animal world do not and cannot torture or frighten him, for he deals with omniscient Light and omnipotent Power. Here a Master of the highest height assumed the form of a tiger not to devour the members of the audience but to remind them that the ferocious animal qualities within them were still looming large. But a Master like Gambhirananda can easily devour all the animal qualities of the audience and illumine them into the divine qualities of God-realisation, God-revelation and God-manifestation.

In a previous story a Master assumed the form of a snake. In that case and here also, the Master came, out of compassion, to tell the seekers that if they want to make the fastest progress, they should look at the world and see that the world is like a venomous snake or a ferocious tiger. The very nature of the earth-consciousness is to bite and devour. If you are not guarded, the tiger will bite you, so be cautious.

IMF 28. *Give what you are and not what you have*

One day a disciple of Gambhirananda brought his own son and his friend's son to the Master. Alas, on that very day his friend's son was attacked by cholera. The doctors said it was a hopeless case; it was only a matter of hours before he would die.

The disciple felt miserable because the boy was his friend's only son. So he went to Gambhirananda and begged him to cure the boy. In his mind the disciple was saying to himself: "Why did I bring this young boy? If he dies, what will I tell my friend?" Then he had another thought: "Oh, I have a few children. I won't mind if one of my children dies instead of my friend's son."

At this point Gambhirananda read his mind. "You great sacrificer!" he said, "You are ready to let your son die! What right do you have to sacrifice your son? Your life belongs to you, but your son's life belongs to him. You cannot claim your son's life. You have not yet learned the ABC of spiritual life, and you are showing off about what a great sacrificer you are. Be sincere! Try to know where you stand in the spiritual life. Start from the very beginning. Learn the ABC of spiritual life and then think of sacrifice."

The Master mocked the disciple, scolded him and insulted him. Then finally he cured his friend's son.

Commentary: It is easy to be generous at the expense of others. In the outer world when we sacrifice something, we are totally aware of the results of our action. At times it is the results — which are glory, name and fame — that prompt us to make an act of sacrifice. But in the inner world there is no such thing as sacrifice. Through our constant prayer and meditation we become fully aware of our universal oneness. When we separate our existence from the blind limitations of the body, we see ourselves not only as unlimited possibilities but also as infinite inevitabilities. Our sense of separativity we sacrifice in order to become great. Our sense of unity we treasure in order to remain always good.

IMF 29. *The joint initiation of the earth-reality and the Heaven-reality*

One day a middle-aged man and his wife went to Gambhirananda and asked to be initiated. The Master said, "Not today, but in a few months' time I shall initiate you."

It happened that the wife was attacked by a severe illness very shortly afterwards and died. The man was very sad, but he still wanted to become a real disciple of Gambhirananda. So he went to the Master and again asked to be initiated. The Master agreed, and set the date.

At the time of initiation, the man begged Gambhirananda to initiate his deceased wife as well. The Master said, "How can I do that? She is dead; she is no longer with you."

The man said, "No, her soul is not dead. You promised you would initiate both of us. While initiating me, you can initiate her too. Please do me this favour." He began crying, and finally the Master agreed.

Gambhirananda placed two small cushions side by side. The man sat on one, and the other remained unoccupied. While the Master was initiating the seeker, he placed one of his hands on the seeker and the other in the space above the empty cushion. In a few minutes' time people saw that the cushion was moving, and they felt certain that it was the wife's presence. In this way, Gambhirananda initiated both of them together.

Commentary: The true operation of initiation takes place mostly in the soul and not in the body-consciousness. When the Master initiates a seeker, he immediately helps the seeker remember his soul's promise to the Absolute Supreme before the soul entered into the world-arena. When the Master initiates the physical in a seeker, he purifies the seeker's outer existence by touching the seeker's physical-reality. When he initiates the spiritual in the seeker, he pours a stream of illumining light into the seeker's system. Physical initiation reminds us of our spiritual duty. Spiritual initiation reminds us of the immortality of our consciousness-light.

IMF 30. *A flood of compassion-heart*

Gambhirananda was a man of few words. Sometimes people used to misunderstand him, thinking he was indifferent to the world, because he used to hide his compassionate heart. But when necessity demanded, he helped people, cured them and illumined them unreservedly and unconditionally.

Gambhirananda was fond of animals — both ferocious animals and tame household pets. Ferocious animals even roamed among the Master's attendants. These animals were very fond of Gambhirananda, and he gave them much affection and love.

One night, a disciple was sleeping beside the Master's room when some noise from inside the room woke him up. He quietly opened the door of the Master's room and saw the Master feeding quite a few mice with small pieces of bread. He was offering them the bread with great affection.

When Gambhirananda saw the disciple, he was a little bit embarrassed to be seen feeding mice at that hour, but the disciple was very moved. The Master quite often showed tremendous indifference to seekers outwardly, but here the disciple saw that his compassionate heart cried even for poor little mice.

Commentary: It is almost impossible to fathom a spiritual Master's compassion-height and justice-light. His justice-light is admired and adored by the brave. His compassion-height is loved and adored by the hopeless and helpless. But his compassion-height and justice-light together prepare the seeker for an integral understanding of God the Creator Supreme and God the creation Manifested.

IMF 31. *The conqueror of two realities: time and space*

Once a woman went to Gambhirananda crying and crying because for a long time she had not heard anything from her son, who was in England. She was terribly worried and she begged the Master to tell her something about her son. The Master said he did not have that kind of occult power, but she cried and cried until finally the Master agreed. He entered into a room for twenty minutes and when he came out he said, "Don't worry. Your son has left England and is now in Bombay. He is coming back to you. In three days' time he will arrive home."

On exactly the third day the son arrived home. When the mother told him the story, the son laughed and laughed. "I have been to Europe," he said, "so I know that this is only a kind of superstition you are enjoying."

The mother said, "All right, but at least come and see this spiritual Master." So the son went with his mother. When he saw Gambhirananda he almost fainted. "Hello, what are you doing here?" he demanded.

The disciples who were with the Master became angry. "Why are you speaking to our Master with such disrespect?" they asked.

The young man said, "I saw him on the ship in Bombay, near my cabin. He was walking around in the same dress he has on now. I was surprised to see him and I wondered why a poor man like him was standing near the first-class cabins. So I asked him the same question: 'What are you doing here'? but he only smiled at me! He didn't speak. Now I see him here."

Then the son bowed down to the Master and said, " Forgive me. Now I know that you are a very great spiritual Master. Forgive my audacity."

Commentary: A spiritual Master is he who has conquered time and space. A spiritual Master is he who lives a forgiveness-life. A spiritual Master is he who cries and dies with the bleeding heart of humanity. A spiritual Master is he who smiles God's Smile and spreads God's Satisfaction-Delight in and through humanity's evolving aspiration-quest.

INDIA AND HER MIRACLE-FEAST:
COME AND ENJOY YOURSELF

BOOK 4:
TRADITIONAL INDIAN STORIES
ABOUT BHASKARANANDA

IMF 32. *The transfer from attachment-life to detachment-Life*

When Bhaskarananda was 18 years old, his parents forced him to marry. The following year, when his wife was blessed with a child, all his relatives were swimming in the sea of delight. But the father of the child was an exception; he was swimming in the sea of suffering. He said to himself, "This is the beginning of my attachment-life," and on that very day he left home for good. Only after he became a great spiritual Master with abundant occult powers did he return home, but by then his child was with God.

Commentary: Often we start with attachment-life and then enter into detachment-life. Attachment-life tells us that we can have everything in the course of time. Detachment-life tells us that we are eternally everything. Attachment-life tells us that hunger is one thing, feast is something else, and that they have to be brought together. Detachment-life tells us that hunger is the birth of satisfaction and feast is the transcendence of satisfaction.

IMF 33. *Master, I wish to possess your will; you possess my ring*

A certain king was a devotee of Bhaskarananda and he used to visit his Master quite often. One day Bhaskarananda took him to a pond and casually asked the king to give him his diamond ring. Bhaskarananda looked at it and appreciated it deeply. Then he threw it into the pond.

The king was not disturbed at all. He thought, "Perhaps I was too attached to it; therefore, the Master has thrown it into the water. Or perhaps the Master is just playing a game and will bring it back to me. He has that kind of spiritual power, I am sure. Anyway, whatever his reason, it is for my good that he has done it."

Bhaskarananda and the king had a long conversation about spirituality, and the Master told many spiritual secrets to the king. Then the Master said, "Don't you want to have your ring back?"

The king said, "It is all up to you. If you want to, you can give it back. Otherwise, you can let the ring remain on the bottom of the pond."

Bhaskarananda said, "All right, I want to give it back to you. Now, just touch the water with your hand."

The Master had thrown the ring from the spot where they were standing, but the king decided to go to the other side of the pond in order to see if the ring would come back to that side. As he touched the water with his hand, sixteen rings of the same type appeared. The king could not tell which one was his.

"Since you are not attached to your ring," said Bhaskarananda, "I am giving it back." Then the Master threw fifteen of the rings back into the pond and gave the king the one that was his.

Commentary: Possession is not happiness. Surrendered oneness with the Master is the only true happiness. With our human will we possess, create and build the world of our imaginary liking. With our divine will we develop the capacity to have a free access to God's ever-transcending Vision and ever-manifesting Reality. The Master is at once the embodiment of God's Vision-Height and God's Reality-Depth.

IMF 34. *Body's strength assails, soul's strength sails*

Once an English military officer who was very devoted to Bhas-karananda was boasting about his latest military achievement. The Master said, "That's fine. I admire your bravery. Now, just give me that pencil that is right in front of you. I have to write something."

The officer bent down to pick up the pencil for the Master, but he could not lift it. Again the Master said, "Please give it to me. I cannot reach it."

The officer tried and tried, but he did not have the strength to lift up the pencil. With utmost affection the Master told him, "Look, it is God's strength and capacity that works in and through you on the battlefield. That is why you are victorious. Without God's strength, you don't have the capacity even to lift up a pencil. So don't boast, my child. It is all God's Will."

Commentary: Military strength is of the vital world, but it applies quite often to the physical world. Spiritual power is of the soul's world, but it can be applied in the physical world as well, to dominate the physical in us. Spiritual power is applied in the body, vital, mind and heart for glowing illumination and fulfilling perfection. Physical strength, vital strength and mental strength sing the song of subjugation. But psychic strength, founded on the soul's power, always sings the song of universal oneness-satisfaction.

IMF 35. *Humility's core owns divinity's lore*

Once Bhaskarananda was supposed to give a talk. A special stage had been built for the speaker, and it was decorated extremely beautifully. There were hundreds of people attending the meeting. Before the Master began his talk he said, "Where is Lakshman Mala? I want Lakshman Mala to be here."

Most of the people did not know who Lakshman Mala was, but somebody said he was a fisherman. Such respected and learned people were there! Who would think that the Master would ask to see a fisherman? But everybody began looking for him. Everybody started calling, "Lakshman! Lakshman!"

Lakshman had been almost afraid to come to this big gathering because so many educated people were there, so he was sitting at the back. When they found him, they escorted him to the Master, who showed him much affection and love. Then Bhaskarananda said, "During my talk, he has to be with me."

So Lakshman stood beside Bhaskarananda with folded hands, swimming in the sea of devotion and surrender. During the talk the Master highly appreciated Lakshman. He said, "You people are learned, cultured, great. But true greatness lies in pure devotion."

When the meeting was over, Lakshman followed the Master home, and from then on he stayed at the Master's house.

Commentary: The intellectual mind does not know and cannot know what God's Compassion-Reality is. It is only the devoted heart of the seeker that knows perfectly well what God's Compassion is. It also goes one step farther. The seeker grows into the very image of his Master by virtue of his heart's devoted oneness with his beloved. The mind always experiences sad defeat when it tries to fathom the mysteries of the inner world, but the heart never fails in discovering the wealth of the inner world. For the heart, there is no such thing as the inner world and the outer world. The heart has only one world: God the world. To the soulful heart the world itself is God.

IMF 36. *Accident-train stopped, experience-train continued*

A certain king who was Bhaskarananda's disciple went to stay with him and spend a few days sitting at his feet. On the fourth day of his visit the king received an express telegram from his palace. A serious catastrophe had taken place and it demanded his immediate attention. His physical presence was also needed.

The king wanted to leave immediately, but Bhaskarananda said, "No, you can't go. No matter how serious the thing is, you can't go today." The king did not want to disobey the Master, but he was very sad. Finally the Master said, "All right, you can go today. But don't go on the afternoon train at two o'clock. I want you to take the evening train."

When the king arrived at the station that evening, he was shocked to hear that the previous train had met with an accident. Many people had been thrown out of it and killed. When he heard this, the king was overwhelmed with gratitude to the Master. Instead of returning home as he had planned, he went back to the Master's house and touched his feet with gratitude.

Commentary: The Master sees the future continuously glowing and spreading itself in the immediacy of the eternal Now. The future is at the command of his vision-eye. The Master saved his disciple's life by asking him not to take a particular train. He could easily have told the station authorities to pay special attention to the train's journey. But he did not warn them, not because he was indifferent or unkind to the ill-fated passengers and the train, but because he got the command from within, from the Supreme Reality, that he could save only his disciple's life. God wanted him to remain silent about the serious accident that the train was destined to have.

A Master does not want to change the cosmic Law unless it is expressly decreed by God Himself, for it is God who has created the cosmic Law. In a case like this, it is not the Master's indifference to the rest of the world and his preference to his own little world that we are seeing. The Master is just executing God's Will in His world of multiple realities. Creation-preservation and destruction-transformation are all of God and for God. In them and through them He binds Himself and enjoys the destruction-death or transformation-life of the finite and the satisfaction-perfection of Infinity's Immortality.

IMF 37. *God knocks only at humility's heart-door*

Once a devoted disciple of Bijoykrishna came up to Bhaskarananda at a gathering and asked him a few questions. The Master had answered everybody else's questions, but he would not answer Bijoykrishna's disciple. Instead he insulted the disciple and told him to go away.

Everybody was shocked at the Master's behaviour, and the disciple went home very sad. But that night he had a dream and, in the dream, Swami Bhaskarananda answered his question with utmost affection.

The next day the seeker told Bhaskarananda's disciples why the Master had not answered his question in front of others. Others had asked their questions with utmost sincerity and humility, but he had had tremendous pride when he had asked his question. That is why Swami Bhaskarananda had insulted him instead of answering his question. But at night Bhaskarananda had forgiven him and had answered the question in his dream. The seeker was very pleased with the answer and extremely grateful that Bhaskarananda had punished him for his undivine pride.

Commentary: Pride separates, humility unites. Pride is the vision of a blind man. Humility is the vision of a God-man. It is not beneath the dignity of the Master to deal with the pride-existence of the seeker, for the Master knows that the seeker will not and cannot receive anything from him if pride is what he has and what he is. Humility is receptivity in the purest sense of the term. Humility welcomes both God the Creator and God the creation in its ever-expanding life and ever-soaring heart.

IMF 38. *God wills, time executes*

A highly respected man had been suffering from a kidney problem for a long time, and the doctors were not able to cure him. He was a disciple of Bhaskarananda, so he went to his Master and cried and cried to him for help.

The Master concentrated on his disciple and then said, "Well, I don't have to do anything for you, and the doctors do not have to do anything either. Just wait for thirty-nine days. After thirty-nine days your kidney problem will be totally cured."

At the end of thirty-nine days, the man was totally cured.

Commentary: True, time cures everything, but we have to know that inside time is God's Will. If God's Will does not operate in and through time, then time is like a lifeless bud that has no soul, no eternal life.

IMF 39. *You cannot touch my feet now*

Once a group of seekers was going up to Bhaskarananda one by one to bow to him and touch his feet. When it was the turn of a certain man, the Master said to him, "You cannot touch my feet now; you are not pure. Your father has died. Go home; there will be a telegram for you from your family." The man left for home immediately, with a sorrowful heart, and when he arrived at his own home, the messenger was waiting with a telegram from his mother. The telegram read: "Come home immediately. Your father has passed away."

Commentary: When someone dies, usually the soul of the person first looks around its own dead body, then flies to the dear ones who are not around the body. There are various reasons why souls do this. Sometimes the souls want to see whether they were really needed by the world, so they watch to see whether or not their dear ones are crying for them. Sometimes they try to console their near and dear ones by telling them that it is God's cosmic Law that they are fulfilling: nobody can stay on earth forever. Every soul has to leave the body after it has played its role on earth.

It is good to know what is happening all around, but if you will create undue suffering, by telling people, then it is not advisable to do so. Perhaps the Master could have told the seeker, "Go home quickly. You are needed there." But telling him about his father's passing and not allowing him to touch his feet was not correct from the highest spiritual point of view. He should have been allowed to go home and read the telegram. If everything is done in its due course, then we do not create sorrow in others before it is actually necessary.

In Indian tradition when someone dies, members of the immediate family are supposed to become impure for some time.

God alone knows how difficult it is for a spiritual Master of the highest order to appreciate this kind of theory. Who can understand why Indians think that the dear ones are impure? I pray to God to bless all these foolish theories, along with the practitioners of the theories. First of all, one has the pain of losing one's dear ones. Then at the same time he has to undergo humiliation for that very loss. No matter what kind of justification people give with regard to impurity invading the physical body of the dear ones — saying that an evil spirit possesses the body of the deceased after the soul has left, and because of their connection with him, the near and dear ones also become impure — from the spiritual point of view there is no truth in this theory. There is no justification at all.

IMF 40. *Don't think of anything else: just eat and be happy*

Once three renunciates came to Bhaskarananda's home. They meditated with him and asked him a few questions, and were very pleased with the answers. After a while Bhaskarananda asked them to stay and eat with him.

"Oh, no, we can't," said the renunciates. "You are poor and we will not be able to get the things we want."

Bhaskarananda said, "Just let me hear what you want to eat."

The renunciates mentioned four different kinds of Indian sweetmeats, and also asked for a few oranges. Then they resumed their conversation with Bhaskarananda.

In a few minutes' time, to their wide surprise, three most beautiful young boys came up to the Master and placed at his feet a large plate of sweetmeats — the ones the renunciates had wanted — plus a basketful of oranges. The renunciates asked Bhaskarananda how this was possible.

The Master smiled and said, "Just eat and be happy. Is anything impossible in God's creation?"

Commentary: Blessed are those who get spiritual food from the Master. Doubly blessed are those who get both spiritual food and material food from the Master. With the material food the Master energises their earthly reality-body so that the body can be of service to the spirit. With the spiritual food the Master keeps the immortality of the soul glowing, flowing, manifesting and fulfilling.

IMF 41. *Marriage predestined*

A couple who were disciples of Bhaskarananda once came to him with a serious problem. An astrologer, who also happened to be a disciple, had cast the horoscope of their only son, Ganesh. The astrologer told them that their son would die in an accident at the age of sixteen, and he advised the parents not to allow the son to marry. The father wanted to listen to the astrologer's advice, but the mother wanted the son to get married, so they came to the Master to learn what they should do.

Bhaskarananda said, "Yes, your son should marry. It is predestined. You are right that it will be a deplorable experience for his wife to become a widow at a very tender age. But I clearly see that this girl has a special connection with him in the soul's world, and both of them are destined to get married. Both he and she need this experience. Ganesh is now thirteen years old. It is true that he is supposed to die at the age of sixteen, but I shall delay his death for a couple of years. I will not allow him to die until I die."

So Ganesh got married. A few years went by, and he passed his sixteenth birthday without incident. Then one day Bhaskarananda was attacked by the most fatal disease in India, cholera. On the same day, Ganesh fell from a horse and was knocked unconscious. Ganesh remained senseless for three days and

Bhaskarananda suffered from cholera also for three days. Bhaskarananda passed away at noon on the third day, and at that very moment Ganesh also left the world.

Commentary: Experience is of prime importance. Sometimes the experience of union, sometimes the experience of separation, sometimes the experience of re-union, sometimes the experience of eternal separation are necessary for the physical reality in us. To make progress and, while making progress, to realise that there is only one Reality Supreme — this is the experience that is constantly needed both here on earth and there in Heaven. And that Reality Supreme is God Himself.

With his yogic power, Bhaskarananda kept Ganesh on earth for a few years more than his due; otherwise, Ganesh would have passed away before. To give him and his dear ones experiences that would help them in future incarnations, the Master gave Ganesh an extended lease on life. True spiritual Masters can do this, but they do it only when it has been decreed by the Absolute Supreme.

IMF 42. *The Master tested and stupidity exposed*

Once a certain king was jealous of Bhaskarananda's name and fame, although in his heart he secretly admired the Master. The king wanted to test Bhaskarananda to see if he had conquered his senses, his lower vital. So one night he sent three most beautiful women of ill repute to Bhaskarananda's home to tempt him in various ways.

Bhaskarananda got furious and ordered them to leave his house immediately; otherwise, he threatened to punish them mercilessly. Two of the women left out of fear, but one of them was brave enough or foolish enough to stay. So Bhaskarananda used his occult power and brought a huge snake into the room.

The snake encircled the woman and pinned her to the ground so that she was unable to escape. The woman was frightened almost to death.

Because the woman did not come back, her two friends thought that she had been successful with the Master. Her friends were happy and miserable both — happy because at least one of them had succeeded in lowering the Master's consciousness, and miserable because they were jealous that she was the one who had been successful. After a few hours they went back to Bhaskarananda's home, and then they saw the pitiful condition of their friend.

The two women went and reported the matter to the king, and the king became sad because he was the cause of that particular woman's suffering. So the king went to Bhaskarananda's house to see the pitiful plight of this woman. He begged the Master to forgive her, and admitted that he was the one who was behind all this.

Bhaskarananda forgave the king and the woman and said, "Don't try to tempt spiritual people. This time I am allowing her to go with her life, but in the future, if she or anybody else comes to tempt me, I will just destroy that person immediately. Nobody should deliberately try to tempt spiritual people." Then gradually the snake disappeared.

Commentary: Temptation is the order of the day; it attacks almost everyone. But real spiritual Masters are true exceptions. The human tendency is such, however, that it is difficult for a human being to see in others striking capacities that are not manifested in himself. He sees others according to his own capacities. But he forgets that there can be and there are people who far surpass him and who do not have the same weaknesses that he has.

When people try to tempt the true spiritual Masters, the Masters either ignore them or threaten them. If they ignore them, these undivine people may wait for another occasion to come and tempt the Master. But if the Master is strict with them and threatens them or frightens them, then the culprits will not dare to try to tempt the Master again.

IMF 43. *My food, my oneness universal*

Once a disciple of Bhaskarananda brought some fruits to his Master. The Master distributed the fruits to the disciples who were around him, and there was none left for himself. But Bhaskarananda did not feel at all sorry, because his joy came in feeding his spiritual children.

The next day the same disciple brought quite a few mangoes, but he kept aside two delicious ones for the Master. After the Master had distributed all the mangoes, the disciple gave him the two that he had saved. But Bhaskarananda scolded him, saying, "You can't do that. Whatever you have brought, you have to give to me. Whatever I want, I will keep for myself. Don't you know that I eat everything in and through my disciples? When you people eat, it is more than enough for me, for I enjoy eating and doing everything in and through you all."

Commentary: Once we offer something to the Master, our claim on that thing must totally disappear. If we give something to the Master and want him to do something with it in accordance with our desire, then we are not making a real offering. We are only trying to bind him with our desire-gift. We should give to the Master not only devotedly and unreservedly, but also unconditionally. Then only will we have peace of mind, happiness in our heart and fulfilment in our life.

We must give for God's sake. The God within us wants to give to the God within others. So one God gives, and another God receives. The giver and the receiver are expected to be equally happy in the act of giving and receiving unconditionally.

IMF 44. *Three supreme valuables: God's Compassion, God's Light And God's Delight*

Once a certain king came to Bhaskarananda and offered him a golden dish with quite a few diamond rings. Bhaskarananda refused to accept them, saying, "I do not value these things. I value only God's Compassion, Light and Delight. What shall I do with things that I do not value?"

The Master Bijoykrishna happened to be there at the time with a few of his disciples. Bhaskarananda's renunciation amazed Bijoykrishna and all of his disciples. Bijoykrishna immediately composed a song in utmost adoration of Bhaskarananda, and sang it most soulfully.

Commentary: Earthly wealth is necessary for those who value it, but when we ourselves are pinched with inner thirst or when we want to create inner thirst in others, we can never be happy with earthly things, no matter how valuable they are. With earthly possessions we satisfy the needs of the human in us. With Heavenly possessions such as God's Compassion, God's Light and God's Delight, we satisfy the needs of the eternally real in us, the soul.

INDIA AND HER MIRACLE-FEAST:
COME AND ENJOY YOURSELF

BOOK 5:
TRADITIONAL INDIAN STORIES
ABOUT DEVADAS MAHARAJ

When Ramdas was a young boy, one night he and his Guru, Devadas Maharaj, were meditating separately at different places. It was snowing heavily and the weather was extremely cold. Each one had an open fire in front of him to keep him warm. Ramdas meditated a few hours; then he fell asleep. When he woke up, he saw that the fire was totally extinguished. He was frightened to death, for he knew that his Master would be furious if he went to him to get a few burning coals. But at the same time he was unable to bear the cold weather. Finally he mustered courage and went to his Master for a few burning charcoals.

Devadas Maharaj came out of his trance and insulted Ramdas mercilessly. "Who asked you to leave your parents and your family if sleep is so important in your life?" he shouted. "This is my last warning. If you ever fall asleep again when you are supposed to be meditating, I shall not keep you as my disciple. You do not deserve to be my disciple."

Commentary: Spirituality means discipline. Discipline means conscious progress. Conscious progress means the transcendence of nature. Man's transcendence of his nature is his awareness of his immortal self for God-Satisfaction in God's own Way.

Discipline is always indispensable, especially in the beginning of the seeker's spiritual adventure. Today we call something discipline; tomorrow we call that very thing a natural and spontaneous habit. Today's forward movement carries us to tomorrow's door. Once we are at the door, we do not even have to knock at the door. The divine owner opens the door from inside and then takes us inside to introduce us to three most important friends: Eternity's Beauty, Infinity's Delight and Immortality's Light.

SRI CHINMOY

IMF 46. *To you my heart of infinite gratitude*

Once Guru Devadas Maharaj left his small ashram for a few days and asked his dear disciple Ramdas to remain seated at a particular place and continue meditating until he came back. For five or six days Ramdas meditated day and night until his Master returned. The Master immediately blessed Ramdas and said, "Today you have highly pleased me. You could have slept, you could have left the place, you could have deceived me in various ways. I clearly see that you have not deceived me in any way; therefore, my heart of infinite gratitude and my life of infinite pride I offer to you."

Commentary: The command from the divine Master is never a command as such. His voice may sound very strict and stern, but inside him is the flow of his compassionate oneness. His compassionate oneness awakens the sleeping heart and illumines the doubting mind of the disciple even before the disciple is asked to do anything.

Divine obedience is not only soulful but fruitful. Divine obedience gets tremendous delight by virtue of its inner, spontaneous oneness with the Master's will. Here it is not actually the oneness of the superior and the inferior; it is the oneness of one reality that has two heights. The first reality enters into the second reality to manifest God the Unmanifest. The second reality enters into the first to realise God the infinite and ever-transcending Vision.

IMF 47. *This eternal slave is yours*

Once Ramdas made a mistake and his Master got furious. He struck the disciple severely and scolded him mercilessly. "You are a low-caste fellow! What can I expect from you? Spirituality is not meant for you. For God's sake, leave me immediately!"

But Ramdas only said to his Master, "Lord, beat me as long as you want to, beat me as hard as you want to, insult me as mercilessly as you want to, but grant me only one boon and that boon is that you will keep this eternal slave of yours always at your feet."

Commentary: The Master advocates oneness, conscious and constant oneness. The disciple tries to realise that oneness with the Master and with the rest of the world. Such being the case, scolding and insulting never indicate punishment. The Master is just adopting a method which will immediately awaken the disciple more fully to expedite the disciple's progress. As outwardly he shouts and barks, inwardly he knows what he has for the disciple and what he is to the disciple. What he has for the disciple is oneness-delight. The Master feels it is his bounden duty to do the things that are necessary in order to accelerate the disciple's progress, no matter how badly he is misunderstood by the world or even by the disciple himself. The Master always remembers the promise that he made to the disciple's soul and to God that he would leave no stone unturned in order to make the disciple make the fastest progress in his spiritual adventure.

IMF 48. *Not advisable: two tigers in one den*

One day both the Master Maharaj and his disciple Ramdas were meditating separately in an open field. A young man came and bowed down before each one, and offered some money to Ramdas. Ramdas immediately protested and asked the young man to take the money away and place it at his Master's feet instead. In spite of being repeatedly requested to do so, the young man did not comply with Ramdas' request.

When the young man left, Ramdas went to his Master and offered him the money, only to be rebuked ruthlessly by the Master for accepting the money. Ramdas said that he had repeatedly asked the man not to give him the money, but to give it to his Master instead. But Devadas Maharaj's anger still remained at the transcendental height. He said, "I am sure he saw greed in you; therefore, he gave the money to you and not to me."

Ramdas felt sad. Then his Master said, "Don't feel sad. Now I am telling you the truth. Like me, you have also become a tiger in the spiritual life; therefore, the young man felt that if he gave it to you, it was as good as offering it to me. The time has come for you to have disciples of your own and to move to a different place."

Ramdas fell at the Master's feet and said, "My eternal place is here and nowhere else."

Commentary: Indeed, it is at times difficult, if not almost impossible, to know what the Master wants. If the disciple has a pure heart and if he has a sincere attitude, then he is bound to please the Master. Because of his purity's striking luminosity and his sincerity's spontaneous oneness, there is every possibility that he will do the right thing. Again, if the disciple does not do the right thing, but his mind is still searching and his heart is crying, then the Master does not blame the disciple for his mistakes, for he knows perfectly well that these so-called mistakes are the pathfinders of true truth.

Two tigers — the Master the tiger and the disciple the tiger — cannot live together. The Master thinks not in human terms — that if they stay together then each will not get full importance from the rest of the world; therefore, it is advisable to stay separately so that both can get due attention. If this is what the human mind thinks is the reason, then it is a deplorable mistake. When the Master says that the disciple has come up to his standard and asks the disciple to stay separately in the world, what the Master wants from the disciple is very simple: he wants the disciple to spread light as the Master is spreading light. If both of them do the same thing for the same people at the same time, then it is totally redundant. But if they share their achievements with the rest of the world, staying away from each other geographically and physically, then only the larger world will receive light from both God-realised souls. What the Master wants is not possession but the expansion of the God-reality in him and in his disciple. God's creation is very vast. The more who can manifest God with the help of illumined, liberated and realised souls, the better; and the sooner God's infinite Manifestation can take place here, there, everywhere.

IMF 49. *The Master comes first*

Ramdas and his Master were both heavy smokers, and they often took arsenic to keep themselves warm. One night Devadas asked his disciples to go and buy two rupees' worth of arsenic, but his disciples had no money and they were also a little bit hesitant to go to the town at that hour. Ramdas offered to go, but he had no money either. The Master said, "Don't worry. You just go to the town. There will be somebody there to give you some money."

Ramdas believed his Master and left without any money. When he reached the town, it was quite late and everything was dark. He saw a light in only one house, so he went there and knocked at the door. When the owner opened the door, he was so happy to see a sadhu standing there. He said, "All day I have been thinking of offering two rupees to a sadhu, and now you have come. I am so grateful to you. Please take these two rupees."

Then Ramdas took the money and bought two rupees' worth of arsenic. On his way back to the ashram he thought that since he had such a large quantity, he would take a very small portion and his Master would not notice it.

Ramdas was so happy to bring the arsenic and offer it to his Master, but Devadas Maharaj showed him a sad face. Ramdas said, "At this hour I went all the way to town and got you arsenic. How is it that you are sad?"

The Master replied, "I am sad because you come first in your life, and not me. You should have given me the full quantity; then I would have given some to you. Always think of me first. Only then shall I be pleased with you, and I shall give you not only much more than you need, but much more than you deserve."

Commentary: The Master's faith in the disciple and the disciple's faith in the Master are of equal importance. But sometimes the Master does not reveal to the disciple all aspects of the reality-tree, for it may confuse the seeker's unripe mind. If he does not tell the story of the reality-life all at once, that does not mean that the Master is mean or not generous. But the Master feels that like a child the disciple has to receive things little by little so that he can assimilate everything.

When the disciple has to deal with the Master, the story has to be different, for no matter what he has or what he is, it will not confuse the Master's illumined mind. The Master gives to the disciple according to the disciple's limited receptivity and easily measured capacity, whereas if the disciple wants to give something to the Master, he can do so unreservedly, for the Master's receptivity and capacity is immeasurable. Again, if the disciple does not give his whole existence to the Master, the Master does not become the loser — far from it. But the disciple weakens his capacity, shortens his vision of the Master and falls down from the reality-oneness with the Master. Finally, insincerity-dragon and ingratitude-insect threaten his aspiring existence.

So give to the Master unreservedly what you have and what you are. The Master will give you according to your need and according to God's Need. The fulfilment of your need entirely depends on God's Will.

IMF 50. *The Hindu-Muslim compromise*

Once Devadas went to live and meditate in a Muslim area. In the middle of the night he would blow a conch and ring a bell. The Muslims are dead against using conches and bells, and they warned the Hindu sadhu that they would punish him severely if he did not stop doing this. The following night he blew the conch and rang the bell louder than ever. The Muslim soldiers came to arrest him, but when they entered his room, to their wide surprise they saw that his head had been severed from his body and was lying on a chair, and his limbs were all scattered around the room. But there was no blood. The soldiers did not want to touch the body, so they left.

In a few minutes' time they heard the same bell and the sound of the conch, so they rushed back, only to see the same scene again. Again they left, only to hear the conch and the bell once more. This time they were furious. When they returned to the room, Devadas was there in his normal human form.

"What can you do to me?" he said. "You have just seen twice what I can do. Before you arrest me, I shall disassemble myself."

When the soldiers went to report the matter to the Muslim chief, the chief said to them, "It is not advisable to fight with a man who has such extraordinary spiritual power. The best thing is to surrender to him and ask him if he would like to have a temple built. I shall pay for it. Let him peacefully pray and meditate there and do whatever he wants to do."

Devadas was extremely pleased with the Muslim chief's offer. The Muslim chief erected a beautiful temple for him, and Devadas in deep gratitude stopped blowing the conch and ringing the bell.

Commentary: The Hindu and the Muslim are like two powerful branches of the reality-tree, which is all oneness-freedom. But the outer life of the human beings is so complicated that no matter what other persons do, they will get irritated or feel insecure or inferior.

The Master showed on the one hand that he had the body-reality of the Supreme to manifest the Supreme. On the other hand, he showed that he had the soul-reality of the Supreme to realise the Supreme. The Master disassembled and assembled his body in order to show to the naked eyes of human beings that medical science does not have the last word on God's creation and man's life and death. It is only the inscrutable Will of the Supreme that operates in and through the spiritual Master.

INDIA AND HER MIRACLE-FEAST:
COME AND ENJOY YOURSELF

BOOK 6:
TRADITIONAL INDIAN STORIES
ABOUT RAMDAS KATHIYA BABA (PART 1)

IMF 51. *I have definitely realised God*

Ramdas Kathiya Baba realised God by repeating the Gayatri Mantra one million times at the foot of a banyan tree. Then he composed a sweet, soulful and fruitful song. It said: "I have realised God. My God-realisation is for the holy ones to believe and for the wicked ones not to believe. But I know, I know I have definitely realised God."

Commentary: True, a God-realised soul does not have to depend on man's belief or disbelief. But if people believe in him, then he can without fail accelerate humanity's progress and divinity's manifestation on earth. Not only the non-believers but also the disbelievers will one day turn into believers, but God does not force anyone. He waits for His choice Hour. Again, God's Compassion-Power on rare occasions overrules His Justice-Light. At that time it forces the non-believers and disbelievers to see the Light devotedly the way the Light wants to be seen.

Human belief is transitory; it has a fleeting breath. Divine belief is nothing short of our inmost faith. It sees constantly through the Vision-Eye of God and feels with the Compassion-Heart of God.

IMF 52. *Temptation-force never to be forgiven*

In the middle of the night Ramdas was seated on his bed meditating. His disciples were sleeping in adjacent rooms. Suddenly a middle-aged but beautiful widow came into Ramdas' room and embraced him. Ramdas became furious and wanted to strike her. When he shouted aloud, his disciples came in. All of them wanted to beat the woman mercilessly, but she immediately cried out, "I was sent by the head of the village to test your celibacy. I am innocent. Please forgive me." And she began to weep bitterly.

The disciples were moved to tears and sympathised with her. But the Master did not forgive her. He said to her, "I will not forgive you, for I know you could have easily ignored the request or command of the head of your village. It is not his request or command, it is his money-power that has compelled you to come to me; therefore, I shall not forgive you. Go home."

The widow went home crying and sobbing.

Commentary: Money-power and temptation-power are two neighbours. These two friends are extremely fond of each other. In course of time they look around and find a few more friends. Money-power makes a special attempt to make friends with pride and vanity. Temptation-power makes a special attempt to make friends with the lower vital. In most cases, members of a family or friends all stay together. Here we try to separate them and put an end to their friendship so that we can hear the message of perfect oneness.

After we have separated them they will be weakened, true, but there is no guarantee that they will lose all their power. What shall we do then? We shall have to transform them radically. In order to transform them, we advise money-power to enter into the world of dedicated service. We advise temptation-power to enter into the world of aspiration. We advise the lower vital to enter into the pure heart, the heart that always listens to the soul and devotedly sees eye to eye with the soul. Money-power becomes satisfaction-power only when it is used in service to God. Temptation-power becomes satisfaction-power only when it is used as aspiration-power. The lower vital becomes satisfaction-power only when it is used as illumination-power.

IMF 53. *Deception — no, compassion — yes*

Whenever Kathiya Baba wanted his disciples to meditate for many hours at night, he used to play a trick on them. He would tell them that he was getting the inner message that at night there was every possibility that some thief would commit a theft in the ashram. To prevent a serious type of robbery, they all must remain awake and there was only one way to do so — that is, to remain in constant meditation. If they could really meditate well, they would be able to remain alert and there would be no theft.

The following day Kathiya Baba would tell them that it had been a false alarm. Although they were deceived each time by the Master, the disciples enjoyed their meditation and offered their Master most soulful gratitude, for they knew that it was not deception after all, but true compassion on his part that had wanted to keep them awake even by telling them a white lie.

Commentary: There are so many ways for a Master to increase the aspiration of his disciples. Sometimes the end justifies the means. If the Master feels that a negligible white lie has tremendous power to raise the consciousness of the disciples, then he will not hesitate to tell that white lie, for he knows precisely what God wants from him. God wants him to help his disciples make progress as fast as possible. God Himself will take care of the Master's white lie, as the Master is taking care of the disciples.

If Kathiya Baba had simply asked his disciples to meditate for hours, they would all have made friends with sleep. The Master and the disciples had practically no material possessions, but by telling them that there was every possibility of a theft, the Master made them alert. This alertness helped them tremendously in their sincere effort to meditate, and by meditating for many hours they definitely made tremendous progress. So when we make a comparison, the harmless white lie that the Master told is next to nothing when we see the Joy, the Light, the Delight and the other achievements of the disciples which resulted from the Master's harmless lie.

IMF 54. *Look at this great Bengali soul*

Pushkar was Ramdas' cook. He was extremely greedy, and he was wicked to the backbone. Three times he intentionally poisoned his Master. Once he put poison inside the bread, once inside the rice pudding and a third time in something else. With his occult power Ramdas saved himself, but he suffered miserably. He told his disciples the reason for his suffering, and Pushkar confessed each time.

Once when Ramdas had been poisoned, Bijoykrishna was at that time in a distant city. When he heard that Ramdas was dying, Bijoykrishna said to one of Ramdas' disciples, "I can't believe it. Only poison can take his life. No disease can kill him, for he never allows any disease to enter into him. Somebody has definitely poisoned him."

Ramdas' disciple went to his Master and told him about this. Ramdas said to his disciples, "Look at this great Bengali soul! Where is he and where am I? Although he is so far away, from there he understands what is happening here. You people are here with me, but even then you didn't recognise that I had been poisoned."

After this incident Ramdas' disciples wanted to throw Pushkar out of the ashram, but Ramdas said, "No, he will have his own karma. What I know, I do: I know how to forgive. What he knows he does: he knows how to steal. As God is taking care of me, even so He will take care of him."

Commentary: The disciple poisoned the Master to get his money. This was the height of the disciple's ignorance. But the Master wanted to offer the height of his wisdom to the disciple. He could do this either by forgiving him or by punishing him.

If the disciple is a sincere seeker, then the Master's forgiveness-power itself will invariably act like punishment-power, for it will create tremendous remorse in the sincere seeker's heart for deceiving the Master. Again, if the disciple is punished, he will take it not as justice-light, but as forgiveness-power. He will think that this punishment is absolutely nothing in comparison to the crime he has committed. He will feel very grateful to the Master, for he will say to himself, "The Master has punished me. That means he has taken some interest in me. He could have easily ignored me. He could have easily paid attention to other disciples who are good, sincere, devoted and surrendered. How is it that he is thinking of me?"

Even the Master's punishment is not real punishment; it is only the Master's divine concern which wants us always to make progress. The punishment itself is forgiveness. Something more: it is true concern that the culprit-seeker should become the all-fulfilling truth-seeker.

IMF 55. *God will punish him in His own Way*

Ramdas used to wear a wooden belt which his Master had given him. He wore it twenty-four hours a day. Devadas Maharaj wanted him to wear it all the time so that he could not enjoy comfort, even while he was resting. Pushkar was under the impression that his Master was hiding money inside the wooden belt; therefore, quite a few times he had tried to steal money from his Master by removing the belt while he was resting or sleeping. But each time he had approached his Master to steal the belt, he saw that his Master was actually wide awake.

Finally Pushkar poisoned his Master so that he could get the belt. When Ramdas drank the poison, he suffered terribly, and he asked his disciples to cut and remove the wooden belt. When the disciples removed the wooden belt, they saw that there was nothing inside it. When Pushkar saw that there was no money inside the belt, he confessed that he felt sorry, not for the Master's suffering, but for his own stupidity.

The disciples wanted to throw Pushkar out of the ashram or kill him. But Ramdas said, "Don't throw him out. Don't kill him. God will punish him in His own Way. God wants me to show forgiveness; therefore, I forgive him. We must surrender to God's Will. But God Himself will not forgive him."

Commentary: Man's temptation-power wants to destroy the world. God's Compassion-Power does not permit temptation-power to destroy the world. God's Compassion-Power knows perfectly well that if temptation-power does not succeed in tempting others, it will eventually destroy itself instead of destroying others. God never wants anything or anybody to be destroyed. What He wants is illumination. When illumination takes place, the night of human ignorance becomes the light of divine knowledge. And what is divine knowledge? Divine knowledge is to know God as the Supreme Seeker and as the Beloved Supreme.

IMF 56. *The rogue consoles the saint*

Once Ramdas was meditating at the foot of a small hillock. His cook Pushkar employed two unparalleled rogues to throw a heavy stone on him from the top of the hill. The hooligans succeeded in their wicked adventure, and dropped a heavy piece of stone on Ramdas' lap. He was severely injured. And who came to console him first? The worst possible rogue — Pushkar.

The Master's cries and shouts finally brought some of Ramdas' other disciples to the spot. He immediately told them that it was Pushkar who had employed two of his friends to drop the stone. Pushkar wanted to deny it, but the Master's fiery eyes frightened him; therefore, he had no choice but to tell the truth, to confess. Then Ramdas said to Pushkar, "I shall always forgive you, but God will not forgive you, although He easily can."

Commentary: Pushkar knew what deception was. Ramdas knew what compassion was and what forgiveness was. An individual usually acts according to his nature, but at times one can change this nature. If a spiritual Master feels that by exposing a person he will be able to expedite that person's progress, then he will definitely do so. What the Master wants is progress from the disciples, and for that progress he will adopt any means and do everything he can.

IMF 57. *Take your tongue back*

Ramdas Kathiya Baba had a disciple who had a very foul tongue. Everybody was horrified at his foul language. Many times he had insulted and scolded even his Master, Ramdas. Finally it came to the point when his language was unbearable for everyone. Then Ramdas said to him, "To punish you I am taking your tongue away for twelve years. Now try to talk."

Ramdas did not actually remove the man's tongue, but he took away the disciple's speech-power. From that moment the disciple could not speak, and for twelve long years he did not utter a word.

At the end of twelve years Ramdas Kathiya Baba said, "Take your tongue back," and the disciple could talk again.

Commentary: Silence prepares; speech offers. If there is no preparation, then there can be nothing worth giving. First we dive deep within; then we can either march forward or fly upward.

INDIA AND HER MIRACLE-FEAST:
COME AND ENJOY YOURSELF

BOOK 7:
TRADITIONAL INDIAN STORIES
ABOUT RAMDAS KATHIYA BABA (PART 2)

A certain disciple of Ramdas Kathiya Baba became a victim to lethargy. He had been an excellent aspirant, but somehow he had lost his intense aspiration. A few times his Master, Ramdas, had asked him to give up his lethargy and go back to his intense inner cry. Unfortunately, the seeker did not fulfil his Master's wish.

Then one night, while he was sleeping, a solid brick fell on him and woke him up. He was hurt, but the strange thing was that the mosquito net over his bed remained intact. There was no hole in it, although the brick had fallen from above. The disciple could not account for this.

The following day Ramdas said to him, "I did not want to pass through your mosquito net; therefore, I sent the brick as my representative to wake you from your sleep. I am glad that you are hurt. From now on get up early in the morning and meditate for a few hours. During the day also try to meditate. And at night you must meditate for a few hours if you really want to please me."

Commentary: A spiritual Teacher's only concern is his disciples' progress. If he has to administer punishment to a disciple, he does not mind, for he knows that the disciple is going to benefit from this eventually. At times it is absolutely necessary for the Master to be strict with the disciple, for there is no other way.

Lethargy is a most powerful force. Softness, kindness, sweetness, and politeness sadly fail to fight against lethargy. Strict discipline is the only weapon that can defeat the formidable strength of lethargy. Such being the case, Ramdas did not feel at all sorry when he hurt his dear disciple.

IMF 59. *Protection guaranteed*

A disciple of Ramdas Kathiya Baba had to go out of town on business for a few days. For various reasons he could not take his young wife with him, although she was terribly afraid of staying alone at night, so the Master said to the husband, "You tell your wife not to worry. I shall take care of her."

That night the young woman had a dream that her whole room was flooded with light. When she woke up and opened her eyes, she saw the Master in a corner of the room. It was not the Master's physical body she saw, but his luminous subtle body, but she felt that it was actually his physical body. The Master said to her, "My child, until your husband comes back, always feel that I will be here to protect you," and the Master's subtle body with its luminosity protected her until her husband returned.

Commentary: Human responsibility is such that we can either minimise it or maximise it, contract it or expand it, decrease it or increase it. In the case of a spiritual Master, his responsibility only increases at every moment. A spiritual Master enjoys the increase of responsibility, for his responsibility is nothing short of a golden opportunity for him to manifest more divine Peace, Light and Bliss on earth.

In this case Ramdas showed that a spiritual Master takes care not only of his dear disciples, but also of those who are closely connected with them. The teacher accepts the student not only with what he is, but also with what he has.

IMF 60. *Compassion forgives, compassion liberates, compassion illumines*

One day Ramdas Kathiya Baba was smoking heavily. Three young men wanted to join him, but he refused to smoke with them. They demanded, "What kind of Master are you? You should be generous."

He said, "I don't want to show my generosity to thieves. You three are thieves."

The young men protested vehemently, and a serious argument took place. Finally Ramdas said to the three young men, "You will see! Before the day ends you will be arrested."

His words were irrevocable. That day the three young men were arrested for a previous theft they had committed. Three weeks later two of the thieves were released on bail. They went to Kathiya Baba, sat at his feet and cried and cried. "Please help us! We want to be free! You have the power to set us free. We shall not steal anymore," they said.

Ramdas replied, "Now you are on bail. You will be freed on the condition that you promise not to steal anymore."

Then the two thieves said, "We shall never, never steal again."

The Master's words again proved true. The two young men were freed from prison. Their friend, however, remained.

A few months later Ramdas was going to a nearby town. As he was walking along a young man came up to him crying.

The Master asked, "What is the matter with you?"

The young man said, "Don't you recognise me? You forgave my two friends. Now they are free, while I am working so hard fixing the road. Please, you have the power to free me, too." And again he started crying pitifully.

Ramdas said, "All right, in three days you will also be free."

The man laughed at Ramdas. "Yes, yes, I will be free in three days. You are just joking. How can I be free in three days?" He did not believe Ramdas, but Ramdas gave him a compassionate smile, so to some extent he was consoled.

In three days the village authorities were advised by the government that each prison had to release a certain number of prisoners, for the government was finding it difficult to meet with the expenses of so many prisoners. Those whose crimes were not serious should be given the first chance to go free. This particular young man was one of those whose crime was not extremely serious; therefore, he was set free along with others on the third day.

Commentary: An ordinary person finds it difficult to accept the prophecy of a spiritual Master unless and until it has been proved. What is prophecy? Our human belief feels that prophecy is the ability to see something that will occur in the future and then tell when this incident is due. But in the case of a spiritual Master, prophecy is only a spontaneous revelation of truth-embodiment. This truth-embodiment has to be revealed in God's own Way at God's choice Hour, for He alone knows when prophecy will create unnecessary worries and anxieties, and when it will create illumining aspiration and fulfilling satisfaction.

IMF 61. *Revolver-power surrenders*

One morning Ramdas Kathiya Baba was walking along the bank of a river where a British boat was anchored. The British sailors were in a very undivine mood on that day. When they saw a man practically naked walking along the bank of the river, one of the sailors took offence and wanted to shoot the man with his revolver. He fired a few times, but all in vain. He could not seem to aim properly at this man, who was walking very fast.

His friends were amused and, at the same time, non-plussed, for this sailor happened to be a good shot.

When his friends started to laugh at him, the sailor became furious. He could not understand what was wrong with him. Suddenly he felt an unseen hand very powerfully force him to drop the revolver, which fell into the water. When he told his friends what had just happened, they immediately raised their hands and cheered the Indian sadhu, and begged him to forgive them, for they were afraid that he would create some calamity for them.

Commentary: Destruction is a human tendency. Preservation is a divine tendency. The sailor wanted to destroy the Indian sadhu; God wanted to preserve him. The power that creates and the power that preserves can easily smash the pride of the power that destroys. The sailor, who represented destruction, had to challenge God the Creator and God the Preserver at the same time; therefore, he and his friends quite naturally realised that he would lose to the sadhu if he continued his destructive efforts.

IMF 62. *Questions and answers in the Silence-World*

Once Bijoykrishna went to visit Ramdas Kathiya Baba while he was holding a meeting. His disciples were asking their Master questions, but Bijoykrishna remained silent. When he was about to go away, the disciples of Kathiya Baba said to him, "You came all the way from a distant village to meet with our Master. Do you not have anything to ask?"

Bijoykrishna said, "I have already asked him many, many questions. He has answered all my questions inwardly."

Ramdas smiled and said, "It is absolutely true."

Commentary: When silence asks a question and silence answers, both the question and the answer are most powerful, for the question and answer start their journey in the silence-heart and end in the silence-heart. When the question and answer are not from the silence world and are not in the silence world, the mind wants to add something to the question and to the answer. What the mind adds is nothing but a doubtful, hesitant and discouraging existence-reality. When the mind is involved, the reality-experience is not and cannot be spontaneous; therefore, it is infinitely inferior to the reality-experience which lives in the heart, with the heart and for the heart. In the heart spontaneity always reigns supreme.

IMF 63. *I want justice-light*

Early in the morning Ramdas was meditating in his garden when he saw a young man. "What do you want?" he asked the youth.

The boy replied, "I have come here to take some pomegranate leaves. My doctor has asked me to bring him some leaves of this plant so that he will be able to cure me."

"No, you can't take any leaves; they are my possession," said Ramdas. "Go and ask your doctor to get them from someone else."

The boy could not believe his ears. "You are a spiritual Master. You have so many disciples. You should be generous. You can't part with a few leaves, a few insignificant leaves?"

Ramdas said, "I have not come here to learn your philosophy. Get out. If you don't leave this place, I shall break your head with my stick."

The young man became so angry that he wanted to strike the Master with his stick. Ramdas shouted until many people came.

Then he explained, "This boy wanted to take away some leaves without my permission."

"I am asking your permission," said the boy.

"But I am not granting you permission," replied the Master.

What could the disciples do? They compelled the boy to leave without the pomegranate leaves.

Then the disciples said to Master Ramdas, "We shall never understand you."

"You don't have to understand me," Ramdas said. "Only do what I want you to do. I want justice-light."

The disciples said, "We shall never understand you. At one moment you don't need anything. Even if someone places the whole world's wealth at your feet, you ignore it. But now you are fighting over a few leaves. When you receive nice gifts, like a child you come and tell us how beautiful they are. The other day the girls from the King's family sent you a shawl. Everybody saw how happy you were to have it. You ran into the market place, telling everyone, 'Look, look, how beautiful this shawl is! And who has given it to me? The girls from the King's family'. This moment you act like an innocent child; the next moment you act like a cruel man."

Kathiya Baba said to his disciples, "Don't judge me. You will never be able to fathom me. Only have faith in me and do whatever I ask you to do. This is the only way you will realise me."

Commentary: What is justice? Justice is the execution of God's Will. God's Will is infinitely higher than man's mental grasp can reach. God is not bound by any law. He wants to enjoy the Infinite in the finite. He wants to bring down the message of Immortality into the very heart of death. A spiritual Master is God's representative. Out of His infinite Bounty God has granted him boundless Peace, Light and Bliss. The Master wants to share these gifts with the rest of the world.

The human mind did not know, could not know, that the young boy carried very impure vibrations which were affecting Kathiya Baba's meditation. It was not really a question of a few pomegranate leaves. If the young man had not carried an impure vibration and disturbed Ramdas' peace with his impurity, perhaps the Master would have given him the leaves. But the teacher had every right to throw the boy out, for stealing is one kind of ignorance, and carrying impurity is another. Why should a spiritual Master condone two acts of ignorance?

IMF 64. *I am going Home*

Once, in the middle of the night, Ramdas Kathiya Baba asked a particular disciple of his to bring him a glass of water. Then he said to him, "Now you go back to sleep. I am going Home." The disciple could not understand what the Master meant, but since it was late in the night and he was feeling drowsy, he went back to sleep.

The following morning the disciple heard the Master's cows lowing and he went into the Master's room. The Master's room was flooded with light. The disciple could easily see that the Master had left the body, and he began shouting and crying.

When the rest of the disciples came into the Master's room, they also saw that the Master had left the body. On the one hand the Master was often so hard with the disciples; on the other hand he had a very soft heart for animals. He was extremely fond of his dear cows. The cows felt that the Master had left the body, so they were lowing, they were shedding tears.

Commentary: When a spiritual Master leaves the body, his dear ones suffer terribly. This suffering is an experience not only of the human world, but also of the animal world. As a matter of fact, this is an experience of God's entire universe. All the worlds in God's universe are intertwined. When one becomes a spiritual Master, his oneness-heart with God's Heart permeates all the worlds exactly the way his Beloved Supreme has permeated this reality-existence right from the dawn of His creation.

The disciples of Ramdas cried; the cows cried; humanity as such cried, for they all thought that it was a terrible loss. But divinity knows that there is no such thing as loss. It is only a transformation of the visible into the invisible, which will open up a new chapter in God's ever-illumining and ever-fulfilling cosmic Game.

INDIA AND HER MIRACLE-FEAST:
COME AND ENJOY YOURSELF

BOOK 8:
TRADITIONAL INDIAN STORIES
ABOUT SWAMI NIGAMANANDA

Before the great spiritual Master Nigamananda was known by that name, he was called Nolini Kanto. When his wife died, he could not bear the loss, and for a while he literally became insane. Finally he went to a spiritual Master and begged the Master to show him his wife in the other world.

The Master said with utmost affection, "My son, do not cry for things that are transitory. The body came, the body left; but the soul remains eternally. If you pray and meditate, you will see the soul of your wife everywhere. You have all along been attached to the body. Now you should be attached to the soul. When one is attached to the soul, it is not actually attachment; it is devotedness. I see that a day will come when you will give illumination to many. God wants you to be totally freed from earthly bondage. But God will not be satisfied with only your personal liberation. After you have achieved liberation, He wants you to liberate all those who will be with you, at your feet."

Commentary: The body's attachment-cry is always most painful. The soul's detached oneness is always fruitful. The body knows how to cry the loneliness-cry. The soul knows how to fly in the oneness-sky.

IMF 66. *Temptation-power almost succeeds*

One day, during the period that Nigamananda was practising austerities, he passed by a temple owned by an elderly woman. The woman begged the sadhu to stay in her temple for some time, and he kindly listened to her request. Finally she begged him to take charge of the temple and he agreed. Afterwards, both of them became very fond of each other. She showed him all her motherly affection and he showed her all his heart's good qualities.

One day a beautiful young woman came into the temple. She became deeply enraptured with Nigamananda's soulful beauty, and she did not want to leave the temple. Nigamananda and she had serious spiritual conversations, and he was very moved by her sincere spiritual qualities and deep spiritual understanding.

The owner of the temple did not like this at all. She felt that Nigamananda's spirituality was being ruined. She insulted the young woman like anything in order to make her leave the temple. But the young woman had fallen desperately in love with Nigamananda, so she was adamant about staying there. And gradually Nigamananda also became weak.

One day the young woman said to him, "I have amassed wealth, and I will take you to my house. I assure you, your spirituality will not be ruined. On the contrary, I shall help you to meditate all day and night. Let us get married. If we get married, then it will be natural for me to help you, and society will not criticise us. You will be able to expedite your Godward journey." So they decided to get married in two weeks' time.

Before the two weeks had elapsed, Nigamananda's Master appeared before him one night in a dream with a luminous face. The Master had a stick, and soon Nigamananda was shocked to see his Master striking and beating his girlfriend black and blue. The Master insulted her and beat her senseless. Then he blessed Nigamananda and said to him, "Leave this place immediately! This woman will not help you in your God-realisation, but will take away all the aspiration that you now have and turn you into a street beggar."

Needless to say, Nigamananda obeyed his Master immediately.

Commentary: The sincere seeker has to be extremely alert all the time, for the forces of the lower vital can easily rob him of his aspiration. Until God-realisation dawns, he can always be tempted, and he can easily swerve from the path of Truth and Light. The very nature of the outer world is temptation. In order to overcome temptation, the seeker has to be constantly vigilant and always abide by the dictates of his inner will, not by the suggestions of the outer world.

IMF 67. *Body's beauty fails; soul's beauty sails*

In order to achieve liberation Nigamananda had been practising severe austerities in Benares for quite a few months. One day he was extremely hungry, but he had nothing to eat. In silence he said to the goddess of plenitude, "Annapurna, how is it that I don't have any food to eat?"

Just then a very ugly elderly woman with filthy clothes brought him a bag and said to him, "Please hold this bag of food. Let me go and bathe in the pond nearby. Then we shall eat together."

Nigamananda waited two or three hours, but there was still no sign of her returning. Finally he opened the bag and saw most delicious food and fruits inside. He ate everything himself.

That night in a dream Nigamananda saw the goddess Annapurna. She said to him, "So you see, nobody remains hungry. I feed everyone."

"You feed everyone?" Nigamananda exclaimed. "When did you feed me? I invoked you when I was hungry, but an ugly, dirty, old woman gave me food. You are so beautiful and luminous!"

The goddess explained, "It was I who came to you in that form."

"Why did you do that?" he asked.

"I wanted to show you that all forms are mine," said the goddess. "Still you care more for physical beauty than for the soul's beauty. So I wanted to show you that even ugly people can have good hearts. From now on try to feel that physical beauty has nothing to do with a kind, sympathetic heart."

Commentary: The beauty of the body ultimately fails. The beauty of the soul eventually sails in the boat of perfection-oneness towards God's Satisfaction-Shore.

IMF 68. *Not the outer form, but the inner essence*

Swami Satchidananda had a statue of a particular god. He asked his disciple Nigamananda to worship it, but Nigamananda did not care for this statue. One day the Master said to him, "Why do you not worship the statue which I worship? How is it that you do not see or feel anything inside my beloved Lord?"

Nigamananda said, "You may see your beloved Lord there, but I see only a piece of lifeless wood."

At this the Master became furious. He insulted Nigamananda mercilessly and told him, "If you show disrespect once more to my beloved Lord, I shall throw you out of my ashram! Be careful!" Then the Master left the room and went to his office to attend to ashram business.

Nigamananda was humiliated and very angry. He immediately took the statue off the shrine and gave it a smart slap, exclaiming, "You! For you I have got such a severe scolding from my Master. You deserve my punishment." Then he placed it again on the shrine.

A few minutes later the Master came back and said to him, with a broad smile, "You said my Lord is a lifeless piece of wood, but does anybody strike a lifeless thing? Only when we see that someone or something has life do we get satisfaction by striking it. One does not speak to a lifeless thing, for a lifeless thing cannot understand or respond. No, you do see something inside the statue. I was so pleased when I heard you speaking to my Lord. My Lord not only has life, but embodies the universal and transcendental Life. So from now on please worship this statue."

Nigamananda bowed to his Master and said, "Please forgive me. I shall worship this statue, and inside the statue I shall see and feel you, Master."

The Master said, "That is absolutely the right thing for you to do, my son."

Commentary: Faith is of paramount importance. One needs faith in infinite measure in one's Master. The human mind may sometimes find it difficult to believe in the Master's way, but the aspiring heart is always one with the Master's inner and outer operations. The seeker always has to remain in the heart. To have faith in one's Master is to feel God's own Presence here, there and everywhere. It is not what the object is, not who the man is, but whether or not one retains faith in one's Master's spiritual realisation. Then one achieves success in the outer world and progress in the inner world convincingly, easily and rapidly.

IMF 69. *My Guru is the highest*

Once Nigamananda went to visit the Kumbhamela, India's most famous fair, which literally countless people attend. He was delighted to see his Guru, Swami Satchidananda, there. A different spiritual Master presides over each fair, and this time the great Master Shankaracharya, Satchidananda's Guru, was presiding over the fair. Everybody was full of adoration for Shankaracharya, who was sitting near Satchidananda.

When Nigamananda arrived, he bowed to his Master first and then bowed to Shankaracharya. Everybody was shocked. How was it possible for him to bow to Satchidananda first when Shankaracharya was sitting right beside him? Some people said to Nigamananda, "You are such a fool! Don't you know how to discriminate?"

Nigamananda replied, "I do know how to discriminate. I tell you, nobody can be superior to one's own Guru. My Guru is and will always remain highest to me. Therefore, I did the right thing by bowing to him first."

On hearing this Shankaracharya gave Nigamananda a broad smile and said to him, "You are right, my son, you are right." Then he asked Nigamananda a few spiritual questions which Nigamananda answered perfectly. Then Shankaracharya said to Satchidananda, "What are you doing? Why are you not asking this disciple of yours to have his own disciples and to help illumine mankind? I clearly see that he is ready for that."

Then, in front of Shankaracharya and all the seekers who were nearby, Satchidananda declared, "My spiritual son Niga-mananda has realised God. From now on he will accept disciples and illumine their minds and fulfil their hearts."

Commentary: At the journey's start the Master is the boatman, the boat and the river. At the journey's end, the Master becomes the Goal itself. A beginner-seeker sees the Master as the boat. When he crosses beyond the barrier of the mind, he sees the Master as the boatman. When he establishes his constant one-ness with the Master, he sees the Master as the river. And when he becomes the most perfect instrument of the Master, he sees the Master as his Goal itself. When the hour strikes for the disciple, the disciple also has to play the role of a Master, for progress must continue in the world of self-giving and God-becoming.

IMF 70. *Divine love consoles human loss*

A middle-aged disciple of Swami Nigamananda died of an incurable disease. His mother and his wife were thrown into a sea of sorrow. The mother became practically insane with grief. She said to a picture of their Master which was hanging on the wall, "Why do we have to keep you? You have no power; you are useless! I am throwing you into the pond!"

She grabbed the picture and started carrying it towards the pond. All of a sudden she heard someone behind her crying, "Mother! Mother!" with a tearful and sorrowful voice. She turned around and saw their Guru, Nigamananda, with tearful eyes saying to her, "Mother, let us go back home. Do not cry for your son any more. I will be your son. Your son is with me, inside me and for me."

The woman was greatly consoled and returned to her house with the picture of her Guru. At the hour that all this occurred Nigamananda was actually four hundred miles away, giving spiritual lessons to his disciples who were living at his ashram.

Commentary: Unlike divine love and divine worship, human love and human adoration are always based on personal interest. Whenever personal interest is in the picture, the closeness of inner oneness can never be achieved. At that time the seeker finds himself divided even from his dear ones by inner walls. Attachment-world eventually has to meet with an atom-bomb-destruction.

IMF 71. *The Master's protection-arms*

Another most striking incident took place in the same family. One night a group of hooligans came to the house of the old mother and the widow and were about to strike them. The hooligans wanted to take away their valuable possessions and all their money.

Both the mother and the wife shouted, screamed and cried for help at the top of their voices. Who appeared before them to save them? Their Master, Nigamananda. He appeared in a most beautiful and powerful form and threatened the hooligans with a trident, saying he would destroy them all. Then he made a circle and said that if the family stayed inside the circle, they would be safe. In Nigamananda's presence the two women brought all their valuables and money into the circle, and there they were well-protected by their Master's spiritual and occult power.

Before daybreak the hooligans, finding that they were help-less, left the house.

Commentary: The Master's compassion-heart can always play the role of protection-arms. The Master loves his dear ones infinitely more than the dear ones can imagine. It is the unconditional love and concern of the Master for his dear ones that keeps the seekers' aspiration-flames burning.

IMF 72. *Dream becomes reality*

Once a well-known military officer decided to accept the spir-itual life. He wanted to give up the world of attachment for good, so he began praying to God every day to take him to his real Guru.

One night in a dream he saw a most beautiful luminous being, and at the same time he saw a word written on his heart: Nigamananda. This officer knew nothing about Swami Nigamananda, who was then living a thousand miles away in a different city. But the officer made inquiries, and soon he found someone who knew of Nigamananda, and could tell him where the Master was to be found.

In a few days' time the officer-seeker reached Nigamananda's ashram. As soon as he saw Nigamananda he knew that this was the Master he had seen in his dream and he fell at his feet. Nigamananda said to him simply, "So, you believe in dreams?"

Commentary: The dream-world is next door to the reality-world. Today's beautiful dreams are tomorrow's fruitful realities. A seeker's soulful aspiration-dreams can be transformed into fruitful manifestation-realities. A sincere, self-giving seeker can easily acquire a free access to the dream-moon-world and to the reality-sun-world in the process of his inner evolution.

IMF 73. *A mere God-lover*

Swami Nigamananda's disciples always considered their Master to be an Avatar, although he had never told them that he was one. But they all believed that this was the case, and they did not hesitate to speak of his greatness to others.

One day Swami Nigamananda told his small group of disciples that he was not an Avatar. "Nobody should call me an Avatar," he said. "Nobody should even think of me as one. I am a mere God-lover."

The Master continued, "Like you, I have been evolving from the stone life, and I have had quite a few human incarnations. In this incarnation I have realised God. I have achieved perfection, and I know what the transcendental Truth is. I want to give you all my possessions. I have already given you the key. You have just to unlock my heart-door and then take whatever you want and as much as you want. It is not necessary to have an Avatar of the highest order as your Guru. An ordinary God-realised soul can give you everything you need for your own God-realisation.

Commentary: It is the Love-Oneness aspect of God, not His Sovereignty-Height aspect, that makes us truly love God and worship Him as the universal Beauty and the transcendental Reality.

INDIA AND HER MIRACLE-FEAST:
COME AND ENJOY YOURSELF

BOOK 9:
TRADITIONAL INDIAN STORIES
ABOUT BAMA KSHEPA

IMF 74. *The widow's marriage*

One day a young, beautiful girl and her father came to see Bama Kshepa. The young girl bowed down to the Master and offered him some Indian sweets which she herself had prepared. Bama was extremely pleased with her and said, "I am blessing you. You will be blessed in the future with a beautiful son."

The girl cried out, "Father, Father, look what this sadhu is saying! How can I have a child when I have lost my husband? I am a widow."

Bama said, "You are a widow. So what! You will be remarried. My words will prove true."

In three months' time a very rich young man fell in love with her. Although in those days it was not at all appreciated if a widow remarried, this girl did get married in a special Hindu Vaishnava manner. Needless to say, in a year's time after she got married, she was blessed with a beautiful son.

IMF 75. *A suicide attempt*

Once in the thick of the night a middle-aged man named Nimai was tying a rope to the branch of a tree and was about to hang himself. He could not support his family, and for this reason the members of his family had tremendous disrespect for him. Therefore he wanted to commit suicide.

At that moment Bama appeared in his subtle body and said, "What are you doing? You rascal, don't you know that committing suicide is the worst possible sin? Don't you believe it?"

Nimai said, "All right, I will not commit suicide, but I will never go home again."

Bama said, "You don't have to go home. Come and stay with me, in your real home. God will take care of your family, I assure you."

Bama's words proved true. Very soon, two of Nimai's older sons got jobs and were in a position to support the rest of the members of the family.

IMF 76. *The dying man*

A young man suffering from a serious case of tuberculosis was brought by his relatives to Bama. The young man's days were numbered. Bama said to them, "Why did you bring him to me? Am I a doctor? You rascals, you will never give me peace of mind."

Then the Master stood up and started strangling the patient. Everybody was stunned. The man was already so weak. The disciples started crying because if the young man died, the Master and all of them would be in serious trouble.

But Bama continued to strangle and abuse the man like anything, saying, "When you do bad things, unbearable things, don't you know you will pay the penalty?" Then he said, "All right, I have forgiven you," and he threw the man down on the ground. Everybody thought he was dead.

But in a few minutes, to everyone's astonishment, the young man stood up and said, "I am so hungry. Please give me something to eat. I have never felt this kind of hunger in my life." The dying man was now totally cured. The relatives left the Master's house offering utmost gratitude to Bama, whom they affectionately called the "insane spiritual Master."

IMF 77. *The leper*

Bama had a dear attendant named Nanda, who had developed leprosy. Even then, Bama used to take food from him regularly and not from other disciples. Gradually, Nanda's case became extremely serious. His hands and arms were totally covered with infected wounds and it was a very ugly sight. So he stopped coming to his Master's place.

One day, Bama's attendants said to their Master, "Master, you have the capacity to cure your dear disciple, Nanda. Why don't you cure him?"

Bama said to them, "All right, bring him today."

When Nanda came, Bama started striking him, saying, "Can you count on your fingertips how many times you have done unthinkable things? I say you can't, you rascal. I have forgiven you and I am curing you, but in the future never, never do anything immoral or undivine."

In a month's time Nanda was totally cured. Then he once again started preparing meals for Bama and serving him with utmost love and devoted surrender.

IMF 78. *The stomach ailment*

One day Bama saw a man in the street suffering from severe stomach pains. He had a very serious ailment in his abdomen. When Bama passed by him, he asked Bama to cure him. Bama scolded him most mercilessly. Then he touched the man's stomach and said, "Now you are cured, but lead a good life."

The man said to Bama, "O Master, I know that you are a God-incarnate soul."

Bama immediately replied, "I am not a God-incarnate soul. I am the dust of the dust of my Divine Mother Tara. It is the dust of Her dust that has cured you. I am a mere instrument."

647

IMF 79. *The disciple-thief*

Bama had a close disciple who was in the habit of stealing. From time to time he used to steal money and material things that belonged to Bama. Once he stole a very large sum of money, and both the disciples and the Master were furious. Bama asked a lawyer-disciple of his to press charges against the individual.

The day the case was supposed to go to court, Bama quite unexpectedly came before the judge and pleaded with him to forgive the disciple.

The lawyer-disciple said, "You asked me to be so strict with him. We have filed the case, and today I am here with the judge. What will the court think of us?"

Bama said to his lawyer-disciple, "Rascal, do I have to be afraid of your court?" Then, pointing to the judge, he added, "Here is another rascal. It seems he is not going to listen to my request."

The judge knew Bama's spiritual power, so he said, "No, sadhu, I am at your command. The court listens to me, but I listen to you. You take back your disciple-thief."

The Master said to the judge, "I am so grateful to you, I am so proud of you. Now again, I can chat with my dear disciple. He has stolen my money, but who needs money? I need his devoted love and service."

IMF 80. *Meditating on one's shoes*

One day a certain gentleman bathed in a holy river and then sat down to meditate on its bank. A few minutes later Bama came to the spot and watched the man for some time. Then he entered into the water and, from there, started sprinkling water and throwing sand on the gentleman.

The man said to Bama, "What a rascal you are! Can't you see that I am meditating? Is this the time for you to disturb me?"

Bama replied, "What a liar you are! You are meditating on what? Are you meditating on God or are you meditating on the beautiful, fine shoes that you are going to buy today from the shoe shop? I don't approve of that kind of meditation."

The man was so surprised. He said, "Please, please tell me something about meditation."

But Bama only said, "Meditation is not meant for you for quite a few years." Then Bama started running away.

The man followed him, but Bama ran so fast that he could not catch him. When the man reached Bama's village, he asked people where the Master's house was and went there. But Bama told his disciples, "I will never speak to him. Let him meditate on his shoes. You people meditate on God."

The gentleman felt sad and miserable, and he went away without seeing Bama. Bama knew that this was the only way he could inspire the man to meditate sincerely.

IMF 81. *Dogs are human beings*

One day Bama and his dogs were eating together. Sometimes his dogs were eating food from his plate; sometimes he was reciprocating by eating food from their plates. On seeing this unusual scene, some young boys said to Bama, "How can you do this, and why do you do this? Are you a human being?"

He said to them, "Just because I am a human being I can do this. Now, come here near me."

The three boys came and stood before him. Bama placed his finger on the spine of each boy, one after the other. Using his occult power, Bama brought forward a human face and consciousness on the face of each dog, and a dog's face and consciousness on the face of each human being. Immediately, each boy saw that the dogs were all human beings whereas the other boys who were watching were dogs. They were so astonished and baffled.

Then Bama explained, "You think that a human being can eat only with other human beings. But look at the animals around you. Are they not also human beings? Again, aren't human beings also animals? I wanted you to see this; that is why I used my occult power in this way."

IMF 82. *Bama's affection*

Bama was quite often unkind to people outwardly. Inwardly he was all kindness and concern, but his outer behaviour was quite often shocking. Therefore, nobody expected kindness from him, especially in the outer world.

One day a certain doctor and some of his admirers came to Bama. Bama was extremely kind and affectionate to the doctor and pleaded with him to eat something. The doctor said that he was not hungry and that he did not eat food at odd hours. But Bama pleaded and pleaded. His disciples were so surprised, for Bama never did this kind of thing. He always remained in his own trance. Who had eaten and who had not eaten — these things never bothered him. Since he kept pleading with the doctor to eat something, the doctor finally did so and then went home.

On reaching home, he found that his only daughter had just died. She had had a stroke and in ten minutes' time she had passed away.

Bama had known that this tragedy was going to take place in the doctor's family and therefore had become so kind, so affectionate and so loving. He showed tremendous concern for the bereaved family even before the tragedy took place.

IMF 83. *Bama's magic circle*

Bama lived across the river from his family. When his mother became seriously ill, he did not go to see her because he was practising austere disciplines. Then she died. Bama's family wanted to bring the dead body to the other side of the river so that Bama could offer his last expressions of love and devotion to his mother. But a hurricane was in full swing and it was raining heavily. Therefore, they decided not to bring the dead body to the other side.

From his side of the river Bama saw quite a few people crying and lamenting, so he knew that a dead body had been brought to the river bank to be cremated. He wanted to see who had died, so he jumped into the water and swam across the river. Lo and behold, he saw his younger brother in the crowd of people. His younger brother had not informed him about his mother's death, for Bama often did peculiar things, and he was afraid that Bama would do something unpleasant and embarrass the entire family.

When Bama saw his younger brother crying and weeping, he immediately realised what had happened. He didn't say a word. He just grabbed his mother's dead body and put the body into a nearby sack, which he placed on his shoulders. Then, chanting "Tara, Tara," the name of his beloved Goddess, he brought his mother to the other side of the river where he practised his yoga. His brother and relatives were compelled to come to the other side by boat during the hurricane.

When they arrived, Bama said to his younger brother, "On the thirteenth day we must feed thousands of people."

His brother said, "How? You know how poor we are."

But Bama replied, "You don't have to worry about it."

His relatives, who did not appreciate Bama's craziness, started laughing. They knew that Bama had practically nothing to eat for himself. Bama got furious and said, "I tell you, I will feed them."

Early in the morning on the thirteenth day, many, many people began bringing all kinds of food to Bama's house. They said that they had had a vision of a goddess that previous night. The goddess had told them that Bama was her dearest son and that, because his mother had passed away, today there was going to be a religious festival. The goddess had commanded them to bring food to Bama's family so that the family could feed all the relatives, well-wishers and villagers who would come.

As soon as everybody had come, all of a sudden it started raining very, very heavily. Bama's brother came to Bama and started crying, "O brother, you wanted to feed so many people. Now, by your grace, food has come, but we have no place to feed them. It is all open space. How can we feed people when it is raining so heavily? We can't feed them in our house because it is too small. Food we have, but we have no shelter. So everybody is sad and unhappy."

Bama said, "All right, come with me." His brother followed him to his house. Some onlookers started laughing at Bama, while others showed him respect. No one knew what this crazy man was going to do and his presence created a commotion. Then Bama took a small stick and made a very big circle and said, "All of you come inside this circle. If you are inside the circle, you will not be affected by the rain at all."

When they all came inside, everyone was amazed, for it continued raining heavily right outside the boundary of the circle. But inside, all of them were perfectly safe; inside the circle they ate to their heart's content. But as soon as the meal was over and they walked out of the circle to go home, they got thoroughly drenched. So they all came back into the circle and stayed there for a couple of hours until the rain finally stopped.

IMF 84. *Bama eats the temple prasad*

Bama used to frequent a temple dedicated to the goddess Tara that was owned by a queen. One day he went into the temple and ate all the prasad that had been offered to the goddess. When the head priest and the guard saw what Bama had done, they struck him mercilessly.

That night the queen had a most frightening dream. She saw the goddess Tara weeping in front of her. On the one hand, she was so delighted to see the goddess, who was the goal of her life. On the other hand, she was so sad to see the goddess weeping.

The goddess Tara showed the queen her back, which was bleeding. "My dearest son, Bama, ate the food that was meant for Me in the temple. Your priest and your guard have beaten him mercilessly. If the son can't eat his mother's food, who can eat it?"

The queen did not know who Bama was, but the next morning she asked the priest and the guard to bring him to her. They looked for him, but he was nowhere to be found. It took them three days to find Bama. He was still suffering from the pain of the beating, so they were very kind, affectionate and apologetic to him. When they brought him to the queen she looked at him and felt miserable.

The queen said to Bama, "From now on this temple is yours. Before we place food in the temple, we shall feed you first. This is what the goddess Tara wants from me. I shall have to feed you first before I offer food to Her in the temple." Bama was very happy and delighted. From that day on, his poverty was over.

IMF 85. *Far above human standards*

A few months after the queen had offered her temple to Bama, the Master one day got inspiration to pass water and sprinkle it all over the temple.

The priest and the guard were horrified, but Bama just said to them, "She is my Mother, I am her little child. What else do you expect me to do if I don't pass water on Her? I have a right to do these kinds of things. What does the little child do with the mother? The child passes water."

The priest and the guard thought that if they made complaints to the queen, the queen would be really angry with Bama for his bad behaviour. They were already jealous of him because the queen always showed him tremendous concern and love. So they went to the queen and told her what had happened, expressing tremendous anxiety, worry and fear.

The queen scolded them mercilessly. "You fools!" she said. "This is a matter entirely related to the Mother and the son. Bama's Mother is the goddess Tara; he is his Mother's dearest son — her darling little child. Mother and son are one. This is none of our business; we should stay totally out of it. Let the problem be solved by the Mother and the son. They are dearer than the dearest to each other, so mind your own business. Don't make any complaints against Bama. He is far above our human standards."

IMF 86. *The beautiful woman*

One night Bama was lying down in his room meditating. His disciples were fast asleep in the adjacent rooms. Suddenly a beautiful girl came into Bama's room on tiptoe and started massaging his feet. Bama made no sign that he was awake. Then she said to him, "Bama, you are so beautiful."

Bama sat up and told her to get out of the house immediately. But instead of leaving, she embraced Bama most passionately. Bama screamed and shouted at the top of his voice, and the disciples came running in. Bama gave the beautiful woman a smart slap and asked the disciples to compel her to leave.

The woman placed at Bama's feet the money that had been given to her by the zamindar who had sent her to test Bama's spiritual celibacy. But the Master returned the money to her and told her, "You can return the money to the zamindar, since you have not been successful in your attempt."

IMF 87. *Bama Kshepa's passing*

The day of his passing, Bama Kshepa showed tremendous affection to his dear disciples and also to his dogs. His dogs were shedding bitter tears in silence. Their oneness-heart with their Master could only be felt and never described. Finally, Bama uttered in a loud voice only one word — "Tara!" — which was the name of his supreme goddess. Then he breathed his last.

Commentary: Outer beauty and material wealth Bama always shunned. He did not care for religious principles as such. His only religion was his love for his deity, the Divine Mother Tara. His legacy to humanity was his soulful oneness with the human world and the animal world.

INDIA AND HER MIRACLE-FEAST:
COME AND ENJOY YOURSELF

BOOK 10:
TRADITIONAL INDIAN STORIES
ABOUT BALANANDA

IMF 88. *Balananda's initiation*

The day of his initiation, Balananda said to his Master, "Today you are going to initiate me. On the one hand, I am so happy and delighted that out of your infinite kindness you are going to initiate me. On the other hand, I feel extremely sorry that I don't have anything to offer you in return. I am so poor."

The Master, Brahmananda, said to his dearest disciple, "My son, you should not think of that. I do not need any material wealth or earthly possessions. I need only one thing from you and that is your God-realisation. One day you will definitely realise God, and your God-realisation itself will be my best reward. I am initiating you with my heart's infinite love and concern. I shall guide you at every moment in your spiritual journey.

"God-realisation for you is destined in this incarnation and today's initiation is going to expedite your journey. I am extremely glad to have found in you a true disciple, a perfect disciple. Today I want to tell you not to worry about anything. You do not have to give anything to me now. Your God-realisation at God's choice Hour in this incarnation will be the supreme reward which I shall receive from you."

IMF 89. *The king's surrender*

One day a great king sent his representative to Balananda to invite him to come to the king's palace. Balananda said to the king's representative, "Well, you are coming from one king to another. You must know that I am also a king — in the inner world. Since one king is inviting another king, I feel that I must go. But first I wish to tell you a story."

Balananda asked his disciples who were nearby to come and sit in front of him, as he was going to tell a significant story:

Once there was a great spiritual Master who used to meditate for days on end without eating or drinking anything. It happened that on one occasion he got an inner urge to meditate for three days sitting in the middle of a public road. On the second day of his austere discipline, he heard a very loud noise. He opened his eyes and he saw that a big procession honouring a certain king was coming down the road, heading towards him. Three of the king's guards came rushing up to him and said, "Look, look, the king will soon pass by. Leave way for him. Move aside and leave the road free."

The Master said, "Who? Who?"

"The king himself!" the guards replied.

The Master said, "Don't bother me. I am also a king."

The guards threatened him, "We will strike you!"

He said, "How dare you touch me! Just try!" Then the guards looked at his eyes and saw that they were emitting fire. They got frightened and ran to narrate the story to their king.

After he heard the story, the king went up to the Master and said in a mocking manner, "O saint, I understand that you are another king. Please tell me how many soldiers you have."

The spiritual man said, "I don't have any soldiers — not even one."

"How can you be a king without any soldiers?" the king asked.

The saint replied, "I have no enemy to fight against. Why do I need any soldiers?"

Then the king asked, "Tell me, please, where is your house? Where do you live?"

He answered, "The whole world is my house. Why do I need a particular house? All the houses in God's creation belong to me, for God is my Father, my only Father. The father's house the son can legitimately claim. So all the houses of this world are mine. I don't need any special house to live in." The king now realised that this man was not an ordinary human being. He fell down at the feet of the spiritual Master and begged him for forgiveness. The Master immediately granted him forgiveness and, with a smiling face, moved away from where he had been seated in the middle of the road so that the king's procession could freely move on to its destination.

After hearing the story the king's representative got the point. He was very embarrassed and went and told his king the story. The king was also embarrassed. He went running to Balananda to beg him for forgiveness, and then asked him to initiate him.

After Balananda had initiated him, the king said, "Please tell me how I can rule my kingdom. I am always assailed by fear, doubt, anxiety and worry."

Balananda said, "It is very easy. From now on, let all your possessions remain with you, but feel that they are not yours. They belong to God. God is the sole owner of all the things that you claim to be yours; you are only His manager. He has asked you to manage these things on His behalf, but He is the real owner. You are the false owner. Since the real owner always takes care of His own property, the false owner must surrender to His Will. Pray to God to make you an unconditional instrument of His. In that way you will never be assailed by fear, worry, anxiety and doubt; you will be only a dear instrument of His."

IMF 90. *Four most important things in life*

One day Balananda said to his disciples, "I know all of you want to become my good disciples, but it is quite a difficult task. Each of you needs to develop four most important things in your life. You need to develop the capacity to tolerate the world and to tolerate your own life. You need to develop the capacity to sacrifice everything that you have and everything that you are. You need to cultivate the capacity to remain silent even when you are mistreated mercilessly, without rhyme or reason, by a hostile world. You need to develop the capacity to remain calm, quiet and tranquil without being completely shattered when you lose in the battlefield of life or extolling yourself to the skies when you succeed in the battlefield of life."

The disciples said to him, "Master, is it at all possible to do all this in one incarnation?"

Balananda said, "Why not? Why not? I, too, was once upon a time a disciple in this incarnation. In this incarnation I realised God. You also can realise God, provided you always do the right thing at the right time, with the help of the right Master."

IMF 91. *The mother's vision*

A high-ranking railway officer who was head of a railway line was once in serious trouble. It happened that a particular tram on his line met with a severe accident and hundreds of people were killed. He was accused of being responsible for the accident and he was about to lose his job. He had a big family so he was very sad and disturbed.

His mother started praying to God to forgive her son. One night she had a vision in which she saw a most beautiful sannyasi who said to her, "Mother, don't worry. I shall save your son."

The next morning she was extremely excited. She told her son all about her dream and he was very pleased to hear it.

The following day Balananda came to the mother's house quite unexpectedly. As soon as she saw him she was astonished, for the man she had seen in her dream looked exactly like Balananda. Balananda said to her, "Do not worry. I am the same person you saw in your dream. Now, I know that your son is a good hunter, so please give me a tiger skin."

Her son, the great officer, happened to be there. He was very moved to see Balananda and he offered him not one, but three tiger skins. He said, "Please make your choice. If you want all three, I will be happy to offer them all to you."

Balananda said, "I am sorry. I don't like any of these three."

The officer replied, "Then I will go out and buy some to offer to you."

Balananda said, "No, I have changed my mind. I don't need one now. God has asked me to come to you and save you. In a few days time they will withdraw the case against you. They will prove that the accident was not due to your negligence at all, but to some other reason. You do not have to worry. You will be acquitted; nothing will happen to you."

Both the son and the mother fell at Balananda's feet and said, "We are offering you our gratitude-hearts. Please accept us as your disciples."

Balananda smilingly said, "I have already accepted you both as my true disciples."

IMF 92. *The Master-chloroform*

A few months later, after the railway officer and all the members
of his family had become Balananda's disciples, an unfortunate
thing happened. The railway officer got a dangerous and poisonous carbuncle on his back. The doctor wanted him to undergo
an operation and he readily agreed. On the day of his operation
he prayed in silence to Balananda, who lived seven hundred
miles away, and asked for his Master's protection.

Before the operation, the doctor wanted to give him chloroform, but he said, "Oh, no! My Master is my chloroform."

The doctor said, "Do not mix medical science with spirituality.
You need chloroform. You will not be able to bear the pain. It
will be excruciating."

The railway officer said, "No harm. I will be able to bear it. I
am taking full responsibility for my operation." The doctor did
not argue any further and he started to operate on the carbuncle.
During the operation the patient kept his eyes wide open and
the whole time he kept smiling at the window before him.

When it was over, the doctor asked him why he had been
smiling and how it had even been possible for him to smile while
he was undergoing such a painful operation. The railway officer
said, "Why was I smiling? It was quite easy for me to smile
because I was seeing my Master standing by the window. How
was it possible? I saw my Master taking away all the pain from
me. Therefore, I was smiling at him with my heart's boundless
gratitude."

After a few hours the patient was taken back to his home.
Early that evening he received a telegram from his Master which
said, "My son, your Master-chloroform was quite effective, was
it not? Love and blessings, your Master, Balananda."

Needless to say, the Master had not been informed on the
physical plane as to the actual day and hour of the operation.

IMF 93. *The snake bite*

Two new disciples, a father and son, were living together in Balananda's ashram. One night the son was bitten by a poisonous snake. The father called in a doctor who said it was a hopeless case, and that it was just a matter of hours before his son would die.

Then the father said, "There is also another doctor. Let me go to him." So he left the doctor and his son in one room and entered into his meditation room. He sat down in front of his shrine and prayed to his Master to save his son. In half an hour's time he came back and said to the doctor, "I have received an inner assurance that my son will be saved by my Master."

The incident took place at three o'clock in the morning, and the father did not dare to inform the Master outwardly at that hour. By seven o'clock the son was completely cured and he was very happy and cheerful.

The father said to his son, "When I was meditating on our Master, I saw four messengers of death, very ugly-looking, who came to take you, and I saw our Master chase them away with his trident. Therefore, I was quite confident that you would be saved, my son." The father, the son and the doctor were all in a very cheerful frame of mind.

Just then, quite unexpectedly, the Master's main attendant came in and said that the Master wanted to hear the snake story. They told the attendant what had happened, and then he said, "Now I have a story to tell you. Around two o'clock this morning I heard Master's voice saying to someone, 'Get out, get out of this place'. I rushed into his room, turned on the light and saw a snake with its hood spread, about to strike the Master. I was horrified. The Master again said, 'Get out, get out'. After a few minutes the snake left. Even now the thought of that particular scene is frightening me."

The father said to the attendant, "I knew, I knew. Master came to me in a vision. I saw him chasing away the messengers of death. Our Master is all compassion. I have only one prayer, and that prayer is to have a heart of constant gratitude."

IMF 94. *The Master's true disciples*

One day, some of Balananda's dear disciples said to him, "Master, some of your disciples also go to other Masters. Do you approve of this?"

He said, "I do approve of it. They are acting like bees. Bees enjoy collecting honey from various flowers, so my disciples also can do it."

The disciples said, "No, we will never do that. We don't want to act like bees. We want to be all yours. What you have is infinitely more than we need."

The Master said, "I knew it. I knew it. I knew that you people are not of that type, but there is one thing you can do. You can go to other spiritual Masters for metaphysical knowledge. You have all been initiated by me. I am your Master for God-realisation and others can be your Masters for philosophy and mental expansion."

The disciples said, "We don't need a mind, we don't need mental expansion. What we need is a heart, a oneness-heart with you."

The Master said to them, "Who else can be my true disciples, if not all of you?"

IMF 95. *Pitambar*

Balananda's original name was Pitambar. Pitambar's father died when he was six years old. After his father's death, his family became very poor. During this period Pitambar was very restless and he paid no attention to his studies. His mother begged him to study and to give up his restlessness and mischievous pranks, but he did not listen to her.

One day her anger reached the highest height and she said to her son, "Oh, I see you are going to become a sadhu. Since in every way you are hopeless and useless, you are destined to become a sadhu."

The word "sadhu" immediately transported the child's mind and heart to a higher world. He said, "Mother, I am going to become a sadhu." Then he entered into his room, collected all his clothes and set them on fire. He besmeared his whole body with ashes, put a sadhu's mark on his forehead and, putting on a loincloth, started clapping. "Mother, Mother," he said, "look at me. I have really become a sadhu." His mother smiled and cried.

Later, at the age of nine, Pitambar left his mother and his earthly home. His mother tried in so many ways to see him. Her heart was all sorrow and grief, but the son would not see his mother under any circumstances. He was adamant. He thought that she would create attachment for him and that he would not be able to pursue his spiritual life if she came to him with all her emotional demands. So he refused to see her until he reached the age of fifty. At that time the son and the mother met for the first time since he had left home.

Indeed, his spiritual discipline and inner cry made Balananda a spiritual giant. At the age of ninety Balananda returned to his Heavenly home.

APPENDIX

PREFACE TO ORIGINAL EDITIONS

Editor's preface to the original edition of Great Indian meals: divinely delicious and supremely nourishing

Most of the stories in this and other books in this series are Sri Chinmoy's retelling of traditional Indian tales. On rare occasions the Master has modified a story to make it more acceptable to the Western palate. And a few of the stories are Sri Chinmoy's own.

These tales are not only delicious and nourishing, but also encouraging and illumining. Some are quite entertaining. Others are surcharged with morality-flames and spirituality-fire, which easily enlighten the Western mind, strengthen the vital and quicken the journey of the body-consciousness. Together they represent two trees standing side by side: entertainment-tree and enlightenment-tree. Both trees are at your disposal. Appreciate their flowers and fruits to your heart's content.

*

Editor's preface to the original edition of Illumination-experiences on Indian soil

The stories in this book, many based on historical incidents or traditional tales from India's past, offer an illumining glimpse at some of the experiences that helped shape the consciousness of Mother India. The stories have been adapted and retold by a master storyteller whose spiritual insights will benefit Easterners and Westerners alike.

BIBLIOGRAPHY

EIT. THE EARTH-ILLUMINATION-TRUMPETS OF DIVINITY'S HOME
(3 VOLUMES)

SRI CHINMOY:
    – *The Earth-Illumination-Trumpets of divinity's Home, part 1*, New York, Agni Press, 1995.
    – *The Earth-Illumination-Trumpets of divinity's Home, part 2*, New York, Agni Press, 1995.
    – *The Earth-Illumination-Trumpets of divinity's Home, part 3*, New York, Agni Press, 1995.

IE. ILLUMINATION-EXPERIENCES ON INDIAN SOIL (4 VOLUMES)

SRI CHINMOY:
    –*Illumination-experiences on Indian soil, part 1*, New York, Agni Press, 1982.
    –*Illumination-experiences on Indian soil, part 2*, New York, Agni Press, 1982.
    –*Illumination-experiences on Indian soil, part 3*, New York, Agni Press, 1982.
    –*Illumination-experiences on Indian soil, part 4*, New York, Agni Press, 1995.

GIM. GREAT INDIAN MEALS: DIVINELY DELICIOUS AND SUPREMELY
NOURISHING (10 VOLUMES)

SRI CHINMOY:
    −*Great Indian meals: divinely delicious and supremely nourishing,
part 1*, New York, Agni Press, 1979.
    −*Great Indian meals: divinely delicious and supremely nourishing,
part 2*, New York, Agni Press, 1979.
    −*Great Indian meals: divinely delicious and supremely nourishing,
part 3*, New York, Agni Press, 1979.
    −*Great Indian meals: divinely delicious and supremely nourishing,
part 4*, New York, Agni Press, 1979.
    −*Great Indian meals: divinely delicious and supremely nourishing,
part 5*, New York, Agni Press, 1979.
    −*Great Indian meals: divinely delicious and supremely nourishing,
part 6*, New York, Agni Press, 1979.
    −*Great Indian meals: divinely delicious and supremely nourishing,
part 7*, New York, Agni Press, 1979.
    −*Great Indian meals: divinely delicious and supremely nourishing,
part 8*, New York, Agni Press, 1979.
    −*Great Indian meals: divinely delicious and supremely nourishing,
part 9*, New York, Agni Press, 1979.
    −*Great Indian meals: divinely delicious and supremely nourishing,
part 10*, New York, Agni Press, 1982.

IMF. INDIA AND HER MIRACLE-FEAST: COME AND ENJOY YOUR-
SELF (10 VOLUMES)

SRI CHINMOY:
   –India and her miracle-feast: come and enjoy yourself. Part 1 -
Traditional stories about Troilanga Swami, New York, Agni Press,
1977.
   –India and her miracle-feast: come and enjoy yourself. Part 2 -
Traditional stories about Shyama Charan Lahiri, New York, Agni
Press, 1977.
   –India and her miracle-feast: come and enjoy yourself. Part 3 -
Traditional stories about Gambhirananda, New York, Agni Press,
1977.
   –India and her miracle-feast: come and enjoy yourself. Part 4 -
Traditional stories about Bhaskarananda, New York, Agni Press,
1977.
   –India and her miracle-feast: come and enjoy yourself. Part 5 -
Traditional stories about Devadas Maharaj, New York, Agni Press,
1977.
   –India and her miracle-feast: come and enjoy yourself. Part 6,
vol. 1 - Traditional stories about Ramdas Kathiya Baba, New York,
Agni Press, 1977.
   –India and her miracle-feast: come and enjoy yourself. Part 6,
vol. 2 - Traditional stories about Ramdas Kathiya Baba, New York,
Agni Press, 1977.
   –India and her miracle-feast: come and enjoy yourself. Part 7 -
Traditional stories about Swami Nigamananda, New York, Agni
Press, 1981.
   –India and her miracle-feast: come and enjoy yourself. Part 8
- Traditional stories about Bama Kshepa, New York, Agni Press,
1981.
   –India and her miracle-feast: come and enjoy yourself. Part 9 -
Traditional stories about Balananda, New York, Agni Press, 1981.

POSTFACE

Publishing principles

This edition of *The works of Sri Chinmoy* aims to obey the Author's wish: scrupulous fidelity to his original words, use of typographical style by him selected, specific spelling choices, end placement of any editorial content (i.e. not written by Sri Chinmoy himself), particular treatment of some personal nouns in special cases, etc.

Textual accuracy

The text of this edition has been checked to ensure faithful accuracy to the originals. Although much effort has been put in proofreading and comparing different versions of the text, this print may still present a few lingering errors.

The Publisher would be grateful to be apprised of any mistypes via postal mail or facsimile, possibly with scan of the original page where the text is different. Please use original books only, specifying the year of publication. Online versions may be not as accurate and should not be considered authoritative.

Acknowledgements

The Publisher is very grateful to the late Professor Lambert and his équipe for his invaluable advice. For many decades Prof. Lambert conducted a small publishing house specialising in hand-made prints of philological edition of the classics. The standard of this edition would not have been the same without his scholarly advice.

The Publisher is also grateful to the international team of collaborators that spent countless hours proofreading and checking the current text against the originals.

Our deepest gratitude to Sri Chinmoy. His living presence can be felt breathing throughout his writings. It is a privilege to be involved with his works, in any form.

Citation keys

Citation keys are used throughout *The works of Sri Chinmoy* to allow accurate cross-reference of texts across titles and editions. Examples: EA 13, ST 50000, UPA 7.

Sri Chinmoy Canon

We could not use better words than Professor Lambert's, who kindly offered the name *Sri Chinmoy Canon*:

> «By defining Sri Chinmoy's first editions as *editio princeps* we chose to follow classical scholarship criteria, not because we consider Sri Chinmoy's work antique, but because we believe it is among the few post ‹classical antiquity› works to rightly deserve to be considered a *classicus*, designating by that term *superiority, authority* and *perfection*.
> «The monumental work Sri Chinmoy is offering to mankind is awe-inspiring and supremely pre-eminent in proportions and quality. It is manifest that Sri Chinmoy's work — which we feel right to call *The Sri Chinmoy Canon* — will be of profound help and source of enlightenment to anyone seeking a higher wisdom, truth and reality supreme.»

[Translated from French by M. G.S.]

TABLE OF CONTENTS

Composition typographique par imprimerie
Ab Academia Aoidon, Paris & Lyon.

Un grand merci à Prof Knuth pour
l'utilisation avancée de TeX.

A LYON, LE 7 OCTOBRE LXXXV Æ.G.

www.ingramcontent.com/pod-product-compliance
Lightning Source LLC
Chambersburg PA
CBHW020814300326
41914CB00075B/1770/J

9 780993 308048